INSIGHT GUIDE

EGYPT

APA PUBLICATIONS
Part of the Langenscheidt Publishing Group

INSIGHT GUIDE
EGYPT

ABOUT THIS BOOK

Editorial

Editor
Dorothy Stannard
Editorial Director
Brian Bell

Distribution

UK & Ireland
GeoCenter International Ltd
The Viables Centre , Harrow Way
Basingstoke, Hants RG22 4BJ
Fax: (44) 1256-817988

United States
Langenscheidt Publishers, Inc.
46–35 54th Road, Maspeth, NY 11378
Fax: (718) 784-0640

Canada
Prologue Inc.
1650 Lionel Bertrand Blvd., Boisbriand
Québec, Canada J7H 1N7
Tel: (450) 434-0306. Fax: (450) 434-2627

Worldwide
Apa Publications GmbH & Co.
Verlag KG (Singapore branch)
38 Joo Koon Road, Singapore 628990
Tel: (65) 865-1600. Fax: (65) 861-6438

Printing

Insight Print Services (Pte) Ltd
38 Joo Koon Road, Singapore 628990
Tel: (65) 865-1600. Fax: (65) 861-6438

©2000 Apa Publications GmbH & Co.
Verlag KG (Singapore branch)
All Rights Reserved

First Edition 1987
Fifth Edition 1998 (Updated 2000)

CONTACTING THE EDITORS
Although every effort is made to provide accurate information, we live in a fast-changing world and would appreciate it if readers would call our attention to any errors or outdated information that may occur by writing to:
Insight Guides, P.O. Box 7910, London SE1 1WE, England.
Fax: (44 20) 7403-0290.
e-mail:
insight@apaguide.demon.co.uk

NO part of this book may be reproduced, stored in a retrieval system or transmitted in any form or means electronic, mechanical, photocopying, recording or otherwise, without prior written permission of *Apa Publications*. Brief text quotations with use of photographs are exempted for book review purposes only. Information has been obtained from sources believed to be reliable, but its accuracy and completeness, and the opinions based thereon, are not guaranteed.

This guidebook combines the interests and enthusiasms of two of the world's best known information providers: Insight Guides, whose titles have set the standard for visual travel guides since 1970, and Discovery Channel, the world's premier source of nonfiction television programming.

The editors of Insight Guides provide both practical advice and general understanding about a destination's history, culture, institutions and people. Discovery Channel and its Web site, www.discovery.com, help millions of viewers explore their world from the comfort of their own home and also encourage them to explore it firsthand.

Land of Exploration

The great 19th-century explorer of Africa, Henry Morton Stanley, offered this advice: "To those who wish to be wise, to be healthful, to borrow one month of pleasure from a serious life, I would say, come and see the Nile."

How to use this book

Insight Guide: Egypt is structured to convey an understanding of Egypt and to guide readers through its many attractions.

EXPLORE YOUR WORLD®

Discovery
CHANNEL

◆ To get the most out of Egypt's wealth of sights, it's important to understand its past. The first section, therefore, explains the country's history, from the days of the pharaohs to the lives and times of its modern presidents.
◆ The Places section of the book provides a run-down of the towns and regions worth visiting, beginning with Cairo and working south. Places of major interest are cross-referenced by number or letter with full-colour maps.
◆Travel Tips provides practical information on all aspects of your trip. Information can be located quickly by using the index on the back cover flap.

The contributors
Like other Insight Guides, *Insight Guide: Egypt* is a joint effort. It involved a team of expert writers and contributors, many of whom are long-term residents of Egypt.

This new edition builds on the work of the first edition that was supervised by **John Rodenbeck**, Professor of English and Comparative Literature at the American University in Cairo and the co-founder of Hoopoe Press based in Cairo.

Together with native Egyptian and harvard graduate **Hisham Youssef**, Rodenbeck commissioned **Jill Kamil** (early history and Abu Simbel); **Elizabeth Maynard** (Upper Egypt and the Red Sea); **Max Rodenbeck** (The Egyptians, Markets and Bazaars, Suez and Sinai); **William Lyster** (Egypt under Islam); **Carina Campobasso** (Muhammad Ali and Modern Egypt); **Alice Brinton** (Alexandria); **Cassandra Vivian** (Travel Tips) and photographer **Albano Guatti**.

This edition was expanded and updated by **Sylvie Franquet**, an Arabic scholar who worked in Cairo as a model, translator and tour operator before starting to write. As well as fully updating the book, Franquet added new chapters on Egyptian cuisine and its dynamic popular culture, expanded the text on Middle Egypt, Upper Egypt, Nubia and the Red Sea and wrote the five "Insight on..." picture stories. New images were supplied by **Axel Krause**.

The book was edited by **Dorothy Stannard** with help from **Julia Roles** and **Kate Mikhail**.

Map Legend

Map Legend

— ‥ —	International Boundary
⊖	Border Crossing
— • —	National Park
— — — —	Ferry Route
Ⓜ	Metro
✈ ✈	Airport
🚌	Bus Station
ℹ	Tourist Information
✉	Post Office
✝ ⚲ ♂	Church/Ruins
⚲ ⚑	Mosque
✡ ✡	Synagogue
♂ ⚑	Castle/Ruins
∴	Archaeological Site
★	Place of Interest
𝟙	Statue/Monument

The main places of interest in the **Places** section are cross-referenced by letter or number (e.g. ❶), with a full-color map. A symbol at the top of every right-hand page tells you where to find the specific map.

CONTENTS

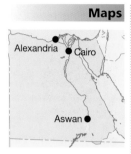
Introduction

History

People and Culture

The colours of
the Nile Valley,
Upper Egypt

THE SPELL OF EGYPT

Egypt is the Nile and the Nile is Egypt, the saying goes.

But there's much, much more to it than that...

The Land of the Nile has often exercised a potent spell over quite ordinary people. Egypt – or someone's idea of it – has inspired styles in everything from Western architecture and furniture to paper packaging, modern American condoms and cigarettes.

Egypt has even influenced Western fashion in matters of life and death, often grotesquely so. Interest in mummified flesh, for example, arose when word spread in medieval times about the therapeutic value of powdered *mumia* in the treatment of a wide variety of ailments. By the 16th century, mummies so fascinated visitors to Egypt that an active trade in their desiccated flesh began. Ancient burial grounds were dug up, mummies were stripped of their coverings and sent piecemeal to the apothecaries of Europe.

Descriptive accounts and sketches of Egypt made in the 18th century joined with a trickle of small objects – scarabs, amulets, and a multitude of fakes – to excite interest in Egypt as a source of the "primitive", a search for which was one of the century's preoccupations. Napoleon's expedition to Egypt, with assorted savants, took place largely in response to this new fashion.

An event that captured English interest in 1821 was the opening of the Egyptian Hall in London as a museum of "natural curiosities". It displayed the latest finds, casts and sketches by the Italian Giovanni Belzoni, who had cleared the Temple of Abu Simbel and shipped tons of treasures back to England. There was no restriction on grave-robbing, and ancient burial grounds were pillaged for anything movable. Museums all over Europe and beyond were soon acquiring Egyptian collections.

The event that captured world attention to a degree unrivalled by anything archaeological before was Howard Carter's discovery of the Tomb of Tutankhamun in 1922. Its 5,000 works of art were widely publicised. Thousands of sightseers made their way to the Valley of the Kings. They wanted to be in on the discovery, and they wanted to have a relic from the tomb. Local antique dealers, ready to fulfil the demand, ordered their collections from Cairo to be returned. The best local craftsmen turned out instant *antikas* bearing the royal cartouche. When the treasures went on tour later in the century (Paris in 1967, London in 1972, Russia in 1973 and the United States in 1975) the number of people wanting to visit Egypt skyrocketed. Tour companies began devising affordable package-tours and Nile cruises were no longer the preserve of the rich and cultured. The spell of Egypt retained its potency. ❏

PRECEDING PAGES: the Nile just south of Aswan; Giza pyramid looms through the fog; life in the desert; inside a festival tent, Cairo.
LEFT: obelisks often stand at the entrance to Egyptian temples.

Decisive Dates

EARLY DYNASTIC PERIOD (3100-2649 BC)
1st and 2nd Dynasties: Memphis founded as the capital of Egypt. The rulers are buried in tombs at Saqqarah, where the first pyramids were built.

OLD KINGDOM (2686-2181 BC)
2649–2575: 3rd Dynasty. Zoser complex at Saqqarah.
2575–2465: 4th Dynasty. Centralised government; pyramids at Dahshur, Giza and Abu Ruwash.
2455–2134: 5th and 6th Dynasties. Pyramids and sun temples at Abu Sir and Saqqarah. Tomb reliefs at Saqqarah and Giza. Pyramid texts.

FIRST INTERMEDIATE PERIOD (2134-2040 BC)
7th–10th Dynasties. Collapse of government; country divided among local rulers; famine and poverty.

MIDDLE KINGDOM (2134-1633 BC)
11th–13th Dynasties. Reunification by Theban rulers; powerful central government. Pyramids at Dahshur and Hawarah built by Amenemhet III (1842–1797). Pyramids at Al-Lisht, Mazghunah and south Saqqarah.

SECOND INTERMEDIATE PERIOD (1640-1532 BC)
14th–17th Dynasties. Country divided again. Asiatics ("Hyksos") rule in Delta.

NEW KINGDOM (1551-1085 BC)
1550–1307: 18th Dynasty. Reunification under Theban kings; expulsion of Asiatics in north and annexa-

tion of Nubia. Period of greatest prosperity, with Thebes (Luxor) as main royal residence. Pharaohs include Akhenaten (1353–1335) and Tutankhamun (1333–1323).
1307–1196: 19th Dynasty. Ramesses II (1290–1224) embodies ideal kingship, builds many monuments.
1196–1085: 20th Dynasty. Invasions by Libyans and "Sea Peoples". Weak kings rule from the Delta.

THIRD INTERMEDIATE PERIOD (1085-712 BC)
21st–24th Dynasties. Tanis is capital, displaced as Egypt is divided among several rulers.

LATE PERIOD 716-332 BC
716–657: 25th Dynasty from Kush (Sudan) unites country. Assyrian invasions in 667 and 663.
664–525: 26th Dynasty rules from Sais in Western Delta. First settlement of Greeks at Memphis.
525–405: 27th Dynasty (Persian). Canal linking the Nile with the Red Sea completed under Darius I. Fortress called "Perhapemon" (Babylon in Greek) built at the Nile end of the canal on future site of Cairo.
404–342: 28th–30th Dynasties. Slow decline.
342–330: 31st Dynasty (Persian).

PTOLEMAIC EMPIRE (332-30 BC)
332–30: Alexander the Great conquers Egypt, founds Alexandria. Ptolemy I rules as governor after Alexander's death in 323 BC, then after 304 BC as first king of dynasty.

ROMAN PERIOD (30 BC–AD 324)
Rule from Rome. Fortress rebuilt at Babylon in AD 116 under Trajan (98–117). Visits to Egypt by Vespasian, Trajan, Hadrian (twice), Septimus Severus and Caracalla. High taxes, poverty and revolt. Spread of Christianity, despite persecution from AD 251 onward.

BYZANTINE PERIOD (AD 324–AD 642)
Rule from Constantinople (Byzantium).
324–619: Christianity made state religion, 379. Coptic Church separates from Catholic Church, 451. Last pagan temple (Philae) converted into church, 527.
619–29: Third Persian occupation.
629–39: Re-establishment of Byzantine rule.
639–42: Arab conquest under Amr ibn al-As, who founds new capital, Fustat, next to Babylon.

ARAB EMPIRE (AD 642-868)
Rule by governors on behalf of caliph.
642–58: The Rashidun ("Orthodox") caliphs.
658–750: The Umayyad caliphs rule from Damascus.
750–878: The Abbasid caliphs rule from Baghdad. Al-Askar built. First Turkish governor appointed, 856.

TULUNID EMPIRE (AD 878-905)
Ahmad Ibn Tulun, Turkish governor, declares independence, founds Al-Qatai, builds great mosque which carries his name, 876–9.

ABBASID INTERIM (905–935)
Reassertion of power from Baghdad.
FATIMID EMPIRE (969–1171) Golden age.
969: Al-Qahirah, royal enclosure, founded.
970–72: Al-Azhar built.
996–1021: Reign of Al-Hakim, "The Mad Caliph".
1085–92: Mosque of al-Guyushi, walls of Al-Qahirah, Bab al-Futuh, Bab an-Nasr, Bab Zuwaylah built.
1168: Frankish invasion, Fustat destroyed.
AYYUBID EMPIRE (1171–1250) Saladin (Salah ad-Din) and his successors conduct campaigns against Franks and other invaders.
1174: Crusader invasion repelled.
1187–92: Jerusalem and most of Palestine retaken.
1219–21: Frankish invasion by sea; occupation of Damietta and advance on Cairo culminates in Muslim victory at Mansura ("The Victorious") in the Delta.
1249: Frankish invasion under St Louis culminates in second Muslim victory at Mansura.
BAHRI MAMLUK EMPIRE (1250–1382) Era of expansion and prosperity.
1260–79: Reign of Baybars al-Bunduqdari. Defeat of the Mongols, reduction of Frankish states to vassalage, extension of empire.
1279–90: Reign of Qalawun.
1293–1340: Three reigns of An-Nasir Muhammad ibn Qalawun. Period of architectural splendour in Cairo.
1340–82: Reigns of sons, grandsons and great-grandsons of An-Nasir Muhammad.
BURGI (CIRCASSIAN) MAMLUK EMPIRE (1382–1517) Continuation of massive building programmes under the rule of 23 sultans.
OTTOMAN PERIOD (1517–1914)
Egypt is a province of the Ottoman Empire.
1517–1798: Ottoman rule through 106 governors. Cultural decline, commercial prosperity.
1798–1805: French invasion and occupation.
1805–48: Muhammad Ali Pasha. Massive programme of modernisation and creation of new empire.
1848: Ibrahim Pasha
1849–54: Abbas Pasha
1854–63: Said Pasha. Suez Canal concession granted. Cairo–Alexandria rail link, Nile steamship service established.
1863–79: Ismail the Magnificent. Programme of modernisation. Chamber of Deputies established (1866), principle of primogeniture accepted by Sultan. Title of "Khedive" (sovereign) granted (1867). Suez Canal opened (1869).

PRECEDING PAGES: the sphinx and Pyramids of Giza.
LEFT: Amenhopis II.
RIGHT: Napoleon meets the vizir.

1879–92: Khedive Tawfik. British Occupation begins (1882).
1892–1914: Khedive Abbas Hilmi II .
POST-1914: PROTECTORATE–REPUBLIC
1914–17: Sultan Husayn Kamel. British Protectorate declared, martial law instituted.
1917–22: Sultan Fuad. Revolution of 1919.
1922–36: King Fuad I. Monarchy established.
1936–52: King Faruq. During World War II Egypt is neutral, but is reoccupied by Britain. Fires of Black Saturday (1952) lead to military coup.
1952–53: The July Revolution deposes Faruq in favour of his infant son, Ahmad Fuad, then declares Egypt a republic. Gamal Abdel Nasser becomes leader.

1956: Suez Canal nationalised. Tripartite aggression of British, French and Jewish interests against Egypt.
1967: The Six-Day War against Israel.
1970: Nasser is succeeded by Anwar Sadat.
1973: The October War against Israel.
1974–77: Open Door Policy, political liberalisation.
1979: Camp David accords lead to peace treaty with Israel. Egypt boycotted by the rest of the Arab World.
1981: President Anwar Sadat assassinated. Hosni Mubarak succeeds him.
1996-7: Spate of terrorist attacks on tourists in Cairoand at the Temple of Hatshepsut, Luxor.
1999: The discovery of a major 1st–2nd-century cemetery in the Bahariyyah oasis, 370km (230 miles) southwest of Giza. Excavations reveal some 10,000 decorated mummies. ❑

ANCIENT EGYPT

Egypt's ancient civilisation saw the rise of the great pharaohs
but also their fall, which opened the floodgates to years of foreign rule

Egypt produced one of the earliest and most magnificent civilisations the world has ever witnessed. Five thousand years ago, when Mesopotamia was still the scene of petty squabbling between city states and while Europe, America and most of western Asia were inhabited by Stone-Age hunters, the ancient Egyptians had learned how to make bread, brew beer and mix paint. They could smelt and cast copper, drill beads, mix mineral compounds for cosmetics, and glaze stone and pottery surfaces. They had invented the hoe, the most ancient of agricultural implements, and had carried out experiments in plant and animal breeding.

Egypt is a land of unusual geographic isolation, with well-defined boundaries. To the east and west are vast deserts. To the north is the Mediterranean Sea. To the south there was, before the construction of the High Dam at Aswan, a formidable barrier of igneous rock, beyond which lay the barren land of Nubia. Within these recognisable boundaries, however, was a land divided; Upper Egypt extended from Aswan to a point just south of modern Cairo and was largely barren, apart from a narrow strip of land flanking the river; the Delta, or Lower Egypt, spread from the point where the Nile fanned into a fertile triangle some 200 km (125 miles) before reaching the Mediterranean Sea. Linking Upper and Lower Egypt was the vital artery, the River Nile.

Before the Nile was harnessed by technology, the annual flood, a result of the monsoon rains on the Ethiopian tableland, spilled into the flood plain, leaving a thick layer of alluvial soil. Since rainfall in Egypt is almost nill, the people depended on the river for their crops; and it was ultimately on the fertility of the soil that ancient Egyptian civilisation was based.

The earliest human inhabitants of the Nile Valley were hunters who tracked game across northern Africa and the eastern Sudan, later joined by nomadic tribes of Asiatic origin who filtered into Egypt in sporadic migrations across the Sinai peninsula and the Red Sea.

Late Paleolithic settlements (*circa* 12000–8000 BC) reveal that both these newcomers and the indigenous inhabitants had a hunting and

food-gathering economy. As time went by, their lives became bound to the ebb and flow of the annual flood.

As the water rose each year in July, the inhabitants were obliged to draw back from the banks. By August, when the river waters swept across the lowlands, they took to the highland plateaux and pursued hunting activities, tracking antelope, hartebeest, wild ass and gazelle, with lances, bows and arrows. During the first half of October the river attained its highest level, and thereafter began to subside, leaving lagoons and streams which became natural reservoirs for fish.

A variety of plants grew from the fertile, uniform deposit of silt. During this season

LEFT: a 19th-century engraving of the Temple of Philae, showing traces of the original colours.
RIGHT: scene in the tomb of Nakht (mid-XVIIIth Dynasty), the Tombs of the Nobles, Thebes.

of plenty, hunting activity was at a minimum. From January to March seasonal pools dried out and fishing was limited, but in the swampy areas near the river there were turtles, rodents and Nile clams. At low Nile, during April, May and June, game scattered, food became scarce, and hunting was actively pursued once more.

Despite their diverse origins, therefore, there was a natural tendency for the people to group together during the "season of abundance" when there was plenty of food to eat and then to split up into smaller

LIFE AFTER DEATH

As inevitably as the sun rose each morning and the flood arrived each year, man, it was believed, would rise again.

death and rebirth that left a profound impression on the people: the sun that "died" in the western horizon each evening was "reborn" in the eastern sky the following morning; and the river was directly and unfailingly responsible for the germination or "rebirth" of the crops after the "death" of the land each year.

This natural sequence of rebirth after death undoubtedly lay at the root of the ancient Egyptian belief in the afterlife. As inevitably as the sun rose at a certain time each morning and the river flood

groups or communities during the low-flood season or during periods of drought.

Religion and agriculture

As a certain rhythm formed in their lives, they observed that the gifts of their naturally irrigated valley depended on a dual force: the sun and the river, both of which had creative and destructive powers. The life-giving rays of the sun that caused a crop to grow could also cause it to shrivel and die. And the river that invigorated the soil with its mineral-rich deposits could destroy whatever lay in its path or, if it failed to rise sufficiently, bring famine. These two phenomena, moreover, shared in the pattern of

arrived each year, man, it was believed, would rise again from death.

Agriculture was introduced into the Nile Valley about 5000 BC. Once grain (a variety of domesticated barley from Asia) could be cultivated and stored, the people could be assured of a regular food supply, which was an important factor in the movement away from primitive society towards civilisation. Agriculture made possible a surplus of time and economic resources, which resulted in population increase and craft specialisation. Polished stone axes, well-made knives, and pottery vessels were produced, as well as ivory combs and slate palettes, on which paint for body decoration was prepared.

Slowly, assimilation took place. Some villages may have merged as their boundaries expanded; or small groups of people may have gravitated towards larger ones and started to trade and barter with them. The affairs of the various communities became tied to major settlements, which undoubtedly represented the richest and most powerful. This tendency towards political unity occurred in both Upper and Lower Egypt. In Upper Egypt, the chief settlement was Nekhen, where the leader wore a conical White Crown

PYRAMID AGE

The Old Kingdom, from the 3rd to 6th Dynasties, is considered by many historians as the high-water mark of achievement.

portrayed wearing both the White Crown and the Red Crown. He stands at the beginning of Egypt's ancient history, which was divided by an Egyptian historian called Manetho – who lived *circa* 280 BC – into 30 royal dynasties starting at Menes and ending with Alexander the Great.

The dynasties were subsequently combined and grouped into three main periods: the Old Kingdom or Pyramid Age, the Middle Kingdom and the New Kingdom. Although further divided by modern historians,

and took the sedge plant as his emblem. In the Delta or Lower Egypt, the capital was Buto, and the leader wore the characteristic Red Crown and adopted the bee as his symbol.

The Old Kingdom

Unification of Upper and Lower Egypts has been ascribed to Narmer (Menes), in 3100 BC. He set up his capital at Memphis, at the apex of the Delta, and was the first king to be

LEFT: ibex depicted in the Mastaba of Kagemni, a VIth Dynasty official, at Saqqarah.
ABOVE: *View of the Sphinx and the Great Pyramid*, painted by Nicolas Jaques Conté in the 18th century.

these periods remain the basis of ancient Egyptian chronology.

The Old Kingdom, from the 3rd to 6th Dynasties (2686–2181 BC), is considered by many historians as the high-water mark of achievement. A series of vigorous and able monarchs established a highly organised, centralised government. The great Pyramids of Giza, on the western bank of the Nile southwest of Cairo, have secured undying fame for Khufu (Cheops), Khafre (Chephren) and Menkaure (Mycerinus).

These kings ruled during a period of great refinement, an aristocratic era, which saw rising productivity in all fields. Cattle and raw materials, including gold and copper, were taken in donkey caravans from the Sudan and Nubia. Sinai was exploited for mineral wealth and a fleet of ships sailed to Byblos (on the coast of Lebanon) to import cedar wood. The "Great House", *peraha*, from which the word pharaoh is derived, controlled all trade routes throughout the land, as well as all the markets.

The end of the Old Kingdom
In the Old Kingdom the power of the pharaoh was supreme and he took an active part in all affairs of state, which ranged from determining the height of the Nile during the annual inundation, to recruiting a labour force from the provinces,

to leading mining and exploratory expeditions.

Naturally, such responsibility was too much for one person and he therefore delegated power to the provincial lords, who were often members of the royal family. The provincial nobility became wealthier, began to exert power, and the result was an inevitable weakening of centralised authority. At the end of the 6th Dynasty some of the provinces managed to shake themselves free from the central government and establish independence. The monarchy collapsed. The Old Kingdom came to an end.

The era known as the First Intermediate Period, between the 7th and the 10th Dynasties,

A LOVE OF BEAUTY

Most of the buildings of ancient Egypt, including the royal palaces, were built of perishable materials such as brick, wood and bundles of reeds, while tombs were built of stone, to last for eternity. This distinction gives the erroneous impression that the ancient Egyptians were preoccupied with thoughts of death. Evidence to the contrary is abundant. Wishing to ensure bounty in the afterlife similar to that enjoyed on earth, they decorated their tombs with a wide variety of farming scenes, manufacturing processes and leisure activities such as hunting parties and musical gatherings, as well as scenes from their own personal lives.

The Old Kingdom tombs at Saqqarah, south of Giza, are adorned with painted relics of the deceased, his wife and children, overseers of his estates, supervisors of his factories, scribes, artisans and peasants. The graphic portrayals of everyday life are clear evidence that the ancient Egyptians took great pride in beautiful possessions: chairs and beds (which often had leather or rope-weave seats or mattresses fastened to the frame with leather thongs) had legs carved in the form of the powerful hind limbs of an ox or lion, for instance; the handle of a spoon was fashioned to resemble a lotus blossom.

saw anarchy, bloodshed and a restructuring of society throughout Egypt. The provincial lords who had gained power and prestige under the great monarchs began to reflect on the traditional beliefs of their forefathers. It was a time of soul-searching; and great contempt was voiced for the law and order of the past.

A powerful family of provincial lords from Herakleopolis Magna (near Bani Suwayf in Middle Egypt) achieved prominence in the 9th and 10th Dynasties and restored some degree of

END OF AN ERA

The period known as the First Intermediate Period saw anarchy, bloodshed and a restructuring of society in Egypt.

and the arts, as well as a breakthrough in literature, established the 12th Dynasty, one of the most peaceful and prosperous eras known to Egypt. Political stability was soon reflected in material prosperity. Building operations were undertaken throughout the whole country. Amenemhet III constructed his tomb at Hawarah (in the Fayyum) with a funerary monument later described by classical writers as "The Labyrinth" and declared by Herodotus to be more wonderful than the pyramids of Giza.

order. In Upper Egypt, meanwhile, in the Theban area (near Luxor), a confederation had gathered around the strong Intef and Mentuhotep family, who slowly extended their authority northwards until there was a clash with the family from Herakleopolis. A civil war resulted in triumph for the Thebans.

The Middle Kingdom

The Middle Kingdom covers the 11th and 12th Dynasties (*circa* 2133–1633 BC). Amenemhet I, whose rule heralded a revival in architecture

LEFT: coffin interior showing Anubis and Horus.
ABOVE: tomb painting in the Valley of the Kings, Luxor.

Goldsmiths, jewellers and sculptors perfected their skills, as Egyptian political and cultural influence extended to Nubia and Kush in the south, around the Eastern Mediterranean to Libya, Palestine, Syria and even to Crete, the Aegean Islands and the mainland to Greece.

In the Middle Kingdom an increasingly wealthy middle class led the ordinary man to aspire to have what only members of the aristocracy had had before: elaborate funerary equipment to ensure a comfortable afterlife. To pay homage to their legendary ancestor, Osiris, thousands of pilgrims from all walks of life made their way to the holy city of Abydos each year, leaving so many offerings in pottery vessels that the site acquired the name of Umm al-Gaab, which means "Mother of Potsherds".

According to legend, Osiris was a just and much-loved ruler who taught his people how to make farm implements, rotate crops and control the waters of the Nile. He also showed them how to adapt to a wheat diet and make bread, wine and beer. Isis, his devoted wife, was also popular. She taught the people how to grind wheat and weave linen with a loom.

Osiris had a brother, Seth, who was secretly jealous of his popularity and conspired against

HERO WORSHIP

The cult of Osiris captured the popular imagination in the Middle Kingdom.

forth an heir, Horus. She raised her son in the marshes of the Delta until he grew strong enough to avenge his father's death by slaying Seth. Horus then took over the throne on earth and the resurrected Osiris became king of the underworld.

The story became a classic. The traditions of the loyalty and devotion of Isis to her husband, of the piety of Horus, who avenged his father's death in a triumph of good over evil, and of the benevolence of Osiris, who was killed but rose to rule again, survived for centuries. The cult of

him. Seth tricked Osiris into climbing into a chest, had it sealed, then cast it into the Nile. Broken-hearted, Isis went in search of the body of her husband, eventually found it, and hid it. But Seth was out boar-hunting and discovered the body. He tore it into 14 pieces, which he scattered over the land. Isis again went in search of Osiris, in the company of her sister Nephthys.

The two sisters collected the pieces and, according to one version of the myth, bound them together with bandages. They lamented over the body of Osiris, fanning it with their wings in order to breath life back in to it. Isis then descended on her husband in the form of a winged bird, received his seed, and brought

Osiris captured the popular imagination of the Egyptians in the Middle Kingdom; and it became desirable to have a *stele* or tombstone erected at or near Abydos, so that the spirit of the deceased could join in the annual dramatisation of his resurrection enacted by the priests.

Later, during the New Kingdom, when Thebes became capital, it was traditional for deceased noblemen to be borne to Abydos and placed in the precinct of the temple there, before being interred at Thebes. If for some reason they could not make this pilgrimage after death, it was made symbolically: their tombs were decorated with handsome reliefs of boats bearing their mummified bodies to Abydos.

End of the Middle Kingdom

At the end of the 13th Dynasty the provincial rulers once again rose against the crown. During this period of instability the Hyksos (a Manethonian term corrupted from *Hekakhasut,* meaning "rulers of foreign countries"), who are believed to have come from the direction of Syria, challenged Egyptian authority. With horses and chariots (hitherto unknown in Egypt), they swept across the northern Sinai, fortified a stronghold at Tel ad-Deba, south of Tanis in the northeastern Delta, then moved towards the apex of the Delta, from where they surged southwards.

The damage done to Egypt's great cities can only be guessed at. Pharaohs of later times inscribed declarations that they "restored what was ruined" and "raised what had gone to pieces", but the almost total absence of contemporary documents during the Hyksos occupation leaves scant evidence of what actually took place. The humiliation of foreign occupa-

MILITARY MIGHT

Out of the desire for national security was born the spirit of military expansion characteristic of the New Kingdom.

tion came to an end when Ahmose, father of the New Kingdom (18th–20th Dynasties, 1551–1085 BC) started a war of liberation and finally expelled the hated invaders from the land. This first unhappy exposure to foreign domination left a lasting mark on the Egyptian character. The seemingly inviolable land of Egypt had to be protected from invasion and to do so meant not only to rid the country of enemies, but to pursue them into western Asia. Out of the desire for national security was born the spirit of military expansion characteristic of the New Kingdom.

LEFT: 19th-century engraving of the grand portico of the Temple of Philae near Aswan.
ABOVE: frieze showing captives at Abu Simbel.

The New Kingdom

The New Kingdom (1551–1085 BC) was the empire period. The military conquests of Thutmosis III, in no fewer than 17 campaigns, resulted in the establishment of Egyptian power throughout Syria and northern Mesopotamia, as well as in Nubia and Libya. Great wealth from conquered nations and vassal states poured into Thebes (Luxor). The caravans were laden with gold, silver, ivory, spices and rare flora and fauna. The greater part of the wealth was bestowed upon Amun who, with the aid of an influential priesthood, was established as Amun-Ra, "King of Gods". Thebes flourished, and some of Egypt's most extravagant monuments were built.

The 18th Dynasty was a period of transition. Old values were passing and new ones emerging. The spirit of the age was based on wealth and power. But grave discontent, especially among the upper classes, was apparent in criticism of the national god Amun and the materialism of the priests who promoted his cult.

slight innovations had become radical reforms. For many centuries portrayals of the pharaohs had been highly stylised; they were always depicted as being strong and powerful, and artists were not permitted to divert from this image in any way.

Now, with the consent, it seems, of Akhenaten, figures in a variety of movements and postures were sculptured in exquisite low relief. Akhenaten himself wished to exaggerate his physical imperfections in order to create the impression of

Akhenaten's revolution

It was in this atmosphere that Amenhotep IV (Akhenaten) grew up, the pharaoh who would revolt against the priests and order temple reliefs to be defaced, shrines to be destroyed, and the image of the god Amun to be erased. Akhenaten transferred the royal residence to Al-Amarnah, in Middle Egypt (*see page 208*), and promoted worship of one god, the Aten, the life-giving sun. The city was called Akhetaten ("The Horizon of the Aten").

Certain innovations had already begun to transform the character of Egyptian art in the early years of Akhenaten's reign. By the time of his move from Thebes to Al-Amarnah, these

a pharaoh who was mortal – a stark contrast with the representations of earlier pharaohs, which had portrayed them as physically perfect god-kings.

Unfortunately, the ideal needs of a religious community and the practical requirements of governing a large empire were not to prove compatible demands. After the deaths of Akhenaten and his half-brother Smenkare, the boy-king Tutankhamun (famous today as one of the few pharaohs to have escaped the early tomb-robbers) came to the throne. Tutankhamun abandoned Al-Amarnah and returned to Memphis and Thebes. The priests of Amun were able to make a spectacular return to power.

Empire-builders

Horemheb, the general who seized the throne at the end of the 18th Dynasty, was an excellent administrator. He re-established a strong government and started a programme of restoration, which continued into the 19th Dynasty, when the pharaohs channelled their boundless energies into reorganising Akhenaten's rule. Seti I, builder of a famous mortuary temple at Abydos, fought battles against the Libyans, Syrians and Hittites; Ramesses II, hero of a war against the Hittites, with whom he signed a famous peace treaty, was also celebrated as a builder of great monuments, including the famous temples at

within shrine, where almost all the pharaohs wished to record their names and deeds for posterity. As new pylons, colonnades and shrines were built, valuable blocks of inscribed stone from earlier periods were often used. The Sun Temples of Akhenaten suffered this fate: thousands of their distinctly uniform, decorated sandstone blocks, known as *talatat*, were buried in various places in Karnak, such as beneath the flagstones of the great Hypostyle Hall.

Ramesses III (1182–1151 BC) was the last of the great pharaohs. His ever-weakening successors fell more and more under the yoke of the priests of Amun who controlled enormous

Abu Simbel; and Ramesses III not only conquered the Libyans, but successfully protected his country from the "People of the Sea".

All these warrior kings of the 19th Dynasty raised magnificent temples in honour of Amun. It was both a duty and privilege to serve the state god, who granted them military success; and successive pharaohs systematically tried to outdo their predecessors in the magnificence of their architectural and artistic endeavours, especially in the great Temple of Amun at Karnak. It became a temple within a temple, shrine

LEFT: mosaic of Akhenaten, Al-Amarnah.
ABOVE: the Ramesseum, Thebes.

KARNAK'S GLORY

The Hypostyle Hall at Karnak is the largest single chamber of any temple in the world. It covers an area of 4,983 sq metres (53,318 sq ft). To support the roof, 134 columns were arranged in 16 rows, with the double row of central columns higher than the others. According to Napoleon's savants, who examined the hall in 1798, the whole of the cathedral of Notre Dame could be accommodated within its walls. Seti I was responsible for the northern half of the hall and Ramesses II built the southern portion, but many other 19th-Dynasty pharaohs recorded their names there, honouring the god Amun.

wealth. According to a text known as the Harris Papyrus, written in the reign of Ramesses III, they possessed over 5,000 divine statues, more than 81,000 slaves, vassals and servants, well over 421,000 cattle, 433 gardens, 691, 334 acres of land, 83 ships, 46 building yards and 65 cities. Naturally such a priesthood wielded enormous power. Gradually the priests came to regard themselves as the ruling power of the state and, at the end of the 20th Dynasty, in 1085 BC, the high priests of Amun overthrew the dynasty. Theoret-

STATE OF CORRUPTION

Anarchy blighted the land and occupation by successive foreign military powers was the result.

ically, the country was still united. In fact, the government became synonymous with corruption. Anarchy flourished and occupation by successive foreign military powers was the result.

Centuries of foreign rule

In 945 BC, Sheshonk, from a family of Libyan descent, but completely Egyptianised, took over leadership. His Libyan followers were probably descendants of mercenary troops who had earlier been granted land in return for military service. The Libyan monarchs conducted themselves as pharaohs and their rule lasted for two centuries.

In 748 BC a military leader, Piankhi, from the region of Kush (northern Sudan), marched northward. Because his people had absorbed Egyptian culture during a long period of Egyptian rule he did not view himself as a conqueror, but as a champion freeing Egypt from the barbarism that had engulfed it. The Egyptians, however, did not regard the Kushites as liberators and it was only after a military clash at Memphis, when the foreigners surged over the ramparts, that they surrendered. Like the Libyans before them, the Kushites established themselves as genuine pharaohs, restored ancient temples and were sympathetic to local customs.

The Assyrians, reputedly the most ruthless of ancient peoples, conquered Egypt in 667 and 663 BC. With a well-trained army they moved south from province to province, assuring the local population of a speedy liberation from oppression.

In these long centuries of foreign rule Egypt had one short respite: the Saite Period, ensuing after an Egyptian named Psamtik liberated the country from Assyrian occupation. He turned his attention to reuniting Egypt, establishing order and promoting tradition.

The unflagging efforts of this great leader, and the Saite rulers who followed him, to restore former greatness led them to pattern their government and society on the Old Kingdom, a model 2,000 years old. Instead of channelling their energies into creating new forms, they fell back on the traditions of the past.

Egypt's revival came to an end when the Persian King Cambyses occupied the land in 525 BC and turned it into a Persian province. The new rulers, like the Libyans and the Kushites, at first showed respect for the religion and customs of the country in an effort to gain support. But the Egyptians were not deceived and as soon as an opportunity arose they routed their invaders. Unfortunately, they were able to maintain independence for only about 60 years before another Persian army invaded.

When Alexander the Great marched on Egypt in 332 BC, he and his army were welcomed by the Egyptians as liberators.   ❑

LEFT: Ramesses III depicted in the tomb of his son, Amun-Khopshef, in the Valley of the Kings, Thebes. **RIGHT:** hieroglyphs combined alphabetical signs, pictures (ideograms) and symbols representing sounds (phonograms).

A PARADE OF THE MORE IMPORTANT GODS

The ancient Egyptians explained the mysteries of nature and the creation of the world through myths concerning the origins and powers of their gods

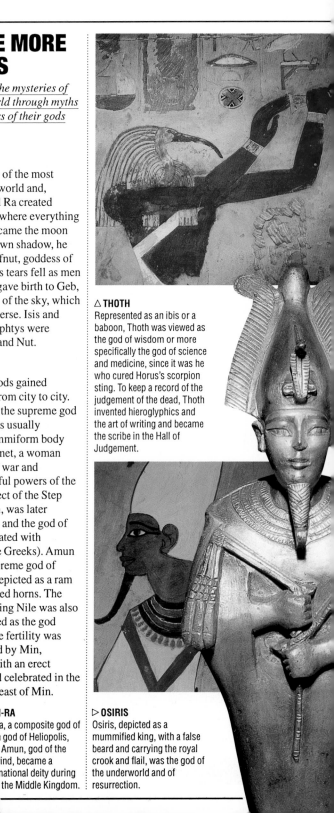

THE CREATION OF THE SUN GOD

The movement of the sun was one of the most significant forces in the ancients' world and, according to his myth, the sun god Ra created himself from the primeval waters where everything was dark and chaotic. His eyes became the moon and the sun and, mating with his own shadow, he created Shu, god of the air, and Tefnut, goddess of mist. At this point, Ra wept and his tears fell as men and women. Shu and Tefnut then gave birth to Geb, god of the earth, and Nut, goddess of the sky, which completed the creation of the universe. Isis and Osiris, Seth and his sister-wife Nephtys were created through the union of Geb and Nut.

RISE AND FALL OF GODS

Through the centuries, different gods gained importance as the capital moved from city to city. In Memphis, Ptah was considered the supreme god and creator of the universe. He was usually depicted as a bald man with a mummiform body and false beard. His consort Sekhmet, a woman with a lion's head, was goddess of war and represented the harmful powers of the sun. Imhotep, architect of the Step Pyramid at Saqqarah, was later deified as their son and the god of medicine (and equated with Asklepios by the Greeks). Amun was the supreme god of Thebes, depicted as a ram with curved horns. The life-bringing Nile was also personified as the god Hapi, while fertility was represented by Min, depicted with an erect phallus and celebrated in the important Feast of Min.

△ **THOTH**
Represented as an ibis or a baboon, Thoth was viewed as the god of wisdom or more specifically the god of science and medicine, since it was he who cured Horus's scorpion sting. To keep a record of the judgement of the dead, Thoth invented hieroglyphics and the art of writing and became the scribe in the Hall of Judgement.

◁ **AMUN-RA**
Amun-Ra, a composite god of Ra, sun god of Heliopolis, and Amun, god of the wind, became a national deity during the Middle Kingdom.

▷ **OSIRIS**
Osiris, depicted as a mummified king, with a false beard and carrying the royal crook and flail, was the god of the underworld and of resurrection.

◁ **HATHOR**
An early Egyptian Earth Mother, depicted as a cow, or as a woman with cow's ears or horns, Hathor was the goddess of beauty, love and music (identified by the Greeks with Aphrodite).

▽ **ISIS**
Like Hathor, Isis was often depicted with cow horns, encircling a solar disc. As the sister-wife of Osiris and mother of Horus, she embodied marital fidelity and maternal devotion.

△ **HORUS**
The falcon-headed god Horus was foremost a sun god, but also a protector of kings and a guide to the dead in the underworld.

◁ **ANUBIS**
Depicted as a jackal, or a man with a jackal head, Anubis greeted the dead in the underworld and protected their bodies from decay.

THE MURDER OF OSIRIS

The myth of the murder of Osiris and his sister-wife's hunt for his body clearly illustrates the Egyptian belief in the afterlife. Osiris was born a god but grew up as a man who became the king of Egypt. His brother Seth was so jealous of his popularity and success that he locked him in a coffin, which he threw into the Nile. Isis, mourning her husband's death, went looking for the coffin and eventually found it near Byblos (modern Lebanon) where it had been surrounded by a tree.

Having recovered the body, Isis took the form of a bird (symbol of the spirit) to revive Osiris, but only managed to stir him long enough to impregnate herself with a son, Horus the Younger. While Isis was giving birth to her son, Seth was cutting Osiris's body into 14 pieces, which he scattered across Egypt. Isis later recovered all of them except his penis, which had been eaten by Nile fish. She reassembled the parts and made a mould of the missing organ, while Horus, having fought a battle with Seth, brought the eye of his father's murderer and placed it in Osiris's mouth, ensuring his eternal life.

The image above depicts Isis on the canopic shrine of Tutankhamun.

THE PTOLEMAIC PERIOD

*Under the Ptolemies, Egypt again became a powerful empire with Alexandria
as its capital and the infamous Cleopatra VI as its queen*

When Alexander the Great marched on Egypt, the Egyptians had no reason to fear that this would mark the end of their status as an independent nation. He first made his way to thickly populated Memphis, the ancient capital, where he made an offering at the Temple of Ptah, then lost no time in travelling to Siwah Oasis to consult the famous oracle of Amun-Ra. When he emerged from the sanctuary he announced that the sacred statue had recognised him, and the priests of Amun greeted him as the son of the god.

Before he left Egypt, Alexander laid down the basic plans for its government. In the important provinces (*nomes* in Greek), he appointed local governors from among Egyptian nobles; he made provision for the collection of taxes and he laid out the plans for his great city and sea-port, Alexandria, so situated as to facilitate the flow of Egypt's surplus resources to Greece and to intercept all trade with Africa and Asia.

When Alexander died from a fever at Babylon, his conquests fell to lesser heirs. Egypt was held by a general named Ptolemy, who took over leadership as King Ptolemy I. During the three centuries of Ptolemaic rule that followed, Egypt became the seat of a brilliant empire once more.

The first of the Ptolemies

Ptolemy did not continue Alexander's practice of founding independent cities. With the exception of Ptolemais, on the western bank of the Nile in Middle Egypt, and the old Greek city of Naucratis in the Delta, only Alexandria represented a traditional Greek city-state. Ptolemy chose instead to settle his mercenary troops (Greeks, Macedonians, Persians and Hellenised Asiatics) among the Egyptian population in towns near the capitals of the provinces into which Egypt was

divided. Many settlers married Egyptians and by the second and third generations their children bore both Greek and Egyptian names.

In Alexandria Greeks formed the bulk of the population, followed in number by the Jews. But there was also a large Egyptian population, which lived west of the city, in the old quarter

of Rhacotis. Alexandria occupied the strip of sandy soil between Lake Mareotis and the sea, where the island of Pharos stood, surmounted by its famous lighthouse, one of the Seven Wonders of the World.

The Serapis cult

Ptolemy I introduced a cult designed to provide a link between his subjects, Greek and Egyptian. He observed that the Apis bull was worshipped at Memphis and assumed, wrongly, that the cult was popular and widespread. The deceased Apis was known as Osiris-Apis or "Oserapis", from which Serapis was derived. Ptolemy supplied Serapis with anthropomor-

---

PRECEDING PAGES: the Temple of Khnum at Esna has reliefs recording the names of the Ptolemies.
LEFT: a statue of Herhor displayed in the Greco-Roman Museum, Alexandria.
RIGHT: Sobek, the crocodile god, is celebrated at the Ptolemaic Temple of Horus at Kom Ombo.

phic features and declared him to be a national god. To slot the new deity into the path of his own career, Ptolemy announced that he had had a dream in which a colossal statue was revealed to him. No sooner had he communicated his revelation to the people than a statue of Serapis was put on view, closely resembling his vision.

The cult of Serapis was to have some success throughout Greece and Asia Minor, in Sicily, and especially in Rome where, as the patron god of the Ptolemaic Empire, its presence

CULTURAL UNITY

The Ptolemies regarded Egypt as their land, conducting themselves both as bearers of Greek culture and as guardians of Egyptian culture.

ematicians, geographers, historians, poets and philosophers gravitated to the *Mouseion* or Museum attached to the Library in Alexandria, which was a research institution.

Alexandrian astronomers revised the Egyptian calendar, then, some two centuries later, the Roman one, creating the Julian calendar that was used throughout Europe until the end of the Renaissance. Literary critics and scholars edited classical texts, giving them the editions we now know. Many living poets such as Theocritus, Callimachus and

enhanced the empire's prestige. In Egypt Serapis was worshipped in every major town, but especially in Alexandria and Memphis, where the Serapeum, the temple of Serapis in the necropolis of Saqqarah, became a famous site.

Alexandria, seat of learning

Alexandria became capital in place of Memphis and was soon to become the major seat of learning in the Mediterranean world, replacing Athens as the centre of culture. Ptolemy II commissioned Egyptians to translate their literature into Greek; and a priest, Manetho, wrote the history of his country. Research was also fostered; and distinguished astronomers, math-

Apollonius Rhodius received generous financial support.

The Ptolemies regarded Egypt as their land and they played a dual role in it, conducting themselves both as bearers of Greek culture and as guardians of Egyptian culture. They resided in Alexandria, yet as pharaohs they lavished revenues on local priesthoods for the upkeep of temples or at least exempted them from taxes. One aspect of the power of the pharaoh was his capacity to uphold religious order; and the Ptolemies thus continued an ancient tradition. Ptolemaic temples were built on traditional lines, often on the sites of more ancient temples. The walls were adorned with scenes depicting

Ptolemaic kings in the manner of the ancient pharaohs. Like the ancient pharaohs, the kings fulfilled religious duties and and made ceremonial journeys up the Nile, enjoying the public worship of political leadership that was a long-standing feature of life in Egypt.

The Greek language

Bilingual Egyptians realised long before the conquest by Alexander that if they transcribed their own language into the Greek alphabet, which was well known among the middle

SHARED IMAGERY

The resemblances between Biblical and Egyptian imagery are not surprising in view of the centuries of contact between Egyptians and Jews in Egypt.

the Ptolemies. When Palestine fell under the control of Ptolemy I in 301 BC, he brought back Jewish mercenaries, who joined the established communities. Unable to speak Hebrew, which had disappeared as a living language, Egyptian Jews soon felt a need to translate their sacred books into Greek, which resulted in the version of the Old Testament known as the *Septuagint.*

The striking resemblances between Biblical and Egyptian expression and imagery are not all that surprising in view of the

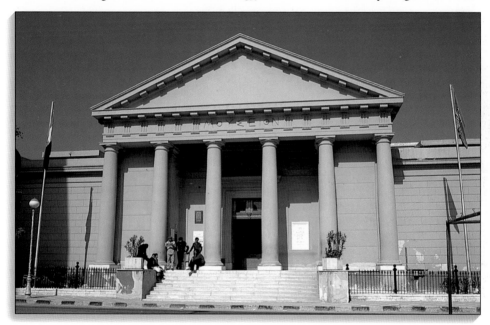

classes and was simpler to read, communication would be easier. Scribes started the transliteration, adding seven extra letters from the Egyptian alphabet to accommodate sounds for which there were no Greek letters, and created a new script, now known as Coptic.

Greek also became the mother-tongue of the Jews in Egypt, who constituted the second-largest foreign community. Many had been imported as soldiers, even before the arrival of

---

LEFT: column at the catacombs of Kom Al-Shuqafah, Alexandria, Egypt's largest Roman funerary complex.
ABOVE: the Greco-Roman Museum in Alexandria has a superb collection of Ptolemaic artifacts.

centuries of contact between Egyptians and Jews in Egypt. For example, an Egyptian sage called Amenemope (*circa* 1320–1080 BC) admonished, "Set thyself in the arms of God," while Moses declaimed, "The eternal God is a dwelling place, and underneath are the everlasting arms." "Yahweh weigheth the hearts," says Proverbs 2:12; and it has not passed unobserved that the only other doctrine in which a god weighs the human heart is the myth of the court of Osiris in the underworld, where it is weighed against the feather of truth.

The Ptolemies encouraged other foreigners to come to live in Egypt, including Syrians and Persians, as well as Greeks. There was a strong anti-Egyptian feeling among the sophisticated Greeks, who did not encourage Egyptians to become citizens of Alexandria and the Greek cities. Although they held Egyptian culture in reverence in many ways, they did not learn the Egyptian language or writing. Even the Greek masses, fascinated by the "sacred mysteries" and "divine oracles" of the Land of Wonders, nevertheless held the Egyptians in contempt.

There was also anti-Greek feeling among the Egyptians, who had a strong sense of cultural

NATIONALIST FERVOUR

This era saw the emergence of a landed and wealthy Egyptian population that was ardently nationalistic.

superiority towards anyone who did not speak their language. Although there is evidence that Egyptian priests and officials collaborated with the Ptolemies, there are also indications that they rebelled frequently, resentful of the fact that they were being treated as a conquered race. Prophetic writings were widely circulated among the Egyptian people, promising the expulsion of the foreigners.

The last of the Ptolemies

Towards the end of the 2nd century BC there were economic problems and political unrest in Egypt, along with a decline in foreign trade. Some territories outside Egypt were lost, and the pros-

perity of the kingdom waned. The court, rich in material wealth and lax in morals, became the scene of decadence and anarchy.

By the last century of Ptolemaic rule, the Egyptians had acquired a position that was somewhat nearer in equality to the Greeks than they had enjoyed under the earlier Ptolemies. This era saw the emergence of a landed, wealthy Egyptian population, who were ardently nationalistic with little respect for the settlers. It was from their ranks that Coptic Christianity's great spiritual leaders were to arise.

Cleopatra VI, the most famous of the Ptolemies, came to the throne at the age of about 18, as co-regent with her even younger brother Ptolemy XII. They were at that time under the guardianship of the Roman Senate and Romans interfered in the rivalry between them, which led Ptolemy to banish his 21-year-old sister from Egypt. Cleopatra sought refuge in Syria, with a view to raising an army and recovering the throne by force. When Julius Caesar came to Alexandria in 47 BC, he took the side of the banished queen and set her on the throne. Soon afterwards Cleopatra bore his only son, Caesarion.

A little over five years later, she met Mark Antony at Tarsus. Their legendary love affair brought her three more children, but succeeded in alienating Antony from his supporters in Rome. His purported will, stating his wishes to be buried at Alexandria, angered many Romans, and gave Octavian (later known as emperor Augustus) the excuse he was looking for to declare war on Antony. Octavian marched against him, defeating him at Actium and capturing Alexandria. Antony committed suicide and Cleopatra is recorded to have caused her own death by the bite of an asp. Caesarion, who had been co-regent since 43 BC, was murdered; and Octavian became sole ruler in 30 BC.

Egypt thenceforth was a province of the Roman empire, subject only to the rule of the emperor in Rome, and to viceroys or prefects nominated by the emperor, who followed the example of the Ptolemies and represented themselves to the Egyptians as successors of the ancient pharaohs. ❑

LEFT: Cleopatra delivers the fatal bite of an asp.
RIGHT: funeral mask, Greco-Roman Museum.

21995

THE ROMAN PERIOD AND EARLY CHRISTIANITY

Early Christians were brutally persecuted under the Roman rule of force –
until, that is, the revelation of Emperor Constantine

The Roman occupation of Egypt, ostensibly a mere extension of Ptolemaic rule, was actually markedly different. While a mutual hostility towards the Persians and a long history of commercial relations bound Egyptians and Greeks together, no such affinity existed between Egyptians and Romans. Alexander the Great had entered Egypt without striking a blow; Roman troops fought battles with Egyptians almost immediately. The Ptolemaic kings had lived in Egypt; the Roman emperors governed from Rome and their prefects took over the position formerly held in the scheme of government by the kings.

To the Egyptians the prefect, not the emperor, was therefore the royal personage. And the prefect did not perform the ceremonial functions of divine kingship, which was by tradition highly personal. There was thus a drastic change in the climate of leadership throughout this period.

The emperor Augustus made the mistake of arousing the ire of the Greeks when he abolished the Greek Senate in Alexandria and took administrative powers from Greek officials. Further, in response to an appeal by Herod, king of Judaea, he not only agreed to restore to him the land that had been bestowed on Cleopatra during her short refuge in Syria, but also agreed to grant self-government to the Hellenised Jews of Alexandria. This caused great consternation among the Greeks. Fighting soon broke out, first between Greeks and Jews, then with the Romans when they tried to separate the two. The unrest that marks the beginning of the Christian era in Alexandria had already begun. Ships in the harbour were set on fire, the flames spread and the Mouseion Library was burned. An estimated 490,000 rolls of papyrus perished in the process.

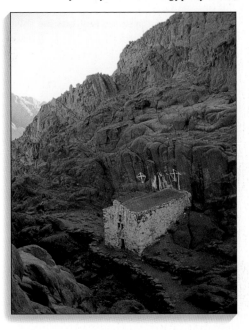

The Romans thenceforth stationed garrisons at Alexandria, which remained the capital; at Babylon (Old Cairo), which was the key to communications with Asia and with Lower Egypt; and at Syene (Aswan), which was Egypt's southern boundary. They controlled Egypt by force, and regarded the land as no more than a granary supplying wheat to Rome. Consequently, an enormous burden of taxation was placed on the people of the Nile Valley. A census was imposed on villages throughout the land and house-to-house registration of the number of residents was made, which might have been considered normal procedure in Rome, but was regarded as an infringement of privacy by Egyptians. Calculation of the wheat quota was based not on the productivity of the land, but on the number of men in a village.

Those Egyptians who had enjoyed certain privileges under the later Ptolemies and acquired considerable wealth received no

---

PRECEDING PAGES: St Anthony's Monastery in the Eastern Desert dates from the 4th century.
LEFT: Coptic painting with Byzantine influences.
RIGHT: chapel on Mount Moses, Sinai.

special consideration by the Romans, but had their problems compounded when the emperor Trajan declared that peasant farmers should be recruited for the Roman army. Hadrian reduced rentals on imperial lands and exempted citizens of Greek cities and Greek settlers in the Fayyum from taxation, but the Egyptian rural population was assessed at a flat rate, without regard for income, age or capacity for work. Hardship followed. There are records of men having "fled leaving no property", 43 in

PUBLIC PROPERTY

Egypt was treated as a private estate of the emperor and as a pleasure-ground for the Roman upper classes.

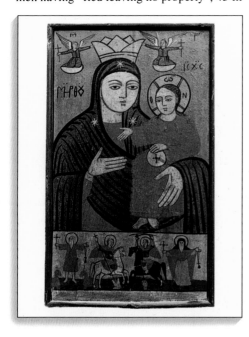

number, then 60, then 100 from a single village. Some took refuge in remote areas of the desert, while others hid in caves and ancient tombs flanking the Nile Valley. When men fled or hid, their families suffered the penalties.

Strategic planning

The Romans made an overt show of respect for Egyptian priesthoods by constructing new temples or completing older ones built by the Ptolemies. The temple to the goddess Hathor at Denderah, for example, which was started under the later Ptolemies, was completed some 185 years later under the emperor Tiberius; and temples in the traditional style were completed

at Esna, Kom Ombo and Philae. It is worth noting, however, that these sites were chosen for their strategic position as well as the sake of ancient tradition. Esna had been a centre for local commerce from earliest times; Kom Ombo, situated on a hill, commanded the trade routes to Nubia in the south; and Philae was situated on Egypt's southern border.

Temple lands elsewhere, however, were annexed and placed under the control of the Roman government. Local priests were allotted only a small part of sacred property and their own material wealth was curbed. The produce of vineyards, palm groves and fig plantations owned by temples was collected by Roman officials and taxes were levied on sheep, oxen, horses and donkeys. A Roman official held the title of "High Priest of Alexandria and all Egypt". Egypt was treated as a private estate of the emperor and a pleasure-ground for the Roman upper classes.

Early Christianity

Such were the conditions in Egypt during the 1st century of the Christian era, when the apostle Mark preached in Alexandria. Remains from the period showing the diffusion of Christianity in Egypt are scant, but New Testament writings found in Bahnasa in Middle Egypt date from around the year 200, and a fragment of the gospel of St John, written in Coptic and found in Upper Egypt, can be dated even earlier. They testify to the spread of Christianity throughout Egypt within a century of St Mark's arrival.

The Catechetical School of Alexandria was the first important institution of religious learning in Christian antiquity. It was founded in 190 by Pantanaeus, a scholar who is believed to have come to Alexandria approximately 10 years earlier. Significantly, the emergence of the school coincides with the first direct attacks by the Romans on the Christians of Alexandria.

Clement (160–215), a convert from paganism who succeeded Pantanaeus, is regarded as an early apostle of Christian liberalism and taught in Alexandria for more than 20 years. He was succeeded by Origen (185–253), the theologian and writer who is considered as the greatest of the early Christian apologists. Like Clement, he was highly critical of the Gnostic movement (from the Greek *gnosis* or "knowledge").

Gnosticism

The origin of the Gnostic communities is obscure and until recently not much was known about them: the Gnostics were hounded into silence, in the name of orthodox Christianity, from the 4th century onward and their writings were burned.

Fortunately, however, a collection of manuscripts was discovered in Nag Hammadi in Upper Egypt in 1945. These texts, which have raised some important questions about the progress of development of

MIND OVER MATTER

Neoplatonists understood reality as the spiritual world contemplated by reason and allowed the material world only a formal existence.

Zoroastrianism and Manichaeism. Little wonder that the Gnostics, with such diversity, came under attack by orthodox Christians.

Neoplatonism

A more formidable rival to Christianity in the long run came directly from pagan thought: Neoplatonism. Coalescing in Alexandria during the 3rd century, this philosophical school revived and developed the metaphysical and mystical side of Platonic doctrine, explaining the universe as a hierarchy

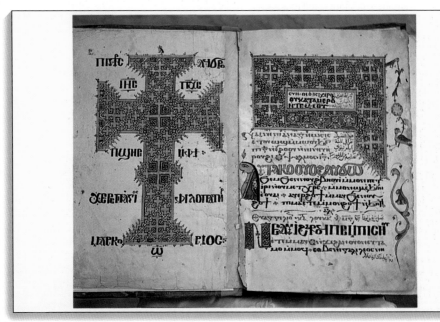

Christianity in Egypt, are copied from original writings that may date from the second half of the 1st century.

The 12 Nag Hammadi codices were collected by Egyptians and translated into Coptic, the Egyptian language of the time. They vary widely in content, presenting a spectrum of heritages that range from Egyptian folklore, Hermeticism, Greek philosophy and Persian mysticism to the Old and New Testaments. The codices include a "a gospel of Thomas", a compilation of sayings attributed to Jesus; extracts from Plato's *Republic*; and *apocrypha* ("secret books") related to

LEFT AND ABOVE: in the Monastery of St Bishay.

rising from matter to soul, soul to reason and reason to God, conceived as pure being without matter or form. Neoplatonists understood reality as the spiritual world contemplated by reason and allowed the material world only a formal existence. Ascetic disciplines were part of their ethical code, which urged them to ascend from the bonds of matter to the spiritual world, to become ecstatically united with the divine.

The first Neoplatonist, Ammonius Saccas, had been the teacher of Origen and was a lapsed Christian, while his famous successors – Plotinus, Porphyry, Iamblichus, Hypatia and Proclus – were all pagans. Plotinus, born in Asyut, was the most influential, making many converts at the imperial court in Rome. Porphyry, who was his student, came to be regarded by the Christian bishops as their greatest enemy – they burned his books in public – and the last important work of the school was Proclus's defence of the pagan philosophical tradition against Christianity. More than one Christian was a student of Neoplatonism, nevertheless, and even Porphyry found Christian readers and translators, by whom Neoplatonic ideas were co-opted into the teachings of the early Church.

ENFORCED PAGANISM

Decius ordered Egyptians to participate in pagan worship and to submit certificates of sacrifice.

Major Neoplatonic works survived intact, and by the end of the Middle Ages a handful of Europeans could read them in the original. As knowledge of Greek began to extend outside the clergy, aristocratic study-groups sprang up, most notably in Florence, and Neoplatonism rapidly became a fashion, then a movement. Within a few years its influence had spread from northern Italy throughout Western Europe, largely creating that cultural consensus we call the Renaissance. Thus a common element in the paintings of Botticelli or Titian, the engravings of Dürer, the sculpture of Michelangelo, or the poetry of Shakespeare, which distinguishes them from earlier European art, is their rootedness in Neoplatonic images and ideas. For two centuries or so, while a 1,000-year-old Christian orthodoxy came increasingly into question, these images and ideas were to be the conceptual currency of every educated European.

They were also modern man's first key to an understanding of the ancient pagan culture that the early Church, in Egypt and elsewhere, had conscientiously set out to destroy.

Religious persecution

The first systematic attempt to put an end to Christianity by depriving the Church of both its leaders and followers took place under the emperor Decius (249–251), who ordered Egyptians to participate in pagan worship in the presence of Roman officers and to submit certificates of sacrifice. Those who refused were declared to be self-avowed Christians and were tortured. Some Christians sent in false certificates; others managed to escape to the solitude of the desert. Many, however, were willing to die rather than abjure their faith, and their martyrdom further accelerated the Christian movement.

Beginnings of Monasticism

St Paul the Theban, orphaned as a youth, and - St Anthony, who came from a family of landowners with a certain status in society, were two of Egypt's earliest and greatest spiritual leaders. Both lived lives of meditation and prayer at about this time; each, unknown to the other, had chosen a retreat in the Eastern Desert in a range of mountains near the Gulf of Suez. St Paul, older than St Anthony and with the gift of healing, is believed to have retired to the desert at the age

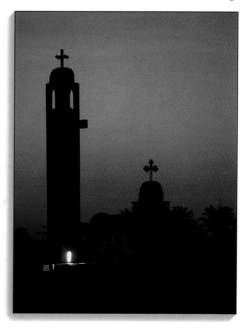

of 16 to escape the persecutions of Decius. St Anthony was born of fairly wealthy parents but, as a result of visionary inspiration, sold his inheritance and gave his money to the poor, then retreated to the cliffs flanking the Nile Valley, later settling beneath a range of mountains known today as the South Qalala.

These two men became regarded as having special powers and a special relationship with the divine, attracting other eremites to draw near them. By this time thousands of ascetics, whose original models may be traced to pre-Christian times in Egypt, were living either alone or in small groups and were looking for guidance from masters, like St Paul and St Anthony, who would be able to give instruction in an atmosphere of security and spirituality.

As with most great movements that went on to spread beyond the borders of the country in which they first took root, contradictory traditions as to the origins of Monasticism have emerged. St Jerome credits St Paul the Theban with being the first hermit. In both Coptic and Western tradition, however, St Anthony holds a more prominent position, and Copts regard him as the prototype of the Egyptian anchorite.

THE FINAL SOLUTION

Egyptians were dismissed from government service, their property confiscated, and their houses levelled.

Unification of the Roman empire was undoubtedly the reason for these reforms, but Egyptians had had enough. They rebelled so violently that Diocletian decided that if they could not be subjugated, they should be eliminated. They were dismissed from government service, their property was confiscated, and their houses levelled. Searches were made for Christian literature and copies of the scriptures, when found, were burned. Though thousands of people died during the terrible persecutions of Diocletian, unknown numbers

In 284 the Roman army elected Diocletian emperor and his reforms mark a turning-point in the history of Christianity. The appalling social and economic conditions throughout the Roman empire led him to reorganise it along military lines. He divided Egypt into three major provinces, separated civic and military powers, then imposed new methods of tax assessment based on units of productivity. Under Diocletian's reforms Egyptians were forced into public service and, to facilitate control, Latin was introduced as the official language.

escaped to refuge in the deserts, taking their zeal for Christianity with them, to create new converts.

Early Monastic reform

St Pachom (Pachomius in Latin, referred to as Anba Bakhum in Arabic), born about 285, first saw the benefits of organising the widespread anchoritic communities, and therefore became the founder of a form of Monasticism that took his name. A native Egyptian who learned Greek only late in life in order to communicate with strangers, Pachom established a community near Akhmin, where the caves in the hills flanking the Nile floodplain were populated with large numbers of ascetics. Pachom drew them

LEFT: St Bishay in the Natrun Valley.
ABOVE: St Anthony's Monastery.

together and introduced a schedule of activities for every hour of the day and night, emphasising that a healthy body provided a healthy spirit, and stressing that there should be no excesses of any kind, even in spiritual meditation.

Pachom's aim was to establish a pious, enlightened and self-sufficient community that would set an example to others. An applicant for admission did not have to exhibit spectacular feats of mortification of the flesh. Although there are numerous examples of physical self-torture in the lives of the Desert Fathers, a candidate for Pachomian Monasticism merely had to undergo a period of probation, after which he

dict, who founded monasteries in the West in the 6th century, used the model of St Pachom, but in a stricter form.

Conversion and controversy

The famous revelation of the emperor Constantine in 312, which resulted in his conversion to Christianity, was followed by the Edict of Milan, which established Christianity as the favoured religion throughout the Roman empire. It was at last safe to admit to being a Christian in Egypt. Unfortunately, the theological disputes that had plagued the early Christian movement became even fiercer in the 4th and following centuries.

was clothed in the habit of a monk and officially joined the community.

Pachom's first monastery was so successful that he moved on to found a second similar institution and yet another, until he had established no fewer than 11 monasteries in Upper Egypt, including two convents for women, although not all the ascetic communities adopted St Pachom's Rule.

All Christian Monasticism stems, either directly or indirectly, from Pachomian Monasticism: St Basil, organiser of the Monastic movement in Asia Minor, visited Egypt around 357; St Jerome, translator of the Bible into Latin, made it known to the West; and St Bene-

St Pachom's Monks

Leading disciplined lives, the monks brought productivity to the soil, revived crafts and, more importantly, were in communication with non-Christian neighbouring communities. There is much evidence in the surviving records of various monasteries that monks aided the people economically by providing them with their crop surpluses and products from craft industries. They dispensed medication and even acted as mediators in grievances, whether between members of a family or in disputes over land or water rights between neighbours. Their monasteries were usually within easy reach of settlements.

The controversies centred on the attempt to define the Incarnation: if Jesus was both God and Man, had He two natures? If so, what was their relationship? Defining the nature of Jesus was of crucial importance to a new religion that attracted people from many backgrounds, with different traditions, concepts of godliness, and styles of worship, and proved extremely difficult. It concerned such definitions as "Father", "Son", "begotten" and "unbegotten".

The chief antagonists were the Arians, named

CHRISTIAN DEBATE

Defining the nature of Jesus was of crucial importance to a new religion that attracted people from many different backgrounds

atmosphere and reached such an impasse that Constantine felt impelled to define officially a dogma to unify Christian belief. The Council of Nicea, convened in Asia Minor in 325 for this purpose, was the earliest and most important church council, the first meeting between the Church and the State. Although the bishop Alexander officially led Egypt's delegation, it was his deacon, Athanasius, who was his chief spokesman. And it says a great deal for his eloquence, reasoning and persistence that the

after Arius, an elderly Alexandrian presbyter, and the Monophysites, led by Alexander, bishop of Alexandria. The former held that "a time there was when He was not", in other words that Jesus did not have the same nature as God the Father. The Monophysites regarded this doctrine as recognition of two gods and a reversion to polytheism. They believed that Father and Son were intrinsically of one nature, and that Jesus was therefore both divine and human.

The dispute was discussed in a highly charged

LEFT: drawbridge leading to the keep at the Monastery of St Baramus, Wadi Natrun.
ABOVE: St Bishay Monastery.

Nicene Creed, to the effect that Father and Son are of the same nature, was sanctioned and remains part of the Christian liturgy. Constantine formally accepted the decision of the bishops, and issued a decree of banishment against those who refused to subscribe to it.

The decline of Alexandria

Soon after the Council of Nicea, Constantine moved his capital to the ancient Greek town of Byzantium, which became Constantinople or "Constantine's city", and was to gain much of the importance and prestige that had once belonged to Alexandria. The new metropolis was embellished with great monuments from many ancient cities, including an obelisk over 30 metres (100 ft) high shipped from Egypt. Known as "New Rome", Constantinople became a storehouse of Christian and pagan art and science. It rapidly usurped the reputation Alexandria had held as a seat of learning since Ptolemaic times.

Thus began an era when ecclesiastical dignitaries excommunicated one another in Egypt and mobs sacked churches of opposing factions. Athanasius was driven into exile five times and sought shelter with hermits in their isolated caves.

Under Theodosius I Christianity was formally declared the religion of the empire and the

PILGRIM CENTRE

Pilgrims came from all over the Christian world to visit the monasteries in Egypt. The bishop of Bahnasa estimated the number of monks in Middle Egypt at 10,000 and nuns at 20,000. Archaeology has revealed a huge monastic settlement in Al-Khargah Oasis, in the Western Desert, dating from the 4th century, with a necropolis at Bagawat containing over 200 chapels. Wadi Natrun once had 50 monasteries and over 5,000 monks. In the biography of St Macrufus, who lived in the 6th century, the Ishnin an-Nasarah is reported to have had "as many churches as there were days in the year".

Arians were again declared heretics. The Monophysite bishops of Alexandria were reinstated but, as a result of the partition of the empire between the emperor Honorius of Rome and the emperor Arcadius of Constantinople, their power was limited. Egypt fell under the jurisdiction of the latter and the so-called Byzantine rule of Egypt began.

Byzantine Period

Theophilus was made Patriarch of Alexandria and displayed tremendous zeal in destroying heathen temples. A wave of destruction swept over the land of Egypt. Tombs were ravaged, walls of ancient monuments scraped, and statues toppled. In Alexandria the famous statue of Serapis was burned and the Serapeum destroyed, along with its library, which had replaced the Mouseion as a centre of learning. It was a folly of fanaticism in the name of orthodoxy not, ironically, so different from that which had earlier opposed Christianity. In 415, under Theodosius II, Patriarch Cyril expelled the Jews of Alexandria from the city.

In the 4th and 5th centuries many ancient temples were converted into monastic centres – Deir al-Medinah and Deir al-Bahri, both in the Theban necropolis, are two well-known examples – or churches, as in the second court of the mortuary temple of Ramesses III at Medinat Habu and the Court of Amenhotep III in Luxor Temple. One of the earliest Christian buildings in Egypt was constructed between the Birth House and the Coronation House of the Temple of Hathor at Denderah, using some of the blocks from the Birth House. It is possible that this church was the famous Christian centre somewhere in the neighbourhood of Denderah that St Jerome alludes to as sheltering an assembly of 50,000 monks to celebrate Easter.

Despite the growth of the Christian movement, factional disputes continued, especially when the see of Alexandria officially lost precedence to the see of Constantinople at the Council of Constantinople in 381. There had been riots so violent that the Catechetical School, a central force in intellectual life at Alexandria for nearly two centuries, had been destroyed.

The Coptic Orthodox Church

Convened in 451, the Council of Chalcedon showed Byzantine determination to exert authority throughout Egypt. A new statement of dogma declared that Christ had two Natures "concurring" in One Person. When the Egyptians refused to endorse this revisionist doctrine, their Patriarch was excommunicated. In the struggle that followed, several Egyptian leaders were killed, and Alexandria was pillaged by imperial troops.

From this time onward, Egypt generally had two Patriarchs, one representing the orthodoxy of Constantinople, the other upholding the "One Person" beliefs of the majority of Egyptian Christians, embodied in the Coptic Orthodox Church,

COPTIC HERITAGE

Copts continue to be identified with the intense patriotism that distinguished their forebears.

nority, who officially constitute about nine percent of the population and who continue to be identified with the same intense patriotism that distinguished their forebears.

The Emperor Zeno's attempt in 482 to mend the breach between Churches was unsuccessful, but after strengthening his garrison and deporting the more obstreperous Copts to Constantinople, he let matters rest. There were no more significant disturbances involving the Christians until the reign of Justinian (528–565).

the national Church of Egypt, which emerged as a separate entity. The English word Copt, meaning "Egyptian Christian", is derived from the Arabic *qibt*, which is derived in turn from *Kyptaios*, the Coptic form of the Greek word *Aigyptios*. It also designates not only the last stages of the ancient Egyptian language and script, but also the distinctive art and architecture that developed everywhere in Egypt except Alexandria – which remained attached to cosmopolitan forms – during the country's Christian era. It is used, finally, to refer to most of modern Egypt's Christian mi-

LEFT: entrance to the chapel of St Baramus.
ABOVE: amphorae in the Monastery of St Bishay.

The end of Byzantine rule

Under Justinian, the Copts were saved from persecution only by the interest of the empress Theodora, his wife. After Theodora's death, however, Justinian sent Alexandria a patriarch-prefect determinedly armed with both civil and religious powers. Greeted by a mob, which stoned him when he attempted to speak in church, the new bishop retaliated with force by ordering the troops under his command to carry out a general slaughter. This act effectively quelled immediate resistance, but completed the alienation of the Copts, who henceforward simply ignored any ecclesiastical representatives sent from Constantinople. ❑

EGYPT UNDER ISLAM

In the age of the Crusades the Mamluks, a formidable slave army, seized power from their Sultan and became the saviours of Islam

I n the early 7th century, while the great rival Byzantine and Sasanian empires were exhausting themselves in a futile and costly struggle for supremacy, the Arabs were being spiritually and politically united by the Prophet Muhammad. His call for the creation of a Muslim community (the *Umma*) obedient to the commands of God, as revealed in the Holy Qur'an, cut across tribal conflicts and forged the Arabs into a single nation. Under the leadership of his successors, the caliphs, the energy of the Arabs was directed outward against the contending empires of the north, who were too weak to resist an unexpected invasion from the heart of the Arabian Peninsula. Inspired by both the duty of waging *jihad* (Holy War) against non-believers and the promise of rich booty, the Muslim armies conquered all of Persia and half of the Byzantine empire between 636 and 649.

The Byzantine province of Egypt was invaded in 639 by 'Amr ibn al-'As, one of the ablest of the early Muslim generals, who had visited Alexandria in his youth and had never forgotten the Egyptian capital's obvious wealth. Acting on his own initiative, 'Amr justified his actions by saying that the people of Egypt were sheep, that its land was gold, and that it belonged to whoever was strong enough to take it. Masters of hit-and-run tactics, his horsemen easily defeated a Byzantine army near the ancient ruins of Heliopolis in 640. He then set about besieging both the fortress of Babylon, at the head of the Delta, and Alexandria itself. Paralysed by internal problems and foreign wars, the Byzantines were unable to reinforce their army in Egypt. Babylon fell in 641 and the rest of the country was formally surrendered soon after.

The Arabs were aided in their conquest by the indifference of the native Egyptians, the Copts, whose political and religious disputes with Constantinople, never resolved, had made them deeply hostile to Byzantine rule. Not yet interested in converting subject peoples to Islam, which they still viewed as a purely Arab religion, the Muslim conquerors favoured the Coptic Church over the Byzantine establishment and allowed it autonomy, using it to assist them in collecting the poll-tax levied on all non-Muslims.

During the siege of Babylon, the Muslims had camped to the north of the fortress and it was here that 'Amr founded Fustat, a garrison city, for the control of the Nile Valley. Arabic began to replace Greek as the language of government, culture and commerce in the city and in time filtered down to the rural population, causing the local Coptic language to be all but forgotten.

The Abbasid caliphs

The rapid growth of the new Islamic empire brought in its wake a host of problems. Tribal differences among the Arabs began to reassert themselves as various factions fought over the spoils of conquest and the leadership of the Umma.

PRECEDING PAGES: detail of marblework from the 14th-century Mosque of Aqsunqur, Cairo.
LEFT: inside the Mosque of Sultan Hasan, Cairo.
RIGHT: part of Luxor Temple is topped by a mosque.

These conflicts, usually expressed in religious terms, deeply divided the Arabs and resulted in more than a 100 years of rebellions and civil wars. A semblance of Muslim unity was eventually re-established in 750 when the Abbasid family seized control of the empire. Brought to power by a coalition of Arab and Iranian forces, the Abbasids established a more international state, centred on Baghdad, that drew upon the services of all Muslims.

In Egypt a new administrative capital was built to the north of

their internal authority to prevent the establishment of an independent state in Egypt.

The result was oppressive taxation and widespread official corruption, which brought Egypt to the verge of economic collapse in the early 9th century. This state of affairs also reflected the progressive decline of Abbasid authority throughout the empire, which was simply too large to be effectively ruled by one man.

In order to hold their state together the caliphs in Baghdad began to employ Turkish slave

POWER SHIFT

During the first 200 years of Muslim rule, Egypt was a pawn rather than a player in the wider political issues of the Islamic empire.

the former capital Fustat. Known as Al-Askar or "the Cantonments", this military suburb became the official residence of the provincial governor, his attendant army and the large bureaucracy.

During the first 200 years of Muslim rule, Egypt was a pawn rather than a true participant in the wider political issues that dominated the affairs of the Islamic empire. Controlled by a series of military governors appointed by the caliphs in the east, most of the country's great agricultural wealth was channelled into the coffers of the central treasury. The power of these governors was severely curtailed by short terms of office and by restrictions placed upon

armies to act as a counterbalance to their turbulent Arab and Iranian subjects. Far from being slaves in the Western sense of the word, these Turks were groomed as a ruling caste, loyal only to the Abbasids. The power of the Turkish generals became so great and the upkeep of their armies so expensive that the caliphs were compelled to distribute whole provinces to them in lieu of pay. In this manner Egypt became a private fief of the new Muslim military elite in 832. Unwilling to leave the political nerve centre of Iraq, which might result in a loss of influence, the generals appointed their own governors for Egypt, who acted independently rather than as agents of the caliphs.

Independence under Ibn Tulun

The most famous Turkish governor was Ahmad Ibn Tulun. The son of a Turkish slave, he had been raised and educated in the Abbasid court and was posted to Egypt in 868 at the age of 33. Taking advantage of rivalry among the Abbasid family and its Turkish armies, Ibn Tulun was able to gain total control of the provincial government, establishing the first autonomous Muslim state in Egypt. By drastically reducing the imperial tribute to Iraq and by reinvesting the country's wealth in his new

POLICY OF INVESTMENT

Ibn Tulun brought about a period of prosperity for ruler and ruled alike.

Ibu Tulun died in 884 and was succeeded by his 20-year-old son Khumarawayh. With his father's army he extended the borders of the Tulunid state to the Euphrates, forcing the Abbasids to recognise his sovereignty.

In 896 Khumarawayh was murdered by slaves from his harem and was succeeded by his two sons and a brother, noteworthy only for the extravagance of their lifestyle and incompetence of their rule. After exhausting the state treasury and alienating the army, they were deposed and murdered, leaving Egypt too

domain, Ibn Tulun brought about a period of prosperity for ruler and ruled alike. One of his first actions as independent sovereign was the creation of a strong army made up of Turkish, Greek and Sudanese slaves, with which he conquered all of Syria in 878.

In order to celebrate his independence Ibn Tulun built a new royal city to the north of Al-Askar called Al-Qatai or "the Wards" after its division into separate districts, each housing a different contingent of his multi-racial army.

LEFT: engraving of the Mosque of Ibn Tulun from Napoleon's *Description de l'Egypt.*
ABOVE: vaulted *iwan* in the Mosque of Sultan Hasan.

weak to resist the reestablishment of direct Abbasid rule in 905.

For the next 30 years Egypt was again ruled by a series of oppressive and ineffectual provincial governors, appointed from Iraq. The growing threat of the Shi'i Fatimid dynasty, centred in Tunisia, however, demanded a more effective form of government in the Nile Valley. The Abbasids were therefore compelled to allow the establishment in 935 of a new semi-autonomous state in Egypt, founded by Muhammad Ibn Tuglij, known as "the Ikhshid". His main task was the creation of a strong Egyptian buffer state to prevent further Fatimid eastern expansion.

On his death in 946, he was nominally

succeeded by his young sons, but the real power was held by their regent, the Nubian eunuch Kafur. Kafur's strong rule held the Ikhshid state together, but on his death it fell in the face of the Fatimid invasion of 969.

The origins of the Fatimids

The Fatimids were a radical Shi'a sect that believed their *imams* (leaders) were the only rightful rulers of the Muslim world. Basing their claim on their direct descent from the Prophet Muhammad through his daughter Fatima, they viewed the Abbasids as usurpers, and dreamed of uniting all of Islam under the banner of Shi'a Islam.

The origins of this rivalry date back to the first years of the Islamic era, when the early Muslims were divided over who was to succeed Muhammad on his death in 632. The majority of his followers, who were to become the Sunnis, favoured the election of one of them as caliph, while a minority, who became known as the Shi'a, supported a hereditary principle, which would preserve the caliphate within the Prophet's family.

Among the most extreme of the various Shi'a sects that grew out of this conflict were the Isma'ilis, of whom the Fatimids were the most successful members. They attributed a semi-divine status to their imams, the Fatimid caliphs, who they believed were the only men capable of leading the Umma to perfection. The imams controlled a vast secret organisation, the Da'wa, which would send highly trained agents throughout the Muslim world, winning converts and preparing the way for the eventual takeover of the Isma'ili caliphs.

The conversion of the Kutama Berbers of Algeria by an Isma'ili agent in the early 10th century supplied the Fatimids with an army and a North African kingdom, but their dreams were set on Egypt. The death of Kafur supplied the Fatimid caliph Al Mu'izz with the chance he had been waiting for.

The founding of Al-Qahirah

In 969 Egypt fell to general Jawhar, a military slave of European origin, whose first action was the construction of a new royal enclosure to house the victorious Al-Mu'izz and his Shi'a government. The new Fatimid capital was named Al-Qahirah, "The Subduer", later corrupted by Italian merchants into Cairo.

The initial military success of the Fatimids was short-lived. After gaining control of Palestine and the holy cities of Mecca and Medina, they encountered stiff Byzantine resistance in northern Syria. To offset their military failure the Fatimids turned to the realm of trade. Fustat became a major trade emporium, and Fatimid Egypt became fabulously wealthy.

Plans for the conquest of the Abbasid empire were postponed indefinitely and little effort was made to convert the Christian and Sunni Muslim native population to Shi'a Islam. As a minority sect in Egypt, unconcerned with proselytising, the Fatimids were extremely tolerant, employing Sunnis, Christians and Jews equally.

INSIDE THE ROYAL ENCLOSURE

Separated from the predominantly Sunni population of Fustat by a mile of wasteland, Al-Qahirah's high walls could be penetrated only by the Isma'aili elite. Within were two great palaces, the home of the imam and his court bureaucracy. Its religious and intellectual centre was the mosque of Al-Azhar, the headquarters of the Da'wa and the main congregational mosque of the city. The rest of Al-Qahirah's 300 acres were filled with gardens, hippodromes and military barracks. Secluded in the luxury of their fortress city, the Fatimid imams underwent a dramatic change and the more radical aspects of their esoteric teachings were toned down.

The mad caliph

The shift to a conservative and materialistic state deeply concerned the third Fatimid caliph, Al-Hakim (996–1021). Universally described as insane by medieval Arab historians, Al-Hakim was preoccupied with revitalising the spiritual mission of the Isma'ili movement and with the maintenance of his personal power in the face of Fatimid governmental opposition. His fervour resulted in measures that were invariably both extreme, and brutal, but rarely without a purpose.

RELIGIOUS TOLERANCE

The Fatimids were tolerant rulers and employed Sunnis, Christians and Jews equally in the running of their state.

stage too far. Riots of protest broke out in Fustat and his devotees were forced to flee to Lebanon, where they founded the Druze religion, a sect that still believes Al-Hakim to have been the incarnation of God.

The Fatimid hierarchy eventually decided the unstable imam had to go. While he was riding his donkey alone in the Muqattam Hills at night, Al-Hakim mysteriously disappeared, almost certainly murdered on the orders of his sister and the Fatimid elite, who now took over the reins of government.

Decrees aimed against women, forbidding them from leaving their houses or possessing independent wealth, besides being a concession to public morality, were probably directed against his sister, Sitt al-Mulk, who was an influential opponent of his policies. When he allowed a group of extremist Iranian Isma'ilis to proclaim his divinity in 1017, he was only carrying the spiritual pretensions of his family to their ultimate limits.

In this, however, Al-Hakim had finally gone a

LEFT: the large congregational Mosque of Ibn Tulun, built by the Abbasids.
ABOVE: interior of the Sultan Hasan Mosque.

Fatimid heyday

During the long reign of Al-Mustansir (1036–94), Fustat reached the peak of its prosperity. With a population of almost half a million living in five-storey buildings, complete with running water and sophisticated sewer systems, it was one of the great cities of its age.

Despite its wealth the Fatimid state rapidly began to decline. The Turkish troops, who had largely replaced their Berber rivals, were unruly and a constant threat to internal security. A series of seven low Niles between 1066 and 1072 plunged the country into further chaos. Famine and plague spread throughout the Nile Valley, reducing the people of Fustat to cannibalism. The

Turkish soldiers looted the Fatimid palaces on the pretext of arrears of pay, and Al-Mustansir secretly called in Badr al-Jamali, the Fatimid's Armenian governor at Acre in Palestine, to restore order.

A surprise attack on Al-Qahirah in 1072 crushed all opposition and won Badr al-Jamali full dictatorial powers. He now had to face an impending invasion by the Seljuk Turks and the enclosing walls of Al-Qahirah were rebuilt, incorporating massive new gates, to withstand the expected siege.

> **DIVIDED FORCE**
> The crusaders were more concerned with their individual needs than with establishing a single, strong Christian kingdom.

The sudden break-up of the Seljuk empire after 1092 saved the Fatimids from certain defeat, but left the Middle East crowded with petty Muslim states. Their lack of unity facilitated the victories of the first Crusade of 1099, launched in response to the Seljuk conquest of Jerusalem a few years earlier. The crusaders were themselves divided into four, often hostile, principalities, more concerned with their individual short-term needs than with the establishment of a single, strong Christian kingdom.

The rise of the Zangids of Mosul, who began absorbing their Muslim neighbours and preaching *jihad* against the crusaders in the first half of the 12th century, meant that it was just a matter

of time before the Christians were encircled and picked off one by one. Both sides realised that Egypt, weakened by dynastic and military rivalries, yet incredibly wealthy, was the key to victory. Whoever controlled her vast resources could dominate the whole region.

Saladin
The Fatimids tried to play one side against the other, but in 1169 were compelled to submit to the Zangid general Salah-ad-Din (Saladin), who abolished the Fatimid caliphate in 1171, re-establishing Sunni Islam in Egypt. The Fatimids were the last Arab dynasty to rule Egypt. From this point on the country would be under the control of Turks and related peoples from the eastern Islamic world, a situation that would continue until the 1952 revolution.

In theory Egypt was now a part of the Zangid empire, ruled by Nur ad-Din, a man dedicated to *jihad* against the crusaders; in reality it was firmly in the hands of his Kurdish general, Saladin. Refusing to leave Egypt until it was secure from crusader attack and Fatimid resurgence, Saladin fell out with his master, who wanted Egypt's resources for his own war effort.

Sending only apologies and excuses, Saladin set about building a power base. His enlarged army was stationed in the newly constructed Citadel, situated about halfway between Al-Qahirah and Fustat. The two urban centres were linked to the new fortress by a series of walls, to facilitate the defence of the Egyptian capital, setting the stage for the future development of one unified city.

Resisting the Crusades
The death of Nur ad-Din in 1174 and the subsequent break-up of this empire left Saladin undisputed master of Egypt. He spent the next 13 years conquering the divided Zangid principalities of Syria and placing them under the control of his family, the Ayyubids. With Egypt and Syria once again united, Saladin turned his attention to the crusaders, who were decisively defeated in 1187.

The capture of Jerusalem and Palestine established Saladin as a champion of Islam, but also triggered off the Third Crusade in 1189. Led by Richard the Lion-Heart of England and Philip II of France, the Christians retook Acre, but were unable to advance further. The peace settlement of 1192 recognised Saladin's gains, leaving the crusaders in possession of a small coastal strip of Palestine. Saladin died the following year a satisfied man.

The Ayyubid empire created by Saladin was a federation of sovereign city states, loosely held together by family solidarity. The rulers of Egypt, the wealthiest and most centralised of the provinces, exercised a vague suzerainty over their kinsmen, which they used to try to limit the endless intrigues and power struggles that dominated Ayyubid politics. As the head of the family, the sultans of Egypt had the right to demand military aid from their brothers and cousins in Syria, but this was often reluctantly given, the minor princes being more afraid of their Ayyubid neighbours than òf an external enemy. The sultans, as a result, were hesitant about engaging in serious warfare, preferring to use diplomacy to achieve their aims.

The Sultan Al-Kamil (1218–38) was able to defeat a Christian invasion of the Nile Delta in 1221, but to avoid a repetition of the experience came to a peaceful agreement with the Holy Roman Emperor Frederick II in 1229, whereby Jerusalem was declared an open city, accessible to Muslims and Christians alike. This solution to the crusading problem proved unpopular with religious fanatics on both sides and hostilities were soon resumed.

The last major Ayyubid sultan, As-Salih (1240–49), whose ruthless rise to power had made enemies of most of his relatives, could no longer rely on the support of his Syrian kinsmen. Faced with the growing threat of a Mongol invasion from the east, As-Salih began building a Turkish slave army, loyal only to him, to defend the Ayyubid state.

The fighting abilities of As-Salih's new military slaves or Mamluks were put to the test in 1249, when the 6th Crusade of St Louis IX of France invaded Egypt. During the course of the hostilities As-Salih died, but news of his death was concealed by his wife, Shagar ad-Durr (Tree of Pearls) and the Mamluk amirs, to allow his son, Turan Shah, to reach Egypt and claim the sultanate. Turan Shah arrived in time to

BIRTH OF THE MAMLUKS

Faced with the threat of a Mongol invasion from the east, As-Salih began building a Turkish slave army, loyal only to him.

witness the defeat of the French king by the Mamluks in 1250. Alarmed by the growing power of the Bahris, the new sultan began to replace them with his own men. But the Mamluks were not to be ousted so easily. Instead, they murdered Turan Shah and seized control of Egypt.

The Bahri Mamluks

To legitimise their *coup d'état*, the Mamluks then proclaimed Shagar Ad-Durr sultan on the strength of her marriage to As-Salih. The Ayyubid princes of

Syria, refusing to accept the loss of the richest province of their empire to a woman, prepared for war. Needing a man to lead her army, Shagar ad-Durr married the Mamluk commander, Aybek, who now ruled as sultan with his new wife. The Ayyubids were defeated in 1250 and Aybek, encouraged by his victory, conquered Palestine.

To strengthen his position, in 1257 Aybek began negotiating a second marriage with a princess of Mosul. Unwilling to share her power with another woman, Shagar Ad-Durr had her husband murdered. Aybek's Mamluks, enraged by the death of their master, seized his queen and handed her over to the former wife of Aybek,

LEFT AND RIGHT: Mamluk soldiers dressed to kill.

whom he had been compelled to divorce by Shagar Ad-Durr upon becoming sultan. Egypt's only woman sultan was then beaten to death in front of her rival.

The Mamluks had proved their military prowess against the crusaders and the Ayyubids, but were now called upon to face a far greater threat; the heathen Mongols, who in 1257 swept through Iraq into Syria, crushing all Muslim resistance. Undefeated in battle, the Central Asian hordes seemed on the verge of extinguishing Muslim civilisation in the Mid-

> **SAVIOURS OF ISLAM**
>
> The Mamluks were called upon to face the heathen Mongols, who swept through Iraq into Syria, crushing all Muslim resistance.

dle East. Only the Mamluks remained to stop them and at the battle of Ayn Jalut in 1260 they did, becoming the saviours of Islam.

Under the sway of their first great sultans, Baybars al-Bunduqdari (1260–79) and then Qalawun (1279–90), the Mamluks emerged as the foremost military power of their age. Kept in top fighting shape by the constant threat of the Mongols, now centred in Iran, the Mamluks recaptured Syria and expelled the last of the crusaders from the Palestinian coast.

The Mamluk system

The political system created by Baybars was based on a military slave oligarchy. Young Qipchaq Turks would be brought to Egypt as slaves, converted to Islam and given a thorough military training. On completion of their education they would be freed and enrolled in the private army of one of the great Mamluk amirs, who collectively controlled all of Egypt's resources and governmental positions. The most powerful amir would be chosen as the sultan.

The foundation of the system was the intense loyalty the individual Mamluk felt for his military house (*bayt*). His political fortunes were linked to those of his amir. If his *bayt* was successful, the common Mamluk could expect to be promoted to the rank of amir and in time even to the sultanate. The Mamluk political environment was therefore dominated by intrigue and the constant striving for power among the *bayts*. The sultan tried to manipulate these conflicts to maintain his position but, if he was unsuccessful, he would be destroyed by the ambitions of his amirs.

Position within the Mamluk hierarchy was dependent upon slave origins. The children of Mamluks were prevented from following their fathers' military career and as a result the army required a steady flow of new Turkish slaves to replenish its ranks.

The reign of An-Nasir Muhammad

The one exception to this rule was that the son of a sultan often succeeded his father as a stop-gap ruler without power, allowing the amirs time to determine who was the strongest without resorting to civil war. In this manner Qalawun's son An-Nasir Muhammad was made nominal sultan in 1293, at the age of nine. After ruling for a year he was deposed, but then reinstated in 1299, when the amirs fell out amongst themselves.

Having been raised in an atmosphere of intrigue and double-dealing, An-Nasir emerged at the age of 25 as a ruthless, suspicious and absolutely despotic sultan. Resolving to rule alone after enduring the miseries of his youth, he murdered the amirs of his father one by one, replacing them with his own men. Unwilling to trust even the amirs of his own *bayt*, An-Nasir inaugurated an era of peace to prevent arming a potential rival with the command of an army. A period of flourishing trade and great prosperity ensued, the apex of Muslim civilisation in Egypt.

An-Nasir's success in mastering the Mamluk system brought about the beginning of its decline. So firmly did he grip the reins of power that, on his death in 1340, none of the amirs was strong enough to replace him. Instead he was to be succeeded by a series of ineffective sons and grandsons.

An-Nasir's policy of peace filled the state's treasury but caused the Mamluks to neglect their military training. A whole generation therefore grew up without ever having fought a major war, a serious deficiency for a state that had been founded on martial superiority.

they arrived in Cairo with clear ideas of how to manipulate the system to their own benefit. Ambitious, unruly and deficient in their military training, they were a terror to the inhabitants of Egypt, but poor soldiers.

Unable to defeat the invading Tamerlane in 1400, the Circassians watched helplessly as the new central Asian conqueror devastated their Syrian province. Repeated outbreaks of plague throughout the 15th century decimated the ranks of the unacclimatised Mamluks, whose replacement was both costly and difficult. The threat of strong neighbours and the chronic outbreak of factional fighting at home further drained the

The Circassian Mamluks

For 41 years after the death of An-Nasir, 12 of his direct descendants ruled Egypt as nominal sultans. In 1382, however, the amir Barquq (1382–99) seized control and began distributing all positions of power to his fellow Circassians. This second Mamluk dynasty maintained the same political system as the Qipchaq predecessors. An important difference, however, was that the Circassians were brought to Egypt not as boys, but as young men. Instead of being moulded by the rigours of a Mamluk education,

LEFT: the Mamluks loved splendour.
ABOVE: *The Turkish Patrol*, by Decamps.

THE BLACK DEATH

The reign of the Mamluk sultan Hasan (1347–61) saw the outbreak of the Black Death, which rocked the economic foundations of Egypt by decimating its population. Whole districts of Cairo were completely wiped out, indirectly benefiting the sultan, who inherited the property and valuables of the plague's victims. With this unexpected windfall Hasan financed his great mosque, completed in 1362 and considered the grandest of all Mamluk buildings, which were many since the Mamluk sultans' lust for political power was matched only by their love of luxury and of grand buildings.

treasury, forcing the sultans to adopt the short-sighted economic policies of excessive taxation, debasement of the currency and the introduction of state-owned monopolies.

The chief failing of the Circassians, however, was their refusal to adopt modern military methods. Bred to be a cavalry elite, they despised gunpowder as unmanly. Their major rivals in the early 16th century, the Ottoman Turks, had no such snobbish qualms. When the two forces finally clashed at the battle of Marj Dabiq in 1517, the Mamluks were literally blown off the field by superior cannon fire. Following this victory, the Ottoman Sultan Selim the Grim

conquered the Mamluk sultanate and Cairo became the provincial capital of a new Muslim empire centred in Istanbul.

Egypt as an Ottoman province

The Ottomans, engaged in continual warfare with Iran and the Christian West, could not afford to spare the necessary men to uproot the Mamluks from Egypt completely. Instead the Mamluks were incorporated into the Ottoman ruling elite and held in check by a provincial governor and a garrison of crack Ottoman troops, the Janissaries.

In the 17th century, military defeats brought steady decline to the Ottoman empire. Rampant inflation, caused by the flood of Spanish silver from the New World, upset the balance of power in Egypt. The office of governor was now sold to the highest bidder, and then resold at the first opportunity, to supply the central treasury with a steady flow of cash. The governors, rarely ruling for more than three years, could never therefore establish effective control over Egypt. The Janissaries, forced into local trade by the steady devaluation of their salaries, became little more than armed shopkeepers and artisans.

The rise of Ali Bey al Kabir (1760–72) saw the remergence of the Mamluks as an international power. By destroying the rival *bayts*, the governor and the Janissaries, Ali Bey became master of Egypt. He was on the verge of re-establishing the Mamluk empire when he was betrayed by his lieutenant Abu'l-Dhahab, secretly in the pay of the Ottomans.

Deprived of its strong leadership, the Mamluk *bayt* of Ali Bey fragmented and Egypt was plunged into a devastating civil war which lasted until 1791. Although order was restored by the victory of Murad Bey and Ibrahim Bey, the economy of the country was in ruins. In this unsettled state, Egypt was invaded in 1798 by the French under Napoleon Bonaparte.

The French expedition

On the morning of 21 July, 1798, the combined musketry and artillery of 29,000 French troops smashed a headlong onslaught of Mamluk cavalry. This, the Battle of the Pyramids, marked a turning of the tide against the East. It also roused Egypt from the slumber of 300 years as an Ottoman province.

The conquest of Egypt was ostensibly carried out on the orders of Bonaparte's superiors in Paris, whose overt objective was to threaten Britain's lucrative Indian trade from a Middle Eastern stronghold. In fact, however, the French expedition was largely inspired by irrational factors, of which by no means the least was Bonaparte's own romantic pursuit of glory.

Bonaparte's expedition was doomed right

NAPOLEON'S SAVANTS

A scientific mission consisting of 60 savants accompanied the expedition. Their task was to compile a complete dossier on Egypt's antiquities, people, topography, flora and fauna, producing a massive *Description de l'Egypte*.

from the start. Within seven days of raising the *tricolore* over Saladin's citadel, the British had sunk the French fleet off Abu Qir and the Mamluks under Murad Bey had fallen back to Upper Egypt, from where they continued to conduct a successful guerilla war.

Hoping to regain momentum and impress his constituency in France, Bonaparte decided to embark on a campaign in Palestine. Again, superior French artillery brought quick victories. These efforts to terrorise their opponents into submission failed, however, and at the fortress of Acre in northern Palestine the French were brought to a halt. Reinforced from the sea by a British fleet, the Turkish garrison held out for two months, while Bonaparte's army was decimated by malaria and dysentery.

FRENCH DEFEAT

Although the French remained in Egypt two more years, the hopelessness of their mission finally forced them to succumb.

marauding British, his own troops disillusioned, he wisely concluded that his personal ambitions were unlikely to be served by further lingering.

Fourteen months after his arrival, Bonaparte slipped home in such apparent haste that General Kléber, his second in command, received the first news of his appointment as the new General-in-Chief of the Army of the Orient scrawled on an abandoned scrap of paper.

Although the French remained in Egypt two more years, defeating two Turkish attempts to

dislodge them, the hopelessness of their mission finally forced them to succumb. Kléber was assassinated at Azbakiyyah in June, 1800 and the task of negotiating with an Anglo-Ottoman force that landed in the Delta in the autumn of 1801 was left to his successor. Mercifully, the French, now numbering only 7,000, were allowed to return to France. In three years of occupation, they had failed to meet any of their strategic objectives. Britain still dominated the seas, the Ottomans had reinforced their hold on the Levant, and the Egyptians, though impressed by the power of European science, technology and military organisation, had rejected what little they saw of the infidel's civilisation. ❑

Despite the propaganda churned out in Arabic by his printing press – the first in modern Egypt – his attempt to portray the Palestine débâcle as a victory was not greeted with enthusiasm in Cairo. At last, with communications to Paris cut by the

LEFT: Napoleon roused Egypt from its slumber.
ABOVE: detail from the *Battle of the Pyramids*, painted by Lejeune.

MUHAMMAD ALI AND MODERN EGYPT

Western intervention may have put the brakes on Egypt's expansionist projects but it indirectly led to the modernisation of the country's infrastructure

Muhammad Ali Pasha, who ruled for nearly half a century, is credited with having laid the foundations of modern Egypt. In addition to building an empire, he carried out reforms aimed at modernising Egypt and founded the dynasty that was to rule the country for a period of almost 150 years, until the revolution of 1952.

Muhammad Ali was born in 1769 in Kavalla, Macedonia, in what is now part of modern Greece but then belonged to the Ottoman empire. He entered Egypt as second in command of an Ottoman army sent to join the British in expelling the French, who had occupied the country since 1798. After the French and British troops left Egypt, the Ottoman troops stayed on to reassert the Sultan's authority.

During the four ensuing years, however, Egypt was reduced to a state of anarchy, with Mamluk beys fighting against one another and against the Ottomans, who were themselves divided along ethnic lines. In 1805, having had enough of chaos, the people of Cairo finally turned to Muhammad Ali to restore order, naming him the new viceroy. Such an appointment was the prerogative of the Sultan in Constantinople, but the Sultan, presented with the *fait accompli*, confirmed the Cairenes' choice.

Nevertheless, Muhammad Ali's position as viceroy was tenuous. Defeating a British force at Rosetta in 1807 consolidated his power, but bold steps were still required. Boldest and bloodiest was his extirpation of the rebellious Mamluk beys (officers). On March, 1811, he invited 470 Mamluks to a ceremony in the Citadel. Assembled to take their leave, the departing Mamluks had to pass through a narrow passageway to a locked gate, where the Pasha had arranged for their massacre. For the next 37 years his authority was absolute in Egypt.

Among Muhammad Ali's best-known exploits are his military conquests. In 1811, at the request of the Turkish Sultan Mahmud II, he sent troops into the Arabian province of the Hijaz to combat the Wahhabi movement, a fundamentalist sect of Islam that threatened the Sultan's authority. In 1816 Egyptian troops entered the Nejd, the Wahhabi's homeland, and by 1818 all of western and central Arabia was under Egyptian control.

After the Arabian campaigns, Muhammad Ali sent an expedition under one of his sons up the Nile to gain control of the Sudan's mineral resources and its active slave trade, which he saw as a possible source of manpower for the army. Next came campaigns in Greece. At the request of the Sultan, an army commanded by his son Ibrahim was sent to Crete in 1822 to quell an uprising against Ottoman control.

In 1824 a second expedition, again commanded by Ibrahim, sailed from Alexandria for the Morea, now known as the Peloponnese. This reassertion of Ottoman power provoked the major European states, Britain, France and Russia. An allied fleet sent to mediate ended up sinking the entire Egyptian fleet at Navarino in 1827.

Syria gained

Muhammad Ali's last successful expansionist venture was his Syrian expedition of 1831. Using a quarrel with a governor as a pretext, he sent in Ibrahim with an army of peasant conscripts. At the end of 10 months all of Syria had acknowledged him as overlord. In 1832 Ibrahim pushed on into Anatolia, defeating the Ottomans at Konya. Before he could occupy Constantinople, however, Russian intervention again brought European interests into play; and in 1833 an agreement was signed between the Sultan and his unruly vassal, by which Egypt was formally accorded rule over Crete and Syria in return for an annual tribute.

With the Sudan, the Hijaz and these new acquisitions, the Egyptian empire rivalled the Ottoman in size, although Egypt itself was still nominally a part of the Ottoman empire and

PRECEDING PAGES: interior of the mosque of Muhammad Ali at the Citadel.

LEFT: a contemporary engraving of Muhammad Ali Pasha with his *shibuk*.

Muhammad Ali still only a Pasha, the Sultan's viceroy. In 1839 the Sultan attempted to regain Syria by force.

Ibrahim's own crushing victory over an Ottoman army at Nezib was followed by the desertion of the Ottoman navy to Alexandria and these two events led to a European crisis. Britain, Russia and Austria sided with the Sultan, while France supported Muhammad Ali. A catastrophe was averted when Muhammad Ali signed an agreement by which his rule was to be made hereditary, but which also confirmed the Sultan's suzerainty, the terms of which were agreed under European pressure in 1841.

HEALTH OF THE NATION

The one subject on which Muhammad Ali was known to have been fanatical was public health. Swamps were drained, cemeteries were moved, hospitals, infirmaries and asylums were built, a school for midwives was established, and French-trained physicians were appointed as public health officers in all provinces. In Cairo accumulated rubbish was cleared and seasonal ponds, like the one at Azbakiyyah, were filled, while a start was made on a street system that would allow the use of wheeled vehicles. The city's dancing prostitutes were banished to Upper Egypt.

Modernising on all fronts

Shorn of his acquisitions abroad, the Pasha turned his remaining energies back to the task of modernising Egypt. The benefits to his country were enormous. They include the massive upgrading and extension of Egypt's irrigation system and the introduction of a multitude of exotic plants. Rice, indigo and sugar cane were massively encouraged, as well as the cultivation of long-staple Egyptian cotton, which later became the country's principal export. By 1840 he had planted more than 16 million trees and built roads and bridges where none had ever existed.

Land tenure and tax systems he reformed by nationalising all property, making himself titular owner of all land and eliminating the iniquitous tax farming system that had prevailed earlier.

Muhammad Ali also created modern industries in Egypt. Beginning with an industrial complex at Bulaq, the Nile port of Cairo, where the famous Bulaq Press was set up, he built shipyards, foundries and armament factories. Textile mills, the basis of the European Industrial Revolution, soon followed. Since a primary aim was to avoid dependence upon Europe, the infant textile industry was protected by embargoes and subsidies, but this step toward economic independence was foiled, like his foreign policy, by European interests: the provisions of 1841 made Egypt subject to the tariffs that prevailed through the Ottoman empire, allowing cheaper imports, mainly from Britain, to flood into Egypt.

In other respects his efforts were more successful. The Bulaq Press was to become the most distinguished publisher in the Arab world. Its production of printed books was an essential element in the creation of a new intellectual élite, which would gradually replace the European experts recruited during his early years in power.

In Alexandria Muhammad Ali established a Quarantine Commission, thus identifying the city once again as the country's main port of entry. And it was here that the Pasha died in 1848, 80 years old, but predeceased by his son, the gallant Ibrahim, to whom he had given the viceregal throne 11 months before.

Muhammad Ali's successors

Ibrahim's death was unfortunate, since he had shown himself to be a good leader. His nephew, Abbas, the only son of Muhammad Ali's second son, Tussun, became viceroy and immediately rejected all his policies. While Muhammad Ali had been eager for Western agricultural and technical ideas, particularly those of the French, Abbas was xenophobic, disliking the French in particular and favouring the British, to whom he granted a railway concession. He summarily expelled all the French advisors upon whom his grandfather had depended, closed all secular or European schools, and turned for support to religious leaders. He was as autocratic as his grandfather, but earned the gratitude of the Egyptian peasants by his negligence, which left them in

THE WEST REJECTED

Abbas was xenophobic and expelled all the French advisors upon whom his grandfather had depended.

best known for his friendship with Ferdinand de Lesseps, to whom he granted a concession for the Suez Canal. As originally granted in 1854, this concession was one of the great swindles of all time, with terms extremely disadvantageous to Egypt. Recognising the enormity of his error later, Said managed to renegotiate and got somewhat more favourable terms, but only at the cost of an indemnity of more than three million Egyptian pounds. To pay this sum he was forced to take Egypt's first foreign loan, thus not only setting

comparative peace. Apart from the British railway completed after his death, the sole positive relic of his six-year rule was that he left full coffers and no foreign debt.

When Abbas was murdered in 1854 by two of his personal bodyguards, his uncle Said succeeded him. Said again reversed the direction of the government, favouring a return to his father's programmes and to abandoned projects in irrigation, agriculture and education.

Open to European influences, Said is perhaps

LEFT: statue of Ibrahim Pasha.
ABOVE: *Grand Cairo*, painted by the orientalist David Roberts from 1839–49.

a dangerous precedent, but planting a time-bomb under Ismail, the third of Ibrahim's four sons, who became viceroy on Said's death in 1863.

Ismail the Magnificent (1863–79)

Under Ismail's rule the modernisation begun by Muhammad Ali moved forward with new dynamism. Reviving his grandfather's policy of independence from the Sultan, Ismail sought to transform Egypt into a country that Europe would respect in European terms.

In 1866, through payments to the Sultan and an increase in tribute, he secured a change in the hereditary principle from seniority to primogeniture, thus guaranteeing the throne to his own line, and permission to maintain a standing army of 30,000. The same year he summoned the first Chamber of Deputies, a move that pleased the Europeans as representing a step towards constitutionality. The following year he obtained the Persian title of Khedive ("Sovereign"), borne by his heirs down to 1914, as well as the right to create institutions, issue regulations and conclude administrative agreements with foreign powers without consulting Constantinople. His new independence was signalised in June 1867 by Egypt's autonomous participation in the Exposition Universelle in Paris.

Ismail had been sent as a student to Paris by Muhammad Ali in 1844, one of a delegation of 70 that also included a young man named Ali Mubarak, who would later serve Ismail as Minister of Education, Director General of the State Railways, Minister of Endowments and Minister of Public Works. Ismail and Mubarak had thus known Paris as it was before the Second Empire: an essentially medieval city, largely slums and only partially touched by modernisation under Bonaparte.

When Ismail saw the transformation wrought by Haussmann – the new city, with its broad boulevards and parks – he was dazzled; and on his return to Egypt he sent Mubarak likewise to have a look, appointing him Minister of Public Works in the meantime. The result was the transformation of Cairo.

The changes made in the city during the few months leading up to the opening of the Suez Canal, in 1869, were the culmination of five years of feverish modernisation not just in Cairo but throughout the country. Two other major canals had already been completed. Municipal water and gas companies had been set up in 1865 and Cairo's main railway station had been inaugurated in 1867. Telegraph linked all parts of the country.

Foreign debts come home

The Sultan's response to the festivities at the Canal opening, however, was to send Ismail a decree forbidding him to undertake foreign loans without approval. A massive bribe secured confirmation in 1873 of all rights obtained earlier, as well as permission to raise a large army.

The American Civil War had brought wealth

PARIS ON THE NILE

When Ismail saw how Paris had been transformed, he was dazzled. Cairo was also soon transformed.

to Egypt by raising the price of cotton, enriching the new class of landowners that Said and Ismail had created. Since the Khedive and his family still owned one-fifth of Egypt's cultivable land, much of the new wealth came Ismail's way. Not enough, however, even coupled with Egypt's tax revenues, to keep pace with his ambitions. In the confusion of public and private exchequers, colossal debts had been run up, prompting alarm in Paris and London, where Ismail's independence was already regarded as a threat to the *status quo*.

Most of the debt was the result of swindles perpetrated by European adventurers. The largest of these, like the first of the debts, was an inheritance from Said: the Suez Canal, built using the *corvée,* at Egyptian expense. In 1875, after swinging another huge loan, Ismail was forced to sell his shares in the Canal Company to Britain. An Anglo-French Dual Control set up to oversee his finances began creaming off three-quarters of the annual revenues of Egypt to pay European creditors.

Ismail was forced to liquidate his personal estates and to accept British and French ministers in his cabinet. Adroitly playing the few cards that were left to him, he evaded a complete takeover of his government until finally the Europeans lost patience. Putting pressure on the Sultan, they had Ismail deposed.

Occupation

His son Tawfiq, whom Ismail himself described as having" neither head nor heart nor courage", was no match for the adversaries who had defeated his father. But the army made a stand. The chief spokesman, a senior officer named Ahmad 'Urabi, was appointed Minister of War and thus found himself at the forefront

FOREIGN TRICKERY

Most of the debt was the result of swindles, the largest of these being the Suez Canal.

government also melted away. Near the end of August, 20,000 redcoats were landed on the supposedly sacrosanct banks of the new Suez Canal and two weeks later the Egyptian army under 'Urabi was crushingly defeated at Tell al-Kabir.

Thus came to an end 19th-century Egypt's double experiment at modernisation, twice halted by European displays of power. The many cultural, social and even physical marks left on the country by Muhammad Ali and Ismail have, however, so far proved indelible.

The Suez Canal

of resistance to further European intrusion.

Presented abroad first as a military dictatorship, then as an anarchy dangerous not only to European interests, but also to the Sultan's, this situation provided the final excuse for intervention. Over the Sultan's protests, British warships bombarded Alexandria on 11 July 1882. Hoping to regain status after repeated humiliations through the instrument of these invaders, Tawfiq abandoned his own government and put himself under their protection. Support for a provisional

LEFT: Khedive Ismail, a visionary ruler.
ABOVE: before the advent of air travel, the Suez Canal was the main link between Europe and Asia.

British rule

Evelyn Baring, who became Lord Cromer in 1891, first came to Egypt in 1879 as the British financial controller during the Dual Control of France and Britain but later returned in 1882 as the Consul-General. In 1882, the British government promised an early evacuation of its troops, but they lingered on and, since the British refused to formalise their presence, the British Consul-General became the *de facto* ruler of Egypt, with absolute authority in both its internal and foreign affairs.

The most important achievements during this period were the completion of the Delta Barrage in 1890 and the building of the first Aswan Dam in 1902. Begun under Muhammad Ali, the Delta Barrage made double and triple cropping possible in the Delta, while the Aswan Dam, coupled with barrages at Asyut (1903) and Esna (1906), extended the same system to Upper Egypt, reducing dependence on the annual flood.

By this time, cotton had become the mainstay of the Egyptian economy. Other food crops continued to be grown, and Egypt was still able to feed its growing population without depending on imports. Its role within the British empire was essentially to supply raw materials and a market for manufactured items, like any other colony or possession. Cromer therefore discouraged both industrialisation and higher education, putting an end to the kind of autonomous development that before the Occupation had made Egypt, with Japan, unique among countries of the non-Western world. It is therefore not surprising that the British occupation helped to solidify nationalist awareness in Egypt.

This awareness received added stimulus after 1892, when Abbas Hilmi Tawfiq's 18-year-old son succeeded as Khedive. Educated at a Swiss school and at the celebrated Theresianum in Vienna, Abbas II was typical of the new Egyptian élite that had been created by Muhammad Ali's and Ismail's educational designs. In Egypt under Cromer, however, there was no real role for this elite or even for Abbas himself to play, as the Consul-General made humiliatingly clear to the young Khedive at the earliest opportunity. Abbas' response was to seek out the young nationalist leaders and provide them with financial support.

Secular nationalism drew growing strength between 1890 and 1906 from the country's enormous prosperity, derived almost exclusively from cotton. The land-owning class created by Said and Ismail grew even richer, merging with the old and new elites. Greeks and Italians chiefly, but also Britons, Frenchmen, Swiss, Germans and Belgians, all received privileges under the Ottoman Capitulations, that granted them immunity from Egyptian laws and taxes.

The Dinshwai Incident

As Cromer approached retirement from Egyptian service in 1906, he was contemplating changes to allow for more self-government, but his autocratic rule had left him few friends in the country. In that year the Dinshwai Incident occurred when a group of British officers were casually shooting domestic pigeons that belonged to peasants in the Delta village of Dinshwai. The villagers tried to stop them, and in the skirmish a woman and four men were wounded. Outraged villagers surrounded the officers, beat them and held them until the police arrived. One officer escaped and ran through the noon-day heat to a British army camp, but died of sunstroke just outside the camp entrance. A peasant who had tried to help him was beaten to death by British soldiers. This murder was subsequently forgotten. To consider charges against the villagers of Dinshwai, however, a special Tribunal was set up.

The Tribunal met in Dinshwai for 30 minutes then sentenced eight villagers to lashes, 11 to periods of penal servitude ranging from one year to life, and four – including a 17-year-old boy and a 60-year-old man – to hanging. Though public executions had been outlawed in Egypt two years previously, the villagers of

---

BOOM TIMES

In line with the Western-influenced thinking of Muhammad Ali and Ismail, Cairo and Alexandria were irrevocably transformed into European-looking cities by the real estate boom of 1896–1907.

Dinshwai were forced to witness the carrying out of these sentences.

Nobody connected with this incident – to which Egyptians could only respond with helpless grief – was ever forgiven.

Cromer's successor as Consul-General, Sir Eldon Gorst, spoke Arabic, having lived many years in Egypt, and was ready to effect change in British policy. He cultivated a friendship with the Khedive, whom he permitted to wield increased power, and undertook several reforms. Egypt's first secular university was

EDUCATION REFORM

Egypt's first secular university was allowed to open in 1908.

well. He introduced regulations for censorship, school discipline and the suppression of conspiracy. Once again the Khedive came under the Consul-General's strict authority. In 1913, however, he introduced what seemed to be a liberal reform: a new constitution that provided for a Legislative Assembly. It had met on only one occasion, when World War I broke out.

The Protectorate (1914–22)

The outbreak of the war was the catalyst for a series of important events. Severing the 400-

allowed to open in 1908 and the provincial councils were encouraged towards more autonomy. Unfortunately, Gorst's arrival coincided with a worldwide economic slump. Blamed for the ensuing crash, his policies were resented by British civil servants in Egypt and misinterpreted as weakness by the Egyptian population. In 1910, recognising their failure, he resigned and Lord Kitchener succeeded.

Kitchener had served as Commander-in-Chief of the Egyptian army and knew Egypt

---

LEFT: cartoon of Lord Kitchener in Egypt.
ABOVE: contemporary cartoon showing anti-British riots at Aswan in 1919.

year-old Ottoman connection, Britain declared Egypt a protectorate, thereby finally formalising the authority it had had for the past 32 years. Abbas Hilmi, who had been in Constantinople when the war started, was forbidden to return, then declared a traitor and deposed. His two young sons being excluded from succession, his uncle, 60-year-old Husayn Kamel, was made ruler, with the title of Sultan, by the British. There was little enthusiasm in Egypt for either side in the war, but much resentment of the arrogance of British power.

At the end of the war, the nationalist movement was stronger than ever and a dynamic new leader had emerged to direct its efforts. Saad

Zaghlul was an Al Azhar-educated lawyer of pure Egyptian peasant ancestry. Imprisoned briefly for his participation in the resistance of 1882, Zaghlul later practised law. During this period he married the daughter of a pro-British Prime Minister, and was shown favour by Cromer, who had appointed him Minister of Education. It was not until the Protectorate was declared in 1914 that, angered by Kitchener's treachery to the constitution he had supported in 1913, Zaghlul joined the nationalist ranks.

WORLD WAR I

There was little enthusiasm in Egypt for either side in the war, but much resentment of the arrogance of British power.

over foreign relations, the protection of foreign interests and the Sudan, Egypt should be declared an independent country. But the report was not published until the end of 1921, and meanwhile Zaghlul was arrested and exiled again.

For his part, Allenby had privately made conclusions similar to those of the mission. In February 1922, upon his return from a visit to England, he bore a proclamation that unilaterally ended the Protectorate, but reserving four areas of British control. Three weeks later, Egypt's in-

Emergence of the Wafd
As soon as the armistice was signed, Zaghlul asked the British government to be allowed to go to London to present Egypt's case for independence, but London refused. This uncompromising position only hardened nationalist sentiment, and by early 1919 they were demanding no less than complete independence, with representation at the Peace Conference in Paris. Following demonstrations in Cairo, Zaghlul and three other nationalists were exiled to Malta.

This provoked the successful uprising that Egyptians refer to as the Revolution of 1919. Violence was accompanied by a general strike and a Field-Marshal, Lord Allenby, was sent to replace Wingate, recalled because of his support of the Egyptians' demands. After appraising the situation, however, Allenby promptly brought Zaghlul home from exile, and gave him permission to go to Paris. With other members of the Wafd, as his followers had come to be called (*wafd* means "delegation" in Arabic), Zaghlul attended the conference, but failed to secure his major objective. On the same day that the Treaty of Versailles was signed Allenby issued a proclamation reaffirming the Protectorate.

The Wafd came to speak for the whole country during this period. In fact, its ranks consisted mostly of Egyptian professionals, businessmen and landowners, whose interests the Wafd represented right up until the time all the political parties were outlawed under Nasser.

In November 1919, the British government decided to send a mission to Egypt to study and make recommendations on the form of a constitution for the Protectorate. The mission's report recommended that, although Britain should maintain military forces in Egypt and control

dependence was officially declared; and Sultan Fuad – who had been chosen by the British from among several candidates to succeed his brother, Husayn Kamel, upon the latter's death in 1917 – became King Fuad. A constitution based on Belgium's was adopted in 1923.

Fuad as king (1922–36)
The Wafdists at first rejected this declaration of independence, with its four "reserved points". When Zaghlul was finally allowed to return, however, they sought to participate actively in the upcoming elections, which they won by an overwhelming majority. And so Zaghlul became Egypt's Prime Minister in early 1924.

As Prime Minister, Zaghlul gave up none of his demands connected with completing independence, which included the evacuation of all British troops and Egyptian sovereignty over Sudan. His hopes for their fulfilment were raised when a Labour government came to power in England. Less than a year after the Wafd's landslide victory, however, the assassination of Sir Lee Stack, the British Commander-in-Chief (*Sirdar*) of the Egyptian army and Governor-General of the Sudan, put an end to such optimism.

FREEDOM FIGHTER

As Prime Minister, Zaghlul gave up none of his demands connected with completing independence.

During this crisis, in December 1924, King Fuad took the opportunity to dissolve the Wafdist Parliament and rule by decree. When elections were held in March 1925 and the Wafd won by an overwhelming margin, the king again dissolved parliament. A third set of elections in May 1926 also gave the Wafd a majority, but the British vetoed Zaghlul's reinstatement as the Prime Minister. His health, already shattered by Stack's murder, which had betrayed him, deteriorated further. Zaghlul died a few months later.

Allenby then delivered an ultimatum to the Egyptian government, though it had clearly not been responsible for the murder, making punitive demands. Badly shocked, Zaghlul accepted most of them, but refused to agree to the withdrawal of Egyptian troops from the Sudan, the right of Britain to protect foreign interests in Egypt, or the suppression of political demonstrations. Defiance seemed impossible, however, and he could only resign, leaving it to a successor to accept all the British conditions.

LEFT: European dress was the norm for middle-class Egyptians in the early 20th century.
ABOVE: King Faruq admiring a bust of his father.

Royal dictatorship

Mustafa An-Nahhas succeeded Zaghlul as the leader of the Wafd, and during the following four years the struggle between the Wafd and King Fuad took the same pattern, with the Wafd winning general elections and the king dissolving the parliament to appoint his own ministers. In 1930, Fuad appointed Ismail Sidqi Pasha as Prime Minister and replaced the 1923 constitution with his own royally decreed one. Two successors managed to maintain Fuad's constitution until 1935, when nationalist, popular and British pressure combined to force him to restore the constitution of 1923.

Negotiations for an Anglo-Egyptian treaty

concerning the status of Britain in Egypt and the Sudan had long been underway, and the treaty was finally signed in August 1936. It became the basis of the two countries' relations for the next 18 years.

King Faruq

After 1936, political leadership and the internal political situation both deteriorated. King Fuad died in April 1936 and his son, Faruq, still a minor, succeeded him. The Wafd split, and a new party – the Saad Wafd – was formed.

to invest in factories. The process of industrialisation began again, in a modest way initially, but greatly stepped up after the end of World War II. Along with industrialisation inevitably came urbanisation. Population pressure in the rural areas encouraged large numbers of rural poor to migrate from the countryside to the city in search of jobs. Beginning during the inter-war period, this population shift has since made Cairo one of the most densely packed cities in the world.

Wishing you a Happy Christmas and a Bright New Year.

Extremist organisations also emerged, such as Misr Al-Fatat, an ultra-nationalist pro-royalist group that combined elements of religious fanaticism, militarism and a deep admiration for Nazi Germany and Fascist Italy.

In 1928, Hassan Al-Banna had founded the Muslim Brotherhood, the stated aim of which was to purify and revitalise Islam. But the Brotherhood had political aspirations as well and began to take an active part in politics in the late 1930s. It has since been a force with which every Egyptian government has had to contend.

During the inter-war period, agriculture remained the backbone of the Egyptian economy. But the native Egyptian middle class started

World War II

When World War II broke out, in accordance with the terms of the Treaty of 1936 Britain took control of all Egyptian military facilities, although Egypt itself remained officially neutral for most of the war. The government necessarily supported the British, but many Egyptians did not, while clandestine army groups and Al-Banna's Muslim Brotherhood not only rejected the idea of co-operation but secretly plotted the government's overthrow. In February 1942, with tanks drawn up in front of Abdin Palace, the British installed their own candidate, the Wafdist An-Nahhas, as Prime Minister at gun point. This not only poisoned Anglo-Egyptian relations for more than a decade, but also discredited the Wafd itself.

At the end of the war, Egypt was in a precarious situation. Prime ministers and cabinets changed often; the Wafd, the Saadist party and the king were mutually hostile, and even communist elements were gaining strength.

A SECOND DINSHWAI

Rioting broke out in Cairo, which the authorities would not or could not control.

In addition, a new political force had appeared, the Free Officer movement in the army, led by Gamal Abdel Nasser. Fiercely nationalistic, completely disillusioned with the government, it denounced what it saw as Britain's humiliating occupation of Egyptian soil. The leaders of the Free Officers were in contact with the Muslim Brotherhood and, although some of the two groups' aims coincided, the Free Officers refused Al-Banna's offer to join forces.

The disastrous defeat of the Arabs – the Egyptian army at their forefront – in Palestine in 1948–9 fed fuel to the Muslim Brotherhood, whose volunteers had fought bravely, and its membership rapidly increased. The defeat also increased the disaffection of the army with both the palace and the government, which it accused of complicity in a scandal involving defective arms. Both the Muslim Brotherhood and the Free Officers plotted to take power; and to this end the Brotherhood carried out a series of terrorist operations, including the assassination of the Prime Minister, Noqrashy Pasha, in December 1948. By now aware of the danger that the Muslim Brotherhood represented, the government retaliated with massive arrests of its members and Al-Banna himself was assassinated in February 1949.

Black Saturday
In 1950, riddled with corruption and bad leadership, the Wafd was again elected to power. It instituted disastrous economic policies, but sought to hold onto popularity by releasing many members of the Brotherhood, abrogating the 1936 treaty and calling for the evacuation of British troops from the Canal Zone. Resistance to the British troops in the Canal area took the form of guerilla action with the tacit approval of

LEFT: British servicemen had these cards printed to give their correspondence an Egyptian flavour.
RIGHT: Nasser's stamp of authority.

the government. In January 1952, a second Dinshwai occurred when the British besieged and overran a post manned by Egyptian auxiliary police, who fought to the last man. Rioting broke out in Cairo, which the authorities either would not or could not control. On 26 January, the day known as Black Saturday, foreign shops, bars and nightclubs were burned and British landmarks such as Shepheard's Hotel and the Turf Club disappeared for ever.

The climax came in the night of 22 July, when

the Free Officers took over key positions in a bloodless *coup d'état* engineered by Nasser and other members of his organisation. On the morning of 23 July, the Egyptians were informed that the army, commanded by General Neguib, had seized power. Disillusioned by their corrupt government and their dissolute king, the Egyptians greeted the news with joy.

The Nasser Era (1952–70)
The young officers moved quickly to consolidate their power. On 26 July, King Faruq was forced to abdicate in favour of his son, only six months old. The constitution was repealed and all political parties were suspended. In June

1953, the monarchy was formally ended and a republic declared.

General Neguib, brought late into the Free Officers' plans to serve as a figurehead, was declared President and Prime Minister of the new republic. Other Free Officers were installed as his ministers, Nasser becoming Deputy Prime Minister and Minister of the Interior. Neguib tried to assert the authority he only nominally held, but by May 1954 Nasser was Prime Minister and virtual dictator.

Nasser's first important public act as Prime Minister was the amicable negotiation of a new Anglo-Egyptian treaty that provided for the gradual evacuation of British troops from the Canal Zone. The agreement was signed in October 1954 after six months of negotiations. Although his opponents grumbled that it was not favourable enough to Egypt, since it provided that the British could use the Canal base in times of war, Nasser was generally hailed as the leader who finally ended foreign occupation in Egypt.

In April 1955, Nasser attended the Bandung Conference of Afro-Asian states. Soon afterwards he announced Egypt's commitment to positive neutrality, or non-alignment, and its refusal to join the Baghdad Pact, a military alliance including Iraq and Turkey, which the United States and Britain hoped to establish in the Middle East as a way of maintaining Western influence. With Nehru and Tito, Nasser became one of the leaders of the Non-Aligned Movement.

The turning point in political orientation away from the West came in June 1956, after the United States withdrew its financing for the High Dam at Aswan. Nasser nationalised the Suez Canal and announced that he would use the revenues from it to build the dam, provoking the fury of France and Britain, whose nationals owned the Canal; and with Israel they launched a tripartite attack on Egypt. The invasion was ended by the intervention of the United States and the Soviet Union, forcing the three aggressors to withdraw. Nasser had won an important victory with very little effort and became the symbol of the defiance of imperialist domination.

Arab socialism

It was not until July 1961, five years after the Suez War, that Nasser adopted a comprehensive programme of rapid industrialisation, to be financed in part by nationalisation of all manufacturing

firms, financial institutions and public utilities. Created to further the new programme decreed that year, the Arab Socialist Union was to remain the only legal avenue for political activity open to the Egyptian people for more than a decade.

As Nasser built respect for Egypt abroad, he began increasingly to wave the banner of Arab unity. This led in 1958 to a union between Egypt and Syria, later joined by Yemen, called the United Arab Republic. Initially more enthusiastic than the Egyptians, the Syrians were soon disenchanted, first by the Egyptian bureaucracy, then by the July Ordinances, which toppled their government. A new military regime took Syria

REDISTRIBUTION OF WEALTH

One of Nasser's first policies was the institution of land reform. Ownership of land was limited to 200 acres per person. Holdings beyond this limit – subsequently reduced many times – were taken over and redistributed among the peasants. Private property was confiscated from foreigners, members of the royal family and the rich in general. Bank accounts, land, houses, furniture, jewellery and even books belonging to 4,000 familes were seized, in an effort to deprive the old upper classes of their capital assets, political influence and their culture that had set them apart from the masses.

out of the Union in 1961. Egypt nevertheless retained the name of the United Arab Republic until after Nasser's death.

Nasser's next unfortunate undertaking in the name of Arab unity was his five-year embroilment in Yemen. He sent troops to help out the republican forces there in 1962, while Saudi Arabia aided the royalists. But both countries remained put until 1967, when they were forced to come to an agreement in order to face a common enemy: Israel.

> ### MAN OF THE PEOPLE
> After the Six-Day War Nasser resigned, but he resumed his post next day after mass demonstrations for his return.

The Six-Day War
The Arab-Israeli war of June 1967 was a blow from which Nasser never really recovered. Following growing tension in the area, in May 1967 he demanded that UN troops stationed in the Sinai be withdrawn and announced a blockade of the Straits of Tiran. Probably only bluff on Nasser's part, these moves were quickly taken advantage of by Israel. On 5 June, it launched a sneak attack on Jordan, Syria and Egypt, wiped out the entire Egyptian air force on the ground, and in six days had occupied the Golan Heights, Gaza, Jerusalem, the West Bank and the Sinai. Israeli troops crossed the Suez Canal and were ready to march to Cairo. Only a cease-fire quickly worked out by the United States and the Soviet Union prevented further disaster. After the Six-Day War Nasser resigned, but resumed his post the next day following mass demonstrations for his return.

However popular he remained, the old charisma was gone and Nasser was a broken man. Efforts to salvage a wrecked economy, no longer even agriculturally self-sufficient, proved fruitless. His last important act was an attempt to reconcile King Hussein and the Palestinians after the bloody events of Black September 1970, when the king tried to crush the PLO in Jordan. Later in September, he helped to negotiate an accord by which Hussein, Arafat and other Arab leaders agreed to end the fighting. He died of a heart attack the day after the signing of the accord.

The Sadat era
On Nasser's death, Anwar Sadat, his vice-president, succeeded to the presidency. No-one

expected Sadat to last long in this position, but he proved more skilful than his opponents. In May 1971, with what he called a "corrective movement", he consolidated his power by dismissing high-ranking government officials who openly or secretly opposed him. Another surprise move the following year was the expulsion of Soviet teachers and advisors who had been in Egypt for more than a decade. After a long period of close relations with the Eastern bloc, Egypt was turning toward the West.

Sadat's boldest initiative was his launching of the fourth Arab-Israeli war in October 1973. The outcome of this was by no means a total victory, but it did allow Egypt to regain its pride.

It also gave Sadat enough prestige to ignore Arab unity and seek a separate peace with Israel. The dramatic opening of this process was his visit to Israel in November 1977 during which he addressed the Knesset. The treaty process resulted in the Camp David accords, signed under US patronage in March 1979. Furthered by massive infusions of US aid, the accords were greeted in Egypt with euphoria, but this mood rapidly dissipated as differences between Egyptian and Israeli interpretations of

LEFT: Nasser waves to the crowds.
RIGHT: Anwar al Sadat, Egypt's second president.

them became clear. Arab countries meanwhile denounced the accords as treachery and expelled Egypt from the Arab League.

Sadat's economic policies, encouraging foreign investment and private enterprise, created high inflation and widened differences between the new rich and older salaried classes, as well as the poor. The drain of Egyptian brains and brawn to neighbouring oil-rich countries meanwhile became a torrent. Remittances from abroad began to emerge as the single most

important factor in the Egyptian economy. Property prices soared as returning Egyptians sought to invest in something safe. The impact of these revenues was ignored by government planners, whose economic models were geared solely to public-sector revenues.

The high-handed style of Sadat's government, in an atmosphere of corruption and crony capitalism, alienated many followers. Overt opposition gathered round the new political parties, including a revived Wafd, while less public hostility crystallised in Islamic revivalism. Thanks to Sadat's lifting of systematic repression, the Muslim Brotherhood had regained most of its freedom of action, but there were other more radical groupings, one of which was responsible for Sadat's assassination on 6 October 1981 during a ceremony commemorating the crossing of the Suez Canal.

GROWING OPPOSITION

The high-handed style of Sadat's government, in an atmosphere of corruption and crony capitalism, alienated many followers.

The Mubarak years

After nearly three decades of authoritarian rule, Vice President Hosni Mubarak, a former air force commander, became president. While honouring the commitments made under Sadat's liberalised economic policies, Mubarak's regime curtailed corruption and tried to promote more democratic government. However, faced with providing for a rapidly growing population, Mubarak introduced tough financial controls.

His greatest challenge was presented by the Islamic Group (Al-Gama'a al-Islamiya), whose aim was to oust Mubarak and turn Egypt into a fundamentalist Islamic state. A new domino theory was propounded by international diplomats, envisaging the rapid collapse of secular governments in neighbouring countries if Egypt were to fall to the fundamentalists.

The Islamic Group's attacks on tour buses, cruise boats and ancient sites caused tourism, Egypt's biggest foreign currency earner by far, to plummet, further increasing unemployment and social discontent. The government reacted with a harsh crackdown. Hangings of convicted terrorists – the first since the aftermath of Sadat's assassination – were resumed in 1993.

Egyptian society has become very complex. The population eats and sleeps surrounded by walls of concrete rather than mudbrick, and works in industry, commerce, services or the governmental bureaucracy rather than in agriculture. Authoritarian structures, bolstered in the past by middle-class fears of the masses, have come to be seen as inefficient. Increasing democratisation therefore has become the centre of Egyptian hopes.

At the same time, the freeing of exchange rates, easing of import controls, creation of an Egyptian stock exchange and the repatriation of large sums privately invested abroad have helped the middle class. Their support of Mubarak and their ability to stimulate the economy remains the key to Egypt's prosperity. ❑

LEFT: Hosni Mubarak campaigns.
RIGHT: posters of presidents – Mubarak and Sadat.

NINETEENTH-CENTURY TRAVELLERS ON THE NILE

Tourists had been visiting Egypt since the time of the Greeks, but there was a sense of rediscovery as 19th-century Westerners arrived in Egypt

It is hard for us to imagine the shock of arriving in Egypt in the 18th or 19th centuries. By the time we arrive, books, newspapers and television have shown us in minute detail what temples and tombs look like and the ways in which they functioned. Yet for all our information, early travellers were often better equipped to appreciate what they saw. After the French scholar Champollion deciphered hieroglyphics, many of them arrived having learned how to read ancient inscriptions. They would have read their Greek and Roman histories, and their early travellers, as well as the latest accounts.

THE EGYPT THEY FOUND

Most Western visitors spoke no Arabic, though in Egypt few people spoke anything other than Arabic. Until the 1820s, they travelled under constant threat in a country with no strong central authority, but there was romance as well as danger: new tombs and temples were being dug out of the sand, and until the mid-19th century they sailed on a river whose source remained a mystery.

▷ LITERARY TRAVELS

Egypt has long been a favourite place for adventurous writers. Among the crowd who visited in the 19th century, both Gustave Flaubert (right) and Mark Twain (top) left classic accounts, though in Flaubert's case the wonders of ancient Egypt take second place after the marvels of its brothels and baths.

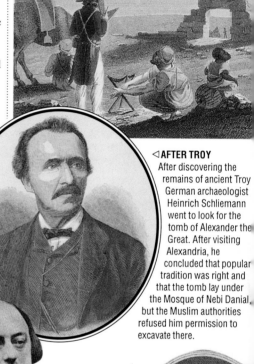

◁ AFTER TROY

After discovering the remains of ancient Troy German archaeologist Heinrich Schliemann went to look for the tomb of Alexander the Great. After visiting Alexandria, he concluded that popular tradition was right and that the tomb lay under the Mosque of Nebi Danial, but the Muslim authorities refused him permission to excavate there.

△ CLASSIC TRAVELS

Sir Samuel and Lady Baker (*right*) left Cairo to explore the Nile sources in 1861 and were the first white people to visit Lake Albert.

LADIES ON THE NILE

In 1849, Florence Nightingale went to Egypt for the winter to recover her health and wrote, "One wonders that people come back from Egypt and live lives as they did before." She did not: by the time she got home she had written some of the finest letters from Egypt and also decided to devote her life to helping the sick.

By then people could sail on the Nile in comfort, but earlier travellers had not had it so easy. Elisa Fay, *en route* to India in 1779, was scared on the river up to Cairo, nearly suffocated under all the layers she was obliged to wear in public and was then robbed, along with the rest of her caravan, crossing the desert to Suez.

Sophia Poole, sister of Edward Lane, the Arabic scholar, lived in Egypt for seven years (1842–49) without having to compromise her Christian values, although she was a little shocked by the public baths. Miss Poole and her contemporary Harriet Martineau were among the first outsiders to write about women in Egypt, an insight furthered by the letters of Lucie Duff Gordon, who had been sent to the Nile for her health. In the year of her death, 1869, conditions were "soft" enough for Thomas Cook to launch the first package tour of the country.

△ **SCHOLARLY ARMY**
When Napoleon invaded Egypt in 1798, he landed with an army of soldiers and a group of 167 savants under the leadership of Baron Dominique Vivant Denon (*above and left*). Denon travelled to Aswan with the army, while the savants spread across the country recording everything from antiquities to wildlife. He published his *Travels* in 1802, ahead of the *Description de l'Egypte* (1809).

▽ **TRAVELLING INCOGNITO**
The extraordinary Richard Burton perfected his disguise as Mirca Abdullah in Cairo before undertaking a pilgrimage to Mecca.

△ **SLAVE WIFE**
Baker had bought his wife as a slave and, although she suffered when her origins were known, she was admired for her endurance.

△ **GREAT DISCOVERER**
Between 1815–19 Giovanni Belzoni, circus strongman turned antiquity-hunter, opened the Second Pyramid at Giza and Abu Simbel's Great Temple, and discovered Seti I's tomb in Luxor.

ENDANGERED MONUMENTS

Conservation in the name of tourism can be far from desirable, as the weakening structure of the Sphinx demonstrates

Until 1965, when the Aswan High Dam held back its first flood, very few of the millions of structures built by Egyptians were ever intended to last more than a few months, or at most a few years. Imhotep's architectural revolution at Saqqarah made the permanence of building in stone possible as early as the 3rd millennium BC, but for most of the ensuing centuries the idea of permanence was extended only to religious structures. Even the pharaohs' palaces were built of perishable materials. Ancient dwellings have therefore disappeared, while ancient religious structures remain. They are the most tangible link between modern Egypt and its ancient past.

The question of conserving pharaonic monuments involves two major considerations: archaeology and tourism. Once a building has been thoroughly documented, its archaeological purpose has been fulfilled; and as far as archaeologists are concerned it can then be filed away for future reference. In 1969, for example, the French Archaeological Institute, working in collaboration with the Antiquities Organisation, excavated and cleared an extraordinary 6th-century monastic complex near Esna, secured the necessary data, then reburied it, publishing a complete report three years later. The site has thus been saved for future generations.

Putting the Sphinx on show

The Sphinx, now an endangered monument, might have been preserved by this tactic. Though cleared many times in its earlier history, it had been allowed to rest safely under sand until 1925, when it was exhumed again and repaired. Since its stone is very soft, it is subject to massive erosion by the sand-blast of Giza's incessant winds. Chemical injection, intended to harden the stone were made, though their long-term effects were still unknown. Unfortunately, they resulted in weakening the

LEFT: paw and head of the Sphinx, a monument that has been heavily restored.
RIGHT: detail from the Temple of Dendarah.

Sphinx, and subsequent erosion is such that there are now fears that its head may topple off.

The Sphinx is thus rapidly being sacrificed to tourism, which is not only an important industry in general for Egypt, but also specifically supports the Ministry of Culture, as well as excavation, restoration and conservation. So Egyptian

archaeologists face a dilemma: their source of funding is also the greatest source of destruction.

Reconstruction may be archaeologically desirable and even necessary at certain sites, such as Saqqarah, but once documentation has been finished most archaeologists can bring themselves to accept even a building's complete destruction with a certain equanimity.

Philae and Abu Simbel

The archaeological outcry over the Nubian antiquities doomed by the construction of the High Dam at Aswan thus had less to do with a wish to preserve what had already been recorded than with the loss or destruction of vast amounts of physical data that had not yet been archaeologically surveyed.

Philae was famous throughout the Mediterranean in antiquity and represented a vital part of an international cultural inheritance. But motives for moving the rock-cut Abu Simbel temples, unknown until 1813, are best understood as a mixture of the aesthetic, the commercial and the sentimental.

It was precisely for the benefits of tourism, however, that both Philae and the Abu Simbel temples were moved to their present positions.

Though Egyptologists are even more thrilled than other people by these two sites, neither of them represents the cutting edge of modern archaeological research; and the sums finally expended on these two projects – nearly US$30 million for moving Philae and more than US$40 million for Abu Simbel – probably amounted to far more than the total that had been spent on archaeology itself since the beginnings of Egyptology.

Urban conservation

Generally standing on rural or desert sites in isolation from present-day communities, pharaonic tombs and temples have little significance for local people unless they can be exploited for immediate material gain. This local indifference allowed them to tumble or be buried under sand, but also created an absence of environmental complication that has since made many of them fairly easy to excavate, clear, reconstruct, record, restore and then eventually conserve.

This situation contrasts totally with that of Egypt's medieval and modern monuments, nearly all of which stand in the urban setting of Cairo. The ancestors of Cairo, moreover, were not only the mudbrick towns of the Old and New Kingdoms, but also the cities of the Hellenistic world, typified by Ptolemaic Alexandria. There the notion of architectural permanence had been extended for the first time in Egypt to secular buildings, making it a "city of marble". Burnt brick and stone thus became the materials of the new metropolis. Coupled with a remarkable history – Cairo has known earthquake, plagues and fires, but (uniquely among Middle Eastern cities) has never undergone the utter devastation that follows political, economic or cultural irrelevance – these materials have ensured that Cairene buildings dating from the 7th century onward still remain more or less intact.

Secular buildings frequently fell victim throughout the Middle Ages to new architectural schemes, but street patterns were maintained and religious buildings were often restored by succeeding generations.

Egypt's first conservation organisation, the Khedivial government's Committee for the Conservation of Monuments of Arab Art, was set up in 1881 specifically to protect medieval Islamic buildings, which had not only fallen into dilapidation, but were additionally threatened by new development. Many had in fact already been sacrificed to Ali Mubarak's masterplan under the Khedive Ismail, while work on reconstructing pharaonic monuments, by contrast, had hardly begun. The committee's criteria and techniques were identical with those of similar European organisations and are now quite outdated, but during its 70-year existence it completed some remarkable tasks, beginning with an index of 800 buildings.

In 1952 it was absorbed into the Antiquities Organisation, under the Ministry of Culture, which carried out almost no urban or medieval restoration or conservation for nearly 30 years, largely because it had no access to its revenues. The result, by 1980, was near-disaster. Apart from declining conditions caused by traffic, industrialisation, declining cultural and economic levels, and increasing population density, the city's water and sewerage systems had collapsed, raising the water-table in some places almost to the surface, well above the impermeable footings installed by medieval builders. Walls soaked up water or drew it up by capillary action and began to disintegrate, while badly restored or unrepaired roofs began to collapse.

COST OF NEGLECT

Walls soaked up water while roofs began to collapse.

which they are often directly related. Awareness of their value to the city as a whole, however, has spread recently even into the public sector. A stiff new law passed in 1983 brought regulations up-to-date, covering all historic buildings and their environs with new protection but excluding those less than 100 years old from registration on the index except by specific decree. The fate of Cairo's later neo-Islamic, Beaux-Arts, Art Nouveau and Art Deco buildings thus still hangs in the balance. Moratoria on building permits, arising directly out of public dismay at what seemed

Great changes have taken place since 1981. There is no programme for urban rehabilitation but from 1982 onward the organisation at least tackled the problem of the medieval monuments themselves. An earthquake in 1992 showed that there is still a great deal to be done, however, and many monuments remain under scaffolding.

But Cairo's special quality comes from its combination of the medieval and the modern: its 19th and early 20th-century buildings are as important to its character as its great Mamluk monuments, to

LEFT: Mosque of Amr ibn al-'As being repaired. Many of Cairo's mosques are in a precarious condition.
ABOVE: work in progress at Karnak.

to be the city's wholesale destruction, have slowed the pace of their disappearance dramatically, however, and a campaign mounted since 1985 has already succeeded in indexing a handful of the most important.

Beyond all these concerns, of course, is the question of caring for the environment throughout Egypt as a whole. Today's tourist is attracted by those qualities that will make the country attractive to future Egyptians themselves. To squander natural and cultural resources now is therefore to make the country not only less habitable in the future, but also less viable as a place anyone would want to visit. That fact is beginning to be thoroughly understood. ❏

THE EGYPTIANS

*Egyptians as a whole are said to be humble, pious and a touch mischievous,
but the people of every region have their own defining characteristics*

When God created the nations, so Arab - wisdom has it, he endowed each with two counterbalanced qualities: to the intelligence of the Syrians he thus added fatuousness; to Iraq he gave pride, but tempered it with hypocrisy; while for the desert Arabs he compensated hardship with good health. And Egypt he blessed with abundance at the cost of humility.

It does not require a deep understanding of the past to feel that, as far as Egypt is concerned, God has withdrawn the first half of his covenant – or that, at any rate, He's made a new deal with the desert dwellers. As any Egyptian will explain, it is not many generations since Egyptian donations fed the poor of the holy cities of Mecca and Medina, in what is now Saudi Arabia. To the desert Arabs, however, God has recently given abundance, in the form of oil, while Egypt, formerly the land of plenty, has received unaccustomed hardship, in the form of war and overpopulation. Once the breadbasket of the Roman Empire, Egypt now follows only Japan and Russia as an importer of food and only India in the league of aid recipients.

Yet poverty is a relative thing and, perhaps because of their humility, Egyptians bear it with considerable grace. In the poorest hinterland of the south, a foreign traveller overheard a conversation between two venerable farmers: "These poor Europeans," said one, "they will do anything to escape their horrible climate. I saw one the other day who'd come all the way here on a bicycle." "Yes," replied the other, "their land is covered with ice all year round. Look at us. We've got sunshine, water, everything." "It is indeed terrible," concluded the first. "The *khawaga* I saw didn't even have money to buy proper trousers – he was riding about in his underwear!"

Egyptian humility takes many forms. One is a tragic sense of life, arising from a tragic view of history. While the West embraces the idea of progress as a solution to all man's ills, the Egyptians have an impulse to turn towards a utopian past, perhaps to a time when Muhammad's successors, the four Rightly Guided Caliphs, brought justice, prosperity and true belief to the land.

The humiliating defeat suffered by Egypt in

the 1967 war would have brought on a revolution in another country. Yet when Nasser, in an emotional speech, offered to resign, the response was dramatic: millions of Egyptians poured into the streets demanding that he stay. His willingness to share their humiliation brought forth instant sympathy from the masses, who saw it as more important that his intentions had been morally right than that he had failed to realise them.

Islam and popular piety

Any visitor to Egypt will be struck by the piety of its people. Humility is inherent in the very word Islam, the religion of nine-tenths of Egyptians. Islam (from the Arabic roots *salima*, to be safe; *aslama*, to surrender and *salaam*, peace) means "submission", whether it be to God, fate or the social system framed by the Qur'an.

Most Westerners find the continuing dominance of Islam in what purports to be an age of reason perplexing. The important thing to recognise is that the Qur'an – literally, a "recitation" – is the word of God in Arabic as directly transmitted by Muhammad. The power of the Word thus has a strength in Islam unmatched by the literature of any other "revealed" religion; and the beauty of the Qur'an,

SUPERNATURAL POWER

Magicians, witches and priests do a brisk trade in spells and potions.

vanished from European speech proliferate in everyday language in Egypt. "God willing", "By God's permission", "Praise God" and "Our Lord prevails" are as common as the word "Goodbye" is in English. But goodbye long ago lost its religious connotation whereas in Egypt such meanings have not been forgotten. The proper response to the greeting *Salam aleikum* (Peace be upon you) is *Aleikum as-salam wa rahmat Allah wa barakatu* (Upon you be peace and the mercy of God and his blessings).

Apart from piety, however, this exchange also

by definition "inimitable", is cited as a miracle in its own right. It is not extraordinary that many Egyptian tastes, habits, and preferences are referred directly back to the Qur'an.

While there are many atheists and agnostics in Egypt, the vast majority sticks as tenaciously to belief in a supreme deity and the imminence of the Day of Judgement. The month-long, dawn-to-dusk fast of Ramadan, still officially observed by the entire country, bears witness to Islam's pervasiveness, but even the Coptic minority, conscious of being members of one of the earliest Christian sects, maintains a degree of devoutness that is often bewildering to Western Christians. Religious expressions of a kind that have almost

reflects a point of Arab etiquette – any greeting must be followed by a response that outdoes the first speaker's in politeness. Religiosity, though abundant, is not always heartfelt.

For many, particularly the poor, belief in the supernatural extends beyond orthodoxy to a world of genies and spirits of the dead. Fertility rites are still held in Upper Egyptian temples; and magicians, witches and priests do a brisk trade in spells and potions.

Jests, gibes and practical jokes

Egyptian piety is also balanced by a deep love of mischief. If anything can compete in public esteem with holiness, it is wit; and Egyptian humour holds nothing sacred. Political jokes are particularly sharp and irreverent, but Egyptians make use of the smallest incident to provoke laughter. In a café or bar, wise-cracks are fired back and forth with increasing hilarity until the whole company falls off its chair.

Sages have often remarked that, while the condition that formulates much of Western behaviour is a sense of guilt, arising from an individual "conscience", in the East in general it is shame, arising from a sense of public disapproval or contempt. Egyptian children, raised with the idea that whatever you can get away with socially is morally permissible, must rank among the world's naughtiest. Historically, Egyptian mischievousness has its roots in the legacy of centuries of repressive government. Numerous are the stories that celebrate the victory, through a mix of cunning and trickery, of the poor fellah over wicked pashas or foreigners.

This love of trickery has its drawbacks, as the 15th-century Egyptian historian Al Maqrizi noted in an unflattering portrayal of his countrymen: "That which dominates in the character of the Egyptians is the love of pleasure… They are extremely inclined to cunning and deceit."

Maqrizi notes, among other things, that the Egyptians of his time showed a distinct disdain for study. This indifference, it must be said, is very pronounced to this day, and most evident in a tendency to attempt to achieve goals by means other than hard labour and careful planning. It is a habit of mind that even President Mubarak castigates in his fellow citizens. Although much of it can be attributed to overcrowding and a faulty educational system, the degree of cheating in Egyptian schools and universities is scandalous.

Coercion and conformity

Shame has other manifestations. Unjustly, Egyptians are generally not trustful of one another, believing that it is only by overt pressure that people can be prevented from overstepping the bounds of morality. This attitude explains, more than political exigencies, the

> ### BATTLE OF WITS
> In a café or bar, wise-cracks are fired back and forth with increasing hilarity until the whole company falls off its chair.

heavy presence of police in the country. Belief in the need for coercion and forced restraint is strengthened by religious attitudes. It is commonly presumed that without the just guidance of Islam, society would fall apart.

Attitudes to sex are also framed by the same phenomenon. Women are constantly pestered in the streets, largely because it is believed that really masculine men cannot resist the temptations of sex. The same is held to be true of women. Thus foreigners often find the atmos-

phere highly charged sexually in Egypt. Sex is not only openly discussed by both men and women, but also lurks at the edges of even ordinary conversation. Since the Arabic language itself is full of sexual innuendoes, its richness lends a wonderful bawdiness to Egyptian talk.

The mazes of matrimony

Marriage, however, is deemed an absolute prerequisite for sex, as well as for full adulthood and respectability. Particularly among women, whose freedom is still very much limited by rigid social norms, finding and keeping the right husband is thus the major focus of life. Since the 1920s, when the veil was finally discarded,

LEFT: Friday prayers at Al Hussein Mosque, Cairo.
RIGHT: pile them high.

substantial progress towards equality of the sexes has been made, but it is still the rule for a girl to remain in the care of her father until the day she is passed into the care of her husband.

Respect for parents and elders is so strongly ingrained that it is likewise uncommon for even a male child to leave home before marriage; and these days, few urban Egyptians can afford to marry before the age of 25. Despite Islam's flexibility on the subject – easy divorce and polygamy are both sanctioned – marriage is regarded as a binding agreement, made more absolute by economics. For this reason, young couples are expected to work out every detail of their future life – housing, furniture, a dowry for the wife as a form of divorce insurance – before signing the contract.

"Money and children," the Qur'an says, "are the embellishments of life." Egyptians adore children, and large families are the norm. In many ways, the family is more important than the individual as a social unit, extending not only over several generations but also to distant cousins. The fierce vendettas that still rage in Upper Egypt, often claiming dozens of lives over many decades, illustrate this point. Family honour and prestige are serious matters, particularly in the countryside. The crime columns regularly tell of adultery-related murders: a woman's honour, it is said, "is like a matchstick: it can only be used once".

In the cities, political and business alliances are often reinforced through marriage. Because numerous children enlarge the family's potential for wealth and influence, and also because it is believed that it is healthier for children to grow up with lots of brothers and sisters, the family planners have had a hard time bringing down the birth rates.

Egyptian mothers are notoriously soft on their children. Centuries of high infant mortality, sexual roles that give housebound wives complete responsibility for children, and lingering belief in the power of the evil eye mean that mothers are inclined to cater to their child's every whim for fear that some harm may befall him or her. This is particularly true in the case of favoured boys. It is not uncommon, in fact, for a woman's strongest emotional tie to be with her eldest son rather than her husband. As infants, children are wrapped up in swaddling and thoroughly doted upon. By the time they are old enough to walk, however, they are usually

left to spend time as they wish. This unorthodox combination of coddling and freedom is often cited as a reason for the self-confidence and even obstinacy of the Egyptian character.

Life-support systems

Beyond the family, Egyptians have a strong attachment to their immediate community. Village solidarity – when not torn apart by blood feuds – is very strong. In the big towns the *hara* (alley) is the main unit of social bonding.

The main function of *hara* solidarity is to defend the interests of the community. Gangs of local toughs, whose mandate varied from

WILD WEDDINGS

Extravagant weddings testify to the importance of marriage. Wealthy families will blow thousands of pounds on a binge in one of Egypt's five-star hotels, complete with a fanfare of trumpets, lurking video crews, famous belly dancers, singers and other entertainers. And the weddings of poor families are equally extravagant, as they too are expected to flaunt their pride. Whole streets are closed off and the affair takes place in the open air. Street musicians, acrobats, boy dancers and slick masters of ceremonies keep things lively as the male guests tuck into the free beer, hashish and opium.

protection of neighbourhood women against strangers to simple extortion rackets, formed part of the urban landscape until quite recently.

Peculiarities of places

Regional loyalties persist strongly as well. Each major town and province has its acknowledged characteristic, from Alexandria in the north to Aswan in the south. Like the inhabitants of other port cities, Alexandrians are known chiefly for their toughness and willingness to fight, but also noted for their cosmopolitan out-

THE JOKE'S ON ME

Saidis joke even about themselves, being too open-hearted to pass the buck.

that their country cousins do not find endearing.

The Saidis are the Polacks of Egypt, with the difference that the traits attributed to them – simple-mindedness, credulity and impulsiveness – have a remarkable ring of truth. Saidis joke even about themselves, being too open-hearted to pass the buck. A sample joke: an Alexandrian, a Cairene and a Saidi are dying of thirst in the desert when a genie appears and allows each a single wish. The Alexandrian says, "I wish I were on the beach at Muntazah surrounded by girls", and

look and business acumen. The peasants of Lower Egypt and the Delta are regarded as hardworking, thrifty and serious-minded. Rashidis, from Rosetta, are supposed to be kind-hearted, while Dumyatis, from the town of Damietta at the Nile's eastern mouth, are reckoned to be very untrustworthy.

Cairenes, like New Yorkers or cockneys, are seen as slick, fast-talking and immoral. Simply being from the capital allows them to sneer at less sophisticated compatriots, a Cairene habit

LEFT: wedding couple in the Bahariyya Oasis.
ABOVE: funeral cortège in the Fayyum. Bodies are buried on the day of death.

vanishes. The Cairene says, "I wish I were praying in the mosque of Hussein in Cairo," and vanishes. The Saidi, looking dismayed, turns to the genie and says, "I'm so lonely. Couldn't you please bring my friends back?" On the positive side, Saidis are noted for their generosity, courage, virility and sense of honour.

The dark-skinned Nubians of the far south, an ancient people with their own languages, are considered to be the most gentle and peaceful of Egyptians. Long isolated by the cataracts that made the Nile above Aswan impassable, Nubian life, relaxed and carefree, had a unique charm. Nubian villages are spotlessly clean, the spacious mudbrick houses always freshly painted, and both men and women are apt to be more enterprising than their Egyptian neighbours.

The desert Bedu have not given up their ancient occupation of smuggling, and fierce tribal loyalty is still maintained. The Bedu are feared, scorned and envied for their aristocratic wilfulness. The old rivalry between these free-wheeling bandits of the desert and the hardworking peasants of the valley has all but died out – largely through intermarriage – but their pure Arab blood and the beauty of their women are still admired.

HIGH AND MIGHTY

The Bedu are feared, scorned and envied for their aristocratic wilfulness.

exception, naturally, of the Saidis – that they prefer compromise to conflict. By inclination, habit and training, Egyptians are tactful and diplomatic, sometimes even to the point of obsequiousness.

Forms of address in Egypt are complex and varied, as befits a highly stratified society. A taxi driver may be addressed, for example, as "O Chief Engineer" or "O Foreman". (Note that, when sitting in a taxi, one is a temporary guest and not merely a fare; so it is insulting for a lone male passenger to sit in the back seat by himself.) A person of

Pride and prejudice

This catalogue of regional differences obscures an essential homogeneity of attitudes and feelings, however. Despite differences and despite the bitter legacy of imperialism – of defeat, occupation and dependence – pride in Egypt and "the Egyptian way" is fervent. An old Arab adage: "I and my brothers against my cousins, I and my cousins against my tribe, and I and my tribe against the world" serves to illustrate this point. The purpose of all allegiances, from the family to the neighbourhood to the region to the nation and even beyond, is to prevent one from being being pushed around.

It is characteristic of the Egyptians – with the

high social standing should be addressed as "Your Presence", while a person of respectable but indeterminate standing is "O President" or "O Professor". An older person is "O Teacher" or "O Pilgrim", the latter referring of course to someone who has made the pilgrimage to Mecca. Even Turkish titles – bey, pasha, hanem – survive, though they have no legal standing, and are used for courtesy's sake.

This diversity, while lending a great deal of charm to the simplest of exchanges, in fact underlines the cohesiveness of the society rather than its disparateness: the Egyptian sees all men as equals, but allots to each a specific status and with it a role.

Making do

As in many other Third World countries, sharp disparities of wealth exist. There are some 50,000 millionaires, and for a time in the late 1970s poverty-stricken Egypt was importing more Mercedes cars than any other country in the world. On Cairo's streets the contrast between the elegance of imported luxury and the rolling slum of a packed bus or the pathetic heap of a trash-collector's donkey cart is particularly shocking.

Trash collectors, known as *zabbalin* or "garbage people", live in conditions of appalling squalor, their homes nestled among mounds of refuse, which they bring from the city, sort through and sell for recycling. The *zabbalin* represent the absolute bottom of the social pile, but their very existence testifies to the general poverty of the nation. It would take the average worker a year to earn the price of a Cairo-New York return ticket.

Display of wealth in Egypt is often, to Western eyes, vulgar. But the flaunting of riches only confirms that, in a society forced to count its pennies, money carries a special prestige. As a rich merchant, whose lifestyle is otherwise modest, commented, "Yes, I would rather have spent my money on something other than a Mercedes. But you wouldn't believe how much it saves me. I don't have to waste time – or money – proving myself. I get instant respect."

Open doors, closed options

Materialist ostentation became rife after the mid-1970s, when President Sadat reversed 20 years of socialist legislation with the announcement of his Open Door policy. Before him, Nasser had worked to redistribute the country's wealth, parcelling out the great feudal estates, seizing the property of the richest families and reinvesting it in new state industries. Nasser's policies brought dignity to the majority at the expense of the few, but also frightened off private initiative. Not many landlords bothered even to paint their houses, for fear of attracting the tax man. With the Open Door policy, the lid was abruptly removed; and luxury imports

boomed as money came out of Swiss banks or from under the floorboards.

Allowing Egyptians, who were underpaid at home, to work profitably abroad, the Open Door policy brought improved living standards in the form of more TVs, more cars, better clothing and a richer diet. It also inflated expectations and undermined social cohesiveness, something which President Mubarak's new economic reforms – stressing private initiative – have since exacerbated. Neither the poor nor the

old elites approve of today's nouveau riche.

A country without dreams can be a depressing place. The primary condition of Egypt – too many people – doesn't help. In 1968, when Israel was revelling in its conquest of the Sinai peninsula and half a million inhabitants of the cities along the Suez Canal had been made homeless, a journalist asked President Nasser what his major worry was. Without hesitation, he replied, "The thousand new Egyptians born every day." A generation later, the population pyramid looms still more menacingly on the horizon. Schools in Cairo already operate three shifts and a new school must be built every day.

Products of a school system that stifles

LEFT: three generations of a Cairene family.
RIGHT: an *erqsusi*, a vendor of liquorice drink.

curiosity and promotes learning by rote, more and more young Egyptians feel a sense of frustration regarding the future. Among men, those who do not go on to university or manage to obtain an exemption must face three years of military service, often under conditions of extreme hardship. In the bigger cities, many younger women find jobs before marriage, but the majority stay at home and hope for the best. Better prospects await the one in 10 young Egyptians of both sexes who attend university, but the country's dozen institutions of higher learning are appallingly overcrowded, understaffed and disorganised.

before they reach the stage when they require medical care. Money, in particular, causes endless anxieties; feeding, educating and underwriting the marriages of children is not cheap, especially when respectability must be maintained. While families and neighbourhoods provide a degree of support unimaginable in the West, they also eliminate privacy; and even the smallest problems quickly become everybody's business.

The housing shortage means that too many people are often cooped up in the same house, and there are some districts of Cairo where the average density is three to a room.

New anxieties

Low pay and a general loathing for the bureaucracy has meant that government jobs have lost most of their prestige. Increasingly one finds university graduates working as taxi-drivers, plumbers, mechanics and the like. The money is better and tradesmen stand a likelier chance of saving in order to get married, though with inflation and the limited availability of decent apartments, many are obliged to scrimp for years before they can establish a household.

Universally aspired to in Egypt, marriage provides no passport to a life of ease. The typical lifespan is not long – perhaps 55 years – and many Egyptians appear to die of worry or grief

CAN'T PAY, WON'T PAY

Until recently, the government followed a policy of providing employment for every university graduate. The result is that the Egyptian bureaucracy and public-sector industry, which together employ half of the non-agricultural workforce, is catastrophically overstaffed. Studies have shown that an average government employee actually works for between six and 30 minutes a day. Low salaries and lenient employment policies have encouraged apathy and abuse at every level – with obstruction, absenteeism, corruption and intolerable rudeness to the taxpayer who foots the bill.

Compensations

An atmosphere of melancholy pervades life but, strangely enough, the salient characteristic of the Egyptians is their cheerfulness. They are past masters at coping. All problems and situations are so endlessly discussed and analysed that they end by becoming mere topics of amusement. The tales of intrigue, frustrated love, good fortune or catastrophe that even the simplest people in this country relate in connection with their own personal lives retain a quality of wonder reminiscent of *1,001 Nights*. Everyone has a story.

> ### STORY TELLERS
> The tales of intrigue, frustrated love, good fortune or catastrophe retain a quality of wonder… Everyone has a story.

The protective structure of society, based on the strength of family ties, allows Egyptian men and women to give free rein to their emotions. Families, neighbours and countrymen at large can all be relied on for compassion, commiseration or help. This solidarity makes Egypt one of the safest countries in the world. When someone shouts "Thief!" on the street, every shop empties as all and sundry help to chase the culprit, who is almost invariably caught and hauled off to the nearest police station by a gesticulating mob. Following the terrible attack by Islamic fundamentalists on tourists at the Temple of Hatshepsut, Thebes, in 1997, the murderers were pursued across the hill (and caught and killed) by outraged locals. Throughout Egypt fewer murders are committed in a year than take place annually in any typical large city in America – a comparison reflecting the fact that Egyptian society allows fewer people to be marginalised. Every person has his recognised place in the scheme of things.

Taking time out

Egypt's true carnivals, in the form of *mawalid* or saints' days, offer a glimpse of this street energy in concentrated form. Push-carts hawking everything from plastic guns to chick peas sprout overnight, vying for space with the tents and sleeping bodies of country pilgrims. On the Big Night, while dervishes dance to exhaustion to the *dhikr* rhythms (chanting in remembrance of God), local kids try out the swings, shooting galleries and assorted tests of strength.

LEFT: family outing to Cairo's Citadel.
ABOVE: Bedu women gathering firewood.

But even fun is not what it used to be. Respectable middle-class folk scorn the dowdy and unorthodox *mawalid*. Video tapes or television, with their melodramatic soap operas, trashy foreign serials and official sloganising, now provide the entertainment of the majority. These appurtenances of modern life have a powerful effect in a traditional society. Glorifying the bourgeois and "liberal" attitudes of the city and thus homogenising Egyptian life, television has also deprived it of much of its vitality.

It will be a long time yet, though, before the Egyptian people lose their appeal. Sensitivity and kindness still abound. Solicitous for the welfare of their fellows, Egyptians are invariably helpful, hospitable and friendly – indeed, almost to a fault: asking directions needs care, for example, since the response may be generated by a sense of social duty rather than by actual knowledge. Generosity is taken so much for granted that it is considered unseemly to offer thanks too profusely for a gift for fear of being insulting.

The warmth of human relations brings Egypt a soft sweetness, even extended to visitors, that has always been the best part of its charm. ❑

MARKETS AND BAZAARS

To understand a city, you must know its markets. They are the hub of everyday
activity and in Cairo will introduce you to some of the city's oldest quarters

The best way to get a feel for the living energy of any city, beyond the epidermis of its monuments and museums or the skeleton of its streets, is to examine its circulatory system: the mainstream and tributaries of its economic life.

For Cairo, at the crossroads of continents and

area of free trade within the Muslim empire.

Throughout the Middle Ages, as it added more quarters and spread to the north, Cairo boomed. It was an international entrepôt for slaves, ivory, textiles, livestock, spices and luxury goods; and until the 15th century, the dinars and dirhams of the Cairo mint were the most stable currency in

the nexus of the Nile, the function of the marketplace has always been vital. Like Rome, the city's origin lay in its location at an easy crossing of a river. Commerce grew out of the transit of merchandise. Egyptian Babylon was already a settlement of buyers and sellers; and the arrival of Islam in the 7th century brought a new impetus to business, for despite its Bedu origins, Islam was an urban-centred religion. The Prophet Muhammad had himself been a merchant; and the codes of his revelation, detailed in the Qur'an, called for fair play, respect for property and inheritance, and a communal spirit. Egypt, with the new city of Fustat as its capital, became the centre of a huge

the Mediterranean. Long before the Mamluks' extortionate monopoly of the spice trade had pushed Europeans to search for new routes to the East and led indirectly to Columbus's discovery of America, crafts such as metalworking, ceramics, weaving and glass-making had also turned the city into an industrial centre.

The introduction of Ottoman rule in 1517 brought coffee to replace spices, but marked a rigidification of the economic structure and slackening of the entrepreneurial pulse. Guilds and other professional organisations came to dominate economic life. Cairo was divided along ethnic and economic lines into strictly defined districts, each with its own specialisation.

The industrial age came to Egypt in fits and starts. The legacy of the medieval marketplace has therefore had time to adapt, as opposed to being swallowed up by, modern mass-production and marketing. It is this fact that makes Cairo's market life so interesting.

SPICE OF LIFE
Women of the older quarters procure herbal remedies, aphrodisiacs, and fertility potions.

The Khan al-Khalili

At one corner of a triangle of markets that stretches south to Bab Zuwaylah and west to Azbakiyyah is the Khan al-Khalili, a good place to begin exploring the older parts of Cairo. Founded by a Mamluk amir in 1382, the original *khan* or caravanserai grew into the headquarters for merchants of Turkish wares. By the present century, it had become the centre for retailing the products of traditional crafts. Today, while souvenirs and trinkets continue to make headway on the shelves, the narrow lanes of the Khan still conceal articles of fine workmanship and occasionally true works of art, though many things, such as carpets, papyrus, antiques, appliqué work and *gallibiyas* (caftans), are best procured elsewhere. Within the Khan, the better bargains are leather goods, inlaid boxes, silver, gold, jewellery (the stones are mostly artificial, as the dealers will tell you), brass and copper.

The Khan al-Khalili is bordered on the south by Shari' Muski and on the west by the Qasabah, the main street of medieval Cairo, here called Shari' Muizz li-Din Allah. Northwards along the Qasabah from the Khan are gold and silver-smiths, then the Suq al-Nahhasin, the Brass and Coppersmiths' Market.

Shops here cater more to local needs and much of the work is now done in aluminum, but better bargains are to be had than in the Khan. A zone of monumental buildings, Bayn al-Qasrayn, comes next, beyond which are a dozen shops specialising in water pipes, café accessories and cooking pots.

Southwards from the crossroads of Shari' Muski and the Qasabah, a turning to the right alongside the mosque of Sultan Al-Ashraf Barsbay brings us into the Suq al-Attarin, the picturesque Spice Bazaar. Its flagstoned lanes are mere corridors among scores of tiny booths stocked with bottles of essences and bags of spices. Slats of sunlight pick out swirling spice dust kicked up by shuffling feet, as black-clad women of the older quarters procure herbal remedies, perfumes, aphrodisiacs and fertility potions.

A few shops further on, a pedestrian overpass crosses bustling Shari' al-Azhar. On the other side, where the Qasabah plunges into what was the famous Silk Merchants' Bazaar, is the Ghuriyyah. Passages to the right under the mosque of al-Ghuri lead to a lane parallel to the Qasabah. On this tiny street, more of the Spice

Bazaar, truncated with the cutting of Shari' al-Azhar, merges with a market selling carpets, blankets and finally shoes, all at fixed prices.

Bab Zuwaylah

Southwards toward Bab Zuwaylah, the shops along the Qasabah bulge with all manner of useful household goods. Beyond the massive 11th-century gate of Bab Zuwaylah itself, with its spectacular twin minarets, lies a charming square where the Qasabah is crossed by Darb al-Ahmar, which changes its name here to Shari' Ahmad Maher. On the far side of this square the Qasabah dives into the tunnel of the Khayamiyyah, the covered Tentmakers' Bazaar.

LEFT: east meets west at a Cairo market.
RIGHT: Khan al-Khalili wares.

Under the bazaar's wooden roof, the only one currently surviving, are the alcoves where the artisans fashion appliqué tent panels, cushion covers, bedspreads and wall hangings

To the west, Shari' Ahmad Maher leads through an assortment of saddles, colourful tin lamps, rat-traps, beach umbrellas and marble, to Shari' Port Said and the Islamic Museum.

Maydan al-Atabah

Following one of the small streets between Shari' Port Said and Maydan al-Atabah provides a fascinating glimpse of the internal mechanics of Cairo's furniture industry: whole-

Bulaq

The former river port of Bulaq, transformed into an industrial centre by Muhammad Ali, offers an exemplary microcosm of a traditional economy's adaptation to modern needs. Still dotted with Mamluk warehouses as well as small machine works and welding shops, Bulaq is also a huge junk market, which found its niche in World War II dealing in military surplus.

The alleys back from the main streets are crammed with arm's-width stalls, selling car parts that have been cannibalised from wrecks. An astonishing degree of specialisation has been achieved so that a shop may stock only

sale wood merchants give way to vendors of upholstery, stuffing and springs until, toward Atabah, the final flashy product emerges.

Maydan al-Atabah itself is the true hub of Cairene market life. In its vicinity just about anything from transistors to timber, or a whole side of beef can be found. Shari' Muski leads from it eastward parallel to Shari' al-Azhar back to the Khan al-Khalili. Its length crawls with shoppers and wares, street hawkers and black marketeers in a ceaseless buzz of commerce. Just off Shari' Muski, beginning at the Atabah end, are watches, shoes, paper, confectionery, hardware, pipes and hoses, luggage, beads, buttons and textiles.

THE ART OF HAGGLING

Haggling is called for in most transactions in the Khan, though not in every *suq*. Some people are born bargainers, while others botch the business miserably. A few tips: relax and take your time. Shop around and never spend money for politeness' sake. Keep up a cheerful banter and maintain eye contact as much as possible. In Egypt nearly everyone is a softy at heart, so charm is essential. Be sure of what you want and calculate how much it is worth to you before entering negotiations. Couples can let one person do the talking while the other maintains silence and a sour expression.

1950 Cadillac fenders or a variety of radiator caps. Further inside is the used clothing market, a jumble of colourful streets full of America's and Europe's cast-offs, which are auctioned daily. The tall World Trade Centre beside the river could not offer a stronger contrast. Inside, Cairo's rich can buy the latest European fashion or gorge themselves on perfectly prepared sushi.

Further northward is the Wikalat al-Balah, a district named after a former date warehouse, which now serves as a

CAMEL DEALING

Hundreds of the noble yet troublesome beasts are hauled off the trucks, examined, and haggled over by dozens of rustic traders.

Though some of the camels come from the Western Desert – small herds belonging to Bedu may be seen there and in the Eastern Desert and Sinai – the majority originate from the Western Sudan and used to be herded north on an arduous 40-day trek called the *arba'in*. Nowadays only the first 30 days are completed on foot or hoof, bringing the animals as far north as Aswan, where they are then loaded onto trucks for the 24-hour ride to the market at Cairo. Here hundreds of the noble yet troublesome beasts are

market for all kinds of refuse, from bits of old iron grillwork to antiques pilfered from collapsed buildings. Beyond Wikalat al-Balah is the district of Rod al-Farag, which houses Cairo's wholesale fruit and vegetable market.

The Camel Market

Students of native life will probably find the Suq al-Gimal, or Camel Market, more diverting, however. It is held at Birqash, 35km (22 miles) northwest of Cairo, and most lively on Monday and Friday mornings from 6am to 9am.

hauled off the trucks, examined closely and haggled over by dozens of rustic traders, most of whom are either Nubians or hot-headed Upper Egyptians.

Once sold to the best bidder, some of these beasts will be loaded back onto trucks, while others will be herded across one of the city's southern bridges, all of them destined for Cairo's abattoirs. Adventurous tourists who make their way out to the camel market at Birqash are therefore not expected to buy the merchandise there, but to wait until it emerges in finished form: camel flesh is closely textured but prized as *pasturma*, the dried spiced meat that is apparently the origin of pastrami. ❏

LEFT: palm-frond cases carry fruit and live animals.
ABOVE: the camel market at Birqash.

A LOVE OF FOOD

Though not a bastion of haute cuisine, Egypt yields many tasty experiences,
such as memorable mezzes, sensational street food and oriental pastries

I n the Middle Ages, Egyptian cuisine enjoyed a high reputation all over the Islamic empire, but few visitors now travel to Egypt in search of a culinary experience. Those looking for the best of Middle Eastern cuisine will undoubtedly choose countries like Lebanon or Turkey. Nevertheless Egyptians love to eat – and to share a meal – and will endlessly discuss the delight of the dishes, simple as they may be, that have been served. As in most Arab countries the best food is found at home. Restaurants will usually serve only more common Egyptian dishes such as kebabs, *mezze* and, if you are lucky, stuffed pigeon or *meloukhia* (a thick soup made of a deep green leaf, slightly similar to spinach).

Food for the pharaohs

The Egyptians' sense of hospitality and their love of food goes back a long way, according to the evidence of many well-preserved wall paintings and carvings in tombs and temples around the country, which depict large banquets and a wide variety of foods. As well as suggesting that the ancient Egyptians were just as fond of eating and drinking as their descendants, these images also provide proof that many of the dishes enjoyed in Egyptian households today were also regularly on the menu in antiquity. *Meloukhia* soup, roast goose and salted dried fish (*fasieekh*) are obvious examples.

Apart from these few "national dishes", Egyptian cuisine shows signs of a long history of occupation, as the Persians, Greeks, Romans, Arabs and Ottomans all left their mark. More recently, some colonial European influences have been added to the cocktail.

A poor man's table

However elaborate the cuisine enjoyed by Egypt's former kings and sultans, the majority of today's Egyptian *fellaheen* (peasants) are far

PRECEDING PAGES: buffet with an Egyptian flavour.
LEFT: street vendors, with butter beans to the fore.
RIGHT: extremely expensive for the majority of Egyptians, meat is for special occasions only.

too poor to make the most of gastronomic opportunities. As in other Arab countries their diet consists mainly of locally grown vegetables, lentils and beans, with meat for special occasions. With the huge influx of people from the countryside to towns and cities, this vegetable-based peasant cuisine has become commonplace and most middle-class Egyptian families will now elaborate on these basic recipes, adding more expensive ingredients when they can afford them. Even in one of Cairo's most upmarket quarters, the island of Zamalik, colourful carts make their way to street corners early in the morning, where they serve steaming *fuul* (fava beans) for breakfast.

A warm welcome

"If people are standing at the door of your house, don't shut it before them" and "Give the guest food to eat even though you are starving yourself" are two of the many proverbs that insist that hospitality is a duty and that all guests should be offered food and drink. Whatever their social standing, an Egyptian family will always serve guests several salads and a few vegetable and meat dishes. Guests also have a well-prescribed role to play during meals: at first they must refuse the offer, but then must relent after some pressure. They are expected to praise every aspect of the food, without inspecting it too closely. Guests will always be handed the best morsels of fish or the finest cut of meat from the central serving dish or platter.

> **FOOD FOR THOUGHT**
>
> Of all the dishes it is a table full of *mezze* that best reflects the Egyptian and Middle Eastern character.

ture of macaroni, lentils, rice and chickpeas, served with fried onions and topped with a generous dollop of hot tomato sauce.

Make a meal

Of all the dishes on offer in Egypt it is a table full of *mezze*, dips and salads that best reflects the Egyptian and Middle Eastern character. *Mezze* are served with drinks as a light snack or as an appetiser before a meal. With such a variety of dishes, *mezze* can easily turn out to be a pleasurable and leisurely meal on their own.

Fuul above all

Fuul (fava beans), stewed and eaten with bread, is Egypt's staple diet. Usually eaten for breakfast or as a sandwich between meals, it can just as well be served as lunch or dinner in some households. Some people who can't afford any other food will eat it several times a day. At first the brown muddy stew may not look or smell particularly appetising, but with familiarity the dish can be quite addictive.

Fava beans are also used in another of Egypt's favourite dishes, *taameya* (deep-fried fava bean balls), which are often served with *fuul*. Another staple dish, usually sold as street food (and a delicious, inexpensive lunch), is *kushari*, a mix-

> **BEAN FEAST**
>
> In her *Book of Middle Eastern Food*, the Egyptian-born writer Claudia Roden reminisces about *fuul medames* (stewed fava beans): "Ceremoniously, we sprinkled the beans with olive oil, squeezed a little lemon over them, seasoned them with salt and pepper, and placed a hot hard-boiled egg in their midst... Silently, we ate the beans, whole and firm at first; then we squashed them with our forks and combined their floury texture and slightly dull, earthy taste with the acid tang of lemon, mellowed by the olive oil; finally, we crumbled the egg, matching its earthiness with that of the beans..."

Egyptians love to sit and relax at home, on a terrace or in a café, chatting and laughing with friends and savouring a few salads and small dishes. These small dishes can be anything from a plate of hummus (chick pea purée), pickled vegetables or elaborate *mahshi* (stuffed vegetables), to little meat pies.

Celebrations

Meat has always been considered a food for the rich and aristocratic. Poorer Egyptians rely on a diet of wheat, beans and lentils and there is

MEAT'S A TREAT

There is only one day in the year when poor Egyptians are sure to get a taste of meat: Id al-Kebir.

Ramadan, the month of fasting from sunset to sunrise, is another occasion when more meat is consumed than usual. Families visit each other in the evenings and celebrate the end of another day of fasting with a rich display of foods and sweets.

Many Egyptian recipes won't stipulate what sort of meat is to be used as traditionally there was only sheep or lamb, and occasionally camel, goat or gazelle. Islam prohibits pork, but beef and veal are now widely available in Egypt. Meat is usually grilled as

only one day in the year when they are sure to get a taste of meat: Id al-Kebir, the 10th day of the last month of the Muslim calendar. In commemoration of Abraham's sacrifice of his son Ismail, families who can afford it will sacrifice a sheep or a lamb. The animal, which should be fat and young, is ritually slaughtered and roasted whole on a spit and usually some of its meat is distributed to the poor, according to the tenets of Islam. Sheep are also slaughtered to mark other important occasions such as death, birth or marriage.

LEFT: mezze, a great way to dine.
ABOVE: a meal shared with friends.

kebab or *kofta* (minced lamb) or used in a stew. Offal – particularly liver, kidneys and testicles – is considered a delicacy.

Sweet as honey

The traditional end to a meal at home is a bowl of seasonal fruit, but Western-style ice cream and crème caramel will also be offered as a dessert in most restaurants. Even though they are not always eaten as a dessert, there are some delicious Egyptian puddings, including *muhallabia*, a milk cream thickened by cornflour and ground rice, and *roz bi-laban*, a creamy rice pudding, both topped with chopped almonds and pistachio nuts. A more elaborate dessert is *umm ali*, a warm, comforting bread pudding with coconut, raisins, nuts and cream. According to some sources, umm ali was introduced into Egypt by Miss O'Malley, the Irish mistress of the Khedive Ismail.

Pastries are more likely to be served as an offering at parties and special, happy occasions such as weddings and births, rather than as a dessert. *Baklawa* is probably the most famous oriental pastry, a filo wrapping stuffed with a mixture of nuts or almonds and covered with an orange-blossom syrup. More common in Egypt are *basbousa*, a semolina cake of syrup and nuts, and the drier *kunafa*, angel hair filled with

thick cream, ricotta cheese or chopped nuts and syrup. Most pastries are sold in shops, but are usually best when made at home. A housewife who prides herself on making the best – *baklawa* or *konafa* – will often only pass on her recipe to her daughters.

Juicy drinks

Egyptians will tell you that "Once you drink water from the Nile, you will always come back to Egypt". A nice sentiment, but Nile water has also been known to curse as well as bless, and it is definitely safer to stick to mineral water or fresh juices. Brightly coloured juice bars attract thirsty customers and eager photographers with

their picturesque pyramids of strawberries and oranges and baskets of mangoes. Freshly squeezed *asir* (juice) is very cheap, as well as being an excellent refreshment. What's on offer will depend mostly on the season but the most widely available juice is *asir laymun* (fresh lemon or lime), which is often served sweetened unless you ask otherwise.

Usually there will also be a choice of *asir burtuqan* (freshly squeezed winter or summer oranges), *moz* (banana), *gazar* (carrot) and *gawafa* (sweet guava). Depending on the season there could also be deep red *asir ruman* (pomegranate juice), *farawla* (strawberry) and thick *manga* (mango). Some stalls also offer *asab* or *gasab*, the sweet juice pressed out of sugar cane sticks. In summer, street vendors sell glasses of *laymun* (lemon), *tamar hindi* (tamarind) and *ersoos* (liquorice).

Alcoholic pleasures

According to the Qur'an Muslims should not drink alcohol and, with religious tensions rising, much of Egypt is becoming dry. However, it is usually possible to get alcohol in hotels and Western-style bars and restaurants, except during Ramadan when no alcohol will be served to Egyptians even if they are Copts. Some bars close for the whole month, while others may ask to see a passport before they serve beer or wine to foreigners.

Local Stella beer is quite enjoyable, while the more expensive Stella Export is stronger and sweeter. Past problems with quality control might disappear now that the company has been privatised. Foreign brands are planning to open breweries in Egypt, but for the moment imported beers are much more expensive.

The quality of the local wine is even more variable and can be anything from drinkable to downright dangerous.The most famous red is the Omar Khayyam, while the best dry white wine is the Cru des Ptolemées. Wine lists are rarely extensive and, if foreign wine is offered, it will usually be mediocre French or Spanish at an inflated price. Apart from the more reliable *zibeeb*, Egyptian ouzo or arak, locally produced spirits with inspiring names such as Dry Din, Marcel Horse, Ricardo and Johnny Talker are best avoided.   ❑

LEFT: Alexandrian cafés are known for their sweets.
RIGHT: preparing for the lunchtime rush, Cairo.

EGYPTIAN COFFEE HOUSES

*Coffee has had a chequered history in Egypt and, although now integral
to the lives of thousands, it once faced the wrath of the clergy*

In crowded Egypt, Allah can be counted on for two great mercies: endless sunshine and abundant free time. Small wonder that the street café, where much of these two great resources is spent, is so ubiquitous an institution. Few men – for the café, like much else in Egyptian society, is a solidly male preserve – permit a day to pass without killing a few minutes in a café exchanging jokes that turn the trial of life into a spectator sport.

When Edward Lane wrote *Manners and Customs of the Modern Egyptians* in the 1830s, he judged the number of cafés in Cairo to be over 1,000. Given a similar ratio of one café per 400 people, the megalopolis of today would contain over 30,000 such establishments.

Different atmospheres

The *qahwa* – Arabic for both "coffee" and "café" – is defined loosely. It can be anything from a bench, a patch of charcoal, a tin pot and three glasses to a cavernous saloon reverberating with the clack of dominoes, the slap of cards and the crackling of dice.

In Cairo, a café may serve as the headquarters of a street gang, the meeting place for homesick provincials, or the rendezvous of intellectuals. There are cafés for musicians, black marketeers, leftists, Muslim extremists, homosexuals, retired generals and pimps. There is even a café for the deaf and dumb, where absolute silence belies the animated conversation conducted by gesture alone.

The ideal café adjoins a small square in the back streets of a popular quarter. The simple decor of its exterior will reveal the sense of style its patronage demands. The few outdoor tables will be shaded by a tree or vine, while the ground will have been sprinkled with water to keep down the dust. A pungent sweetness emanates from the interior, where sawdust covers the floor. An elaborate brass *sarabantina*, a cross between a steam locomotive and a

samovar, occupies pride of place on the counter at the back of the room, behind which striped glass jugs for smokers' water pipes line the walls. The patron puffs judiciously as he takes in the crime column of the morning paper, while the *qahwagi* or waiter keeps up a continuous banter between forceful shouts to the tea boy.

Liquid incidentals

Atmosphere is only one of the pleasures the classier café offers. To begin with, of course, there is the pleasure of indulging in a hot drink. Tea, introduced in the 19th century, has replaced coffee as the staple. The powerful Egyptian version of the brew takes some getting used to. Since cheap tea dust is the preferred variety, it is no use anticipating delicate flavour. Tea is drunk as a fix, as strong and sweet as possible. It is best to make no compromises with local taste: sugarless Egyptian tea is unpalatable. Some connoisseurs say that the truly classic glass of tea should be only faintly translucent, with a mild aroma of kerosene from extended boiling

---

LEFT: veteran smoker of the *sheesha* or water pipe.
RIGHT: Fishawi, a famous Cairene coffee house.

on a Primus stove. In this form, it is the perfect antidote to the hottest, dustiest and most pestiferous of days in Egypt.

Arabic coffee is still prepared and served in centuries-old style, without the fancy gadgetry of European invention. Sugar, then powdered coffee are added to hot water and brought to the boil in a brass *kanaka*. The *qahwagi* brings the *kanaka* and cup on a tin tray and pours the liquid with solicitude, preserving the *wish* – the "face" or thick mud that sits on the surface before settling. In the better cafés, a dark blend spiced with cardamon is used. In all establishments, the customer must specify how he wants his coffee:

orchids and topped with chopped nuts, is a winter favourite. In summer, cafés serve cooler drinks, ranging from lemonade, *tamarhindi* (tamarind), *ersoos* (liquorice) and *farawla* (strawberry), to the ever more pervasive *Kukula, Bibs* and *Shwibs,* the commercially bottled soft drinks that have run old local brands off the market.

A smoker's paradise

The Egyptian café is a paradise for the serious smoker and has perfected the ultimate tobacco tool. The *sheesha* or water pipe cools, sweetens and lightens the taste of the burning leaves,

saada, or sugarless, *'arriha,* with a dash of sugar, *mazbut,* medium, or *ziyada,* with extra sugar. In some "European cafés", *qahwa Faransawi* or French coffee is served, and more recent cafés have Italian espresso machines.

Of far more ancient origin are the hot medicinal infusions that can still be found in many cafés. The bases of these potations range from ginger, *ganzabeel,* which is recommended for coughs, *erfa* (cinnamon) and *yansun* (aniseed) for the throat, to *helba* (fenugreek) for stomach complaints. *Karkadé,* the scarlet tea of a hibiscus flower, is a speciality of Aswan. Packed with vitamin C, it is delicious hot or cold. *Sahlib,* a steaming cream, concocted from dried

A HEADY BREW

Long used by the Bedu, to whom coffee and the ceremony attached to its serving are a vital part of welcoming friends and strangers, coffee was introduced to the settled inhabitants of Cairo by Sufi mystics in the 16th century. The dervishes' adoption of the stimulant to prolong their ecstatic trances brought the wrath of the orthodox clergy – who saw it as inspiring deviant behaviour – crashing down upon the bean. As with tobacco, controversy raged for years before the weight of popular taste finally concluded the debate and coffee became a respectable part of social intercourse.

makes a soothing gurgle and provides a pleasant distraction for idle hands. It is an instrument of meditation to be savoured serenely.

Two kinds of tobacco are used. Most popular is *ma'assil*, a sticky blend of chopped leaf fermented with molasses. It is pressed in small clay bowls which are fitted into the *sheesha* and lit with charcoal. *Tumbak*, the other variety, is loose dry tobacco wrapped into a cone with a whole leaf. While *ma'assil* is easy to smoke, a cone of *tumbak* may take an hour to exhaust.

YESTERDAY'S CAFÉS

The *ghoraz*, or hash dens, of Cairo were famed throughout the Arab world.

Live entertainment

Every café offers more innocent diversion in the form of cards (*kutshina*), backgammon (*tawla*) and dominoes, played less for intellectual stimulation than as an excuse for exchanging the insults and hyperbole for which the Arabic language is an unparalleled medium.

It is good conversation and companionship that draw the regular crowds. Despite the mass media and the telephone, average citizens still find that the best source of news – not to mention gossip, rumour,

Until recently, hashish smoking was not uncommon in public places. The *ghoraz*, or hash dens, of Cairo were famed throughout the Arab world. Official crackdowns, however, have relegated this once-popular entertainment to seedy back alleys and private homes.

Some of Cairo and Alexandria's grander cafés offer intoxication in the form of liquor but, with the post-Revolutionary departure of the large Greek and Italian communities, and a resurgence of more conservative attitudes, these have lost much of their former glory.

LEFT AND ABOVE: café pursuits – reading, smoking, talking and watching the world go by.

slander and fantasy – is among cronies at the local café.

With the penchant for nostalgia and complaint that characterises the country, aficionados will affirm that cafés are not what they used to be. Like the introduction of radio in the 1930s, which signalled the decline of traditional storytellers and poets, television has led to a decline in public entertainment. Luckily, most café owners leave their sets off except during major football matches.

The best time for dropping in on a café is the late afternoon, when the sun's dying rays turn dun-coloured buildings to gold, and smoke drifts skyward from the *sheesha*. ❑

POPULAR CULTURE

From films to fiction, and soaps to song, Egypt is the hub of popular culture in the Arab world

In *The One Thousand and One Nights*, a mention is made of Cairo as "the mother of the world", a phrase which Egyptians nowadays tend to modify to "Mother of the Arab World". Although in politics and economics that may no longer be true, Egypt can still claim to be in the forefront as far as popular culture is concerned: from Damascus to Casablanca, Egyptian films and television are screened, books by Egyptian writers are read, the country's singers are given airtime on the radio and, to a lesser extent, its theatre is respected.

Word of mouth

The One Thousand and One Nights wasn't composed in Egypt, but Egypt certainly helped to foster the tradition of oral storytelling in which it flourished. Egyptologists claim that ancient Egyptians loved a good story and one of the main entertainments for a community was listening to the passing storyteller. Fifty years ago this was still the case. In Egyptian cities, storytellers would settle in cafés and entertain customers for an evening or more. It was the same at country weddings. The stories were episodic and usually told in verse. Some required a few nights to be told; others, like the million-line epic *The Hilaliya*, could last for months.

This was culture at its most popular, but the storyteller has recently become a rarity, losing his place to television. Occasionally, however, at a village funeral or on stage in Cairo, you can still see these masters of memory performing to a public who now – too late – appreciate an art that has all but disappeared in the country.

The written word

For Egyptian writers, 1988 was a year either of celebration or of sorrow, for that was when Naguib Mahfouz won the Nobel Prize for

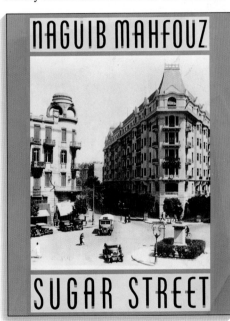

Literature. Even the writer himself was astonished by the award. Not that Mahfouz isn't a world-class writer, but he is seen as a traditionalist – he cites Dickens as a major influence – and the works that were cited by the Nobel committee were written more than a quarter of a century earlier. Mahfouz and the late Taha Hussein are the grand old men of Egyptian letters. They and their younger contemporaries – like Abdel Rahman al Sharqawi (*Egyptian Earth*), Sonallah Ibrahim (*Les Annéss de Zeth*), short-story writer Yusuf Idris (*The Cheapest Nights*), Gamal al Ghitani (*Zayni Barakat*) and Nawal al Saadawi (*Woman at Point Zero*) – have created a tradition of modern storytelling, heavy in allegory (a necessity given the strict censorship laws) and rich in folklore.

Among the other central figures in the development of Egyptian literature this century are Tawfiq al Hakim (*The Prison of Life*), who has defined Egyptian autobiographical writing, and the Alexandrian-Greek poet C. P. Cavafy

PRECEDING PAGES: poster for *Alexandria, Why?* by one of Egypt's best-known film-makers, Youssef Chahine. **LEFT:** Nobel prize-winner Naguib Mahfouz. **RIGHT:** book jacket of Mahfouz's English edition of *Sugar Street.*

(*Collected Poems*) whose explorations of sexuality, memory and history have a universal appeal and extraordinary power.

Post-independence writers have taken different routes. The work of Edward al Kharrat (*Girls of Alexandria*) and Yahya Taher Abdullah (*The Mountain of Green Tea*) move away from dependence on Western literature, while Ahdaf Soueif (*In the Eye of the Sun*) writes in English and has not been translated into Arabic.

Cairo, cinema city

In 1927, while Americans were listening to Al Jonson in *The Jazz Singer*, the world's first

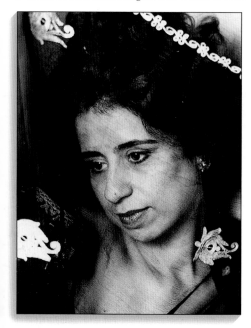

"talkie" film, Aziza Amir released the first Egyptian-made film, *Laila*. Much of Egypt's claim to cultural supremacy in the Arab world has been due to the phenomenal success of the movie industry, which developed in the mid-20th century and peaked in the 1960s, when a new film was released almost every day of the year. With subjects ranging from historical epics to back-alley melodramas, one of the most popular film forms was the musical, whose plots were often copied from Hollywood.

The great Egyptian singer Umm Kalthoum dominated here as she dominated Cairo's concert halls. Her most successful partnership was with the actor Farid al Atrash, an elegant, good-looking man who, like her, combined a talent for acting with an exceptional voice. Umm Kalthoum's main rival in the affections of the cinema-going public was Farid al-Atrash's sister, the beautiful Asmahan, who died young and tragically in a car accident. So important was the musical in the development of Egyptian cinema that the critic Samir Farid noted, "One would say that the Egyptian cinema only became talking in order to sing, without which it would still be silent today."

Salah Abou Seif made some of Egypt's most important post-revolution films, and won the Critics' Prize at the 1956 Cannes Film Festival with *La Sangsue*. Abou Seif directed the leading stars of his day, including the legendary belly-dancer Tahiya Karioka, Hind Rostom, Omar Sharif and his wife Faten Hamama. Abu Seif's films very much reflected the mood of the time – political, questioning, fiercely pro-Arab and anti-royalist.

Youssef Chahine has been directing films on a regular basis since the 1940s and has done more than anyone to bring credibility to Egyptian cinema. Chahine has created a broad body of work, from the realism of the black-and-white *Cairo Central Station*, in which the director also took a key role as a station porter, to the more recent *The Emigrant*, an allegory about corruption, ignorance and injustice, set in ancient Egypt. Part of Chahine's success has been due to his ability to convince European film bodies to provide money or facilities, which also guaranteed him an international audience. Chahine's work was recognised by a lifetime achievement award at the 1997 Cannes Film Festival.

Although he has done much to foster some of

Egypt's younger talent, few other Egyptian directors have achieved anything like Chahine's stature. While directors elsewhere in the Arab world have begun to produce some world-class cinema, the bulk of Egypt's output is low-grade melodrama and weak romantic comedy, with directors treading the fine line between titillating the Egyptian audience and not offending the government's censors, who mostly succeed in keeping nudity, overt political criticism and religious slurs off their cinema screens.

FUTURE HOPES

A new "Hollywood on the Nile", at a cost of US$314 million, is a sign of renewed confidence in the industry.

mentalist groups, *The Terrorist* succeeded in making the public question why such people were driven to violent measures.

Rising costs, a lack of good cinemas, failure to control video piracy and the spread of television have seen film production dwindle in Egypt over the past 10 years, though the opening of a "Hollywood-on-the-Nile"with up-to-date film and TV production facilities 9 miles (15 km) southwest of Cairo, at a cost of US$314 million, is a sign of renewed confidence in the industry.

Adel Imam is probably the most successful leading male actor currently at work in Egypt. Several of his films have tackled serious and topical subjects, most notable, perhaps, being *The Terrorist*, a comedy about an ordinary man getting himself into extraordinary difficulties in the bureaucratic nightmare of Cairo's Interior Ministry building and finding himself being mistaken for a terrorist.

Released at a time when the government was struggling to control the activities of the funda-

LEFT: Ahdaf Soueif, author of *In the Eye of the Sun*.
ABOVE: cinema posters, in characteristically lurid style, on Opera Square, Cairo.

Live on stage

Just as Umm Kalthoum appeared regularly in both film and concert, so many stars of Egyptian cinema also appear regularly on stage in Cairo. The majority of Egyptian theatre is comedy or melodrama, which is carried off by the status of stars like Adel Imam and belly-dancer Fifi Abdou. This sort of theatre is particularly popular during the long nights of Ramadan. An alternative is provided by playwrights such as Mohammad Salmawy, although much of his work owes more to European than Egyptian tradition. Hassan el-Geretly's El Warsha is the most convincing of Egypt's experimental theatre groups. El Warsha's performances often mix storytelling with music and traditional shadow-plays and stick dancing. Needless to say, they are rarely seen at Cairo Opera House.

Television's revolution

It is difficult to appreciate the full impact television has had on the lives of rural Egyptians. The promise Nasser and Sadat made to link every village in the country to the national electricity grid had an unforeseen effect and changed country life for ever, because with electricity came television and with television came later nights and that, in turn, put an end to farmers getting into the fields before dawn.

Television has also become increasingly sophisticated. Ten years ago, an American soap opera (apparently aired for free as part of the US cultural programme) was enough of a draw to empty the streets for an hour in city and country. Sociologists wondered what farmers who had previously seen only Arab films and TV would make of American villas and British Rolls-Royce cars. Satellite television has brought more dramatic changes as Egyptians can now tune into a range of international programmes. Satellite dishes, familiar in cities, are also becoming a familiar ornament in villages along the Nile and deep in the country.

Culture under threat

In the 1960s and 1970s, Egypt was the major producer of film and television programmes in the Arab world. In the past few years, with the advent of a greater variety of foreign programming, Egypt's dominance in the Arab market has begun to wane. In April 1997, an Egyptian journalist working on the BBC's World Service noted that for the first time Egypt's famed Ramadan serial, the *Fawazeer* – a jamboree of song and dance and extravagant costumes which runs each night throughout the month of fasting – had lost ground in the ratings war to Syrian and Jordanian programmes broadcast by satellite. The implication, the journalist suggested, was that before long Egyptian Arabic would no longer be the lingua franca of the Arabic world – an immense loss of status.

Egypt isn't panicking yet – after all, there are more Egyptians than Arabs in the rest of the Middle East – but the authorities have taken action by commissioning Cairo's new multi-million dollar production facility and launching Egypt's first satellite TV station.

The sound of music

Evidence of Egypt's previous domination of the Arab cultural scene is provided by the music of the late Egyptian singer Umm Kalthoum. In the 1960s, when Nasser was president and nationalism ran high, the singer with the trademark dark glasses enjoyed the sort of pulling-power now reserved for American TV soaps. Each week she performed a new song in her inimitable, passionate warble and, the way the story is now told by those who remember, the entire nation came to a stand-still as people listened to the "Star of the East" on the radio. When she died in 1975, the leaders of the Arab world

attended her funeral, and such was her popularity that there were scenes of grief at an exhibition of her personal effects held in Cairo 15 years after her death.

Umm Kalthoum's songs are still played on radio throughout the Arab world in much the same way that the Beatles are played in the West. Her contemporaries, including Mohammad Abdel Wahab (who developed traditional thin *takht* music into a bigger, bolder sound) Abdel Halim al-Hafez and Farid al-Atrash, still have an audience among older Egyptians. But, with over half of the 60-million Egyptian population under 25, the biggest slice of Egypt's music market is taken by modern musicians.

Among the latest sounds to be heard in the country (excluding imports from the West) is *shaabi* (people) music, a sound developed by singer Ahmed Adawiya in the 1970s which mixed protest lyrics with a strong back beat. After a decade and more of phenomenal sales, Adawiya began singing about God, relinquishing his place as king of *shaabi* to Hakim.

In contrast to *shaabi*, *al-jeel* ("the generation") music is a fusion of disco and local rhythms, its lyrics generally confined to love

> **FUTURE PERFECT**
>
> The Neo-Pharaonists believed that a new identity would emerge by examining the ancient past.

and nostalgia. Mohammad Foad and Ehab Tawfiq are two names to listen out for. The sound of Egypt that reached the West during the 1990s was an eclectic mixture of Arab, Egyptian, Turkish and even Indian sounds, produced by musicians such as George Kazazian and Les Musicians du Nil, a group of Saiidi (Upper Egyptian) musicians led by the folk singer Metqal, himself a mix of Sudani, Nubian and Egyptian influences.

LEFT: legendary singer Umm Kalthoum, one of the all-time greats who has fans all over the Arab world.
ABOVE: a member of the Dervish Theatre in rehearsal in Alexandria.

The visual arts

It seems bizarre to Westerners that a country like Egypt might have plenty to show from the visual arts from several thousand years BC until AD641 (think of all those tomb illustrations and the Fayyum mummy portraits, for a start), but little to show since then. The reason for this is very straightforward: the Prophet Muhammad said, "Those who will be most tormented on Judgement Day are image-makers." As a result, Muslims have traditionally frowned on the representation of living creatures. Visual art in Egypt, therefore, can claim an ancient tradition, or no tradition at all.

Contacts with Western culture in the 19th century stimulated a debate about visual art, with the pro-independence nationalists being keen to promote a recognisable Egyptian style of art. Little advance was made, however, until the start of the 20th century, when the Mufti of Egypt suggested that the Prophet's comment should be seen in its context, having been made in an age of idolatry and Prince Yusuf Kamal founded the School of Fine Arts in Cairo.

Egyptian artists started by confronting their ancient traditions, aware of the innovations of Western artists. As sculptor Mahmoud Mukhtar (1883–1934) described it, "When I was a child, there had been no sculpture and no sculptor in my country for more than 700 years."

The Neo-Pharaonists, as they were called, believed that a new Egyptian identity would emerge by examining the ancient past. The work of Modernist artists like Mukhtar, Mahmoud Said and Mohammad Nagui reflected this. It also suited the moment, for around this time Egyptologists were uncovering more of the pharaonic past.

The Contemporary Egyptian Art Group, founded in 1946 and counting Hamid Nada and Abdel Hadi al Gazzar amongst its members, and the Atelier of Alexandria – founded by Mohamed Nagui, his sister Effat Nagui and her husband Saad al Khadem, one of Egypt's most important folklorists – did much to further a purely Egyptian style in a European context. Egypt's contemporary artists, from Adel al-Siwi to Chant Avedissian, continue to work with traditional Egyptian themes while striving for a wider international audience. ❑

MAKING A SONG AND DANCE

Belly-dancers stand alongside farmers, fat pashas and postcard sellers among Egyptian stereotypes, yet their appeal is deep-rooted and very real

Belly-dancing – or *raks sharqi*, Oriental dance, as those in the business prefer to call it – opens a window on Egyptian culture and poses a question: how can a conservative, Islamic society tolerate, much less adulate, curvaceous women dressed in sequin-covered bikinis making provocative gestures in public? The answer most often heard is that belly-dancing is traditional, native and older even than Islam. The other answer is that everyone does it, from children in the street to entertainers at presidential parties.

ANCIENT ORIGINS

The origins of *raks sharqi* are unknown. Tomb paintings (*see below right*) suggest that ancient Egyptians liked to dance, while similarities between dance movements in Egypt, Morocco and India point to a shifting of influence long ago. The legend of Salome, the girl who danced so beautifully that she was granted a wish by the king and asked for the head of John the Baptist, confirms that dance was a court entertainment and that dancers have long commanded high fees.

Nineteenth-century writers, from Lane to Flaubert, refer to the bad reputation of public dancers, Lane with disapproval, Flaubert with pleasure, having slept with one. Flaubert's line seems to have won out as far as foreign expectations go: 19th-century Orientalist painters and 20th-century Hollywood film-makers did as much as anyone to make this sort of dancing universally recognised.

The cinema has helped promote the popularity of public performances in Egypt as well. For a dancer's reputation to survive, she had to mix regular club appearances with screen roles and the famous names that have survived from earlier this century – such as the wonderfully named Tahiya Karioka, Samia Gamal and Naeema Akef – were all successful actresses as well as brilliant dancers.

▷ **BRILLIANT OCCASION**
Dancers have become an indispensable part of society weddings. Celebrations are increasingly lavish, and popular dancers command high fees to make a brief appearance at a wedding between their club shows.

△ **BARE ESSENTIALS**
However extravagant the costume – and some cost a small fortune – decency insists that the belly must be covered, at least with a veil.

▷ **MEN WITH RHYTHM**
Sequinned outfits are for women only, but men like to dance as well. Professional dancers sometimes encourage men to join them on stage, but men also like to dance among themselves.

▽ **A LAST DANCE**
Ancient Egyptians enjoyed dancing, as this painting from a tomb in Thebes suggests.

A FOREIGN AFFAIR

In the 1940s and 1950s, during the heyday of belly-dancing when the great composers were still at work and cinema had a touch of glamour, it was unthinkable that foreigners would star in Cairo's clubs. The biggest names of Cairo's dance scene are still Egyptians, women such as Fifi Abdou (*see below left*), Lucy and Dina, but an increasing number of foreign women are providing competition on Cairo's stages, among them Samasem (*above*).

Some commentators have suggested that foreign women can never attain the heights scaled by Egyptian dancers because, however technically advanced they might be, they will never be able to respond to Egyptian melodies and movements in the same way as the daughters of the Nile.

Since the Gulf War and the rise in the Islamic movement, Egypt's nightclub scene has been in a slump, with dancers facing law-suits on indecency charges and being threatened by fanatics. A number of the more glamorous venues have closed, though the cheaper clubs around Cairo's 26 July Street, where some of today's mega-stars started out dancing for a few pounds a night, are still doing good business. With fewer dance jobs available, the competition has become so severe that many Egyptian dancers have taken early retirement, leaving the stage free for foreigners.

△ QUEEN OF THE NIGHT
At the height of her fame in the 1970s, Nagwa Fouad created a new act with belly-dancing as the centre of a spectacular show.

◁ CLUB, STAGE, SCREEN
Fifi Abdou, known for her energetic and provocative dancing, is a star of club, theatre and cinema. She is also one of the few dancers with international appeal.

IT TATOURS   شركة إيتاتورز للسياحة

PLACES

*A detailed guide to the country, with the principal sites
cross-referenced by number to the maps*

E gypt occupies 1 million sq. km (385,000 sq. miles) of Africa's driest and most barren corner. It adjoins the Sinai peninsula, which is geologically African, but geographically belongs to Asia. South and west, beyond wide barriers of desert, stretches the great body of the rest of Africa, to which Egypt is umbilically connected, in addition, by the slender nourishing lifeline of the the Nile.

As it crosses the Sudanese border into Egypt, the Nile has already travelled 5,000 km (3,000 miles). Leaving mountain lakes, it has roared down cascades, steamed through swamps, and carved a serpentine path through a thousand miles of rock and sand into a massive artificial lake, with the Temple of Abu Simbel on one side. This lake, just south of Aswan, the world's largest, is Lake Nasser, a 20th-century achievement that has changed the face of Egypt forever.

An ancient frontier town, where Africa and Arabia mingle, Aswan is the return point for most Nile cruises, although some companies are now operating in the waters of Lake Nasser. At Luxor the vessels pause in the centre of the largest agglomeration of ancient building the world can offer, anchoring between the East Bank's great temple complexes of Karnak and Luxor and the West Bank's vast funerary cities.

Further north, the river meanders on through fields dotted with ambling water-buffalo. At length it swirls beneath the many bridges of Cairo. Seventeen million people inhabit this metropolis. To the west, the Pyramids of Giza continue to present their mountainous geometry while the Sphinx erodes impassively at their feet.

At Cairo the Nile moves into the Delta, spreading itself lushly until, much diminished, it reaches the Mediterranean Sea. Joined to the Nile by canals is Alexandria, Egypt's most important coastal city, founded by Alexander the Great. From here a flat coastline of fine white sand stretches east and west.

The Nile and its valley are not all there is to Egypt. Deep in the deserts lie miraculous islands of living green: the Oases. More life abounds in the salty depths of the Red Sea – tropical fish and coral. And there is the Sinai peninsula, a landscape of striking beauty.

The Places chapters in this guide begin in Cairo, then make their way steadily south to Upper Egypt with a detour to the oases en route. They then turn to the Delta and Alexandria and travel east to Suez, Sinai and the Red Sea. The main sites are numbered and can be cross-referenced to a map, which can be found on the page shown in the map logo at the top of each right-hand page. ❑

PRECEDING PAGES: inside the Temple of Abu Simbel; air-conditioned ride in the desert; a hobbled camel in the shadow of antiquities. **LEFT:** a felucca reflected in the Nile.

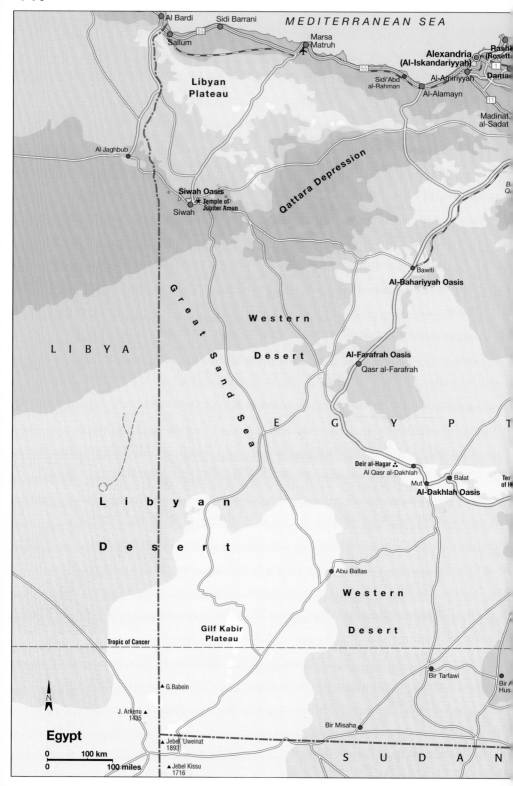

MEDITERRANEAN SEA

Al Bardi
Sidi Barrani
Sallum
55
Marsa
Matruh
Alexandria
(Al-Iskandariyyah)
Rash
(Rosett
Dami
Libyan
Plateau
Sidi'Abd
al-Rahman
Al-Amiriyyah
Al-Alamayn
1
11
Madinat
al-Sadat
Al Jaghbub
Qattara Depression
B
Q
Siwah Oasis
Temple of
Jupiter Amun
Siwah
Bawiti
Al-Bahariyyah Oasis
Western
Desert
Great Sand Sea
Al-Farafrah Oasis
Qasr al-Farafrah
LIBYA
E G Y P T
Deir al-Hagar
Al Qasr al-Dakhlah
Mut
Balat
Ter
of H
Al-Dakhlah Oasis
Libyan
Desert
Abu Ballas
Western
Desert
Gilf Kabir
Plateau
Tropic of Cancer
N
Bir Tarfawi
Bir A
Hus
G.Babein
Egypt
J. Arkenu ▲
1435
Bir Misaha
0   100 km
0   100 miles
Jebel 'Uweinat
1893
S U D A N
Jebel Kissu
1716

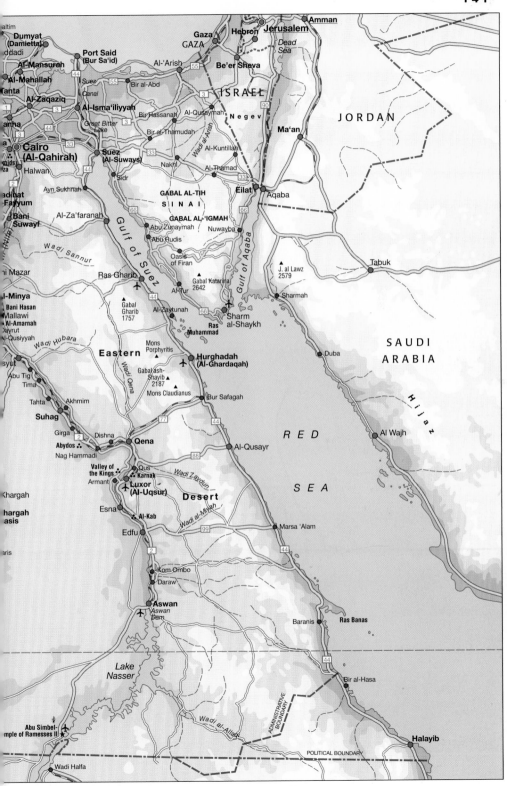

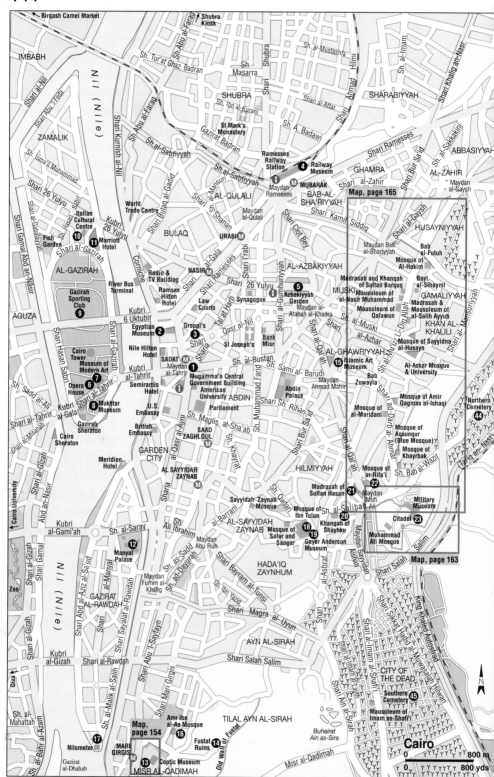

Cairo

CAIRO,
MOTHER OF THE WORLD

Map, page 144

A roaring metropolis of 17 million people, Cairo is loved and hated in equal measure. But most visitors to Egypt spend at least a few days here, sampling its mosques, museums and bazaars

When Ibn Khaldun, the great 14th-century Arab historian and social theorist, visited Cairo, he described it as "the metropolis of the universe, the garden of the world, the anthill of the human species, the throne of royalty, a city embellished with castles and palaces, its horizon decorated with monasteries and with schools, and lighted by the moons and stars of erudition".

What he was looking at was a city that had been devastated by the Black Death three decades earlier and had entered a long twilight of decline. It remained nevertheless the greatest metropolis on earth, still larger in both population and extent than any city west of China. Enriched by the spice trade, by traffic in luxury goods, and by redistribution of urban and rural properties among the diminished population, its sultans and amirs continued to adorn the city with increasingly extravagant architecture.

City of 1,001 Nights

It was during this period, sometime between 1382 and 1517, that *The Arabian Nights* were given their final form in the Cairo of the Circassian Mamluks, a city of wonders, where miraculous reversals of fortune, as history records, were an everyday occurrence. "He who hath not seen Cairo," says a character in one of these tales, "hath not seen the world. Her soil is gold; her Nile is a marvel; her women are like the black-eyed virgins of Paradise; her houses are palaces; and her air is soft, as sweet-smelling as aloe-wood, rejoicing the heart. And how can Cairo be otherwise, when she is Mother of the World?"

The Mother of the World is an old lady now, somewhat long in the tooth. The gold in her soil has ceased to glitter, her Nile has been thoroughly tamed; and, though her women still have many admirers, her palatial houses are being rapidly demolished to make way for concrete high-rises, while her sweet-smelling air has achieved the highest pollution index in the world.

The city's new centre

Modern Cairo spins on **Maydan at-Tahrir ❶**, a huge square from which all distances in Egypt are measured. The square was originally named Maydan Ismailiyyah, after the Khedive Ismail, whose statue was later supposed to be placed on the huge granite plinth at its southeastern corner. An open place, it demarcated one end of the new administrative, commercial and residential quarter of Maydan Ismailiyyah, laid out by the Khedive in 1865. Despite a strategic position near the Nile, however, Maydan Ismailiyyah did not achieve its

PRECEDING PAGES: view of Cairo from the Citadel. **BELOW:** ancient and modern collide in this flyover leading up to Cairo's historic zone.

Model of Maket Ra in the Egyptian Museum.

present importance until after the July Revolution (1952). Its name was changed and the mid-19th century barracks on its western (Nile) side, occupied throughout most of their history by British Guards regiments, were demolished, to be replaced by the **Corniche**, two new administrative buildings, and the **Nile Hilton**, the first major hotel built in Cairo since 1910. On the south side of the Maydan the remains of a palace were removed and a grey concrete block was run up to accommodate those portions of several ministries that deal with the administration of permits, licences, visas, expulsion orders and endless other bureaucratic forms: the **Mugama'a**, a Kafkaesque castle of red tape, notorious not merely for venality, insolence, entrapment, frustration and delay, but also for the number of suicides that have made use of its 14-storey central stairwell.

Situated across the street from this monster, at the extreme southeastern corner of the Maydan, is the only building left from Ismail's era, a small palace dating from 1878, which now houses the **American University**. On the north side of Maydan at-Tahrir is the **Egyptian Museum**.

The Egyptian Museum

Built in 1902 under Abbas II Hilmi and uniquely dignified with Latin inscriptions that may testify to his education at the Theresianum, the **Egyptian Museum** ❷ (Maydan at-Tahrir; open daily 9am–4.30pm, admission charge) holds the world's greatest collection of Egyptian artifacts. Displays on the ground floor are of large objects arranged chronologically running clockwise, so that a left turn from the entrance foyer leads to the famous Menkaure triads from Giza, while a right turn leads to Hellenistic painting and statuary.

No-one should be advised to miss anything if possible, but visitors in a hurry

might turn right and go immediately upstairs to the eastern and northern galleries on the upper floor, where the treasures from the tombs of Tutankhamun and Hetepheres are displayed.

Not to be missed, in addition, is Case H in the upper foyer, containing small masterpieces that are the pride of the Museum, many of them famous from photographs that give no idea of their diminutive size: the ivory statuette of Khufu from Abydos; the black steatite bust of Queen Tiy; the statuette of a Nubian girl with a single earring; the gilded statuette of Ptah; the dancing pygmies carved from ivory, made movable by an ingenious arrangement of strings; and the blue faience hippopotami, of which reproductions have been made that are sold in boutiques all over the world.

Of special interest also are the models that are displayed in Room 27 on the upper floor, mostly from an 11th-Dynasty tomb in Thebes, showing daily life *circa* 2000 BC. In 1994 the Mummy Room reopened, having been locked for many years. The mummies of some of the mightiest pharaohs, including Seti I, Ramesses II and Tuthmosis IV, look rather diminutive and unassuming in their sarcophagi. Most of the mummies were found in a cache in Deir al Bahri, Luxor, in 1875.

Vestiges of glamour

Running northeast from between the front of the Museum and Maydan at-Tahrir (its entrance demarcated on one side by TWA's main office and on the other by an apparently permanent triangular excavation – where, until 1961, Cairo's two most distinguished private houses stood) is **Shari' Qasr an-Nil**. Still the city's main shopping street, it has vestiges of the glamour that Ismail intended when he

Map, page 144

Mummy of Tuthmosis II displayed in the Mummy Room at the Egyptian Museum.

Groppi's Corner House pictured in its heydey in the 1920s, when it staged tea-dances, supper-dances and concerts. Its grandeur has faded but it is still a pleasant, old-fashioned place for pastries, coffee, tea and ice-creams.

BELOW: a choice of sweet sensations.

planned this part of the city. Up the street on the left is the **Automobile Club**, founded in 1924, a favourite haunt of King Faruq, who loved playing poker for outrageous stakes, and 100 yards further on, where the street enters a square, is **Groppi's Corner House ❸** (1924), the second of two luxurious catering establishments founded in Cairo by an Alexandrian-Swiss family.

In the years before World War II, this branch of Groppi's sold Sèvres, Meissen, Lalique and silver as well as afternoon teas, aperitifs, confectionery, pâtisserie and delicatessen items. In the rear were a garden and a rotunda with a stained-glass ceiling, where concerts were given three nights a week during the winter season, with dinner and supper-dancing on the other four nights. But in 1952 the rotunda was burned, the dancing stopped and Groppi's clientele began to change. A handful of old Turkish ladies, who still arrived for tea out of habit, bundled into pre-War furs, gradually found themselves elbowed out of the way by students, prostitutes, pimps and petty gangsters, though the bar remained popular with local businessmen until the place was sold to a teetotaller in 1983.

The Revolution also changed the name and appearance of the square in front of Groppi's. Until then it had officially carried the Arabic name adopted by a Bonapartist officer, Colonel Anthelme Sève, who had entered Muhammad Ali's service after Waterloo, had converted to Islam and, as Sulayman Pasha al Faransawi ("The Frenchman"), had distinguished himself brilliantly. The north-south street running through the square likewise carried Sulayman Pasha's name, which is still used for both street and square by senior residents.

Across the square, opposite Groppi's and on the same side of Shari' Qasr an-Nil, where a later building has been handsomely renovated by a foreign bank, stood the townhouse of one of Muhammad Ali's great-grandsons, which became

the **Savoy**, second only to Shepheard's in glamour among the capital's hotels during the Edwardian era. Royalty stayed here, and several suites were taken every winter between 1898 and 1914 by Sir Ernest Cassel, the international financier, whose guests would include celebrities such as the Duke and Duchess of Devonshire, Sir Winston Churchill or Mrs Keppel, King Edward's last *maîtresse en titre*.

Banks and airline offices line most of Shari' Qasr an-Nil in the stretch to the next square, with shops in between. Another nationalist adorns this second square and the north-south street that crosses Shari' Qasr an-Nil here again has two names – Shari' Emad ad-Din or Shari' Muhammad Farid – between which Cairenes choose according to age and politics. Down the north-south street to the right is **St Joseph's**, Cairo's biggest Catholic church, built in 1909; and nearly opposite is its finest neo-Islamic building, the main branch of **Bank Misr**, built in 1922, which has original woodwork and a particularly splendid Mamluk-style marble floor.

Map, page 144

TIP

Best buys on Shari' Qasr an-Nil are Egyptian yarn goods – printed and plain cottons, silk and wool – and leather.

The pleasures of Azbakiyyah

Shari' Qasr an-Nil leads on into **Shari'al Gumhuriyyah**, formerly Shari'Abdin, which runs north and south and connects **Abdin Palace**, the Muhammad Ali family's chief residence, with the main railway station, where their private trains are on display at a fine **Railway Museum ❹** (Maydan Ramesses; open Tues–Sun 8.30am–1pm; admission charge). An early 18th-century Ottoman mosque on the corner of Shari'al Gumhuriyyah and Shari' Qasr an-Nil indicates the overlapping of Ismail's new quarter with old Misr as it was before the French marched in; and a left turn into Shari'al Gumhuriyyah leads to **Azbakiyyah**, which was founded as a pleasure zone in the 15th century, but had evolved into an upper-class residential area by the time Napoleon Bonaparte made his headquarters there in 1798.

When Napoleon moved in, the focus of the area was a picturesque seasonal lake that filled during the Nile flood. Local resistance and stern punitive measures soon reduced most of the luxurious dwellings along its southern and eastern shores to ruins; and during a revolt of Albanian troops after the French departure, Bonaparte's own palace overlooking the western shore, where his successor had been assassinated by an Egyptian patriot, was also burned.

Under Muhammad Ali, however, who established official residences here for himself and members of his family, Azbakiyyah was soon rebuilt and became dotted with new administrative offices. After 1837, when the lake was drained and its site converted into a park, hotels began to move their premises into Azbakiyyah from the old European quarter along Shari' Muski to the east. One of them, the New British Hotel, was to become world-famous under the name of its first owner – Shepheard's. There was already a French theatre there too, which would soon be joined by restaurants and coffee houses.

In 1868 Ismail reduced the park to an octagonal garden and the remainder of the old lake-site was opened for development. New squares were created in

BELOW: on the Nile, with the Ramses Hilton Hotel in the background.

three of the four corner-spaces left by the octagon's shortest sides and new public buildings were erected, the most striking of which was a theatre for opera. Built entirely of wood and completed within five months during 1869, the old Cairo Opera House saw the premier of *Aida* in 1871 and later became renowned for its collections of manuscripts, scores, costumes and sets, all of which were consumed by fire when the building burned down in 1971. Its site is now identified by one of the city's few high-rise car-parks.

Commissioned by Ismail, later erected (1882) in the square in front of the Opera, and still standing on the same spot, is a heroic equestrian **statue of Ibrahim Pasha**.

Two of Ismail's new streets, both still fashionable – Shari' Abdel Khaliq Tharwat and Shari' Adli, where the largest of Cairo's synagogues stands – lead westward from Ibrahim's statue, while Shari' Gumhuriyyah continues north along the western edge of the **Azbakiyyah Garden ❺**. Reduced in size again in 1872, but elegantly redesigned by Ismail's French city-planner as an enclosed English-style garden of the order of the Parc Monceau in Paris, the Garden at present, even more reduced, retains its octagonal shape, but otherwise shows the devastating result of 20th-century priorities.

Grand hotels

The **Continental Hotel** still stands overlooking the garden from the west, though it has been cut in half and concealed by a row of shopfronts. It was owned at an earlier stage (as the New Hotel) by Ismail himself and came to rank third among Cairo's hotels after the Savoy and, of course, Shepheard's.

Shepheard's itself, destroyed by fire in 1952 – the new Shepheard's on the Corniche has nothing in common with the old one but the name – stood on a site farther north on Shari' Gumhuriyyah now occupied by a high-rise building. In Ismail's time there were at least seven other hotels close by, plus half a dozen restaurants and a dozen or so foreign consulates.

The area had also been known earlier, however, for its prostitutes, pedlars, mountebanks, jugglers, acrobats and beggars, a reputation that deservedly did not diminish until long after World War II, during which the city was occupied by British and ANZAC troops who were eager for such diversions.

Shari' Clot Bey, ironically named after Muhammad Ali's chief advisor on public health, was famous until quite recently for its brothels. And there is still something raffish about other streets just north of the garden, something that breathes of mysterious *Arabian Nights* hugger-mugger despite the superficially European appearance of things.

Farther north and east of Azbakiyyah is an area where tourists never venture and few Cairenes ever visit, the old **Bab al-Bahr quarter**, long identified with Christians, which probably exemplifies the meaning of tradition better than any other area in the city of Cairo. Though it contains very few historic monuments, its streets follow the 15th-century pattern surveyed in 1800 by Napoleon's savants, whose map remains the only accurate guide.

BELOW: on Opera Square.

Gazirah and Zamalik

Newer districts, however, are not without charm. **Al Gazirah** (The Island), joined to the mainland by three bridges, two of them near Maydan at-Tahrir, offers not only **Zamalik**, a suburb popular among European residents, but also several individual attractions for tourists. The **Gazirah Exhibition Grounds**, for example, which were replaced in 1982 as the site of the city's international expositions by the new **Cairo International Fairgrounds** at Madinat Nasr, have since become instead the location of a Japanese-built cultural complex that Cairenes call the **Opera House ⑥**, seeing it as a replacement for the old Opera House in Azbakiyyah.

The **Museum of Modern Art ⑦** (open Sat–Thurs 10am–1pm and 5–9pm; Fri 10am–noon and 5–9pm; admission charge) has meanwhile been moved from outmoded and overcrowded premises on Maydan Finney in Doqqi to one of the old permanent pavilions; and another permanent pavilion has been set aside for exhibitions of work by contemporary artists.

Finally, it was decided to construct a new **Museum of Egyptian Civilisation** as well, to complement the displays of objects at the Egyptian Museum with working models and live demonstrations.

Across the road from the Gazirah Exhibition Grounds, in the park at the southern end of the island, is the **Mukhtar Museum ⑧** (open Tues–Sun 10am–1pm and 5–9pm, Fri 9am–noon; admission charge), housing works by Mahmoud Mukhtar, Egypt's greatest modern sculptor and one of the handful of 20th-century Egyptian artists to achieve international recognition. North is the 152 metres high (500 ft) **Cairo Tower** (open daily 9am–midnight), erected in 1957. The tower offers, when the lifts are working, a remarkable view of the city.

Map, page 144

TIP

If you would like details of upcoming performances at the Cairo Opera House, tel: 02-342 0598 or call in when passing. Alternatively you can consult the weekly English-language *Middle East Times* or the *Cairo Times*.

BELOW: view from the Cairo Tower.

Farther north are the grounds of two clubs: the **National**, home of the national (*Ahli*) football team, with its own stadium; and the once-famous **Gazirah Sporting Club** ❾, which offers a wide variety of facilities for tennis, riding, swimming and other sports. Arab horses from the best studs in Egypt race at the Gazirah track on alternate weeks in the season.

The name Zamalik covers all of Gazirah north of the Gazirah Sporting Club. Opposite the northern entrance to the club is the charming house built in 1927 for *Nabil* (Lord) Amr Ibrahim, a great-great-grandson of Ibrahim Pasha, as a *salamlik* (reception suite) in the Khedival style. Confiscated after the Revolution, it used to house the exquisite Mahmud-Khalil Collection of paintings, which has now been moved to the Khalil's house in Giza (1 Kafour Street).

Sixteen of the Khalil Collection's Orientalist paintings had already been given to the **Muhammad Ali Club** near Maydan at-Tahrir, formerly Cairo's most exclusive private institution, rescued after the Revolution by the Foreign Ministry and transformed into a club for diplomats. They can still be seen there.

Immediately north, landmarked by a huge old banyan tree, one of Muhammad Ali's imported species, is the **Italian Cultural Centre** ❿, outstanding among foreign institutions in Cairo for its support of the arts. The banyan indicates that the land the Amr Ibrahim house sits on formerly belonged to Ismail's **Gazirah Palace**.

The Palace's grounds now survive more or less intact only in two small portions: the **Fish Garden** (open daily 9am–3.30pm; admission charge), 320 metres (350 yards) to the west, between Shari' al-Gabalayyah and Shari' Hasan Sabri, a public park since 1902, which still has the original estate's grotto-aquarium as its most picturesque feature; and the enclosed garden attached to the **Marriott Hotel** ⓫, standing just across Shari' Lutfallah immediately to the east.

The central block of the hotel incorporates Ismail's Palace itself. Legend says it was built for Empress Eugenie to reside in during the Suez Canal inaugural celebrations of 1869, but it was actually begun in 1863 and opened in 1868. Its chief architect was the German von Diebitsch, a pioneer in modular design, and its grounds were laid out by the Frenchman Barillet-Deschamps, who planned Azbakiyyah Garden and every large green space in Cairo.

When the grounds were laid out in 1867, the Nile was diverted on the western side of the island and the resultant dry channel was turned into an irrigation canal for the gardens. Entire displays of masterworks were meanwhile bought at the Exposition Universelle in Paris to serve as the palace's major furniture.

Map, page 144

More palaces

Two other palaces that once belonged to the Muhammad Ali family can still be seen elsewhere in Cairo: **Shubra Kiosk** on the northern edge of the city and the **Manyal Palace** on Rawdah Island.

Built in 1826, the Shubra Kiosk's plain square exterior conceals an Ottoman-baroque fantasy within: an immense marble basin with a marble island in its centre. The building is in the grounds of the Agricultural Department of the Ayn Shams University and quite hard to visit.

The **Manyal Palace ⑫** (open daily 9am–4pm; admission charge) was built between 1901 and 1929 and left to the Egyptian nation in 1955 by Prince Muhammad Ali, the younger brother of Khedive Abbas II Hilmi and a first cousin of King Faruq. It includes a museum exhibiting Faruq's game-shooting trophies; the prince's own residence with its furnishings; and a 14-room museum housing family memorabilia.

BELOW: terrace of the Marriott Hotel.

The modern Greek Orthodox church of St George marks the start of a visit to Old Cairo. It stands on the remains of one of two great circular towers built by Emperor Trajan.

Babylon – "Old Cairo"

The remains of Roman and Christian Babylon can be found in the area **Misr al Qadimah** , which confusingly translates into "Old Cairo" (though it should not be mistaken for representing more than a foretaste of Cairo's medieval glory). Here too are interesting remains from Egypt's Christian era, as well as one monument from the years immediately following the Arab conquest.

History of Old Cairo

Modern Cairo began at a point halfway between Memphis and Heliopolis (*see page 187*), where a road crossed the river, using the present island of Rawdah as a stepping stone. Since there were no other roads across the Delta, this one not only connected the Old Kingdom's administrative and religious capitals, but was the main passage into Egypt from the East, giving access to the rest of the country. During the Late Dynasty period a small fortress was built here and, after a canal linking the Nile with the Red Sea was completed by the Persian occupiers under Darius I (521–486 BC), the site became even more important. The Greeks called it **Babylon,** a name that should not be confused with Mesopotamian Babylon and that probably derives from some such Egyptian name as *Pi-Hapi-n-On* or *Per-Hapi-n-On*, meaning "The Nile House of On". Under the emperor Trajan (98–117 AD), after more than a century of Roman occupation, when Heliopolis had long been moribund, the old canal was reopened and a new fortress was built, one of three to control the whole of Egypt.

Egyptians themselves knew their country by many names, of which the most common during the Roman period was probably *Kemet*, "The Black Land". Throughout the rest of the Semitic-speaking Middle East, Egypt was called

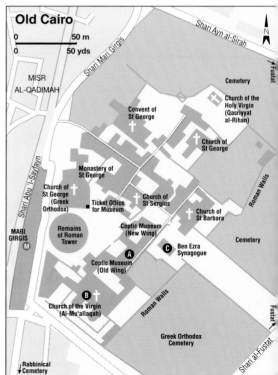

Old Cairo

0   50 m
0   50 yds

Shari Mari Girgis

Shari Ayn al-Sirah

N

MISR AL-QADIMAH

Fustat

Cemetery

Convent of St George

Church of the Holy Virgin (Qasriyyat al-Rihan)

Church of St George

Monastery of St George

Shari Abu 'l-Sayfayn

Church of St George (Greek Orthodox)

Ticket Office for Museum

Church of St Sergius

Church of St Barbara

Roman Walls

MARI GIRGIS
M

Remains of Roman Tower

Coptic Museum (New Wing)

Cemetery

Coptic Museum (Old Wing)

A

C Ben Ezra Synagogue

B

Church of the Virgin (Al-Mu'allaqah)

Roman Walls

Greek Orthodox Cemetery

Fustat

Shari al-Fustat

Rabbinical Cemetery

Misr, the name it still bears in Arabic. When the Arabs conquered Misr in 641 AD and founded a new capital next to the walls of Babylon, this capital acquired the name of the country as a whole. This became more and more appropriate as new quarters with new names were added and it expanded to become the metropolis not only of Egypt, but of the Arab world, a huge city containing many distinct areas with their own lesser names. The Western name "Cairo" derives from "Al-Qahirah", the name of a single one of these later quarters as understood by medieval Italian merchants, who mistook it for a complete city like their walled towns.

Visiting Old Cairo

Largely intact until the British occupation, what is left of the Roman fortress of Babylon can be visited conveniently in conjunction with the **Coptic Museum** Ⓐ (open Sat–Thurs 9am–1pm; Fri 9am–noon; admission charge), and can be reached by taxi or metro. The metro stop is **Mari Girgis** (St George) and stands opposite the modern Greek Orthodox church of the same name. The grounds of the museum begin south of the tower and are entirely within the fortress walls.

Founded by private benefactors on land belonging to the Coptic Church, the museum was taken over by the Egyptian government in 1931. Though there are hundreds of ancient Christian sites in Egypt, there are none in which the churches themselves have not been abandoned, destroyed or extensively rebuilt inside and out. It is therefore only the Coptic Museum that can now give us some idea of what the interior of a 5th, 6th or 7th-century church was like. Objects that were excavated in Upper Egypt and in the ruins of the monastery of St Jeremiah at Saqqarah are of particular interest.

Map, page 154

Textile exhibit in the Coptic Museum. Items in the museum are organised according to the materials used.

BELOW: window in the Coptic Museum.

The museum's most prized relics, however, are the "Nag Hammadi Codices", a collection of nearly 1,200 papyrus pages bound together as books – the earliest so far known with leather covers – sometime soon after the middle of the 4th century. Written in Coptic, the Codices draw syncretically upon Jewish, Christian, Hermetic, Zoroastrian and Platonic sources and have thrown extraordinary light on the background of the New Testament, particularly the Epistles, by revealing that Gnosticism, hitherto supposed to be only a Christian heresy, was in fact a separate religion.

Ancient churches

Babylon is mentioned in St Peter's first epistle, most scholars now concede, in connection with St Mark's Egyptian mission, and local legend claims it as one of the many places in Egypt where the Holy Family rested. The monks and martyrs who elsewhere created the heroic age of the Coptic Church seem to have passed it by, and there are no specific documentary references to any church structure earlier than the Arab conquest. Babylon could not have had much importance as a Christian centre until four centuries later, when it had long since been absorbed into Misr. The **Patriarchate of St Mark**, robbed of the saint's relics by Venetians in 828, was transferred there from a declining Alexandria sometime after 1048.

Not only at Babylon, however, but all over the future site of Misr, there were certainly scattered churches and monastic settlements. Many were later destroyed, but some were undoubtedly incorporated into later structures. Atop the two bastions of the southern gate of the Roman fortress, for example, is the **Church of the Virgin** , referred to locally as **Al-Mu'allaqah** ("The Suspended"), a seat of the Patriarchate for centuries, one portion of which is claimed to date back to the 4th century; and within the walls are several others – the **churches of St Sergius and St Bacchus, St Barbara, St Cyril and St John**; a second church of the Virgin, known as **Qasriyyat al-Rihan** ("Pot of Basir"); and a **convent of St George** – with an almost equal claim to antiquity. Outside the fortress walls, but still within Old Cairo, are no fewer than a dozen more churches that were well documented in medieval times.

A visit to the churches (open 9am–4pm; donations welcomed) within the fortress walls is made particularly pleasant by the fact that this enclosed area is entirely controlled by the Egyptian Antiquities Organisation, which has undertaken a great deal of cleaning and restoration. The interiors of the churches typically follow a basilican plan and cheerfully mix the ancient with the modern, between which local worshippers make little distinction. Pews, for example, are a 20th-century innovation inspired by Western Protestantism, but the use of cymbals or triangles in services may be traced back to the pharaohs. The oldest, finest and most portable objects have all been removed either to the Coptic Museum or to other collections around the world. One of the sanctuaries of the Suspended Church has the remains of some fine frescoes attributed to the 7th or 8th century, however, and the buildings of the convent of St George include an intact reception hall

TIP

Coptic masses can be heard in the Church of the Virgin on Fridays 8–11am and on Sundays 7–10am.

BELOW: inside the church of St Barbara.

belonging to a Fatimid-period house, with magnificent wooden doors 7 metres (22 ft) high.

These churches are all Coptic Orthodox, but during Lent they become pilgrimage sites for Catholics as well. In the 17th and 18th centuries the Franciscan Friars had the right to celebrate mass in the sanctuary of the Holy Family at the church of St Sergius and St Bacchus, which marks a traditional resting-place of the Holy Family and is thus venerated by both Catholic and Orthodox.

Also within the walls is the **Ben Ezra Synagogue** ❸ (open daily 9am–4pm; no admission charge), one of Cairo's 29 synagogues, a reminder of Egypt's role not only in fostering the Saphardic Rabbinical tradition, but also in providing a home for Karaite Jews (before the 10th century) and Ashkenazi Jews (from the 16th century onward). Originally a church dedicated to St Michael the Archangel, the building was closed under the Fatimid caliph Al Hakim (996–1021), then sold to the Saphardic community. Among other functions it served as a *geniza*, a repository for documents made sacrosanct by being sworn under oath, which could not be casually discarded without sacrilege. Since these documents cover several centuries and include such mundane items as contracts, bills of sale and letters of credit, they constitute an extensive record of medieval Mediterranean trade and commerce, an invaluable prize for foreign scholars.

The first Arab capital

Immediately to the east of Old Cairo, in an enormous area slowly being covered with new buildings, is the site of **Fustat** ⓮, the first Muslim capital at Misr, founded by 'Amr ibn al 'As in the course of the Arab conquest. Excavations here have uncovered the remains of elaborate water storage and drainage systems, the foundations of private houses and apartment blocks, and thousands of objects made of wood, paper, ivory, glass, metal or ceramics, ranging in date from the 8th century to the 14th, and in provenance from Spain to China. The most significant of these objects may be seen in the **Islamic Art Museum** ⓯ (Maydan Ahmad Mahir; open daily 9am–4pm; Fri closed during prayers 11.30am–1.30pm; admission charge), including a sensational find made in 1980: block-printed papers that confirmed archaeologically the long-held belief that the art of printing was known in Fatimid Egypt within decades after its invention in China, at least four centuries before its adoption in Europe.

There is little to see at the site now to suggest the importance Fustat still had as a residential, manufacturing and international trading centre even after the government had moved to new quarters farther north. One monument of the early period still remains in Old Cairo, however, and another stands at the tip of Rawdah Island, across an intervening channel of the river.

The **mosque of 'Amr ibn al 'As** ⓰ (open daily 9am–4pm; Fri closed during prayers noon–1pm; admission charge) is 300 yards north of the Roman fortress on the main road parallel to the metro line. Erected in 641 or 642, it was rebuilt in 688, 710, 750 and 791, then doubled to approximately its present size in 827, thus testifying to Fustat's rapid growth. After several subsequent centuries of neglect, it was restored in the 13th

Maps,
**pages
154 & 144**

Beyond Old Cairo, 5km (3 miles) to the southeast, is the Rabbinical Cemetery (considerably older than the synagogue of Ben Ezra). Among the important tombs is that of Ya'kub ibn Killis, the Jewish vizier of the caliph Aziz (975–996).

BELOW: mosque of 'Amr ibn al 'As.

century, rebuilt after the great earthquake of 1303, then partially rebuilt again a century later. Near the end of the 18th century, just before the French invasion, the mosque again underwent massive rebuilding. After all this rebuilding, only an expert could now pinpoint older construction, but the site is important as it marks the first mosque in Africa and inspired the building of Cairo's greatest mosque, that of Ibn Tulun.

The **Nilometer** ⓱ (open daily 9am–4pm; admission charge) at the southern tip of **Rawdah Island** is easy to see from across the river – it is distinguished by a conical cap. The only north-south street on the island giving access to the Nilometer is the easternmost, which can be approached only from the west. The conical dome is a reconstruction made in 1893 of a 17th-century Ottoman dome that had been destroyed by the French in 1800; and its interior is covered with fine Turkish tiles. The substructure, however, which is the Nilometer itself, dates essentially from 861, which makes it the oldest intact Islamic monument in Cairo and the only survivor from the Abbasid period.

Consisting of a calibrated stone column standing upright in a stone-lined pit with a staircase, it is particularly notable for the pointed arches used at the highest intake level, 300 years before the appearance of such arches in Europe.

Medieval Cairo

In 872 the caliph's name was removed from the Nilometer by order of the city's 38-year-old Turkish governor, Ahmad ibn Tulun, who would not only declare himself independent, but within 10 years make Misr the centre of an empire stretching from southern Turkey to Sudan. Cramped by the growth of Fustat, the Abbasid caliphs had already built themselves a new military quarter, **Al**

TIP

An ideal approach to the Nilometer, often used in the 19th century and recently rediscovered by local boatmen, is by water. You should be able to negotiate a ferry ride.

BELOW: Nilometer, Rawdah Island.

Map,
page 144

TIP

Askar, to the north; and Ibn Tulun felt the need for something grander. The result was **Al Qatai'** ("The Wards"), a new town large enough to include a walled hippodrome, a hospital, a menagerie, mews, gardens, markets, baths, residential quarters (classified by occupation or nationality), reception and *harim* ("harem") palaces for Ibn Tulun himself, and a large governmental complex, which was attached to a great congregational mosque. When the Abbasids re-possessed Misr for the caliphate in 905, the **Mosque of Ibn Tulun** ⓲ (Shari' al Salibah; open daily 8am–6pm; admission charge), one of the architectural glories of the Muslim world, was the only building left standing in Al Qatai'.

Though it is now approached by the narrow streets that grew up around it, most taxi drivers can find it, since it is situated between two landmarks, the Citadel and the popular modern mosque of Sayyidha Zaynab, just west of the Qasabah, the great north-south thoroughfare of Mamluk Misr. Several restorations – the earliest was in 1297, the latest in 1981 – have kept it in order without destroying its authenticity, though one must imagine its inscriptions and decorations as painted or gilded.

Built in the imperial style of the Abbasid court at Samarra in Iraq, where Ibn Tulun had lived as a young man, the mosque is constructed of red brick and stucco – original materials, rather than granite, limestone and marble borrowed from other sites, as is often the case in later mosques. The mosque is impressive both for its pleasing simplicity and grand scale – its courtyard alone covers 2.5 hectares (6½ acres) and the sycamore wood frieze of Qur'anic verses around the court is more than 2 km (1¼ miles) long. The unusual spiral minaret was probably inspired by the minaret in Samarra, Iraq, although legend has it that a distracted Ibn Tulun rolled up a piece of paper and told the architect to use that as the design.

The main street of Misr
Adjoining the mosque's northeastern corner is the **Gayer-Anderson Museum** ⓳ (Bayt al Kiridliyyah): two houses, one from the 16th century, the other from the 17th, that have been delightfully joined together to create a larger dwelling with a *salamlik* (reception suite) and *haramlik* (harem suite), both filled with antique furniture from all over the Middle East.

One entrance to the museum leads from the mosque of Ibn Tulun. Another entrance, opposite, can be used as an exit and gives on to a cross-street called Shari' Tulun, which leads eastward (left) after less than 100 yards into the **Qasabah**, medieval Cairo's main street. The Qasabah linked all the city's parts on a north-south axis; and at the height of Cairo's medieval prosperity it had become more than 13 km (8 miles) long.

Shari' as-Salibah
There is so much to see of the rest of medieval Cairo however, that it is best to take the Qasabah piecemeal. The first major cross-street it intersects, for example, about 300 yards up the Qasabah to the north, is **Shari' as-Salibah**, a special joy for the architect or city-planner. On the northeast corner of the intersection is a delightful Ottoman-style *saabil-kuttab* ("fountain school") built in 1867 by the mother of Abbas I, the suc-

The great north-south thoroughfare called the Qasabah, medieval Cairo's main street, can still be followed on foot from Ibn Tulun northward for more than 5 km (3 miles) into the heart of modern Cairo's historic zone (*see page 167*).

BELOW: the minaret of Ibn Tulun Mosque.

"Fountain schools" were endowed by the pious for the public dispensation of the "two mercies" commended by the Prophet – water and religious teaching. They were always constructed in two storeys, with a public water-dispensary below and a school for Qur'anic instruction above.

BELOW: an 18th-century *saabil-kuttab* in the Ottoman baroque style.

cessor of Muhammad Ali, and beautifully restored in 1984 by the Egyptian Antiquities Organisation.

Unmistakable just beyond the northeast and southeast corners of the intersection are the massive facades of two "colleges" built by the Amir Shaykhu, commander of the Mamluk armies under Sultan Hasan ibn an-Nasir Muhammad ibn Qalawun (1334–61), who had him murdered in 1357.

Shaykhu's *madrasah* (built in 1349, on the left) and his *khanqah* ❷⓿ (built in 1355, on the right) represent two classic Cairene architectural types, both introduced two centuries earlier by Saladin. Persian in inspiration, the *madrasah* provided a courtyard mosque made cruciform in plan by building into it four vaulted halls (*liwans*), where instruction could take place simultaneously in the four systems of legal thought regarded as orthodox by Sunni Muslims (Hanafi, Malaki, Shafi'i, Hanbali).

A *khanqah* is a Muslim "monastery", a mosque with attached dwelling areas that are designed to serve as a hostel for Sufis (Muslim mystics). Shaykhu's *khanqah* accommodated some 700 Sufis, though it contains only 150 rooms surrounding a central mosque with a courtyard. These two buildings frame Shari' Salibah as one looks in the direction of the Citadel, creating a gorgeously Oriental-style vista.

Farther up Shari' Salibah in the direction of the Citadel is the first free-standing *saabil-kuttab* in Cairo, built by Qaitbay in 1479, beyond which the street suddenly emerges into the **Qaramaydan** (Maydan Salah ad-Din). This enormous square was the site of Ibn Tulun's hippodrome and the Mamluks' polo-ground, where their pageants, races, matches, musters and military displays took place under the gaze – and the guns – of the Citadel.

The madrasah of Sultan Hasan and the Rifa'i Mosque

At the northwestern corner of this square loom two colossal religious buildings, one on either side of the entrance to a street called Shari'al Qal'ah (but better known under its old name as Shari' Muhammad Ali) confronting each other gatewise just as the Shaykhu *madrasah* and *khanqah* do in Shari' as-Salibah, though on a much larger scale: the **madrasah of Sultan Hasan** ❹ (Maydan Saladin; open daily 8am–5pm, till 6pm in summer; admission charge) Shaykhu's teenage master, built between 1356 and 1363; and the **Rifa'i Mosque** ❷❷ (same hours and ticket as Hasan's madrasah), built to complement it architecturally between 1869 and 1912.

Map, page 144

Visitors sometimes fail to understand that these two buildings were con-structed more than five centuries apart, since the modern mosque shows perfect respect for its older neighbour across the street in fabric, scale and style.

Inside the Rifa'i Mosque Mamluk motifs have been reproduced with luxuri-ous fidelity, demonstrating recognition of the Mamluk style as Cairo's distin-guishing trademark, an almost "official" style and thus particularly suitable in a mosque identified with the ruling dynasty. Originally endowed by the mother of the Khedive Ismail, it houses her tomb as well as those of the magnificent Khedive himself and four of his sons, including Husayn Kamil (1853–1917) and King Fuad (1868–1936). King Faruq's body was laid to rest here after tem-porary interment in the Southern Cemetery.

A great parade of Sufi orders, with chanting, banners and drums, takes place annually in Cairo on the eve of the Prophet's Birthday. Despite the Revolution, it traditionally begins here at the Rifa'i Mosque, marches down Shari' Muham-mad Ali, up Shari' Bur Sa'id, then down Shari' al Azhar – wide new European-

Among the famous tombs inside the Rifa'i Mosque is that of Muhammad Reza Pahleve, the last Shah of Iran, whose first wife was Faruq's sister (also buried here).

BELOW: the Rifa'i Mosque and the Madrasah of Sultan Hasan at festival time.

Prayers in the Madrasah of Sultan Hasan, the grandest of all Cairo's Mamluk buildings.

BELOW: 27 varieties of marble were imported for the floors of the Madrasah of Sultan Hasan.

style streets constructed by the Dynasty between 1873 and 1930 – to end at the popular mosque of Sayyidna al-Husayn (closed for non-Muslims), which was built by the Khedive Ismail.

Sultan Hasan's Madrasah, situated just across the street from the Rifa'i Mosque, provided a daunting model, since it is probably the greatest of the Bahri architectural monuments, and second only to Ibn Tulun's mosque in grandeur of conception among all the historic buildings in Cairo. The walls are 117 ft (36 metres) high and so solidly built that the mosque was twice used as a fortress – first in 1381 during a Mamluk revolt and then again in 1517 during the Ottoman invasion.

Originally four minarets were planned, including two over the entrance portal, but in February 1360, while the building was still under construction, one of these two fell, killing 300 people, and the second was never built. One of the two remaining minarets collapsed in 1659 and was replaced by the present smaller version, an Ottoman construction in the Mamluk style, in 1672, when the dome was also replaced. The architectural daring that caused the difficulties is made clear by the sole original minaret at the western corner; it is over 265 ft (80 metres), taller and larger than any other in Cairo.

The complex originally included a market, apartments and a well at its northern end, of which little now remains. The original wooden doors at the entrance, covered with bronze and filigree silver in geometric patterns, were removed by Sultan Mu'ayyad Sheikh in 1416 to be used in his mosque near Bab Zuwaylah, where they are still visible; and most of the original marble floor was stripped by Selim the Grim for shipment to Istanbul after the Ottoman conquest. What is left, however, is stunningly impressive.

The Citadel

The **Citadel** (open daily 9am–4pm; admission charge) was begun by Saladin in 1176 as part of a grand scheme to enclose all of Misr, for the first time, within a system of walls. By 1182, when he had gone northward again to fight his last series of victorious campaigns against the crusaders, it was virtually complete; and though it was later modified in detail, it has never since been without a military garrison.

In 1218 Sultan al Kamil, Saladin's nephew, took up residence in it and, from that time until the construction of Abdin Palace in the mid-19th century, the Citadel was also the home and seat of government of all but one of Egypt's subsequent rulers, even Ottoman viceroys. The Lower Enclosure contains the famous gate-passage where Muhammad Ali conducted a massacre of Mamluks in 1811, which may be approached by an 18th-century gateway, restored in 1988. It is best seen, however, from the terrace of the Police Museum on the upper level, which contains the Southern and Northern Enclosures, nearly two-thirds of the Citadel's entire area.

Visible from nearly anywhere in the city below on its site at the highest point of the Southern Enclosure is the **Muhammad Ali Mosque Ⓐ**. Built between 1830 and 1848, it was not completed until 1857. Designed by a Greek architect in accord with purely Ottoman models, it owes nothing to Egypt but the materials from which it is made and a few intermingled pharaonic and Mamluk decorative motifs, though it adds a wonderful picture-postcard element to the city's skyline. The clock in the courtyard, a charming touch of the period, was a gift made by Louis-Philippe of France in 1846, a belated exchange for the obelisk of Ramesses II from the Luxor temple, now standing in the Place de la Concorde in

Maps, pages 144 & 163

TIP

If you want to escape the heat and bustle of Cairo for a short while, the Citadel is the best place to head. It has cleaner air, more open space, less noise, lower temperatures and better public facilities than anywhere else in the city.

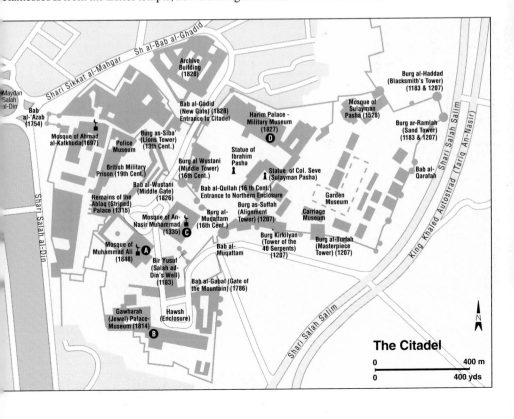

The Citadel

0   400 m
0   400 yds

Map, page 163

👁✓

TIP

One of the best walks in Cairo runs from the Citadel to Bab Zuwaylah (*see the southern section of map on facing page*). Medieval Cairo comes to life in the crumbling palaces and mosques and in the atmospheric street life.

BELOW: mosques clustered below the Citadel.

Paris, which Muhammad Ali had given the French in 1831. The Pasha himself is buried here under a marble cenotaph.

The view over the city seen from the belvedere near the mosque is remarkable on a clear day. Across a little court is the **Gawharah Palace ❸**, built by Muhammad Ali in 1814, gutted by fire during a theft in 1972. The ruins have been intelligently refurbished and converted into a museum of the mid-19th century, when it served as a viceregal *salamlik* (reception) palace.

Below the Muhammad Ali mosque to the northwest, between it and the gateway to the Northern Enclosure, is the great 14th-century **Mosque of An-Nasir Muhammad ❹**, the father of Sultan Hasan. Built in 1318, enlarged in 1335, but stripped of its gorgeous marble by the Ottomans after 1517, it shows Persian-Mongol influence in its unique minarets, and an incredible variety of Egyptian sources in its columns: levied from pharaonic, Greek, Roman and Coptic sites, they constitute a survey of Egyptian architectural styles.

North of the mosque of An-Nasir Muhammad are two gates: one downhill to the left leads into the Lower Enclosure; the other, around a corner to the right, leads into the Northern Enclosure. Within the Northern Enclosure are the **Military Museum ❺**, which is housed in Muhammad Ali's Harim Palace, built in 1827, and an interesting small Museum of Carriages, displaying a few vehicles transferred here from the large collection of royal and viceregal conveyances at the Carriage Museum in Bulaq (now closed to the public). In the far corner of the Northern Enclosure is the first Ottoman mosque built in Cairo (1528). Nestled next to an old Fatimid tomb, it is set in a small garden, which must have afforded a cool and leafy touch of the Bosphorus to the homesick Janissaries who lived there during the centuries after 1517.

Sultanic serendipity

The Citadel was remote from the city: what did a sultan do when he wanted to know what was really going on? Presumably he imitated the Harun ar-Rashid of *The Arabian Nights*, disguised himself, and went out to "wander through the streets and note the quality of people".

Certainly Cairo can be known only on foot: and one of its most magnificent walks begins at the **Bab al Gadid**, the northern gate of the Citadel. From outside the Citadel this point can be reached by leaving a car near the Sultan Hasan Mosque and walking up toward the Citadel, then turning left to climb a road that runs parallel to its walls, bearing on to the first intersection it makes with an old street running downhill.

This old street has many names – Al Tabbana, Bab al-Wazir – but is best known as **Darb al Ahmar**. Connecting the Citadel with Bab Zuwaylah, the southern gate of Al-Qahirah, it runs through an area that had been cleared for pleasure-gardens by Saladin, then became fashionable during the reign of An-Nasir Muhammad, when many of his sons-in-law began building there.

First, on the left down a very short side street, for example, are the ruins of a medieval hospital (1420), the *bimaristan* of Mu'ayyad Shaykh; while on the right appear the *madrasah* and tomb of Amir Aytmish al-Bagasi (1348), the remains of the tomb and *saabil-kuttab* of Amir Tarabay as-Sharifi (1503), and the tomb of Azdumur (early 16th century). A hundred yards farther down the street on the right (east) is the palace of **Alin Aq** (1293), later occupied and re-modelled by the treacherous Amir Khayrbak, who built his tomb (1502), mosque and *saabil-kuttab* (1502) next to it, creating a northward view that is one of the most picturesque and frequently photographed in Cairo.

On the left (west) across the street from **Khayrbak's Mosque ❷** is the beginning of a 14-unit apartment house with several entrances, dating from 1522, which stretches along the street.

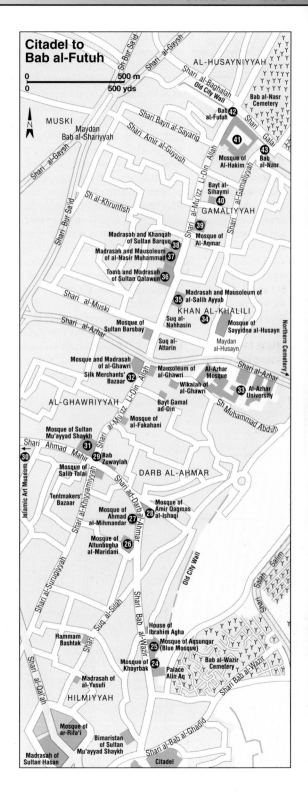

The mosque of Amir Aqsunqur is known as the "Blue Mosque" on account of its blue tiles imported from Damascus.

BELOW: freshly finished chairs get their first airing.

Just beyond Khayrbak's mosque on the right (east), meanwhile, is a 17th-century house, with the mosque of **Amir Aqsunqur** ㉕ (1347) (open 9am–5pm, till 6pm in summer; admission charge), one of An-Nasir Muhammad's sons-in-law, next to it, with tiles from Damascus installed in 1652 by Ibrahim Agha, the first owner of the house. These have inspired guides to call it the "Blue Mosque".

Across the street from the mosque, next to the 16th-century apartment house, is a 17th-century *saabil* and tomb, then on the east side comes another of Ibrahim Agha's houses (1652) with his adjoining *saabil* (1639); and beyond the *saabil* is a small Ottoman religious structure, with an Ayyubid minaret (1260) behind it. A little farther down the street, after an intersection, another 17th-century *saabil-kuttab* appears on the left, then a 14th-century tomb on the right.

Jutting into the street from the left, next comes the **mosque of Altunbugha al-Maridani** ㉖ (1340), notable for its woodwork and marble, which give some idea of what An-Nasir Muhammad's mosque at the Citadel must have been like before the Ottoman conquest; and farther along on the same side of the street is the **mosque of Ahmad al-Mihmandar** ㉗ (1325), with still another 17th-century *saabil-kuttab* next to it. Finally, on the right as the street turns a corner and Bab Zuwaylah comes into view, stands the exquisite funerary mosque of **Amir Qajmas al-Ishaqi** ㉘ (1481) connected with his *saabil-kuttab* by a bridge over a sidestreet.

Darb al-Ahmar now runs east and west and appropriately leads past **Bab Zuwaylah** ㉙ and the Tentmakers' Bazaar – after a change of name – to the **Islamic Art Museum** ㉚ (*see page 157*), Cairo's great storehouse of medieval treasures, which lies 494 metres (1,620 ft) straight ahead, on the northwestern corner of Shari Bur Sa'id and a cluster of cross-streets, at Maydan Ahmad Mahir.

Bab Zuwaylah and beyond

Built in 1092 as the southern gateway of Al-Qahirah, **Bab Zuwaylah** is the most distinguished of all these old quarters. Originally a palace enclosure, it was opened to commercial development by Saladin. Through its heart runs the Qasabah, at once the main artery of the whole medieval city and a single enormous bazaar, straddled at either end of Al-Qahirah by massive Fatimid gates.

High up on the wall next to the gate at Bab Zuwaylah hangs a mysterious trophy of metal objects – weapons, tools, or Sufi instruments – which no-one has ever convincingly identified. Directly on top of the gate are two minarets, which have given it such a specific identity that depictions of it were once used as logos for the modern city. Belonging to the mosque of **Sultan Mu'ayyad Shaykh ⑪** (1420) (open daily 9am–5pm, till 6pm in summer; admission charge), which stands just inside the gate to the left, they also demonstrate that by the end of the 14th century Bab Zuwaylah had ceased to be regarded as primarily military.

It is in this mosque that the splendid doors of Sultan Hasan were finally hung and can still be seen. Across the street, with an attached *saabil-kuttab*, is the facade of a caravanserai-emporium called **As-Sukkariyyah** (from the Arabic *sukkar*, the source of the word meaning "sugar" in every European language), which has given this district just within the southern Fatimid walls its name.

Cruising up the Qasabah

The Qasabah from here northward has been devoted for eight centuries to buying and selling; 450 yards up the street is another famous commercial district, the **Al Gawriyyah**, named after Qansuh al Ghawri, one of the last Mamluk sultans.

Map, page 165

BELOW: tents, sometimes still appliquéd by hand, are used for funeral wakes as well as festivals.

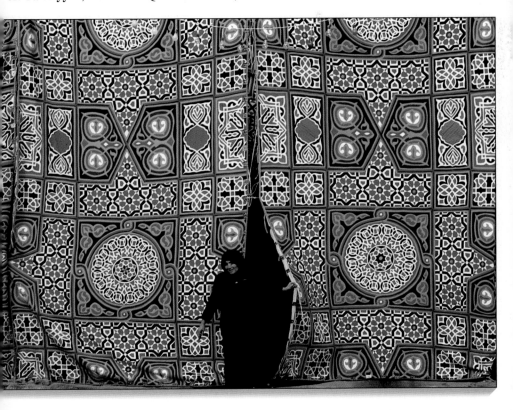

*Khan al-Khalili is
Cairo's most famous
bazaar, selling
excellent, well-made
jewellery and
antiques as well as
kitsch souvenirs such
as this miniature of
Tutankhamun's mask.*

BELOW: minarets of
Al Azhar.

His *madrasah* and mausoleum (1505) stand on the site of the **Silk Merchants' Bazaar ㉜**, a covered street-market that was once the most famous in Cairo. The place is still bursting with trade.

At this point the Qasabah's north-south axis is suddenly sliced by the modern east-west traffic of **Shari' al Azhar**, cut through old Misr in 1930 to provide a tram service for the greatest and most long-lived of the Fatimids' foundations, the **University of Al Azhar ㉝**, which continues to attract Muslim students from around the world. Lying a short distance down Shari' al-Azhar to the east, Al Azhar's oldest buildings represent a variety of endowments from the 10th to the late-19th centuries.

On the other side of Shari' al Azhar, the Qasabah, here called Sharia al-Muizz li-Din Allah, continues north, but is soon interrupted, just beyond a 15th-century *madrasah*, by another modern street, **Shari' al Muski**. Connected with old Christian and European quarters, it soon became favoured by foreign merchants and by the end of the 19th century was lined with European-owned shops.

The Qasabah itself still maintains its traditional character. Around this intersection spices and scents are sold; beyond are goldsmiths; and the first major street off the Qasabah to the right (east) leads to the **Khan al Khalili ㉞**, famous formerly for Turkish goods and now the tourists' bazaar, where locals also go to buy jewellery and antiques.

Between the palaces

Further along, to the right, two *madrasahs* honouring Ayyubid sultans were built over Fatimid ruins. The minaret of the **madrasah-mausoleum ㉟**, built by his widow for Sultan al Salih Nagm ad-Din Ayyub, the last great ruler of the Ayyu-

bid line, past a 14th-century *saabil*, commands a magnificent view over the complex of buildings built by three of the most important Mamluk sultans (open daily 9am–5pm, till 6pm in summer; admission charge). First to the left is the great *maristan* (hospital) tomb-*madrasah* built in 1285 by **Sultan Qalawun ㊱**, and next door are the *madrasah* and mausoleum built 40 years later by his son **Al-Nasir Muhammad ㊲**. The next entrance through heavy bronze-plated doors leads to the *madrasah* and *khanqah* of **Sultan Barquq ㊳**.This section of the Qasabah was known even then as **Bayn al-Qasrayn**, "Between the Two Palaces", in commemoration of the two huge Fatimid palaces that had stood facing each other on this site over a century earlier.

Appropriately, Cairo's principal slave market was also held here in the Bayn al-Qasrayn, where Mamluks and girls, mainly Circassian and Greek, continued to be bought and sold until the time of Muhammad Ali.

To the northern gates of Al Qahirah

Further north, in a stretch of the Qasabah where such items as copper bean-pots and finials for mosques are made, stands the **Aqmar Mosque ㊴**, one of the few remaining Fatimid monuments; and around the corner at the second turning afterwards, on a side-street called the Darb al-Asfar, stands one of the best examples of an 18th-century Cairene townhouse, the **Bayt al-Sihaymi ㊵** (open daily 9am–5pm; admisssion charge). More typical than the Gayer-Anderson house, it illustrates not only the standard division of rooms into a *salaamlik* and a *haramlik*, but also the ingenuity with which architects used courtyards, fountains set in sunken floors, high ceilings and north-facing wind-catchers on the roof to counter the heat of a long Cairene summer.

Map, page 165

TIP

You may find some good buys in functional, well-made brassware in the Suq al-Nahhasin (the Coppersmiths' Bazaar), on the Qasabah, where brass is sold at local prices by weight, regardless of its age.

BELOW: inside Al Azhar Mosque.

Just before the Qasabah exits through Bab al Futuh, one of the two northern gates of Al Qahirah, a space opens out to form another market, where fine agricultural produce from what were formerly the royal family's experimental farms is sold in its various seasons, the garlic being especially prized. Overlooking this area on its eastern side is the congregational **mosque of the Fatimid caliph Al Hakim ㊶** (open 9am–5pm; admission charge), finished in 1013 and restored in 1980 by the Bohora, an Isma'ili Shi'ite sect who are based in Bombay, but trace the ancestry of their leaders back directly to the Fatimids, and who have imported features that give the building a touch of India.

Bab al-Futuh ㊷, the great "Gate of Conquest" (open daily 9am–5pm; admission charge; caretaker sits in the teahouse opposite the gate), **Bab al-Nasr ㊸**, the "Gate of Victory", the other northern gate of Al-Qahirah, and the 330-metre (1,080-ft) stretch of wall between them – all built by the Fatimids' Armenian general Badr al Gamali in 1087 – have been restored and are worth touring. Badr's Armenian architects were skilled military specialists; and their work originally made use of blocks quarried and carved under the pharaohs, some of which were scratched in turn, more than seven centuries later, with Napoleonic grafitti.

Outside the two northern gates is an open area, beyond which the Qasabah moves off from Bab al-Futuh northward through the **Husayniyyah district**, known both as a butchers' quarter and as a hotbed of nationalist sentiment; its patriotic meat-cutters gave the French a great deal of trouble and were bombarded by them from the Fatimid walls. Adjoining the Husayniyyah on the east opposite Bab al-Nasr is a famous cemetery. Ibn Khaldun, the 14th-century historian so dazzled by the city, is among those buried here, though the area is so built up with dwellings among the graves that it looks thoroughly residential.

BELOW:
social gathering.

Living among the dead

This fact, however, makes it a good introduction to Cairo's great **Northern** **and Southern Cemeteries** , which Western journalists delight in calling collectively "The City of the Dead", though they grew up at different times and have always been separated from each other by the limestone spur on which and out of which the Citadel was built.

People live in these cemeteries, a situation journalists explain by quotations from official statistics indicating that the modern city has a terrible housing shortage. Foreigners made the same observations and offered the same rationale, however, as long ago as the 15th century; and the fact is that these cemeteries, as far as anyone knows, have always had inhabitants.

Permanent structures demand caretakers and soon have communities around them, the more so if they are used for occasional purposes other than merely housing the dead. The tombs of popular Cairene saints are always thronged, but on Thursday evenings, Fridays and on major feast days the living Cairenes frequently visit their family tombs – just as ancient Creeks and Romans did or as modern Europeans used to on All Saints' Day – and have large family picnics among the graves.

This custom was elaborated by the Mamluk sultans and amirs. Every guest wore his most extravagant clothes: silks from China (like the cups, bowls and serving dishes) embroidered by the ladies of local *harems*, brocades manufactured in the Mamluks' own workshops. Amid an abundance of flowers, perfume and incense, eating, drinking and music received rapturous attention but, if the tomb-site was suitable, there might also be horse-racing, mounted archery and even hunting expeditions. The Northern Cemetery actually began life in the 13th

Map, page 144

TIP

If you feel uncomfortable about visiting the City of the Dead, perhaps for fear of getting lost or of prying, you could join a small guided tour which will ensure that you see the most important tombs. Enquire at your hotel or at a travel agent.

BELOW: mosque and tomb of local holy man.

century as a hippodrome with viewing stands, evolving into a royal necropolis only later.

The Southern Cemetery is larger – it begins as far north as the mosque of Ibn Tulun – and much older. Several of the tombs have been pilgrimage sites for centuries, particularly the 13th-century **Mausoleum of Imam as-Shafi'i**, a descendant of the Prophet's uncle and founder of the most influential of the four orthodox schools of Sunni jurisprudence, who died in Egypt in 820. Nearby is the **mausoleum of Hawsh al-Basha** built by Muhammad Ali in 1816 for his favourite wife, where her three sons and other family members are also interred, alongside many of their retainers. All around in every direction, interspersed with apartment blocks is a multitude of other tombs. The most notable are those of Burgi Mamluk amirs, set within the remains of complexes that frequently included *khanqahs* and other large residential structures.

What these amirs built in the Southern Cemetery, however, can hardly compare with what their sultans built in the Northern Cemetery. The Burgi period marks the high point in the development of both the carved stone dome and the three-stage minaret – with a square base, an octagonal second storey and a cylindrical upper storey, elaborately carved and topped by a bulb set on colonettes – features that used to dominate Cairo's skyline.

Unhampered in this freshly opened necropolis by considerations of space, the Circassian rulers were free to indulge their tastes for piety and pleasure to the full. The results still visible are the remains of five huge monuments that may represent an epitome in Mamluk architecture. The most important are the **mausoleums of Farrag**, the son of Barquq, and **Qaytbay**, the most famous of the Circassians. Built between 1472 and 1474, they are the jewels of the period.

BELOW: cemetery inhabitants.

Pleasant suburbs

Nearly a quarter of the 140-odd missions in Cairo maintain their chancelleries or ambassador's residence in **Zamalik**. And most of the rest are scattered throughout areas on the Nile's western bank, in Giza, Doqqi, Aguza or Muhandesseen, which were still rural hinterland as recently as 1970. Less green, less exclusively residential and far more crowded than it once was, Zamalik now even boasts cheap nightclubs on its western Nile-side (Shari' Abu al Feda), which have replaced the old house-boat brothels that used to ply this stretch of the river.

Similar nightlife can be found along Giza's Shari' al Ahram, the boulevard leading to the Pyramids, while more elegant diversion is available in the nightclubs of the city's major hotels, most of which also have good discos. Arabic-speaking seekers of down-market pleasure may prowl Azbakiyyah and adjacent streets in the centre of town, but those who are in the petro-dollar fast track simply order their sleazy pleasures by telephone.

Giza, in ancient times merely a stopover between Memphis and Heliopolis, is now a rapidly expanding governorate in its own right. In 1908 the Cairo University was founded as a counterpart to the Islamic University of Al Azhar, but it is now just as much a hotbed of fundamentalism as the latter. Opposite the university are the **Cairo Zoo** and the **Urman Gardens**, designed by the Frenchman Barillet-Deschamps. Established in 1890, the zoo is one of the oldest in the world with a comprehensive collection of animals, unfortunately now often in a rather poor state. It is an outing place for Cairenes, especially on Fridays.

Many foreigners prefer to live in the more modern flats in **Muhandesseen**. The area has taken over from Zamalik for good shopping. Many boutiques selling local and imported fashion recently opened their doors, and most of the city's trendy bars and restaurants are also here.

The older area of **Misr al Gadidah** (Heliopolis) was created as a new upmarket suburb, laid out on the city's northeastern desert edge in 1906. Development was hit by falling property values, but it was so intelligently planned that its density has remained low, its traffic has not become unmanageable and its original neo-Islamic architecture predominates over new slabs of concrete.

Meanwhile the British and Americans have remained faithful to **Garden City**, laid out at almost the same time as Heliopolis but on the site of an old estate of Ibrahim Pasha's south of Maydan at-Tahrir. The British Consulate-General – now the **Residency** – was restored in 1986 to its full late-Victorian splendour. Overcrowded with banks and their customers during the day, Garden City recovers some of its charm at night.

The sprawling city

Most Cairenes live in relatively new "informal sector" housing, which accounts for as much as 80 percent of all residential construction since 1965, when the city had less than a quarter of its present population. The result is that the built-up agglomeration called Cairo has been extended by some 24 km (15 miles) and now covers the eastern bank of the Nile solidly for 35 km (21 miles). It reaches deep into the desert, has satellite cities and in many areas is without running water, drainage, electricity or paved roads. ❑

Map, page 144

TIP

If you fancy a boat trip north of Cairo, public waterbuses leaving from Maspero opposite the radio and TV building regularly make the journey to the barrages, 24 km (15 miles) north. Here the Nile divides into the Rashid (Rosetta) and the Dumyat (Damietta) branch.

BELOW: taking a breather.

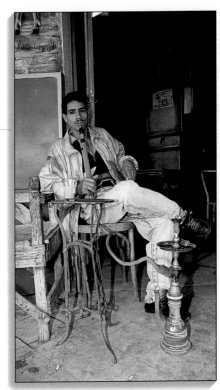

GIZA, MEMPHIS AND SAQQARAH

Maps, pages 177, 178

The Pyramids of Giza are the most famous symbol of Egypt. But also among the country's other highlights are the Step Pyramid and decorated tombs of Saqqarah

The modern city of Cairo occupies a position at the head of the Nile Delta that has been of strategic importance for some 5,000 years and that has consequently seen many urban foundations, of which Cairo itself is merely the largest and the latest.

Memphis

The most important of Cairo's predecessors was the city of **Memphis ❶**, founded by Menes, traditionally regarded as the first king of the 1st Dynasty, on land reclaimed from the Nile in about 3100 BC. The site lies 24 km (15 miles) by road south of Cairo on the western side of the Nile. It can be reached by driving down the eastern band and crossing the bridge over the river south of Halwan; or by crossing the river directly into Giza and then driving south either along the main highway that goes from Giza to Upper Egypt, or along the far more attractive agricultural road that runs south from near the Giza Pyramids.

The ruins of Memphis surround the village of **Mit Rahinah**, which derives its name from a temple of Mithras that was built here under the Romans, long after the days of the city's greatest glory.

There is now very little to see at Memphis (open daily 8am–5pm; admission charge) except one of Ramesses' two colossi (the other stands in front of Cairo's Central Railway Station, Ramesses Square) and the Alabaster Sphinx. More has been brought to light in recent excavations, but visitors are advised to enjoy the serenity of the surrounding groves of date-palms, meditate briefly on the perishability of power, then push on up the road.

Ahead, on the desert plateau overlooking the green of Memphis, is a portion of the ancient capital's necropolis, the vast cemetery of Saqqarah, spanning a period from the 27th century BC to the 10th century AD, standing in the midst of an even larger pyramid field that stretches for miles to the north and south.

Saqqarah

The ticket office at the entrance to the **Saqqarah ❷** necropolis (open daily 7.30am–4pm/5pm in summer; but guards start locking up tombs at 3.30pm) stands above the valley temple attached to the **Pyramid of Unas ❹**. Built by the last king of the 5th Dynasty (*circa* 2375–2345 BC), this houses the earliest Pyramid text. The ceremonial causeway linking the two has been excavated and the pyramid at the end is one of the least difficult for visitors to enter.

Dominating the whole area, however, is the **Step Pyramid of Zoser ❸** (3rd Dynasty, 2668–2649 BC),

PRECEDING PAGES: classic view of Giza's Pyramids. **LEFT:** visiting the Sphinx.

Giza ↗

Abu Sir

Animal Graves

Memphis

❻ Mastaba of Ti

Mastaba of Kagemni

Mastaba of Ankh-ma-hor

❼ Serapeum

Mastaba of Mereruka **❹**

Pyramid of Teti

Rest House **❺**

Step Pyramid of Zoser **❸**

Pyramid of Userkef

Mastaba of Akhet-hotep & Ptah-hotep

Pyramid of Unas **❹**

Mastaba of Idut

Causeway

Mastaba of Horemheb

Pyramid of Sekhemkhet **❽**

Monastery of St Jeremiah **❸**

Ticket Office

Saqqarah

0	500 m
0	500 yds

Pyramid of Pepi I **❿**

N

the earliest of all the pyramids and the first great monument in the world to be built of hewn stone.

The entire complex within the enclosure, including shrines, courtyards and the Step Pyramid itself, was the conception of a single man, Imhotep, Zoser's chief of works, who was perhaps the first recorded genius in history. An inscription left behind by a New Kingdom tourist venerates him as "he who opened the stone" and he was later identified with magic, astronomy and medicine, finally becoming deified in the 6th century BC. Translating motifs from more perishable materials, such as wood or papyrus reeds, into stone, the Zoser complex displays many features that became a permanent part of the Egyptian architectural vocabulary and a few that have apparently remained unique.

The Step Pyramid can be entered only with special permission; the tour takes several hours, and there is no lighting inside. A cross-section, however, would reveal its complexity, arising from the fact that it began as a *mastaba* (from an Arabic word that refers to the usual oblong shape), a one-storey tomb of common type. Even here Imhotep showed his originality, for his *mastaba* was square rather than oblong and built of stone rather than the usual mud-brick.

Quite close to the parking space below the enclosure on the opposite side of the causeway to the pyramid of Unas are the ruins of the **Monastery of St Jeremiah ⓒ**, founded in the 6th century and destroyed in the 10th. It is this monastery that has supplied the objects in Rooms 6 and 7 of the Coptic Museum.

Viziers' tombs

Not to be missed, no matter how short your visit, are two 6th-Dynasty *mastabas*, the **tombs of Mereruka and Kagemni ⓓ**, who were both viziers of King Teti

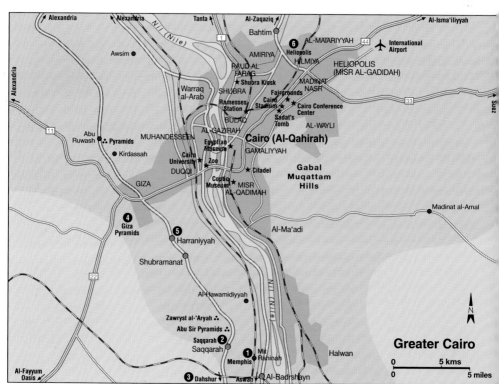

Greater Cairo

(*circa* 2345–2333 BC). Nestled next to the pyramid of Teti, northeast of the Zoser complex, these two structures promise nothing on the outside, but contain the finest tomb reliefs of the Old Kingdom. Carved with lively scenes of domestic life, they show the interests and pursuits of the Old Kingdom nobility: hunting, horticulture, husbandry, music and dancing, preparations to ensure that the next world would be as bountiful as this one. The artist's carved workmen exchange hieroglyphic one-liners; and such is the acuteness of his observations that over 50 different species of fish have been identified by modern experts.

Almost as satisfying are the scenes in the mastaba **of Ankh-ma-hor** (known as the "Doctor's Tomb"), a few steps away, which show similar pursuits but are particularly famous for their depictions of craftsmen (jewellers, metalworks, sculptors) and physicians conducting surgical operations.

Directly west of the pyramid of Teti, a kilometre away and connected with it by a dirt road parallel to what was once an avenue of sphinxes, is a rest house serving cold beer and soft drinks. Near the rest house, left of the dirt road, is the double 5th-Dynasty **mastaba of Akhet-hotep and Ptah-hotep** (his son) **E**, high officials under the kings preceding Unas. To the right of the road is the **mastaba of Ti F**, their slightly older contemporary. Here too are remarkable scenes from daily life, including children's games (Ptah-hotep) and boat-building (Ti).

Bulls and baboons

Below the rest house is the **Serapeum G**, the catacomb of the sacred Apis bull, whose rites were witnessed by Herodotus during his sojourn in Egypt. A circle of statues of Greek poets and philosophers set up by Ptolemy I (323–282 BC)

**Map,
page 177**

*An Apis bull, here
with a sun-disk
between his horns.*

BELOW: The Step
Pyramid of Zoser at
Saqqarah, *circa*
3000 BC.

*When the cult of
Serapis, combining
the characteristics of
Osiris and Apis
(identified with the
Greeks' Zeus), was
invented under the
Ptolemies, the
funerary temple of
Apis became a centre
of pilgrimage for
Greeks and
Egyptians.*

marks the entrance but, except for the size of the bull's sarcophagi, in which no taurine remains have ever been found, the Serapeum itself offers little to stimulate either logic or the imagination, though it makes a nice temporary retreat on a hot day. Situated immediately to the north are graveyards for the mummies of other animals: baboons, now actually extinct in Egypt, though they can still be found in the Sudan; and ibis (three species were known to the ancients, identified by modern experts as Sacred, Bald and Glossy), now extremely rare, though the name is often given locally to the cattle egret.

Just south of the Zoser complex, beyond the pyramid of Unas, is the recently discovered (1950) unfinished **Step Pyramid of Sekhemkhet** , Zoser's successor (2649–2643 BC), overlooking an area where there has been a great deal of archaeological activity. Here in 1975, while looking for the tomb of Maya, an official of Tutankhamun, the Egypt Exploration Society discovered a tomb prepared for Horemheb, Tutankhamun's general, who would become a pharaoh himself (1343–1315 BC). Eleven years later, Maya's tomb was finally found, but not before an enormous amount from other burials had been revealed.

Further south, accessible on foot, by donkey, horse, or camel (which can be rented at the rest house) or by a vehicle with four-wheel drive, are the **pyramid complex of Pepi I** (2332–2283 BC); the **pyramid complex of Djedkare Isesi** (2414–2375 BC) with the pyramid of a queen nearby; the **tomb of Shepseskaf** (2504–2500 BC); the **pyramid complex of Pepi II** (2278–2184 BC); and three other pyramids, one belonging to Userkare Khendjer (*circa* 1747 BC).

In the Saqqarah area alone, in fact, no fewer than 15 royal pyramids have been excavated, creating a zone more than 5 km (3 miles) long. And what has been discovered thus far is only a tiny fraction of what lies still buried under the sands

BELOW: entrance to the funerary complex of Zoser at Saqqarah.

which must cover innumerable unknown tombs, including – somewhere – that of Imhotep, the great architect.

The relationship of all these monuments to Memphis is made clear by the fact that "Memphis" is derived from one of them: the pyramid of Pepi I, which was called *Men-Nefer*, "Established and Beautiful". But the Saqqarah monuments themselves are only part of the Memphite necropolis as a whole, which extends north along the desert plateau beyond Giza to Abu Ruwash and southward to Dahshur and Mazghunah, a total distance of about 33 km (20 miles).

Map, page 178

Pyramids of Dahshur

The peace and quiet beauty of the agricultural countryside around **Dahshur** ❸ have attracted many of Cairo's professional class, who have built rural retreats here. The most pleasant time of year to visit the site (open daily 7.30am–4pm winter, till 5pm summer; admission charge), until recently off-limits for foreigners because of a local military base, is mid-winter, when a lake forms within an artificial embankment below the **Black Pyramid**. This pyramid was built of brick but unused by Amenemhet III (1842–1797 BC), one of Egypt's most colourful kings. Amenemhet's pyramid and temple complex of **Hawarah** on the edge of the Fayyum was visited by Herodotus, who described it as a wonder greater than the pyramids of Giza; and his building of another smaller pyramid here seems to have been a gesture, not uncommon, towards the old capital's prestige. The dark colour that gives it its name arises from the fact that it has been systematically stripped of its original white limestone covering. The view of it across the lake is one of the most charming in Egypt, worth the 5-km (3-mile) drive from Saqqarah. Its inscribed capstone is in the Egyptian Museum.

BELOW: emerging from a pyramid.

There are two other 12th-Dynasty pyramids here, another from the 13th Dynasty, and a third not yet identified. Most striking, however, are two 4th-Dynasty pyramids, built by Snefru (2613–2589 BC). The southernmost of the two is the third largest pyramid in Egypt and is easily distinguished, standing about 274 metres further into the desert beyond the Pyramid of Amenemhet III, not only by its bulk, but by its shape, which has led to it being called the **Bent Pyramid**: the 54-degree slope of its sides changes halfway up to an angle of 43 degrees, for reasons that may have to do with religious symbolism.

Visible a mile and a half away almost directly north is its companion, sometimes called the **Red Pyramid**, which uses a 43-degree angle throughout its height. It is the earliest known to have been completed as a "true" pyramid, built less than 60 years after Imhotep's great discovery.

The Bent Pyramid made internal use of cedar trunks imported from Lebanon, still intact, as beams, and is externally the best-preserved of all the pyramids, thanks to an ingenious construction method that made stripping its surface difficult. About 600 metres northwest of the Bent Pyramid, between it and the Red Pyramid, are the remains of Snefru's mortuary temple, rededicated to him during the Middle Kingdom and under the Ptolemies. Snefru was the father of Khufu (2589–2566 BC), better known by the Greek form of his name as Cheops, builder of the **Great Pyramid** at Giza.

BELOW: for a room with a view, stay at the luxurious Mena House Oberoi.

Khufu's own immediate successor, Djedefre (in power 2566–2556 BC) constructed a pyramid at **Abu Ruwash**, 10 km (6 miles) northwest of Giza, which marks the northernmost limit of the Memphite necropolis; and 5 km (3 miles) south of Dahshur, at **Mazghunah**, are two ruined pyramids possibly marking its southernmost limit.

Pyramids of Giza

The **Pyramids of Giza** ❹ (called *al-Ahram* in Arabic), the only survivors among the Seven Wonders of the World, are not hard to find. Standing at the end of a boulevard (Shari' al-Ahram) on the desert plateau above the western edge of Giza, across the river from Cairo, they can most usefully be seen in combination with a visit either to the sites of Saqqarah or to the modern villages of Kirdassah and Harraniyyah.

Kirdassah, situated at the end of an old caravan route to Libya, 5 km (3 miles) north of Shari' al-Ahram, formerly supplied goods for desert traders and has become a centre for weaving, textiles and ready-made clothing, including the typical flowing *gallabiyas*.

Harraniyyah ❺, 5 km (3 miles) south of Shari' al-Ahram on the road to Saqqarah, houses the famous **Wissa Wassef tapestry workshops** (open daily, 10am–6pm summer, 9.30am–5pm winter; admission free) in a group of buildings that have won international acclaim for their architecture. The workshops export tapestries worldwide, usually made to order, though there is always a good selection on view. Half a mile or so farther down the same road, an outstanding collection of modern Egyptian painting and sculpture is visible at the **Aida Gallery**, which holds special exhibitions throughout the winter.

At the foot of the Pyramids, on the road leading up to them from Shari' al-Ahram, is the **Mena House Oberoi Hotel**, one of the most celebrated hotels in the world. Connected by a tramline to Cairo in 1900 shortly after its opening, it soon rivalled the famous Shepheard's, entertaining statesmen at three historic international conferences, the latest in 1978. Its lavish neo-Islamic decor has been carefully preserved by its new managers.

Map,
page 183

TIP

The Pyramids is a favourite place for hiring a camel or horse. Though most people take only a short ride (overpriced but fun), you can arrange a highly enjoyable day's trek to Saqqarah and back via the Zawiyet al-Aryan pyramids, complete with picnic. Negotiate with the cameleers and horsemen directly.

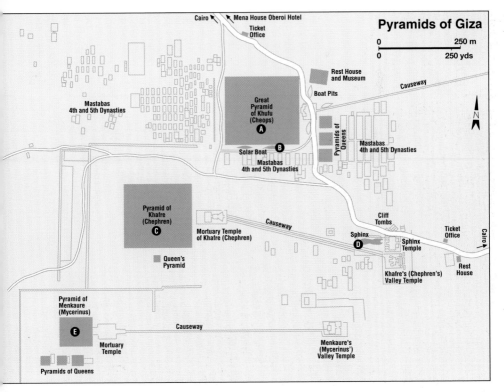

Pyramids of Giza

Cairo — Mena House Oberoi Hotel
Ticket Office

0 ——— 250 m
0 ——— 250 yds

Rest House and Museum
Boat Pits
Causeway

Mastabas 4th and 5th Dynasties

Great Pyramid of Khufu (Cheops) **A**

Pyramids of Queens

Mastabas 4th and 5th Dynasties

Solar Boat **B**

Mastabas 4th and 5th Dynasties

N

Pyramid of Khafre (Chephren) **C**

Mortuary Temple of Khafre (Chephren)

Causeway

Cliff Tombs

Ticket Office

Sphinx **D**

Sphinx Temple

Cairo

Queen's Pyramid

Khafre's (Chephren's) Valley Temple

Rest House

Pyramid of Menkaure (Mycerinus)

Causeway

E

Mortuary Temple

Menkaure's (Mycerinus') Valley Temple

Pyramids of Queens

The most striking thing about the Giza pyramids is their size. The **Great Pyramid of Khufu** was originally 150 metres (480 ft) high and incorporates 2.3 million stone blocks averaging more than 2½ tons in weight. Contrary to popular belief, however, it is neither the biggest pyramid in the world – that distinction belongs, according to the *Guinness Book of Records*, to the Quetzalcoatl Pyramid at Cholula, south of Mexico City, which covers an area more than three times as extensive – nor was it built by slaves. Teams of skilled labourers on three-month hire were supplemented by a permanent workforce of local quarrymen. Other crews cut limestone and granite construction blocks at Tura and Aswan and transported them across or down the Nile to the site. There was housing for 4,000, suggesting large and permanent administrative and support staffs.

Pyramid power

Stripped of their smooth white Tura limestone upper casing and extensively quarried lower down for granite from the 11th century onward, the sides of the **Great Pyramid Ⓐ** slope at an angle of 52 degrees, the normal gradient for all the pyramids built after Snefru's Bent and Red pyramids at Dahshur.

Except for their size, the isolated silhouettes of all the later large pyramids in Egypt would therefore have looked exactly like the Great Pyramid. Each, however, would also have stood within an enclosed complex, like Zoser's at Saqqarah, and would have been further particularised not only by inscriptions, but also by a cap that was possibly either painted or gilded.

The interior of the Great Pyramid (separate ticket; open 8.30am–4pm) can be visited and includes a grand gallery with a corbelled roof that is itself regarded as one of the most remarkable architectural works of the Old Kingdom. East of

TIP

Every evening the Pyramids hosts three performances of a sound and light show, in which an actorly voice relates their history in one of seven different languages. An English-language performance is held everyday except Sunday. For a timetable, consult the Tourist Office or ask at your hotel.

BELOW: The pyramids of Khufu and Khafre at Giza.

the Great Pyramid is the site of Khufu's mortuary temple, identified by the remains of a basalt pavement, north and south of which are two boat pits. Near its base are two more pits, one of which was excavated in 1954, when a complete dismantled river barge was found, probably secreted there in connection with the sun cult. Beautifully reassembled, the cedar-wood vessel can be admired in the **Solar Boat Museum** ❸ (open 9am–4pm; admission charge).

The causeway leading from the Great Pyramid's mortuary temple to its valley temple is largely ruinous and cannot be excavated at its lower end, thanks to the encroachment of modern buildings. But just south of it, close to a group of three subsidiary pyramids, the only undisturbed tomb thus far found of the Old Kingdom was uncovered in 1925. Although the sarcophagus in it was empty, it was identified as the **tomb of Queen Hetepheres**, wife of Snefru and mother of Khufu, and yielded extraordinary objects, including a carrying-chair and a portable boudoir, with linen curtains as well as a gilt bed and chair.

The Sphinx

The pyramid of **Khafre** ❻ (Chephren 2589–2566 BC), just south of the Great Pyramid and second to it in size, not only preserves a considerable part of its limestone casing at the top, but is also the most complete in relation to its surrounding complex, which includes the **Sphinx** ❼. Intended originally to represent a guardian deity in the shape of a lion, the Sphinx had Khafre's face. It is disfigured and beardless, it is said, thanks to Mamluk artillery practice. Later associated with the sun god and with Horus of the Horizon, as a Greek drinking song scratched on one of its toes during the Ptolemaic period attests, it was apparently the object of pilgrimages, especially during the 18th Dynasty. In front

Map, page 183

Inside the Solar Boat Museum. Blocks covering the boat pit bore the name of Redjedef (son of Khufu)

BELOW: the Sphinx.

Corner of the Pharaonic Village on Jacob Island, where actors and actresses recreate the lives and times of the pharaohs. The village also hosts a "Pharaonic Night" featuring dance performances.

BELOW: a passing greeting.

of it stands a granite stele set up by order of Tuthmosis IV (1423–1417 BC), who records a dream he had while still a prince: while he was resting under its shade during a hunting expedition, the Sphinx appeared to him and spoke, promising Tuthmosis the kingdom if he would clear away accumulated sand from around its feet. The story has circulated for many centuries since as a folk tale involving later rulers: in one malicious 20th-century version the hero is Gamal Abdel Nasser and the boon the Sphinx asks for is an exit visa.

And baby makes three

The third of the royal pyramids at Giza was begun by **Menkaure** ❸ (Mycerinus, 2532–2504 BC), Khafre's successor. By far the smallest, it was apparently left unfinished at Menkaure's death and hurriedly completed by his son, Shepseskaf, whose own tomb at Saqqarah has already been mentioned. There are signs of haste through the complex, even in the pyramid itself, which may have been intended originally to be encased entirely in red granite. Brick was used to finish off the mortuary temple, causeway and valley temple, though they had been begun in limestone and some of the blocks weigh 200 tons, showing that the failure to complete it in limestone was by no means due to a decline in technical mastery.

Imitating the past

A fun diversion on the way back into Cairo from Giza is the **Pharaonic Village** (open July to September 9am–11pm, rest of the year 9am–5pm), on Jacob Island 5 km (3 miles) south of central Cairo. Actors and actresses recreate the time of the pharaohs, its daily activities, religious rites, etc. It contains a replica of Tutankhamun's tomb with its treasures.

Heliopolis: City of the Sun

Clustered around Giza's three great pyramids are scores of lesser tombs, originally laid out in orderly rows along the same north-south axis as the tombs of the pharaohs. It seems clear that all the tombs at Giza, including the three great pyramids, were connected not only with Memphis but with the royal cult of Ra, the universal sun god, centred at On, the city the Greeks called **Heliopolis ❻** (City of the Sun). Heliopolis stood 25 km (15 miles) northeast of Giza and thus 32 km (20 miles) almost directly north of Memphis, on the opposite side of the Nile, in the modern district of Al Matariyyah. The primary theological centre of Old Kingdom Egypt, it was finally displaced in importance by Thebes, but not before its priests had developed elaborate rituals, liturgies and mythologies that revolve around the sun god Ra and a host of lesser deities known as the Great Company. Ramesses III (1182–1151 BC) is recorded as endowing Heliopolis with some 12,000 serfs and over 100 towns, not to mention statues, gold, silver, linens, precious stones, birds, incense, cattle and fruit.

Even in ancient times, Heliopolis had begun to suffer a decline that led to systematic pillaging. Strabo, visiting in 24 BC, recorded its desolation and 14 years later a pair of obelisks erected by Tuthmosis III (1504–1450 BC) were removed by the Romans to adorn their new Caesarium, the temple of Julius Caesar in Alexandria. Some 19 centuries later, during the reign of Khedive Ismail, these two monuments found their way out of Egypt and became the "Cleopatra's Needles" of London and New York, which have nothing to do with any of several Cleopatras. Only one obelisk, from a pair erected in the reign of Senusert I (1971–1928 BC), survives on the site. Otherwise there is virtually nothing left of ancient Heliopolis. It is unconnected with the modern suburb of that name. ❏

Map, page 178

BELOW: riding high.

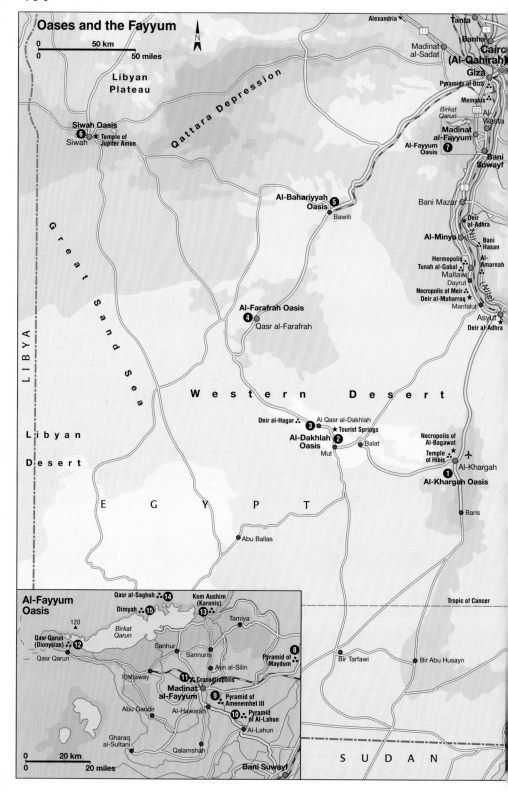

Oases and the Fayyum

THE OASES AND THE FAYYUM

Since at least 5000 BC man has been exploiting nature's gifts in this curve of oasis in Egypt's Western Desert, the most remote of which retains its distinct culture and language

Map, page 190

The very word "Oasis" conjures a string of images – swirling sands, blue-veiled Tuaregs, mirages, the thirsty caravan stumbling into a pool of sweet water set amid swaying palms. Little of this vision has any foundation in modern reality: the caravans have all but vanished, banditry has been suppressed, and the Bedu have traded in their camels for Toyotas. Not even the vestiges of modern man, however, in the form of asphalt, high-tension wires and water pumps, are capable of concealing the truths of a harsh climate, where shifting sands can block roads for days and where the foolhardy can still meet death by thirst, exposure or the sting of a scorpion. Nor have 20th-century wonders obscured the essential miracle of water, gushing hot or cold from barren rock to irrigate acres of garden in the midst of a wasteland.

From the Nile, the Sahara stretches 5,000 km (3,000 miles) westward to the Atlantic. The world's greatest expanse of desert is broken only by dots of green, where human habitation has survived the spread of sands. Contrary to popular imagination, which sees verdure sprouting incongruously from dunes, oases generally lie in rocky lands where wind and time have scratched out vast depressions whose depths allow natural underground aquifers to reach the surface.

In Egypt's Western Desert a single aquifer flows north from Sudan, running in an arc of five oases parallel to the Nile. Prehistoric remains show that man has been exploiting nature's gift since at least 5000 BC. Under the pharaohs the four Nileward oases – Al-Khargah, Al-Dakhlah, Al-Farafrah and Al-Bahariyyah – formed a useful line of defence against Libyan tribes.

Why camels were crucial

The camel, the only beast capable of five days' march without water, was introduced by invading Persians in the 6th century BC and provided the oases with their first great leap forward, matched in importance only recently with the introduction of electricity and the car. The camel helped to revive the desert economy. The new beast was no help to the Persian emperor Cambyses, however, when he dispatched his army from Khargah across the desert to Siwah in 525 BC. According to Herodotus, all 50,000 men were buried in a sandstorm.

The Ptolemies, who administered the country like a vast estate, set about improving desert agriculture. Archaeological remains show that cultivation grew to its furthest extent under their rule; new wells were dug with Alexandrian technology and the complex systems of water distribution that still persist were brought into use. Roman conquest led to a reversal of fortunes. The internal unrest of the late Roman period saw banditry increase at the expense of sedentary agriculture, while persecutions forced Christians into desert refuge, as the

PRECEDING PAGES: Siwah Oasis. **BELOW:** a well-watered region.

many Christian remains in the oases testify. Wells that had been regularly repaired and cleaned were allowed to dry up, as a general decline in population, lasting up to the present century, set in.

Although the date of the last Christian conversions to Islam is not known – the present inhabitants of the oases being solidly Muslim – it is likely that the new religion, so well suited to desert ways, made easy headway in the oases. The charm, generosity and peaceability of the inhabitants owe much to Islam. In a landscape seemingly touched by God – abundance amid waste – a touching humility of outlook is so appropriate as to seem unsurprising.

Al-Khargah (The Outer) ❶ is the most frequented of Egypt's oases, by virtue of its proximity to the Nile and because it is the seat of the New Valley Governorate. Five kilometres (3 miles) north of Asyut, a fine paved road leads past a new industrial complex up into the desert. Two hundred kilometres (120 miles) of barren gravel later, the road descends suddenly down a magnificent cliff into the **Khargah Depression**, which extends southwards, narrowing at its extremity, for 100 km (60 miles).

As one crosses the flat bottom of the depression, a few straggly trees appear on the roadside, inauspiciously announcing the beginning of cultivation. Then Nasserite housing blocks begin to sprout, marking the entrance to Al-Khargah town. Visitors to the oases should not be too disappointed by this; it is merely an administrative centre and a showpiece of the New Valley project, initiated by Abdel Nasser in the later 1950s. The project, the aim of which was to use the vast potential of the oases' waters for land reclamation and new settlement, has met with notable success. Much of Khargah's population consists of resettled Upper Egyptians; and the new hotels, duck farms and packaging industries point

TIP

Al-Khargah is served by twice-weekly flights from Cairo and Luxor, but most travellers prefer the overland route. Since the advent of paved roads, this is no longer the hazardous journey it once was.

BELOW: Coptic cemeteries at Al-Bagawat in Al-Khargah Oasis.

to a fair degree of prosperity. However, with the exception of its old market, there is not much to see here.

Just northeast of the town, not far from the main road, lies a cluster of monuments. Chief among them is the **Temple of Hibis** (not officially open but it is possible to wander around), important as one of the few remnants of Persian rule. Built of local sandstone, it was begun under Cambyses' successor, Darius I, but not completed until the reign of Nectanebo II in the 4th century BC. The temple lies in a palm grove beyond the remains of a ceremonial pool and an avenue of sphinxes. The carving style within shows local influence, while the content of the reliefs – deities, the burial of Osiris, a winged Seth struggling with a serpent – follows a standard pattern.

At the edge of cultivation to the north of the temple lies the 7th-century Christian necropolis of **Al-Bagawat** (open daily 9am–5pm; admission charge), a huge area of mudbrick domes and vaults, some of which preserve decoration. A kilometre's hike across the sand leads to the ruins of a fortified monastery.

South of Al-Khargah town a paved road extends through a string of smaller oases, past some minor antiquities, to **Baris**, the village designed by renowned architect Hassan Fathi.

The silence begins to impress itself as you head towards Al-Dakhlah. The most arresting sight is a line of hills that resembles the pyramids of Giza.

Map, page 190

Dakhlah Oasis

With 12,000 hectares (30,000 acres) under cultivation and a population of 60,000, **Al-Dakhlah (The Inner)** ❷ is the largest of the oases. The New Valley project has more than doubled its size in recent years, but Al-Dakhlah retains

BELOW: pottery at Al-Dakhlah.

TIP

Al-Dakhlah is the only place in Egypt where visitors can still see *saqiyas* (huge buffalo-driven water-wheels constructed from palm timber and clay jars) being made.

more of its original charm than Al-Khargah, to which it is connected by a 200-km (120-mile) road and daily buses.

The first important village in the depression is **Balat**. Here a direct caravan route from Asyut had its terminus, and a hive of mudbrick dwellings testifies to medieval prosperity. Using only mud and straw, builders attained a sophistication in architecture that combines utility, beauty and harmony with natural surroundings. Balat was the seat of the oases' pharaonic governors; and a French expedition is currently excavating extensive remains northwest of the village.

Al-Dakhlah's current capital is at **Mut**, some 30 km (18 miles) further west. The town contains Al-Dakhlah's only hotels, as well as the police station where foreign visitors must register. Most necessities may be obtained here and there are a number of decent restaurants, but little to see – the old town's mudbrick citadel has been allowed to fall into ruins. Outside the town to the northwest are the **Tourist Springs**, which visitors are expected to admire. In fact many of the other springs – most in Al-Dakhlah are warm – are equally pleasant.

No trip to Al-Dakhlah would be complete, however, without a walk through its fields and gardens. The main field crop is wheat, while in the gardens grapevines vie for space with date palms, mulberry trees, figs and citrus.

Thirty kilometres (18 miles) beyond the Tourist Springs, the town of **Al-Qasr al-Dakhlah** ❸ perches on a mound between the desert and the fields. Like Balat, Al-Qasr is a honeycomb of little lanes that run between multi-storied mudbrick houses. Although cement is gaining ground, many locals still prefer the older material, since mudbrick walls retain heat at night and coolness in the day. Qasr has wonderful gardens, a fortress and a mosque dating from the Ayyabid era.

In the desert beyond Al-Qasr to the west are some well-preserved Hellenistic

BELOW: sheikh at Al-Dakhlah Oasis.

tombs, one with a brightly painted zodiac on the ceiling. Farther along the main road lie the ruins of the Roman temple at **Deir al-Hagar**. This 1st-century wreck is a picturesque landmark.

Al-Farafrah ❹ is the furthest of this group of oases from the Nile valley. Although it is also the smallest, with little over 1,000 hectares (2,500 acres) under cultivation, it has the greatest potential for land reclamation. Only recently has Farafrah been connected to the rest of Egypt by decent roads. One now leads south, past the isolated settlement of Abu Mungar and through a 200 km (120-mile) stretch, justifiably called the Sand Sea, to Al-Dakhlah. The other, a more travelled route, goes northeast, through 150 miles (250 km) of some of Egypt's most spectacular desert, to the Bahariyya Oases and then to Cairo.

Qasr al-Farafrah is the only town in Farafrah. It has a three-room rest house, one shop and a coffee house: note that food is not obtainable here. The village, many of its houses gaily painted by a talented local artist, clusters on the lee-ward side of a hill. Farafrah's beautiful gardens, famous for apples and apricots, lie on the windward side. A small natural bath-house at the gardens' edge is a good place for a scrub, while a Roman well within the gardens is of archaeological interest. At the bottom of the hill is a small lake stocked with river fish. The gentle *Farfuris* are not entirely accustomed to foreigners and prefer to avoid them, but visit the *Umda* (Mayor) and, as part of the desert hospitality, tea may be offered in his garden. The springs are a delightful place to swim, while wearing modest clothing.

The **Al-Bahariyyah Oases** ❺ are reached from Cairo by an excellent road that leads westward off the Fayyum desert road behind the Giza pyramids. About 320 rather dull kilometres (200 miles) later is a new settlement attached to

Map, page 190

BELOW: team spirit in Al-Bahariyyah Oasis.

Egypt's only iron mines. Not far beyond the mines the road descends into the **Bahariyyah Depression**. Here, near the town of **Bawiti**, archaeologists revealed, in 1999, the discovery of an enormous ancient Egyptian cemetery, thought to be the biggest ever uncovered. Excavation is in its early stages, but it is thought that there are as many as 10,000 mummies containing the bodies of wealthy members of the Graeco-Roman civilisation that dominated northern Egypt after the time of Alexander the Great. The tomb complex, dubbed the Valley of the Golden Mummies, is not open to the public.

Bawiti sits atop a rock outcrop. To the north, cliffs drop abruptly into a sea of palms. Bawiti's gardens, spread for 5 km (3 miles) along the base of this cliff, are among the most beautiful in all the oases. The view from the cliffs at the spring called 'Ayn Bishmu is breathtaking. Here the water emerges from a gorge to flow into the orchards. Within the gardens, land is so precious that there are few walkways and one must often paddle through the irrigation channels. Dates, olives, oranges, apricots, lemons, pomegranates and tiny apples grow in jungle-like proliferation, set in gardens fenced with mud walls and palm fronds.

Around Bawiti and its sister village of Al-Qasr are numerous ancient sites, not all accessible and not all interesting. More to the taste of tourists are likely to be the hot springs, which range in temperature up to a scalding 47°C (115°F). The waters vary in mineral content, but few things in life are more memorable than a moonlit bath under palm trees in the crisp air of the desert.

Siwah

The most mysterious, the most remote and, until recently, the least visited of Egypt's oases, **Siwah ❻** has been off-limits to tourists thanks to troubles along

The Bahariyyah cemetery was stumbled upon in 1996 when a donkey caught its leg in the opening to the graveyard. The discovery was kept secret until excavations were well under way and the site was secured against looters.

BELOW: following the herd.

the Libyan border, to which it is adjacent. At present, not even a visitor's permit is needed and foreigners can venture freely to the oasis. Daily buses now ply the tarmacked 300 km (190 miles) between Siwah and Marsa Matruh, while 10 years' heavy military presence have contributed to gradual Egyptianisation. Shops now cater to basic needs, and there's a large government-run hotel.

Map,
page 190

The most remote of the oases, Siwah is unique in Egypt in that it has a distinct culture and its own language, related to the Berber languages of North Africa. Unusual customs, such as homosexual marriages, have altogether died out, although the reclusive women of the oasis cling to traditional dress.

The oasis' main population centre is in **Siwah town**, to which the Siwis moved from the **fortress of Aghurmi** in the earlier part of this century. On the rock of Aghurmi, 4 km (2 miles) from the centre, sit the remains of the **Temple of Jupiter-Amun**, home of the famous oracle that confirmed Alexander the Great in his status as a god.

The other major historical site is at **Gabal al-Mawta** (open 9am–2pm; Fri 9am–noon; no official entrance fee but *baksheesh* (a tip) is expected), less than 1 km (half a mile) north of Siwah town. Here tombs have been cut out of the rock of a conical ridge. Paintings cover some of the walls, especially in the tomb of Si-Amun, but much was destroyed when the tombs were used as shelters during the Italian air raids of World War II.

The most impressive sight in the oasis, however, is undoubtedly its agriculture. Siwah is the major producer of dates in Egypt. Some 250,000 palms fill the cultivated area and their production is prized as the finest in the country. Olives also grow in abundance, as well as other fruits and vegetables. Among the groves lie numerous springs, such as the **'Ayn al-Gubah**, the ancient **Well of the Sun**,

I came upon a little single path... and presently, to my delight... we found ourselves by midday at the first bushes of the Siwah Oasis.

— WILFRID SCAWEN
BLUNT 1897

BELOW:
rice growing close to Bani Suwayf, near the Fayyum.

whose waters were said to have purifying properties. Indeed, the water is so plentiful that large salty lakes have formed and drainage is a major problem.

Al-Fayyum

Sprouting from the west bank of the Nile like a tender leaf, **Al-Fayyum** ❼ is referred to by some as Egypt's largest oasis. Others deny that it is an oasis at all, fed as it is by the **Bahr Yusef**, an ancient canal flowing from the Nile.

In prehistoric times the Fayyum was a marshy depression that collected the Nile's overflow in flood season. Its wetlands were a favourite hunting ground of the Old and Middle Kingdom pharaohs until the 12th Dynasty's Amenemhet I (1991–1962 BC) drained the swamps, building a regulator at Al-Lahun, the point where the river periodically breached its banks, and allowing a permanent reservoir to form, Lake Moeris to the Greeks, now called **Birkat Qarun**.

With this lake at the depression's northern end stabilised, agriculture could be introduced; and the Fayyum began to flourish. It received a further boost under the Ptolemies, who reclaimed more than 1,200 sq. km (450 sq. miles) of fertile land, reducing the lake to about twice its present size. Improved agricultural methods were introduced and new-fangled Greek hydraulics – waterwheels of a unique type still in use today – permitted extensive terracing.

The Fayyum, then, was an early and highly successful effort at land reclamation. Further improvements in the 19th century turned it into the "Garden of Egypt". This century has unfortunately brought with it the twin evils of overpopulation and salinisation. Lake Qarun now measures only 40 by 9 km (24 by 5 miles) and is as salty as the Mediterranean, while the population surge has turned Madinat al-Fayyum, the capital city (*see page 199*), into a slum.

Dates flourish in the Fayyum. Palm trees must be pollinated by hand in spring. The female is only susceptible to pollination for two weeks a year.

BELOW:
on Birkat Qarun.

Map, page 190

An excellent road connects the Fayyum to Cairo (two hours away) across the desert, leaving Cairo from behind the Giza pyramids, but the road along the Nile to Upper Egypt is more attractive. Forty-eight kilometres (30 miles) south of Cairo's edge the road draws parallel to the **Pyramid of Maydum** ❽ (open daily 8am–4pm; admission charge,) a huge two-stepped tower silhouetted on the western horizon. A signposted turnoff leads to the pyramid. Dating from the end of the 3rd Dynasty, Maydum represents the transition from the Saqqarah-type step pyramid to the "true" pyramidal forms of Giza. Its present shape resulted from the collapse of the smooth outer casing; some call it the Collapsed Pyramid.

Continuing southwest for 16 km (10 miles) across the desert the road leads over train tracks and along the edge of an army camp. Eventually it forks: the road to the right enters cultivation and ultimately goes to Madinat al-Fayyum; the road to the left goes on towards the **pyramid complex of Amenemhet III** ❾ (1832–1797 BC) at Al-Hawarah (open daily 7am–5pm; admission charge). Having lost its outer casing of limestone, Amenemhet III's pyramid survives as a huge pile of mudbrick. It is easily climbed and the view from its top is superb. Below the pyramid are a number of ruinous tombs and very patchy remains of a mortuary temple. This was the great Labyrinth, which received a rave review from that globe-trotting Greek of the 5th century BC, Herodotus.

Southwest of Hawarah the road crosses a canal to reach the main Fayyum-Bani Suwayf road. Eight kilometres (5 miles) to the left, on a peninsula of desert, stands the 12th-Dynasty **Pyramid of Al-Lahun** ❿ (open daily 7am–4pm; admission charge), the southernmost in the Fayyum pyramid field.

Turning right we reach **Madinat al-Fayyum** after 10 km (6 miles).This town of half a million is the site of ancient **Crocodilopolis** ⓫ and the hub of Fayyum province. Strung out along the Bahr Yusef, it has lost most of its evidently considerable former charm. In the central square a fine example of the Fayyum water-wheel groans away, bemoaning its fate. The main *suq*, its lanes cluttered with wares, has a rustic simplicity.

Lake Qarun

Lake Qarun itself is the Fayyum's greatest tourist attraction. It has an aura of mystery, especially at dusk on a windless day, when the pale sky and stripe of sand on the far side melt into their own reflection. Beaches at its eastern end, where the hotels and an excellent fish restaurant on a pier are located, fill up with Cairenes on holidays. The western end, approached through the villages of **Sanhur** and **Ibshaway**, is more peaceful. The Ptolemaic **temple at Qasr Qarun** ⓬ (open daily 7am–4pm; admission charge) is the site of ancient Dionysias.

Past the eastern tip of the lake, easily accessible from the road to Cairo, is **Kom Aushim** ⓭, ancient Karanis, Egypt's best-preserved Roman city. The site contains the ruins of domestic architecture, two temples and a small museum (closed Mon). Guides can be found here to accompany you into the desert north of Lake Qarun, where the Middle Kingdom temple of **Qasr al-Saghah** ⓮ stands on a rocky hill commanding an exquisite view of the Fayyum. They will also show you **Dimyah** ⓯, 20 minutes' drive away; it was once a caravan town for traders from the Nile Valley and the Western Desert. ❑

TIP

A four-wheel-drive vehicle is essential to get to the Middle Kingdom temple of Qasr al-Saghah and the old caravan town of Dimyah.

BELOW: the long trail home.

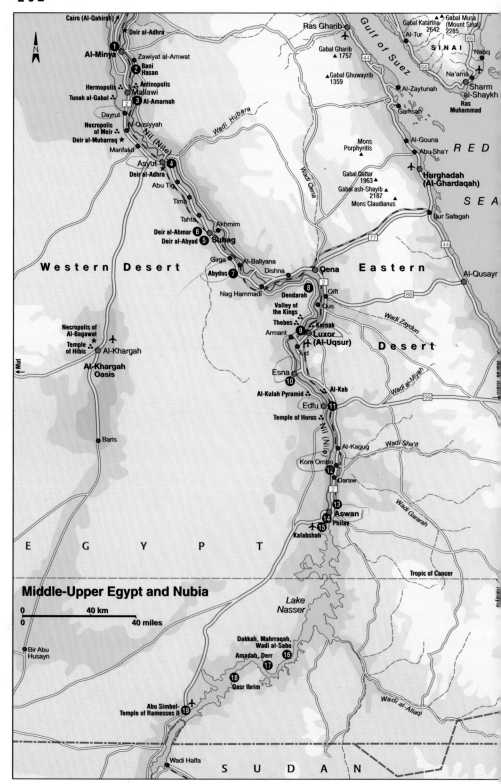

N

Cairo (Al-Qahirah)
Deir al-Adhra
Al-Minya ①
Zawiyat al-Amwat
Bani Hasan ②
Hermopolis
Antinopolis
Tunah al-Gabal
Mallawi ③
Al-Amarnah
Dayrut
Necropolis of Meir
Al-Qusiyyah
Deir al-Muharraq ★
Manfalut
Asyut ④
Deir al-Adhra
Abu Tig
Tima
Tahta
Akhmim
Deir al-Ahmar ⑥
Deir al-Abyad ⑤ **Suhag**
Girga
Al-Ballyana
Abydos ⑦
Dishna
Nag Hammadi
Dendarah ⑧ Qift
Qus
Valley of the Kings
Thebes
Karnak
Luxor (Al-Uqsur) ⑨
Armant
Tud
Esna ⑩
Al-Kab
Al-Kulah Pyramid
Edfu ⑪
Temple of Horus
Al-Kagug
Kom Ombo ⑫
Daraw
⑬
Aswan ⑭
Philae
⑮
Kalabshah

Necropolis of Al-Bagawat
Temple of Hibis
Al-Khargah
Al-Khargah Oasis
Baris

Ras Gharib
Gabal Gharib ▲ 1757
Gabal Ghuwayrib 1359
Al-Zaytunah
Garnsah
Mons Porphyritis ▲
Gabal Qattar 1963 ▲
Gabal ash-Shayib 2187 ▲
Mons Claudianus
Al-Gouna
Abu Sha'r
Hurghadah (Al-Ghardaqah)
Bur Safagah
Al-Qusayr

Gabal Katarina 2642 ▲
Gabal Musa (Mount Sinai) 2285 ▲
Al-Tur
SINAI
Nabq
Na'ama
Sharm al-Shaykh
Ras Muhammad

Gulf of Suez
RED SEA

Western Desert
Eastern Desert

Qena

Wadi Hubara
Wadi Qena
Wadi Zaydun
Wadi al-Miyah
Wadi Sha'it
Wadi Gararah
Wadi al-Allaqi

Nil (Nile)

Mut

E G Y P T

Tropic of Cancer

Middle-Upper Egypt and Nubia

| 0 | 40 km |
| 0 | 40 miles |

Lake Nasser

Bir Abu Husayn

Dakkah, Mahrraqah, Wadi al-Sabu ⑯
Amadah, Derr ⑰
Qasr Ibrim ⑱

Abu Simbel-Temple of Ramesses II ⑲

Wadi al-Allaqi

Wadi Halfa

S U D A N

MIDDLE EGYPT

A visit to Middle Egypt, a region little changed for thousands of years until the building of the Aswan dam, helps to explain the Middle Kingdom shift of power from Giza to the Valley of the Kings

Map,
page 202

For 19th-century visitors sailing along in their comfortable *dahabeyyahs* (sailing boats), the lush countryside south of Cairo offered a first taste of adventure. In recent years the trouble in Middle Egypt, with a series of attacks on tourists and government officials by militant Islamic fundamentalists, has meant that most visitors to Egypt now completely avoid the region and prefer to fly directly to Luxor, which in spite of the massacre at the Temple of Hatshepsut in 1997 is considered safer. Some tour groups and cruise boats are still travelling between Cairo and Upper Egypt, although usually under military escort. A visit to the less glamorous and less visited sites of Middle Egypt provides useful clues to understanding Egypt's long history.

The Middle Kingdom link

The Middle Kingdom tombs at Bani Hasan help to explain the shift away from the Old Kingdom pyramids at Giza and Saqqarah towards the tucked-away royal tombs in the Valley of the Kings in Luxor. Middle Egypt was also the playground for the most radical of all pharaohs, Akhenaten, who moved his capital Akhetaten from Luxor to Al-Amarnah, roughly halfway between the modern towns of Al-Minya and Asyut. It is difficult to believe that it was only 50 years later that Seti I built his magnificent temple complex at Abydos to confirm the restoration of the old regime that Akhenaten had tried to overthrow.

PRECEDING PAGES: a laden *felucca* catches the breeze. **BELOW:** Temple of Sethos, Abydos.

A changing landscape

Compared with the stretch of Nile between Luxor and Aswan, Middle Egypt is much less geared toward mass tourism, and accommodation is pretty basic, apart from a few slightly more upmarket hotels in Al-Minya.

The lives of the *fellaheen* (peasants) changed little for thousands of years until the building of the Aswan dam, which regulates the flow of the Nile and produces hydroelectricity. Before the arrival of electricity, the routines of the *fellaheen* were regulated by the annual rise and fall of the river, and the sowing and harvesting of crops, occasionally interrupted by a *mouled* (local saint's festival). Over the past 25 years, with electricity now reaching most villages, and money coming in from Egyptian labourers earning good pay in other Arab countries, families have become able to buy washing machines and televisions, and to set up small workshops with powertools, or at least to throw parties with strings of lights and amplified music.

Whereas before it was the sun and the Nile that dictated the pattern of the day, it is now often foreign or Egyptian soaps on television that make the *fellaheen* go home a bit earlier.

Copts account for about one-fifth of the population

in Middle Egypt. Until recently their peaceful cohabitation with the Muslim majority was held up almost as a model of Egyptian tolerance. But the population growth demanded building on precious agricultural lands, which in turn brought unemployment and other social problems. These were made worse by the return of Egyptians who had fought with the Mujadaheen in Afghanistan, and of Egyptian migrant workers from the Gulf states after the Gulf War.

Tensions between the two religions have been rising over the past few years and incidents are now rife. Copts and Muslims build new churches and mosques, trying to outdo each other's spires and minarets, which tower higher and higher above the landscape.

Danger spots for tourists

The University of Asyut has long been associated with the Islamic fundamentalist movement. President Sadat's attempt to suppress religious extremism led to a battle between security forces and Islamic groups which escalated to such a point that the president himself was assassinated in 1981. Over a million Egyptians returned home after losing their jobs because of Egypt's involvement in the Gulf War (most were employed in Iraq), and they have created an easy breeding ground for fundamentalist propaganda. In 1992 several groups, especially the Al-Gama'a al-Islamiya, became involved in acts of terrorism to achieve their goals, mainly to make Egypt an Islamic Republic and to deport all foreigners.

Tourists were the obvious target; in a country much dependent on income from tourism, attacks on tourist sites proved an effective way to destabilise the current government. Militants attacked night trains, buses and cruise boats, with some injuries and deaths to foreigners. Most of the attacks occurred in the area

BELOW: trading in cotton, one of Egypt's best-known exports.

around Asyut and Dayrut, which became a no-go area for tourists. Travel in the area remains uncertain. It is sometimes possible to travel unrestricted but it is also possible that a military escort will be provided and that foreigners will be turned away at road blocks at the slightest sign of trouble.

Map, page 202

Al-Minya

The provincial capital of **Al-Minya ❶**, 245 km (153 miles) south of Cairo, has an important university and some derelict colonial architecture from a time when Greek and Egyptian cotton barons did good business in the area. The town itself has no real sights, but a few decent hotels make it a good base for exploring the surrounding countryside and the sites of Tuna al-Gebel, Bani Hasan and Hermopolis Magna. Minya has a large Coptic population and, after several incidents of sectarian violence, security has been tightened.

Across the Nile on the east bank is Minya's vast and impressive cemetery, **Zawiyat al-Mayitin** (Corner of the Dead), with thousands of domes in the Muslim cemetery and just as many crosses in its Coptic counterpart. It is said to be one of the largest cemeteries in the world. Until recently, when a long-awaited bridge was built across the river, the dead were transported on *feluccas* to their final resting place.

Driving 21 km (12 miles) further north on the east bank brings the curious traveller to an extraordinary monastery, the **Deir al-Adhra** (Monastery of the Virgin), perched on top of a cliff and approached by 66 steps hewn into the rock. It is said to have been founded in 328 AD by St Helena, a dubious attribution, but one that corresponds in date at least with the archaeological evidence and the plan of the church. It was built on one of the places where the Holy Family

The mayor of Al-Minya was a fresh-faced, alert, twinkling Muslim in a dazzling loose snowy gown...He dined with us in the garden of the hospitable Coptic house...

– FREYA STARK

East is West, 1945

BELOW: mudbrick domes in Al-Minya's enormous cemetery.

TIP

Visitors to Bani Hasan
can ride up through
the clover fields on a
donkey to visit the
tombs. The view from
the terraces is
impressive.

is supposed to have rested while fleeing Palestine, and many miracles are ascribed to the picture of the Virgin that frequently weeps holy oil. Coptic pilgrims flock here on the feast of the Virgin every 22 August and make the precipitous ascent.

Bani Hasan

On the east bank of the Nile 18 km (11 miles) south of Minya, approached by a battered old ferry with a competent young man of about nine as a pilot, is the village of **Bani Hasan** ❷, above which 39 Middle Kingdom tombs have been cut in the cliffs (open daily 7am–5pm officially, but often closed after 3pm if there is no-one around; admission charge and *baksheesh* (a tip) for the guard who unlocks the tombs).

Powerful feudal lords, who ruled almost independently of the Middle Empire, were buried here. Twelve of the tombs are decorated with scenes similar to those at Saqqarah, but painted in fresco rather than carved in relief. Biographical accounts describing the military and administrative pursuits of the aristocratic owners are depicted, as well as occupations and trades such as hunting, fishing and dyeing cloth. Only the best tombs are open for the public, including the tomb of the governor Kheti I with interesting depictions of daily life in the Middle Kingdom; the beautiful tomb of Khnumhotep with vividly coloured scenes of his family life; and the tomb of Baqet, an 11th-Dynasty monarch, with a catalogue of 200 wrestling positions.

Sixteen kilometres (10 miles) further south is the site of the town of Antinopolis, founded by Hadrian in memory of his friend and favourite, the beautiful boy Antinous, who was drowned here, perhaps willingly, as a human sacrifice.

BELOW: river ride.

Map, page 202

At **Mallawi**, a few minutes further on, a road leads to the right, bending northwards through fields of sugar cane, where a little railway runs in and out to transport the crop to a smoky redbrick Victorian molasses factory nearby. The road passes through the village of Al-Ashmunayn, which partially covers the ruins of ancient **Hermopolis**, city of the moon god Thoth, the reckoner of time, and therefore equated by the Greeks with Hermes. Ancient Egyptians believed that this site was the primeval hill from where the sun god Ra emerged to create the world out of chaos.

It is worth taking the time to wander around the rather confusing overgrown hummocks, which are all that remains of this once flourishing provincial capital. The ruins of a huge temple of Thoth, two giant baboons and a church of the Virgin are about all that can be identified.

Across the fields on the edge of the desert, 7 km (4½ miles) west of Hermopolis, is the necropolis called **Tunah al-Gabal** (open daily 7am–5pm; admission charge) with some interesting graves, in particular that of a man named Petosiris, the decorations of whose family tomb provide a vital link between Egyptian and Greek art.

Petosiris belonged to a family of high priests of Thoth during the time that Alexander liberated the Egyptians from the hated Persians at the end of the 4th century BC. In the decoration of his fine tomb he chose to have the conventional offering scenes depicted in the fashionable new Greek style. Here the stiff virgins characteristic of the New Kingdom are replaced by a parade of buxom young matrons in fluttering see-through draperies, the men are wearing hitched-up *gallibiyas* and straw hats, not unlike the people visible on the roads of Middle and Upper Egypt today.

A baboon at Hermopolis. Baboons were sacred to the ibis-headed Thoth, god of scribes, learning and intellect and the reckoner of time.

BELOW: a close shave in Mallawi.

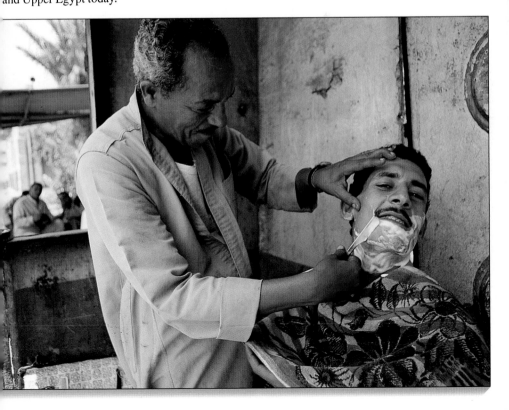

Al-Amarnah

Returning to the main road and heading south, another 10 km (6 miles) will bring the motorist to the turn-off for **Al-Amarnah** ❸ (open daily, 7am–5pm in summer; 7am–4pm in winter; admission charge), the open plain on the east bank of the Nile where Akhenaten and Nefertiti made their brief bid to escape from the stuffy and overbearing establishment at Thebes in the 14th century BC. Though their story is appealing, the hot dusty bowl of the Amarnah plain is rather a disappointment. Archaeologically, however, it has yielded a lot of information and some beautiful objects, including the famous head of Nefertiti. Since their time there has been no further building of any significance on the site, so that the original outlines are still discernible. A cheap local ferry brings tourists and Egyptians across, but for those who want a little more comfort there is a blue tourist ferry, for which tickets are sold at the tourist office on the east bank.

Head of the beautiful Nefertiti. Many such portrait heads were found in the workshop of an Al-Amarnah sculptor called Tuthmosis.

BELOW: the Northern Palace at Al-Amarnah.

Although the site isn't visited very often, or maybe because of that, the tourist office seems to have devised an extremely complicated admission price system. All visitors must pay to enter the site, then subsequent charges vary according to the size of the group and number of sites to be visited. A bus tour to the different monuments is the best way to get around as the city of Akhtetaten was spread out over a distance of 14 km (9 miles).

From what remains of buildings and frescoes, Akhtetaten seems to have been a bright and cheerful place reflecting the king's delight in his family and the everyday world. "Because Thou has risen," he says in his wonderful *Hymn to the Sun*, "all the beasts and cattle repose in their pastures; and the trees and green herbs put forth their leaves and flowers. The birds fly out of their nests; and their wings praise Thy Ka as they fly forth. The sheep and goats of every kind skip

about on their legs; and feathered fowl and birds also live, because Thou hast risen for them."

From the landing stage at Al-Till, a dirt track follows the original Royal Road which cuts straight to the centre of Akhtetaten. Remains of the Great Temple of Aten (now covered in Muslim tombs), the Archives where the famous Amarnah letters were found, and the Royal Palace, are discernible just south of Al-Till.

A pedestrian bridge, from where the royal couple waved at their subordinates, connected the Royal Palace with the State Palace across the Royal Road. The famous unfinished head of Nefertiti (now in Berlin) was found in a sculptor's workshop in the residential quarters, now mostly covered by sand.

Of the 19 southern tombs, about 8 km (5 miles) from the landing, that of Ay is undoubtedly the finest, with wall paintings depicting street and palace scenes, and Akhenaten and his wife presenting Ay with a golden collar. The tomb of Mahu, Akhenaten's chief of police, is the best-preserved on the site.

To the north, outlines of Nefertiti's Northern Palace and courtiers' villas can be traced. Incorporating reception rooms, bedrooms, bathrooms with basins and toilets, kitchens, and storerooms, the houses were surrounded by gardens with trees and pools. Air-conditioning was effected by wind catchers which faced the northerly breezes. These architectural details can be seen in paintings in the Egyptian Museum in Cairo. The seven northern tombs often show depictions of daily life in Akhtetaten, as well as the royal couple and their family.

Map, page 202

After Akhenaten's death, his successor, Tutankhaten (later to change his name to Tutankhamun) abandoned Akhtetaten for Memphis and Thebes and reinstated Amun-Ra as the chief god of Egypt. Akhtetaten quickly went into decline.

Asyut

A few miles further on, **Asyut ④**, the most important town in the region, stands on a bend in the river, 378 km (236 miles) south of Cairo. In the 19th century it marked the end of the Forty Days Road, and in its important market slaves from Sudan and the Libyan desert were sold.

Thanks to the cotton boom during the late 19th and early 20th centuries, its millionaires built themselves palatial villas and lived on a grand scale, with black-tie dinners and weekly races. Most of these families eventually moved north, however, and Asyut is now rather provincial, though it has a university, a huge cement plant and rug factories. A Presbyterian Mission has been established here for over 100 years and there are many Coptic churches and communities.

The large Coptic community takes care of several early monasteries further south. **Deir al-Adhra** (Monastery of the Virgin), 12km (7½ miles) south of Asyut, is believed to have sheltered the Holy Family, and attracts more than 50,000 pilgrims around Assumption Day in August. The **Deir al-Muharraq** (Burnt Monastery) is believed to be the southernmost point in Egypt where the Holy Family stayed.

South of the town of Suhag are two of Egypt's most visited monasteries: the **Deir al-Abyad ⑤** (White Monastery), founded in the 5th century by St Shenute, one of the fathers of Coptic Christianity, has many striking similarities with pharaonic temple design. The nearby **Deir al-Ahmar ⑥** (Red Monastery) was founded by one of Shenute's disciples, St Bishoi. Monasticism started in Egypt around AD 320, after

BELOW: grave of Merires I, Al-Amarnah.

Pachom from Esna founded the first community. He first served in the Roman army, which seems to have convinced him that his monks should be strictly disciplined and of service to the community. Shenute, at the end of the 4th century, went even further and introduced strict rules for every part of the monk's life. The monastery of Deir al-Abyad was once home to over 2,000 monks, but these days only three or four remain.

TIP

As there are no facilities or accommodation for tourists in the immediate vicinity of Abydos, it is usually seen on an all-day excursion from Luxor or is visited from cruise boats.

BELOW: Hall of Osiris, the Temple of Sethos, Abydos.

Abydos

Abydos 7 (open daily, 7am–6pm in summer; 7am–5pm winter; admission charge), 165 km (103 miles) north of Luxor, near Al-Ballyana, is one of Egypt's most spellbinding spots. The earliest-known tomb of a pharaoh, dating back to around 3150 BC, was discovered here in 1993, containing some of the oldest examples of hieroglyphic writing.

In the dawn of history, Wepwawet, the jackal deity and the original god of Abydos, roamed the desert's edge guarding the ancestral burial grounds below the dip in the western hills. At sunset the ancients imagined it to be the dusty golden staircase to the afterworld and they wished to be buried at its foot.

The Osiris legend

Later Abydos became closely associated with the legend of Osiris. The story relates how the just ruler Osiris was killed by his evil brother Seth. Isis, the weeping sister/wife, faithfully searched the banks of the Nile for his dismembered body, which she at length managed to reassemble. He revived sufficiently for their son Horus to be conceived. Thereafter the pieces of Osiris were buried at different places in both Upper and Lower Egypt, but his head was supposed to

have been buried at Abydos; and it was at Abydos that he was resurrected and assumed his powers as the lord and judge of the afterlife. His son Horus grew up and resumed the struggle with Seth.

Every January the great drama was re-enacted as a sort of miracle play, with a cast of thousands and crowds of pilgrims coming from all over Egypt to participate. A gold-plated image represented Osiris, the pharaoh himself took the part of Horus, and the priests and priestesses masqueraded as Wepwawet, Seth, Isis, Nephthys and supporting cast.

From the Middle Kingdom onwards, every pharaoh as well as hundreds of thousands of pilgrims left some token of their presence at Abydos, hoping to gain favour for themselves and their relatives with Osiris in his capacity as Judge of the Court of the Hereafter. The area is a mass of funeral stelae, burial grounds, former temples and memorials. But it was Seti I (1306–1290 BC) of the New Kingdom who was responsible for the most beautiful tribute to Osiris in his seven-sanctuaried **temple**.

Seti came to power in 1306 BC, just 29 years after the monotheistic regime of Akhenaten at Al-Amarnah, some miles to the north, had collapsed. The nation was still recovering from the shock of this apostasy, and Seti wished to reaffirm his faith in the traditional gods and restore them to their former pre-eminence. To this end he rallied all the resources of the land to build and adorn a new temple at Abydos, in which he recorded his devotion to Osiris and his wife Isis and son Horus, as well as to Amun-Ra, Ra-Hor-Akhty and Ptah. He also honoured his forebears by recording their names in a List of Kings, an assemblage of 76 cartouches which has been of immense importance to subsequent researchers and historians.

Map, page 202

The mortuary Temple of Seti (1318–1304 BC) was begun by Seti I and completed by Ramesses II. As well as being unusual for being L-shaped it contains many beautiful reliefs, their colours still visible, and the List of Kings tracing Seti's descent from King Menes.

BELOW: the Temple of Ramesses II at Abydos.

Exquisite reliefs on fine white limestone, which has sometimes taken on the shade of old ivory, show Seti engaged in performing a multitude of rites in honour of Osiris and the company of gods. Seti himself died before the temple was completed, leaving his son Ramesses II to finish the decoration of the courtyards and colonnades.

The cult of Osiris and Isis later moved south to the Cataract Region, but the annual festival of Abydos continued throughout Egyptian history, lingering for almost 400 years into the Christian era. It was the Christians themselves who finally sacked the temple in 395 AD, but mercifully they failed to spoil its essential beauty.

Vestiges of powerful magic still cling to the sacred precincts. Local women can be seen circling the pool of the mysterious building, probably the burial place of Osiris, called the **Osireion**; and quite recently an English mystic deeply versed in Egyptian history and religion spent the last 25 years of her life living at Abydos and working daily in the temple. She was known as Umm Seti, or the Mother of Seti.

Dendarah

The longer cruises visit the **Temple of Dendarah** ❽ (open daily: 7am–6pm; in summer; 7am–5pm in winter; admission charge), near **Qena**, on a bend in the river about halfway between Abydos and Luxor. Like those of Esna, Edfu, Kom Ombo and Philae, and others lost under Lake Nasser, the temple is about a thousand years younger than the New Kingdom temples, and its construction was initiated by the Ptolemies.

Dendarah is dedicated to Hathor, the cow goddess, known as "The Golden

BELOW: the Sacred Lake at the Temple of Dendarah.

One", goddess of women, who was also a sky and tree goddess, sometimes equated to Aphrodite by the Greeks and a great favourite with them. She was supposed to have had healing powers, and the sick journeyed here, as to Kom Ombo and Philae, to be cured.

Despite being damaged by the Christians, who chipped out the faces and limbs of many figures, Dendarah is one of the best-preserved of Egyptian temples and its adjunct structures can all be easily identified. It has retained its girdle wall, its Roman gate, two Birth Houses and a sacred lake, as well as its crypts, stairways, roof and chapels.

Its most immediately distinctive feature is its great hypostyle hall, with its 24 Hathor-headed columns and a ceiling showing the outstretched Nut, the sky-goddess, swallowing the sun at evening and giving birth at morning. The zodiac on the ceiling is the best-preserved in the whole of Egypt. The hall was decorated during the reign of Tiberius and is dated AD 34.

The dark courts and crypts in the interior give evidence of various festivals in which Hathor was involved. The most important of these feasts was the annual New Year Festival, during which the goddess was carried up the western staircase to the roof for the ritual known as the "Union with the Disc", returning down another staircase to the east. On the walls of the stairways the order of procession of the gods in full regalia is clearly shown. There are interesting graffiti on the roof, including names of Napoleon's soldiers. On the back of the temple is one of the very few contemporary representations of Cleopatra with Caesarion, her son by Julius Caesar. Beside the Birth House stand the ruins of one of the earliest structures of the Christian era, a basilica built in sandstone, with a beautifully carved niche inside. ❑

Map, page 202

As for Dendarah and Thebes… My eyes and mind yet ache with grandeur so little in unison with our own littleness…
– BENJAMIN DISRAELI

BELOW: head of the goddess Hathor at the Temple of Dendarah.

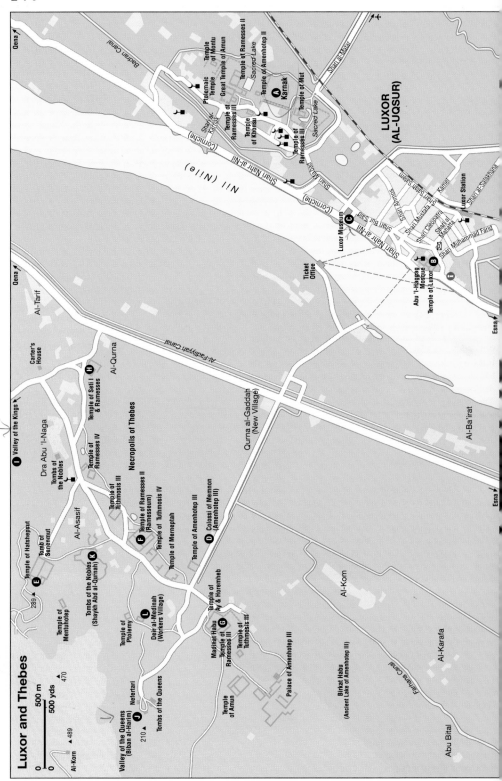

UPPER EGYPT

Map, page 202

The monuments of Upper Egypt are breathtaking. The great temples of Luxor and Karnak and the funerary complexes of the west bank form the largest agglomeration of ancient buildings in the world

During the 19th century, as more and more archaeological discoveries were being made and the mystery of hieroglyphics unravelled, wintering in Egypt became fashionable for the well-to-do. They would hire a private sailing house-boat, complete with crew and cook, at the port of Cairo, and proceed upstream, stopping here and there to explore the ruins and visit local dignitaries. Their impressions were conscientiously set down day by day in letters home or in morocco-bound diaries, as they sat under the awning on deck, glancing up to watch the palm-fringed shore slipping peacefully by.

A river trip between November and March is still the ideal way to visit the magnificent monuments of Upper Egypt. Sightseeing can be interspersed with delicious idleness. Most of the luxury cruise boats run three, five, or eight-day trips starting from Luxor or Aswan. Passengers fly or take the train to meet the boat and go straight on board. Facilities and services are comparable to those in the best hotels and most boats have well-trained guides speaking several languages. For the Egyptology buff, there are select tours led by university lecturers and archaeologists. True romantics can hire a *felucca* (the indigenous sailing boat with tall lateen rig) for the trip from Aswan to Luxor for a fraction of what tourist steamers charge, but these boats are more picturesque than comfortable.

PRECEDING PAGES: on the Road to Thebes, the West Bank, past the colossi of Memnon. **BELOW:** visiting the Valley of the Queens.

The practicalities

There are certain advantages, however, to seeing Upper Egypt by private car or by taxi. Out-of-the-way sites can be visited and alternative routes can be taken for the return trip, either through the Western Oases or over the mountains and up the Red Sea coast.

Whichever way the visitor may choose to travel and whatever his particular predilections, the monuments of Upper Egypt are breathtaking. They have to be seen to be believed. They also require a certain amount of study beforehand.

Sightseeing can be both exhilarating and exhausting, so be prepared. Comfortable shoes, not sandals – there are too many stones to stub the toes – a hat, sunglasses and a flashlight for dark corners are useful additions to light cotton clothes. Sweaters and wraps may be needed for evenings, which can be cold. Parties in the big hotels and cruise ships can be dressy and romantic, but not risqué – remember Egypt is a Muslim country.

Luxor

Luxor ❾, 675 km (420 miles) south of Cairo, is the most important and dramatic site in all Egypt. Al-Uqsur (the Palaces) is the Arabic name for Thebes, the capital city of the New Kingdom (1550–1070 BC), whose glory still glowed in the memories of classical writers a thousand years after its decline. Here the booty of foreign

wars, tribute and taxes poured into the coffers of the pharaohs of the 18th and 19th Dynasties, each of whom surpassed his predecessor in the construction of gorgeous temples and tombs, creating a concentration of monuments that rivals that of any imperial city before or since.

Amun, once just a local god, took on the qualities of Ra, the sun god of Heliopolis, when Thebes became the seat of power, becoming Amun-Ra and rising to a position of ascendancy over all the multifarious gods of Egypt. With his consort Mut and his son Khonsu he formed the Theban Triad.

Two tremendous temple complexes were established in honour of these gods, the temple of Karnak and the temple of Luxor. Both were built over extensive periods of time and were constructed from the inside outwards; the original founders built sanctuaries on spots that had probably been venerated for centuries, and successive pharaohs added progressively more grandiose courtyards, gateways and other elaborations.

Cosmic symbolism

Temples in general all followed the same principles. For the ancient Egyptians the precinct represented a little replica of the cosmos at the time of the creation. It was set apart from the everyday world and demarcated by a mudbrick girdle wall. Usually, but not always, the temple had an east-west axis, so that the rising or setting sun could strike right into its innermost recesses. Giant wedge-shaped pylons or gateways flanked tall gold-plated doors and were decorated on the outside with enormous reliefs of the pharaoh symbolically subduing his enemies and safeguarding the sacred place from malevolent forces.

Within the gates were courtyards, with small kiosks or barque-stations

BELOW: the ceremonial Avenue of Sphinxes at Karnak.

(storage places for the boats of Egyptian gods) for visiting gods. Other shrines appeared in later times, including the Birth Rooms in which the divine progeniture of the pharaoh was established. Before the entrance of the covered part of the temple stood enormous statues of the pharaoh in human or animal form and/or obelisks. Inside was a hypostyle hall, where giant columns, usually with vegetal bases and capitals shaped like papyrus reeds or lotus buds, clustered thickly together to represent the marsh of creation. The conception was completed by the ceiling overhead which was adorned with depictions of heavenly bodies, to recreate the sky. All was lavishly decorated.

In the outer parts of the temple, the reliefs record historical events: the foundation and dedication of the temple itself and details of processions and ceremonies. The pharaoh is very much in evidence, leading the activities. He always faces the interior, while the resident god or goddess, often shown together with a consort and attendant gods, faces the outside world.

Proceeding through a vestibule into the offering court and then the inner parts of the temple, the ground rises by degrees, the roof gets lower, the brilliant daylight is shut out, until the sanctuary, which represents the mound of creation, is quite dark. Only the pharaoh and the priests were allowed into this holy of holies, where a gold-plated image of the presiding god was kept.

From time to time the god would be brought out on his sacred barque from his seclusion, suitably dressed and perfumed, to receive offerings of bread and beer, or to pay visits to other gods. Probably the image could be made to move its hand or bow its head, and its movements were no doubt accompanied by mysterious sounds.

The rooms surrounding the sanctuary were used as the storerooms for cult

Map, page 216

The supporting columns of temples were often carved with reliefs while the capitals were brightly coloured in red, green, yellow and blue. See page 20 for an artist's impression.

BELOW: Karnak Temple and lake.

furniture, vestments, perfumes and incense, and as laboratories and as libraries. Some temples had crypts and secret passages and ducts under the floor.

Karnak

The temple complex of Amun-Ra at **Karnak ⓐ**, 3 km (1¾ miles) north of Luxor, (open daily; 6am–5pm in winter; 6am–6pm in summer; admission charge) and its concomitant accretions constitute the most overwhelming of all the Egyptian monuments. Apart from the immense conglomeration of elements that make up the temple itself, it also has the most complicated form in the country because, unlike most other temples in Egypt, it was developed both on an east-west axis, with six pylons, and on a north-south axis with four pylons. These 10 pylons, together with intervening courts, halls and enclosures, surround the nucleus of the sanctuary.

The vast precinct of the temple at Karnak covers an area of 25 hectares (60 acres) and contains 20 smaller temples.

Karnak, known as the "The Most Select of Places", was one of the most important religious and intellectual centres in antiquity, and for over 13 centuries successive pharaohs were proud to add their share to its magnificence. It would take weeks to explore the temple complex properly, but any visitor should try to put aside two half days to see the most important monuments, one starting early in the morning to be seduced by the temple's mystery, and one in the afternoon when the sun makes the stones glow and adds relief to the carvings on the walls. The local god Amun-Ra became more important during the early Middle Kingdom, and during the 12th Dynasty several temples were erected in his honour. Their foundations were found underneath the later temples.

The origins of the Karnak Temple as we now see it are attributable to the royal family of the 18th Dynasty, who made Amun-Ra the state god and whose rise to

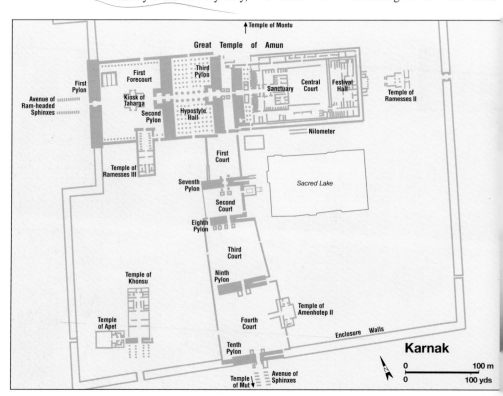

power brought the city of Thebes to the heights of glory. Three Tuthmoses and Hatshepsut, whose relationships are still not satisfactorily sorted out, were responsible for most of the inner parts of the temple. Hatshepsut dominated the family from the time of Tuthmosis I's death in 1492 BC. She was Tuthmosis III's unfavourite wife/aunt, however, and as soon as she was out of the way he proceeded to hack her name away from cartouches, substituting his own, and to wall up the chamber and the bases of the 320-ton obelisks that she had erected. Thus unwittingly he preserved her work in pristine condition. One of Hatshepsut's obelisks remains standing, but the second toppled over centuries ago. The top of the second obelisk has been placed near the **Sacred Lake**. The reliefs show Hatshepsut being crowned Pharaoh by the god Amun.

The third Tuthmosis (1479–1425 BC) proceeded to reign long and brilliantly, waging 17 successful campaigns and extending the Egyptian empire from Syria to the Sudan. He brought back thousands of prisoners and immense quantities of booty, as well as new varieties of trees and plants, new ideas and new fashions. The annals of his career are inscribed on the walls surrounding the **sanctuary** and extend to his great **Festival Hall** and to the southern courts.

Succeeding generations added new pylons, courts and subsidiary temples, all lavishly and colourfully illustrating their conquests, like a great stone history book. Amenhotep III contributed a pylon and the temple of Mut.

The complex was thus already enormous at the advent of the 19th Dynasty, when Seti I (1306–1290 BC) decided to complete the **Great Hypostyle Hall** with its 137 huge columns, covering an area of 6,000 sq metres (19,685 sq ft), started by Amenophis III. This mighty work, the largest hall of any temple in the world, was finally completed by Seti's son, Ramesses II (1290–1224 BC),

Maps, pages 216, 220

Monumental statue of Ramesses II with one of his daughters nestling at his feet.

BELOW: Hypostyle Hall of the Temple of Amun, Karnak.

The karnak sound and light show, which is one of the best in Egypt, is held three or four times a night. As at the Pyramids, performances are held in different languages, with English performed every night of the week. To get to Karnak in the evening, hire a taxi. Your driver will wait while you watch.

who placed the appropriate colossi of himself at the entrance. The northern walls are decorated with remarkable bas reliefs of Seti I's battles in Syria and Lebanon, while the southern walls show similar themes, in a much cruder style, of Ramesses II's Battle of Kadesh.

Though the capital moved away to the Delta and the importance of Thebes declined thereafter, Karnak continued to be expanded and embellished, such was the awe in which Amun-Ra was held. Ramesses III added a complete small temple and at the end of the Ramesside line the temple of Khonsu was built, in which reliefs clearly show the rise to kingly status of the priests.

In the 6th century the Persians did a certain amount of damage when they sacked Thebes, but the incoming Greeks set things to rights. Alexander, his brother Philip Arrhidaeus (who replaced the original sanctuary with one of rose-granite), and subsequently the Ptolemies restored and continued to make additions to the temple. The entrance pylon by which it is approached from the west today, and the enclosure of the first great court were their work.

The two daily performances of the sound and light show start off with a walk through the temple toward the seating area behind the Sacred Lake.

Luxor Temple

The **Luxor Temple** 🅑 (open daily 6am–9pm; admission charge) is relatively long (230 metres/780 ft) and narrow, and lies rather exposed in the centre of Luxor. Like the Karnak Temple, to which it was connected with a 3-km (1¼-mile) long processional Avenue of the Sphinxes, it was dedicated to the Theban triad, but Amun of Luxor had a slightly different form and function, as a divinely fertile figure. Known as the "Harem of the South", the Luxor Temple was the residence of Amun-Ra's consort Mut and her son Khonsu, while the statue of Amun was kept in Karnak. During the annual Opet-festival his statue was brought in a grand procession of holy barges to be reunited with his wife. Nowadays, during the annual *mouled* or festival of Abu ' l-Haggag (Luxor's patron saint, buried in the mosque which hangs above a corner of the court built by Ramesses II), one or more boats are still carried up from the river to the mosque, in a vague reminder of one of the most splendid Egyptian festivals.

The Temple of Luxor is easier to grasp than Karnak, as the major part was built by one pharaoh, Amenhotep III (1414–1397 BC), with substantial later additions by Tutankhamun (1333–1323 BC), Horemheb (1319–1307 BC), Ramesses II (1290–1224 BC), and Alexander the Great (332–323 BC).

The sanctuary area dates from the reign of Amenhotep III. In the Birth Room, his mother Mutemwia is shown being impregnated by Amun and giving birth to the infant pharaoh, whose body and spirit are formed on the potter's wheel by the ram-headed creator-god Khnum. The facts of life are indicated with delicate symbolism. The inner parts of the temple issue into an extensive peristyle court from which a tall processional colonnade with papyrus-bud columns leads northwards.

Amenhotep was succeeded by his son, the revolutionary pharaoh who took the name Akhenaten

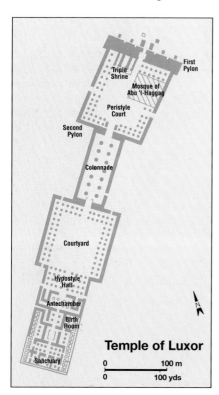

Temple of Luxor

First Pylon
Triple Shrine
Mosque of Abu 'l-Haggag
Peristyle Court
Second Pylon
Colonnade
Courtyard
Hypostyle Hall
Antechamber
Birth Room
Sanctuary

0   100 m
0   100 yds

(1353–1335 BC) and rejected all forms of religion except the worship of the Aten, symbolised by the sun disc, and moved the capital away from Thebes to Al-Amarnah. His reforms collapsed immediately after his death, however, and the capital returned to Thebes, the old hierarchy of priests was re-established, and his successors Tutankhamun and Horemheb dutifully took up the embellishment of the Luxor Temple again.

On the walls of the colonnade their skilful sculptors depicted the annual Opet festival, showing the gods of Karnak, accompanied by a cheerful procession of priests, musicians, singers, dancers and sacred cows, parading down to Luxor on the west, and going back to their own temple on the east. The great peristyle court, which today incorporates the medieval mosque, was added by Ramesses II, who redefined the structure in his usual Cecil B. de Mille style, with a gigantic pylon on which were displayed his triumphs. He also had vast colossi of himself erected within the gates.

The invading French and 19th-century diarists noted the glorious city of Thebes had shrunk to a miserable cluster of villas and squalid mudhuts on top of the metres of dirt and debris that cluttered the Luxor Temple. Only the heads of the colossi of Ramesses, half the granite obelisk of Amenhotep and the capitals of the columns were visible; and these were battered and blackened with smoke. Excavations of the site started in 1885 when houses were bit by bit removed, but the people of Luxor took a stand when it came to removing the mosque of Abu 'l-Haggag, whose annual festival is one of the largest in Egypt.

The riverside road called the **Corniche**, along which the cruise boats and the ferries to the west bank dock, runs parallel to the courts and colonnades of the Luxor Temple. Dilapidated old calashes clatter along the Corniche, the drivers

Map, page 222

Detail from a relief of the Opet festival on the colonnade.

BELOW: the medieval mosque of Abu 'l-Haggag stands above the excavated remains of Luxor Temple.

The Winter Palace Hotel captures a bygone era. Come here by calash (carriage) for afternoon tea on its terrace and views of the sun setting over the Nile.

BELOW: carving of dancers and musicians in Luxor Museum.

cracking their whips and vociferously soliciting business. The sound and smell of the horses and some of the old façades give Luxor a faintly raffish air. Shops, public buildings and big and often luxurious hotels, some old and venerable and others very up-to-date, are strung out along the riverfront. The rest of the town, including the lively bazaar, spreads east toward the station and further toward the airport.

Luxor Museum

The excellent **Luxor Museum** Ⓒ (open daily; 9am–1pm and 5–10pm in summer; 9am–1pm and 4–9pm in winter; admission charge and additional fee to visit the New Hall), further north along the Corniche, houses a small but fine collection of statues and funerary objects found in the area of Luxor. The objects have been carefully placed and lit, and are well-labelled, so that every single item looks like a masterpiece. Most of the ground floor is dedicated to the period of the New Kingdom, and works include a beautiful bust of the young pharaoh Tuthmosis III and a fine wall painting of Amenophis III.

The upper floor has some interesting reliefs from Akhenaton's temple in Karnak as well as some spectacular heads of the same pharaoh in the typical Amarnah style, and smaller objects found in Tutankhamun's tomb. Excavations in 1989 in Luxor Temple, near the Birth Room of Amenophis III, revealed an important cache of statues, now on show in the **New Hall**.

The west bank

The Nile valley is wide at Luxor and the mysteriously pink limestone mountains hovering to the west above the lush green plain are so honeycombed with

treasures and secrets, legends and curiosities, that the average day or two spent among them is not enough.

The west bank can be reached by local ferry which leaves from the landing opposite the Luxor Temple or near the Novotel further south. A slightly more expensive and less characterful tourist ferry also departs from another landing opposite the Mina Palace Hotel. Alternatively, a new bridge, a short distance south of Luxor town, connects the east and west banks for the first time and makes it easy to visit the west bank by taxi.

Tickets for all the sites can be purchased only from the ticket booth on the west bank landing of the tourist ferry or at the inspector's office behind the Colossi of Memnon. Most sites are open daily, 7am–5pm in winter and 7am–6pm in summer unless otherwise stated, and an admission charge is payable for every site. Plan an itinerary for the day and buy the right tickets, as they are not sold at the sites and it can be a long haul back to the ticket office.

An early start is recommended. For one thing the mornings are crisp and delicious, the ferries are less crowded, the donkeys are fresher, the bicycles have not been picked over, and the monuments themselves are better seen by oblique sunlight rather than direct vertical rays. Taking advantage of the cool crystalline air, one can savour the sounds and scents of the countryside.

The fringes of the desert hills lie about 4 km (2½ miles) to the west of the Nile across the plain; and here the great mortuary temples of the New Kingdom pharaohs are spread out over a shallow arc. The Valley of the Queens, the Tombs of the Nobles and the Workers' Village are in the foothills behind them. The road leading to the Valley of the Kings skirts the cliffs before climbing a rocky defile to the northwest.

Map, page 216

Then there were other days at Luxor... I liked getting away from the roads, into the region of country life... Everything there was slow, quiet and regular...
−VITA SACKVILLE-WEST
Passenger to Teheran,
1926

BELOW: a souvenir of Thebes.

One of the two Colossi of Memnon. The colossi are like sentinels beside the road to the tombs and temples in the west bank hills.

BELOW: the Temple of Hatshepsut, Deir al-Bahari, Luxor.

Mortuary temples

The innovative pharaohs of the 18th Dynasty broke with the pyramid tradition and began to have their tombs tunnelled deep into the mountainside, hoping that they would thus avoid the depredations of tomb robbers. On the edge of the valley, at some distance from their final resting places, each pharaoh constructed his individual mortuary temple.

The architecture and decoration of these temples follows essentially the same lines as those of the temples already described, except that in the sanctuary area there is a false door through which the *ka* or spirit of the deceased king (he became a deity after his death) could pass freely back and forth to enjoy the offerings and ceremonies in his honour.

The mortuary temples of Hatshepsut, Seti I, Ramesses II and Ramesses III still stand. The two **Colossi of Memnon ⑩**, standing in the sugar cane fields by the side of the road, are all that remain of the Temple of Amenhotep III, the famous Memnon. After the right one was hit by an earthquake in 27 BC, it made a light singing noise at dawn which the Greeks believed to be Memnon singing for his mother Eos. The Roman emperor Septimus Severus had it restored in AD 199, after which the singing stopped.

Questionable queen

The **Temple of Hatshepsut ⑭** (1492–1458 BC) is somewhat different from the others, being set back in a spectacular natural amphitheatre. Three gracefully proportioned and colonnaded terraces are connected by sloping ramps. The sanctuary areas are backed up against the mountain and partially hollowed out of the rocks. On first approach the temple looks strangely modern, but it is easy

to imagine how grand the complex must have been when the courts were filled with perfumed plants, fountains and myrrh trees. It was here, in 1997, that 58 foreigners and four Egyptians were gunned down by Islamic terrorists (six of whom also died in the massacre).

Probably the daughter, sister/wife and aunt of the first three Tuthmosis, Hatshepsut succeeded her father when she was 24 years old, reigning until her death 34 years later. Her divine birth and exploits are recorded on the walls behind the colonnades. They include an expedition to Punt in Somalia, whence incense trees, giraffes and other exotica were brought back to Egypt. The cutting and transportation of the two great obelisks set up by Hatshepsut at Karnak are also recorded. The temple was designed by Senenmut, evidently a great favourite of the queen. His portrait is hidden behind a door; and his own tomb is nearby.

The glory of the Ramesses

A large section of Ramesses II's (1290–1224 BC) mortuary temple, the **Ramesseum G**, is in ruins, but like other monuments of this prolific pharaoh (who reigned for over 60 years and had 80 children) what remains is majestic. Parts of what is the largest granite colossus on record, the statue of Ozymandias which inspired the poet Shelley, lie collapsed before the entrance of the hypostyle hall. One foot alone measures 3.3 metres (11 ft). The famous battle of Kadesh is depicted on the pylons. More interestingly there is a representation of Thoth, the ibis-headed secretary-god writing Ramesses' name on the leaves of the sacred tree. Both here and at Ramesses III's temple, there are vestiges of adjoining palaces where the kings came to spend a few days supervising work on their "Mansions of Eternity".

Map, page 216

Of all Theban ruins, the Ramesseum is the most cheerful... in the Ramesseum one may thoroughly enjoy the passing hour.

– AMELIA EDWARDS
A Thousand Miles up the Nile, 1877

BELOW: restoration at the Ramesseum.

Ramesses III (1194–1163 BC), however, is not eclipsed by his famous forebear. Although he modelled his mortuary temple, **Madinat Habu** (open daily; 7am–6pm in summer; 7am–5pm in winter; admission charge), on the Ramesseum, the scale of it is even more extravagant. The surrounding mudbrick walls may have partly collapsed but the temple is one of the best-preserved and easiest to understand as it reflects all the the principles of the classical temple. The enclosure is entered through the gatehouse from which stairs lead to the pharaoh's private pleasure apartments. Religious ceremonies took place in the First Court, from where the ruins of the Royal Palace are visible through the windows of the south wall. Coptic Christians later used the Second Court as a church and carved their symbols all over the pillars, but a few Osiris figures survived as well as the vividly coloured reliefs under the western colonnade. The battle reliefs on the exterior of the Ramesses temple are particularly interesting: this pharaoh fought off invading sea peoples from the west and vivid naval engagements are depicted.

Mortuary temple of Seti I

Built during the same period as Seti I's (19th Dynasty) temple at Abydos, his **mortuary temple** is dedicated to the worship of Amun and of Seti's father, Ramesses I. The hypostyle hall and sanctuary contain fine reliefs of Seti and his son Ramesses II in scenes of daily life and making offerings to the gods.

Valley of the Kings

After being embalmed and mummified, the New Kingdom pharaohs were transported in solemn cortège to the **Valley of the Kings** , hidden in a secluded

---

TIP

Isolated on the northern end of the Theban plateau, Seti I's mortuary temple is rarely visited. This adds to its charm for visitors who prefer to avoid the crowds.

BELOW: the Temple of Madinat Habu.

wadi in the Theban hills. Bedecked with gold and jewels, and surrounded by treasures and replicas of all they would need in the afterlife, they were buried in their rock-cut tombs.

As soon as the pharaohs ascended to the throne, they began to build their tomb, which was meant to preserve their royal mummy for eternity. However, many died before the lavish decoration of their tomb was finished, which now gives an interesting insight into the different stages of the whole process. Although, serious precautions were made to dissuade curious intruders, the treasures hidden inside were too much of an attraction to be left alone. As the power of the rulers of the 20th Dynasty decreased, breaking into tombs had become a common sport, mainly by the craftsmen who had worked in them, or by the supervisors themselves. By the end of the New Kingdom the priests reburied the mummies for protection in secret caches in the surrounding mountains, which were only discovered at the end of the 19th century.

There are 63 of these sepulchres, and undoubtedly more to be discovered. A new tomb, the largest found so far and thought to contain 50 of Ramesses II's 52 sons, was discovered in May 1995. Only a few are open to the public at one time, as a rotation system has been introduced to protect the tomb walls from further deterioration caused by too many visitors using flashlights and profuse perspiration which has led to serious damp problems. In most of the tombs, long, elaborately decorated corridors lead down through a series of chambers and false doors to the burial vault. The entrance passage is painted with texts and illustrations from mortuary literature and the *Book of the Dead*. As the pharaoh takes his last journey he passes through the 12 gates of the 12 hours of the night, beset by serpents, crocodiles and other malevolent beings. He arrives at the

Maps, pages 216, 229

BELOW: the Valley of the Kings, looking toward the Nile from the desert.

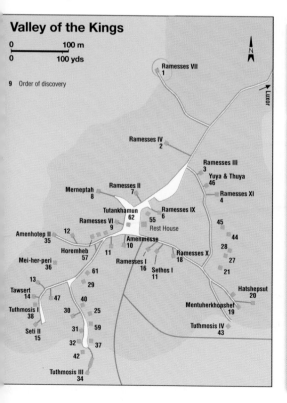

Valley of the Kings

0 ————— 100 m
0 ————— 100 yds

9   Order of discovery

N

▶ Luxor

Ramesses VII
1

Ramesses IV
2

Ramesses III
3

Yuya & Thuya
46

Merneptah
8

Ramesses II
7

Ramesses XI
4

Tutankhamun
62

Ramesses IX
6

Ramesses VI
9

55

Amenhotep II
35

12

Rest House

45

Amenmesse
10

44

Horemheb
57

11

28

Mei-her-peri
36

Ramesses I
16

Ramesses X
18

27

13

61

Sethos I
11

21

Tawsert
14

29

47

40

Hatshepsut
20

Tuthmosis I
38

30

25

Mentuherkhopshef
19

Seti II
15

31

59

Tuthmosis IV
43

32

37

42

Tuthmosis III
34

Court of Osiris where he is met by a delegation of gods; he makes his confession and his heart is weighed for its truthfulness and purity. A hideous monster waits to devour him should he fail the test but, evading the torments of hell, he is eventually received into the company of heaven.

The finest and largest tomb in the valley, often closed to the public, belonged to Seti I. Like the carvings in his temple at Abydos (*see page 210*), the walls are decorated with magnificent, subtly coloured reliefs, and the anteroom to the burial chamber has an important astronomical ceiling. The sarcophagus is now in the Sir John Soane Museum in London, and the mummy in the Egyptian Museum in Cairo.

Other outstanding tombs include that of Ramesses VI where the colours have been well-preserved, the tomb of Ramesses III with unusual depictions of daily life, and the tomb of Horemheb which has a similar plan to Seti I's.

The tomb of Tutankhamun

Only one of these tombs miraculously escaped the attention of tomb robbers, who were already ransacking them, sometimes within just a few years of their construction. The famous small tomb of the boy-king Tutankhamun (1333–1323 BC) was not discovered until 1922, when Howard Carter, under the patronage of Lord Carnarvon, chanced upon it after a search of seven long years. The **tomb** (additional admission charge) contained over 5,000 precious objects buried with the young pharaoh, whose embalmed remains were still in situ in a complex system of gold and jewelled mummy cases and coffins within coffins. A gilded chariot, beds, chairs, stools and headrests covered in gold leaf, alabaster lamps and vases, weapons, sandals, statues of servants, amulets and all kinds of other

...a gasp of wonderment escaped our lips, so gorgeous was the sight that met our eyes: a golden effigy of the young boy-king, of most magnificent workmanship.

— HOWARD CARTER
The Tomb of Tutankhamun, 1923

BELOW: the Tomb of Tutankhamun, the Valley of the Kings.

objects in perfect condition were crammed into the small space of the tomb. The majority of the treasure is now in the Egyptian Museum in Cairo.

Map, page 216

Valley of the Queens

The royal wives were buried in the **Valley of the Queens ❶** in the hills behind Madinat Habu. Very few are open to the public, but in 1995 the restored **Tomb of Nefertari**, one of the most impressive monuments on the west bank, was opened for the first time since its discovery in 1904, albeit to a maximum of 200 people a day (additional admission charge). Also buried in the valley are a number of princes thought to have been killed in a smallpox epidemic, including the nine-year-old son of Ramesses III. The young boy is shown being led by his father to meet the gods.

Until the 19th Dynasty the queens of the pharaohs were buried with their husbands in the Valley of the Kings.

Tombs of the Nobles

Unlike royalty, who were buried with somewhat ominous solemnity, the scribes and dignitaries of the court, whose tombs are scattered in the sandy foothills, departed this world surrounded with scenes of the joyous good living to which they had apparently been accustomed during their lifetime. There are 414 private **nobles' tombs ❿**, from the 4th Dynasty to the Roman period, but the majority are from the New Kingdom. Compared with the tombs of the kings they are small and much more worldly. Many are vividly painted with naturalistic scenes of agriculture, fishing, fowling, feasting and junketing, thereby constituting a fascinating record of everyday life.

The fine decorations in the tomb of Ramose reflect the fact that he was a Governor of Thebes under both Amenhotep III and his son Akhenaten. While the

BELOW: tomb of Menena, the scribe of Tuthmosis IV.

walls show some exquisite carvings in the style of the former, some reliefs on the back wall reveal a clear influence from the Amarnah style. The tombs of Nakht, Userhat, and Menna have fine representations of daily life, as does the tomb of Sennufer which also gives a clear impression of the love between the Mayor of Thebes and his beautiful wife.

Workers' village

Excavation of Deir al-Madinah has thrown considerable light on the lives of ordinary ancient Egyptians. Among the potsherds were found records of wages, religious practices, lawsuits, magical spells and work attendance.

There are records of more humble workmen's lives in the tombs of the village of **Deir al-Madinah ❶**, where the masons, painters and decorators were kept segregated from the rest of the population for generations, in an effort to keep the whereabouts of the treasure-filled royal tombs a secret. They prepared their own tombs in advance.

Even today the country folk on the west bank, known for their independence and secretiveness, cannot be persuaded to move down from the hills to the plain. The government regularly announces plans to move everyone out, and the world-famous architect Hassan Fathy designed a model village for them at **New Qurna**, but they would have none of it. It still stands beside the road, rather the worse for wear, and the wily villagers still guard their secrets.

Esna

BELOW: tomb of Anherkhe at Deir al-Madinah.

The town of **Esna ❿** lies 50 km (30 miles) south of Luxor and is built over the ruins of the **Temple of Khnum** (open daily; 7am–6pm in summer; 7am–5pm in winter; admission charge). Only the hypostyle hall has been excavated and its foundation level is 8 metres (27 ft) below that of the street. It contains most interesting reliefs and inscriptions, however, and is of great historic importance.

The names and activities of Ptolemies and Roman emperors up until the time of Decius, who was murdered in 249 AD, are recorded. French archaeologists have recently deciphered many details of the rituals of the worship of Khnum, as well as a precise calendar specifying when and how they should be celebrated.

Map, page 202

Edfu

By contrast, the Ptolemaic **Temple of Horus** (open daily; 7am–6pm in summer; 7am–5pm in winter; admission charge) at **Edfu** ⑪, another 50 km (30 miles) to the south is the most completely preserved in Egypt and is in near-perfect condition, with its great pylon, exterior walls, courts, halls and sanctuary all in place. Its walls are a textbook of mythology and geopolitics. Building is recorded as having begun in 237 BC by Ptolemy III Euergetes (246–221 BC), and continued until decoration of the outer walls was finished in 57 BC.

Several festivals are depicted: the mock battle commemorating the victory of Horus over Seth; the joyful annual wedding visit of Hathor, who journeyed upriver from Dendarah to be reunited with her spouse, and the annual coronation of the reigning monarch, identified with Horus, which took place in the great forecourt. Regal carved-granite sparrow-hawks stand sentinel at the doors.

Horus, the falcon god of Edfu.

Kom Ombo

The **Temple of Horus** (open daily; 7am–6pm in summer; 7am–5pm in winter; admission charge), at **Kom Ombo** ⑫, dedicated jointly to Horus the sparrow-hawk and Sobek the crocodile, is situated right on a sweeping bend of the Nile 40 km (24 miles) north of Aswan, near a sandy bank where crocodiles used to sun themselves. Part of the front of the temple has fallen into the river and the

BELOW: Titi alabastar shop, painted by a local talent, Luxor.

back parts are roofless. It is built on a double plan with twin sanctuaries for Horus to the north and Sobek to the south. Each has a black diorite offering table. Most of the reliefs were executed by Ptolemy XII (80–58 BC and 55–51 BC) and have some fine details including the personifications of the four winds and an interesting set of medical instruments. At one side a small shrine is used for storing some rather unpleasant crocodile mummies.

The Ptolemies evidently had more than religion in mind when they subsidised the building of these temples, as each one is placed in a strategic position both economically and militarily.

Buying a camel

The dusty town of **Daraw** on the road from Kom Ombo to Aswan (40 km/ 25 miles north of Aswan) distinguishes itself by hosting one of Egypt's largest camel markets. Although this is a daily event, the place comes to full swing on Tuesday and Sunday morning. The camels are brought from the Sudan by the Sudanese and Rachidia herdsmen, through the Libyan desert. This trail, known as the Darb al-Arba'in or the Forty Days Road, is one of the last surviving trading routes through the desert.

Aswan

Ivory, ebony, rose and gold are the defining colours of **Aswan** ⓭ (215 km/135 miles south of Luxor). Here, a wild jumble of glistening igneous rocks, strewn across the Nile, suddenly creates narrows between the highlands of the Eastern Desert and the sandy wastes of the Sahara. The barrier to navigation is known as the First Cataract, and was once where the civilised world stopped.

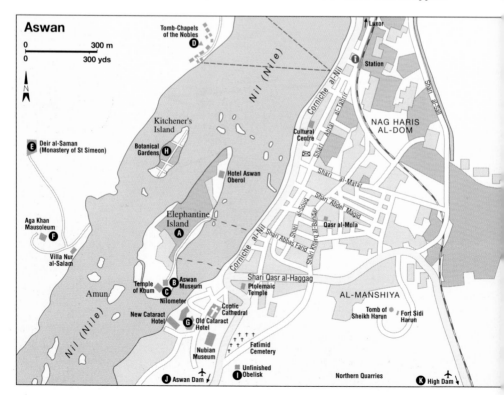

During the Old Kingdom a few travellers ventured further up the Nile in quest of gold, slaves and the occasional pygmy, leaving records of their missions inscribed on the rocks among the islands, but most expeditions were to Elephantine , the island in the middle of the river at the foot of the cataract. Yebu, the main town on the island, was the Old Kingdom border town, and as the Nile was believed to spring up from under the First Cataract, it was also an important religious centre.

Outpost of empires

The excellent winter climate and beautiful setting of Aswan were well-known in the classical world and were described by several writers. They mentioned the temples, the garden and the vineyards of Elephantine, which were supposed to produce grapes all the year round. Both the Ptolemies and the Romans maintained garrisons at this distant southern outpost.

The greatest geographer in antiquity, Eratosthenes (*circa* 273–192 BC), who held a post as librarian in Alexandria under the Ptolemies, established the approximate circumference of the earth from astronomical observations made at Elephantine and Alexandria. He noted that the sun's rays fell vertically to the bottom of a well at Elephantine at the summer solstice, whereas on the same day in Alexandria an upright stake cast a shadow, indicating that the sun was seven degrees from its zenith. Since he knew the distance between the two cities, he could then proceed to work out the total circumference of the earth; and he came within a few miles of the truth.

Juvenal, the satirical Roman poet, died here in exile at the age of 80, towards the end of the 1st century AD. But it was the merchants, more than the scholars,

Maps, pages 202, 234

TIP

Aswan offers some of the loveliest views of the Nile. It's a wonderful place to take a *felucca* trip, either a short voyage around the islands or, for the hardy, to embark on a *felucca* cruise to Luxor.

BELOW: Elephantine Island, Aswan.

scientists, poets and soldiers, who left the greatest quantity of humble reminders of their passage, in the form of *ostraka*, or potsherds, inscribed with records of their commercial transactions. Nineteenth-century travellers were able to pick up a pocketful within minutes.

Some of these remains can be seen in the small **museum** ❸ (open daily; 8:30am–6pm in summer; 8.30am–5pm in winter; admission charge) on Elephantine island, which is due to be replaced by a more ambitious one just south of Aswan. A gold-plated ram, ram mummies, precious stones, jewellery and amulets are on display. At the back of the museum is a shady garden where tea may be offered in return for a small *baksheesh* (tip). The ticket includes entry to the scant **Temple of Khnum** on the tip of the island, and the Nilometer.

Nilometer ❻

From the Old Kingdom onwards a strict watch was kept on the rise and fall of the Nile. Its measurement was one of the important functions of the resident governor of Elephantine and later Aswan. Up until the last century, when western technology started to revolutionise the management of the water, frequent and regular readings were taken from the Nilometer at the southern end of Elephantine island, and the information was communicated to the rest of the country. Those responsible for the cultivation of crops and the maintenance of embankments and canals would thus know in advance what to expect; and other administrators could calculate tax assessments.

According to an interesting text at Edfu, if the Nile rose 24 cubits at Elephantine, it would provide sufficient water to irrigate the land satisfactorily. If it did not, disaster would surely ensue. Just such a failure, which lasted for seven years – though it is not the drought mentioned in the Bible – is recorded on a block of granite a short way upstream: "By a very great misfortune the Nile has not come forth for a period of seven years. Grain has been scarce and there have been no vegetables or anything else for the people to eat."

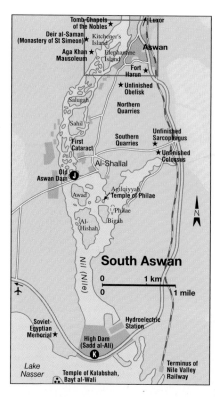

Archaeological remains of the Temples of Khnum on the southern end of Elephantine are sketchy, but there is evidence that Tuthmosis III, Amenhotep II, Ramesses III, Alexander IV (the son of Alexander the Great), Augustus Caesar and Trajan all had a hand either in their construction or maintenance. Parts of them were still standing when the French expedition arrived in 1799, but were demolished about 20 years later by Muhammad Ali's son Ibrahim (at this time viceroy of Upper Egypt) who subsequently used the fine white stone to build himself a palace.

Dome of the Winds

As in so many places in Egypt, there is a multitude of burial grounds and memorials from the different eras of Egyptian history. The hereditary governors of Aswan and other high-ranking officials had their tombs cut out of the cliffs on the west bank of the Nile at a spot called Qubbat al-Hawa in Arabic, or Dome of the Winds. The **Tombs of the nobles** ❿ (open daily; 7am–6pm in summer; 7am–5pm in winter; admission charge) of the Old and Middle Kingdoms depict some interesting scenes

Maps, pages 234, 236

of daily life, and the views over Aswan and the Nile alone are well worth the steep climb. It makes for a pleasant expedition combined with a visit to the Coptic **Deir al-Saman** ❺ (Monastery of St Simeon) (open daily 9am–5pm; admission charge). The 6th-century monastery once provided accommodation for about 300 monks, but these days the ruins lie lost in the desert sands.

Aga Khan III, the grandfather of Kerim Aga Khan and distinguished leader of the Ismaili sect of Islam for many years, loved Aswan for its timeless tranquillity and had his domed mausoleum built high up on the bluffs overlooking the river. He was buried in the **Aga Khan Mausoleum** ❻ in 1957. The building is a close relative of those of his ancestors, the Fatimids, whose followers' mausoleums are on the east bank. The tomb was recently closed to the public by the Begum, who was apparently saddened by the many vendors and souvenir stalls disturbing the tranquillity. There are also many gravestones from the long period of Turkish occupation.

In February 1799, a contingent of Napoleon's invading army arrived, footsore and exasperated, having chased the Mamluk Murad Bey, a survivor from the Battle of the Pyramids, all the way up the Nile Valley. He infuriated them further still by slipping away up the cataract under cover of darkness. The French occupation lasted for less than two years, but it nevertheless brought a long era of somnolence to an end. Aswan was to wake up to great schemes, envisioned by Napoleon and started by the reforming Muhammad Ali.

Nineteenth-century Aswan

In the second half of the 19th century tourists began to arrive by way of Thomas Cook steamers and *dahabeyyas*; and there were plentiful observations to be

If it's too hot to walk, take a camel up to the Aga Khan Mausoleum. Bargain with the cameleers at the landing point.

BELOW: Aga Khan Mausoleum.

TIP

The gardens and islands of Aswan are good places for spotting birds, among them the little green bea-eater, the pied kingfisher, the Nile Valley sunbird, black kites and even the occasional Egyptian vulture. A pair of binoculars are a useful piece of equipment on any Nile cruise.

BELOW: the Old Cataract Hotel.

noted in morocco-bound diaries. Amelia Edwards describes the hustle and bustle of the waterfront, which probably had not changed much in hundreds of years, although slaves and gold were no longer the chief items of merchandise: "Abyssinians like slender-legged baboons; wild-looking Bishariya and Ababdeh Arabs with flashing eyes and flowing hair; sturdy Nubians… and natives of all tribes and shades, from Kordofan to Sennar, the deserts of Bahuda and the banks of the Blue and White Niles. Some were returning from Cairo; others were on their way thither… Each was entrenched in his own little redoubt of piled-up bales and packing cases, like a spider in the centre of his web; each provided with his kettle and coffee pot, and an old rug to sleep and pray upon… great bundles of lion and leopard skins, bales of cotton, sacks of henna-leaves, elephant-tusks swathed in canvas and matting, strewed the sandy bank.'"

A whiff of Africa

Elegant hotels were built to accommodate the fashionable travellers who came to spend the winter at Aswan or to plan the future development of Egypt and the Sudan. The terraces of the **Old Cataract Hotel ⊙** must have been the scene of many a portentous discussion by these cigar-smoking Victorian empire-builders. The construction of the first **Aswan Dam** was successfully financed and the project completed in 1902. King Edward VII's younger brother came out from England for the opening with a host of onlookers, including the young Winston Churchill.

Modern hotels have replaced the grand old ladies of the past, though the Old Cataract survives and the happy hour can still be enjoyed, to the accompaniment of splendid sunsets from its terrace. Below on the shore, the *feluccas* tie

up for the night – nothing beats a *felucca* ride at sunset to enjoy the beauty and peace of Aswan. The nearby **Nubian Museum**, built solely to be dedicated to Nubian history and culture, was not yet open at the time of writing.

Feluccas usually make a stop at the **Botanical Gardens ⓗ** (open daily 8am– sunset; admission charge) on **Kitchener's Island**. In return for his military achievements in the Sudan, Consul-General Kitchener was presented with this island, for which he collected exotic plants and seeds from all over the world.

Aswan's *suq* retains a hint and a whiff of Africa, where small shops sell cotton, baskets, dates, ebony cane and crocheted skull caps. Softly spoken Nubians while away their time in front of coffee shops, and shy women carry home the day's shopping on their heads, still wearing the thin black dresses with flounces that trail behind them. Not so long ago, when they walked across the Nubian sand-dunes, these flounces used to brush away their footprints in the sand. Nowadays they return to their neat stone-built villages in the area, which are quite a contrast to the untidy-looking mudbrick and brick villages further north.

Quarries

Coloured granites, greywacke, syenite, alabaster, ochre and other minerals were quarried and transported down the Nile when the river was in flood to the royal cities of the north. Obelisks, which later made their way to such places as Rome, Istanbul, Paris, London or New York, were ingeniously cut from Aswan granite. In a quarry south of Aswan, the **Unfinished Obelisk ⓘ** (open daily; 7am–6pm in summer; 7am–5pm in winter; admission charge) can still be seen, attached to the bedrock. It would have weighed 1,100 tons had it been completed, but it developed a crack.

Maps, pages 234, 236

TIP

An afternoon walk through the sweet scented-lanes of the Botanical Gardens is the perfect antidote to a hot day. If you come by a *felucca*, your captain will drop you off at one end of Kitchener's Island and then sail round to the other to pick you up.

BELOW: on Kitchener's Island.

Taming the Nile

The taming of the river's unpredictable moods, sometimes bountiful and sometimes enraged, and the year-round conservation of its waters has been at the core of Egypt's history and civilisation since its earliest beginnings. In primeval times, the unharnessed flood roared down annually from the Ethiopian highlands, swamping the valley for three months before it receded, leaving behind thousands of tons of fertile silt which, accumulating over millennia, created the 10-metre-thick (33 ft) blanket of soil which constitutes the Valley and the Delta.

The flood, however, was unpredictable and occasionally failed to appear. The consequences were disastrous; and the co-ordinated planning required to deal with the recurring problem was an important factor in the development of ancient Egyptian civilisation. By systems of dykes and channels, water could be trapped in basins. These systems were improved by waves of conquerors who tried their hand at governing Egypt.

Barrages and dams

In the 19th century Muhammad Ali set about repairing and extending the canals and building barrages, which conserved enough water for a limited year-round supply. They made feasible the production of summer cash crops such as sugar, rice and cotton, which enormously increased the country's revenue.

Continuing this pattern of development, the British in their turn built the first **Aswan Dam ❶** in 1902 at the head of the Cataract, creating a reservoir 225 km (140 miles) long. At the time it was acclaimed as a great feat of engineering, and there was another marked increase in the prosperity of the country.

With the demise of the British occupation and the takeover of Egypt by

BELOW: waiting for the rush.

Colonel Nasser's revolutionary government in 1952, the Nile Valley became a testing ground for international rivalries. The new regime focused its aspirations on the construction of a **High Dam** ⓚ that would generate enough electricity for new industry, as well as for wide rural electrification, and provide enough water to bring millions of new acres under cultivation, but it needed financial and technical assistance to realise the project. The United States was ready to help, but withdrew its offer abruptly when Nasser refused to compromise his non-aligned status. The Soviet Union stepped in with loans and technology.

For 10 years 30,000 workers laboured on the enormous dam, which was built on a new principle of soil mechanics. Hundreds of tons of rubble and rock were shovelled into the Nile to make a barrier 4km wide and 92 metres high (2½ miles by 300 ft). Four huge channels were cut through the granite on the west side to divert the water while 12 turbines (which have since had to be replaced with the help of the United States) were installed on the east. By 1972 the dam was finished; and at last Egypt had a predictable water supply. The massive bulk of the High Dam straddles the Nile 13 km (8 miles) south of Aswan. Beyond it Lake Nasser stretches for 800 km (500 miles), deep into the Sudan.

The beneficial effects of the dam were immediately apparent, though it has fallen short of being the hoped-for panacea for all Egypt's ills. Had it not been for the water stored up behind it, however, Egypt would have suffered as disastrously as Ethiopia and the Sudan during the droughts of 1972 and 1984.

The hydroelectricity produced was sufficient to power new fertiliser, cement, iron and steel plants, and to make electricity available throughout rural areas, though it is recognised that the dam will not be able to produce enough to satisfy the country's ever-increasing demands in the future.

Map, page 236

The first Aswan Dam, built in 1902, was heightened twice – in 1912 and 1932 – before the construction of the High Dam in 1972.

BELOW: monument to Soviet-Egyptian co-operation.

The price to pay

The addition of three million *feddans* (1.2 million hectares/ 30,000 acres) to Egypt's cultivable lands, irrigated by the new assured water supply, was planned, but the leaders were so closely identified with the project that they turned a deaf ear to seasoned advice. The new lands were on poor soil, which took years to attain marginal productivity at exorbitant cost. Eventually Sadat had to admit that grand schemes for land reclamation were unrealistic.

The total containment of the flood has produced other results. Houses can now be built in places that used to be under water for three months of the year; and as a result of vastly improved incomes from the oil boom, together with the pressure of the population explosion, the private sector has responded with a rash of building on precious agricultural land. Moreover, other land is being lost through the constant use of excessive amounts of water, causing waterlogging and salinity. The projected drainage system that would remedy this defect is proving to be more costly than the dam itself.

The Nubians lost their land and were moved from their ancestral home. The Nubian monuments were moved to higher grounds by UNESCO and other international organisations, but the higher water tables and salty water is causing more and more damage to the priceless monuments in Upper Egypt and Cairo. ❑

STILL WILD AFTER ALL THESE YEARS

Despite the ravages made on Egypt's wildlife over the past hundred years, many of the creatures that the ancients revered are still found today

Before the building of the Aswan dams, the Nile flooded each year and its silt-rich water covered the valley. When the water subsided, the first creature that was seen to move was the scarabaeus, the dung beetle. This beetle also laid its eggs in dung or in the corpses of other beetles. Egyptians called it Kheper, and used it to represent the essence of existence, the god Kherpi. Scarab beetles can still be seen rolling their balls of dung, but many of the other animals that lived on land whose re-emergence the scarabaeus celebrated, have long since disappeared.

SURVIVORS

Egyptians used many living creatures to represent their gods, but where now are the Nile crocodile, the African elephant, the lions and ibises, green monkeys and baboons? Long since hunted out of existence or forced off the land as Egyptians spread the cultivation of their buildings.

Amongst the survivors that were common to the ancient Egyptians and are still found in Egypt today are magnificent birds like the short-toed eagle, the long-legged buzzard, the hoopoe and the Egyptian vulture (all were used as hieroglyphics).

The Egyptians domesticated many animals including the cat, ox and cow, which feature on many tomb and temple decorations. In the river, grey mullet, catfish and Bulti fish would have been as familiar to the ancients as they are to Egyptians today.

Finally, while the scarab beetle reminds us of the eternal cycle that ancient Egyptians believed in, the pesky fly, seen in hieroglyphics and ubiquitous in Egypt today, reminds us that then, as now, there were trials and tribulations.

▷ **SNAKE CHARM**
The Egyptian cobra was sacred to the goddess Wadjet. Today cobras are caught for export.

▷ **FOWL PLAY**
One of the great pleasures of well-placed Egyptians in antiquity was to go hunting in the papyrus marshes, particularly in the Delta. Here a hunter is seen raising his throw-stick as birds fly up. Egyptians hunted birds and other animals for sport, not to provide food, which was done using other techniques, such as ensnaring them in nets.

▽ **THE GUARDIAN**
The jackal was sacred to the gods Wepwawet and Duamutef (one of the four sons of Horus), but it was its connection with Anubis, god and protector of the Dead and helper of Osiris, that earned the jackal such a prominent role in Tutankhamun's tomb. Anubis, with dog-like fidelity, was trusted with the protection of the mummy.

PAPYRUS – THE FIRST PAPER

The papyrus plant (*Cyperus papyrus*), a relative of sedge grasses, used to grow abundantly in Egypt, particularly in the marshy Delta. In antiquity Egyptians put papyrus to a number of uses. They wove it into mats, plaited it for ropes, bundled it together to form light rafts – perfect for fishing in the marshes – and pressed and wove it into a suitable medium on which to write.

The creation of this technique was largely responsible for the explosion of literacy in ancient Egypt. Making papyrus sheets was time-consuming and labour-intensive, so even in antiquity they were reserved for writing that was intended to last, for religious texts and important legal works. More ephemeral information was put down on slates or on pottery shards.

Because of its proliferation and importance – the papyrus was one of the symbols of Upper Egypt and its form was recreated in the shapes of pillars in several hypostyle halls.

Papyrus continued to be used for important texts into the 10th century AD, but the manufacturing technique was lost soon after paper was imported from the East and wasn't rediscovered until the 20th century, by which time papyrus had vanished from most of the country. Recently, there has been some replanting.

◁ DESERT PROWLERS
Jackals are still found prowling on the edge of the desert in Egypt and, as that is where Egyptians continue to bury their dead, the association between the jackal and Anubis continues. Today, however, jackals tend to be hunted not venerated. Egypt also has four species of fox, an animal closely related to the jackal.

△ SACRED NO MORE
Like the glossy ibis and bald ibis, the Sacred Ibis is no longer able to breed in Egypt thanks to hunters and population pressure.

◁ GOD OF WISDOM
The ibis was sacred to the highly regarded god Thoth, the scribe of the gods, who was believed to have introduced writing to Egypt.

ABU SIMBEL AND NUBIA

Map, page 202

The popular 19th-century cruises south of the First Cataract were threatened with extinction by the Aswan Dam, but many of Nubia's treasures can once again be viewed from the water

N ubia, the arid sun-seared land of about 22,000 sq km (8,500 sq miles) between Aswan and the northern Sudan, now lies beneath the waters of the High Dam reservoir. Nubia's entire population of some 100,000 people were uprooted from their ancestral homes, half to be relocated in Egypt (in Kom Ombo, about 14 km/9 miles north of Aswan), the other half in the northeastern Sudan (in Kashem al-Girba).

Nubia's major monuments, like its people, were transported to new locations, one as far afield as New York. Both the tragedy of the uprooting of the Nubian people and the technological achievement in saving the monuments can best be understood in the context of Nubia as it was before the deluge.

Old Nubia

Nubia was the link between Egypt and Africa, but it was not a regular trade corridor because of its inhospitable environment. It was a largely barren land, while Egypt, on the other hand, had an abundant agricultural surplus. Even in ancient times Nubians turned to their rich northern neighbour for vital food supplies, especially grain. And Egypt was ready to fulfil the Nubians' requirements in return for the right to exploit their rich mineral resources.

Despite its stark and barren nature, the Nubian people had a strong attachment to their land. In the 20th century their working men went northwards to Egypt to find employment as bargemen, doorkeepers, cooks or government clerks. However, they seldom married Egyptians and inevitably returned to Nubia, bearing cloth, clothing and food for their families, as well as pictures cut out of magazines and newspapers – mostly portraits of political leaders, athletes and film stars – which were used to adorn the walls of their houses.

In the years before the High Dam, Nubian houses were made of sun-baked brick, a mixture of clay and straw. The facade of each house was different from the next. They were painted, both inside and out, with finger paintings of trees, chickens, boats, flags and sacred symbols, and most had porcelain plates (brought from Cairo) inserted into the clay before it dried. Nubia's date-palm groves provided the people not only with food, but also with no fewer than 40 other commodities, such as fibre for ropes, timber for heavy construction and palm "spears" for a variety of uses.

Sailing southwards from Egypt before the land was flooded, one could see Nubian settlements grouped near the banks of the river. Whitewashed shrines of local saints and sheikhs broke the skyline. In the vast distances from village to village, ancient temples could be seen: the great fortress of Kubban which once guarded the Wadi al-Allaqi, one of the richest gold-mining areas

PRECEDING PAGES: the Temple of Philae in silhouette.
LEFT: inscriptions on a boulder at Sehil Island near Aswan.
BELOW: a turban draped in typically casual Nubian style.

in Nubia; the temples of Dabud and Taffah, now reassembled in Madrid and Leiden, or the temples of Qirtasi, Kalabshah and Bayt al-Wali, now reassembled on a new site near the High Dam, all originally built atop jutting sandstone cliffs. And, of course, the great Temple of Ramesses II at Abu Simbel, a symbol of Egyptian power in Nubia in ancient times.

The end of Old Nubia

The trauma for the Nubians, faced with the news that their land was doomed, was compounded by the fact that this was not the first, but the fourth time they had watched their homes being submerged by the River Nile. An old man at Daraw, near Kom Ombo, for example, recalled when the first Aswan dam was built, between 1899 and 1902. It formed an artificial lake 225 km (140 miles) upstream and the Nubians had to move back from the fertile strip at the edge of the river to rebuild their homes.

Less than five years after the dam was completed, it was seen to be inadequate to meet the growing needs of the country and was heightened by about 5 metres (15 ft). The reservoir now created by the thwarted Nile backed upstream 300 km (185 miles) and the Nubians had to move a second time. Between 1929 and 1934 the Aswan dam was raised again, and this time the water extended as far south as Wadi Halfa in northern Sudan. When the Nubians were told that a new dam would be built and that they would have to move once more, this time out of Nubia completely, some of the older generation refused to leave; and, with the water lapping at their feet, they finally had to be helped or even carried bodily to the waiting vessels.

BELOW: sailing by.

The famous Egyptian architect Hassan Fathy was deeply inspired by the

Nubian houses he found in Aswan – "tall, easy, roofed cleanly with a brick vault, each house decorated individually and exquisitely around the doorway with claustra-work mouldings and tracery in mud". After Nubia was submerged the typical architecture started to disappear, but the architect used Nubian crafts-men in several of his projects, and their influence can now be seen throughout the country. The Egyptian government is slowly admitting the cost of the Nubian tragedy and an interesting museum is opening in Aswan, dedicated to Nubian history and culture.

Map, page 202

Salvage archaeology

By 1970, with the water of the High Dam reservoir constantly rising, engulfing more and more of what had once been Nubia, considerable portions of known temples and shrines had been salvaged. But how much more archaeological evidence, in the form of town sites, tombs, temples, churches and documents, was lost to the world for ever under the waters can never fully be ascertained.

Ironically, however, it is due to its disappearance that we now know more of Nubia than we do of many important sites in the rest of Egypt. We know, for example, that when the civilisation of ancient Egypt was in its decline, a king-dom of Upper Nubia prospered, and that around 600 BC the Nubians moved their capital from Napata southwards to Meroe (Shendi). In the fertile bend in the river, free from invasion, well-placed for trade, rich in iron ore and in wood for iron-smelting, they developed a culture that was at once a continuation of the Egyptian-influenced Napatan culture and a totally individual African entity.

The Meroitic Kingdom spread northwards until, by the reign of Ptolemy IV (181 BC), the king of Meroe, Argamanic, controlled the Nile to within sight of

BELOW LEFT:
Trajan's Kiosk, the Temple of Philae.

AN INTERNATIONAL RACE AGAINST TIME

With the creation of Lake Nasser threat-ening to swallow up many important Nubian monuments, the governments of Egypt and Sudan launched an appeal to save and record as many of the monuments as possible.

The international response was immediate. Between 1960 and 1970, in the most concen-trated archaeological operation ever, scholars, engineers, architects and photographers from more than 30 countries fought against time to preserve what they could, with the result that 23 temples were saved. Many of these were left in Nubia but moved or lifted out of harm's way: the Temple of Amadah, for example, was raised as a unit weighing 800 tons, put on rails and dragged up a hill to safety, while the Temple of Derr was rebuilt nearby.

A temple built by Queen Hatshepsut was dis-mantled, crated, loaded onto 28 lorries and taken to the Sudan, where it was reassembled in the National Museum at Khartoum.

Elephantine. There the Nubians remained until the Roman conquest of Egypt in 30 BC, when the Romans signed a treaty with them, turning all northern Nubia into a buffer zone.

Nubia embraced Christianity between the 5th and the 6th centuries, when numerous churches were built and some ancient temples were converted into churches. When Egypt was conquered by the Arabs in the 7th century, they concluded a treaty with the Christian Nubian king and Nubia officially remained Christian until the 12th century, when many Nubians embraced the Muslim faith. Mass conversion to Islam came when tribes from Arabia settled in Lower Nubia and began to impose their religion and political organisation on the people. They intermarried with Arabs and their children came to be called *Bani Kanz*, or the Kenuz tribe. Most of the resettled Nubian population in Kom Ombo belong to this tribe. By the end of the 15th century, Nubians, with the exception of only a few settlements, were Muslim.

Surviving documents in a host of languages, including "Old Nubian" (which has yet to be deciphered), Arabic, Coptic and Greek, provide a wealth of information about the Nubian people in the form of private and official letters, legal documents and petitions, which date from between the end of the 8th and the 15th century. Most of these documents come from Qasr Ibrim (*see page 255*).

Rescued from a watery grave

BELOW:
the Temple of Isis.

During the Ptolemaic period the cult of Isis moved 8 km (5 miles) south of Aswan to the island of **Philae ⓮,** near Bigah Island, identified with the burial place of Osiris. On Philae, a particularly beautiful **temple** (open daily: 7am–6pm in summer; 7am–5pm in winter; admission charge) was dedicated to the god-

dess Isis, and was to become the most important shrine in Egypt over the next 700 years. Pilgrims came from both north and south to invoke the healing powers of the goddess, and continued to do so long after Christianity had been adopted as the national and imperial religion. As well as the Temple of Isis, many subsidiary temples, shrines and gateways were added to enhance the cult centre.

The construction of the first Aswan Dam in 1902 resulted in the partial submersion of Philae during eight months of the year. There had been strong objections by the conservation-minded but, as Winston Churchill caustically observed, to abandon plans for the dam would have been "the most senseless sacrifice ever offered on the altar of a false religion". The dam was built, Philae was indeed inundated and, still more so in 1932, when the dam was heightened for the third time. But visitors were able to row and even swim about among the foliated capitals of the long colonnades and glimpse the ghostly reliefs on the walls in the water below.

Sixty years later, when the High Dam went up, Philae was threatened with total and permanent immersion. This time it was rescued by a huge international mission. A 1.6-km (1-mile) long coffer dam was constructed round the island, and all the water within was pumped out. Stone by stone the temples were dismantled, and transported to nearby **Agilqiyyah Island**, which had been levelled and remodelled to receive the masterpiece of reconstruction that visitors see today. The total cost was in the region of US$30 million.

Stairs from the boat landing on Agilqiyyah Island lead to the oldest part of the Philae complex, the Hall of Nectanebo I (30th Dynasty), followed by the Outer Temple Court, flanked on both sides by colonnades. The entrance to the **Temple of Isis** is marked by the 18-metre (60-ft) high towers of the First Pylon,

Map, page 202

The great Temple of Isis, on the terrace of which I am now writing, is so extremely wonderful that no words can give the least idea of it.

– EDWARD LEAR, 1854

BELOW: the Temple of Isis suffered deliberate damage when the temple became a church in the 6th century.

where reliefs show the Ptolemy in traditional pharaonic poses. To the left of the Central Court is the Birth House of Ptolemy IV (221–205 BC) with fine reliefs depicting the god Horus rising from the marshes. A stairway inside the Inner Sanctuary of Isis leads to the Osiris Chambers, decorated with exquisite reliefs illustrating the Osiris myth (*see page 33*). Inside the sanctuary, reliefs show Isis suckling her son Horus as well as the young pharaoh.

To the right of the Second Pylon is the small temple of Hathor, the patroness of music, with a good relief of musicians. On Hadrian's Gate an interesting relief depicts the source of the Nile as the Nile god Hapi, who pours water from two jars – ancient Egyptians are thought to have believed that the source of the Nile was to be found at the First Cataract, from where it flowed both north towards the Mediterranean and south towards the Sudan. The most photographed part of the temple is probably Trajan's Kiosk with floral columns and reliefs of the Roman Emperor Trajan making offerings to Isis and Osiris.

The Temple of Kalabshah

When the waters of Lake Nasser are high (usually September–December) the only way to get to the **Temple of Kalabshah** ⓫ (open daily 8am–4pm; admission charge) is by boat. At other times it is usually possible to walk from Aswan's shipyard. However great the hassle of haggling with the boatmen, approaching by rowing boat and seeing the temple in all its grandeur from the water is certainly worth the price.

The original site of Kalabshah, ancient Talmis, was 50 km (31 miles) further up the Nile, and today the temple lies somewhat forlorn in the shadow of the High Dam, where it was relocated in 1970.

BELOW: Trajan's Kiosk, Philae.

The **Temple of Mandulis**, dedicated to the Nubian fertility god Marul (Mandulis to the Greeks), was built around 30 BC during the reign of the emperor Augustus, over an older Ptolemaic temple. During the Christian era it was used as a church. An impressive stoneway leads up to the First Pylon. The colonnaded court and hypostyle hall beyond the pylon have varied floral capitals which clearly suggest the idea of a garden. Inside the sanctuary, the emperor is seen in the company of the entire Egyptian pantheon. A stairway leads to the roof, with magnificent views over Lake Nasser.

The smaller temple of **Bayt al-Wali** (House of the Governor), was also relocated here, having stood on a site near the original Kalabshah Temple. Carved from the rocks, it was built by the Viceroy of Kush to commemorate Ramesses II's successful military expeditions in Nubia. The well-preserved and brightly coloured reliefs show the victorious pharaoh receiving heaps of exotic goods as tribute.

Cruising on Lake Nasser

In the mid-19th century, when the Nile attracted tourists from around the world, a cruise south of the First Cataract was considered *de rigueur* if one was to hold one's head up back home. In Nubia the landscape was wilder, the ride rougher, the sun hotter, the wind sharper, the people fiercer. The Aswan Dam put an end to all that, but in the past few years Egyptian entrepreneurs have woken up to Lake Nasser's possibilities and claimed the right to operate services between Aswan and Abu Simbel. Apparently an agreement has been reached limiting the number of boats allowed to operate on the lake, minimising damage to the sites and creating an aura of exclusivity about the cruise – particularly since most of

Map, page 202

A romantic end to an Egyptian day.

BELOW: fishing on Lake Nasser.

the sites (with the noted exception of Abu Simbel) cannot be reached overland.

Leaving from the Saad al Ali maritime station beside the dam, boats pass the temples of Kalabshah and Kirtasi and the Bayt al-Wali, on the western shore, before heading into open water. The lake is broad here and the hills gently sloped, but further south the landscape closes in where the Nile used to run through a narrow passage between steep hills. It is a unique sight. Antiquities used to be spread along the Nile between the First and Second Cataract but, as with Kalabshah, many were grouped together during the salvage operation, which makes seeing them easier, though it has taken some of the drama away.

The next group of **temples** ⑯ – Dakkah, Mahrraqah and Wadi al-Sabu – lies some 140 km (87 miles) south of Aswan, also on the western shore.

Dakkah would have been the first of these temples to be visited. It was built, 40 km (25 miles) north of its present site, by the 3rd-century local king Argamani, reusing stones from earlier buildings. Despite extensive additions under the Ptolemies and the Roman emperor Augustus, the temple was never finished, as is apparent from the lack of decoration on parts of the pylon.

The neighbouring temple of **Mahrraqah** originally stood 30 km (18 miles) to the north of its present site at the frontier marker of Ptolemaic Egypt. It is a later building than Dakkah, constructed during the Roman period and dedicated to Isis and Serapis.

Wadi al-Sabu (the Valley of Lions) is the most complete of this group. The temple, originally located 2 km (1¼ miles) further southwest, takes its name from an avenue of sphinxes that lead to a temple built by the Viceroy of Kush for Ramesses II. Colossal figures of the pharaoh stand at the entrance and line pillars in the court. The outer areas of the temple were built of sandstone, but the

BELOW: Nubian man.

vestibule, antechamber and sanctuary were carved out of the rock. The figures of Ramesses, Amun-Ra and Ra-Harakhte, which once occupied the sanctuary, gave way to an image of St Peter when the temple was converted into a church.

Forty kilometres (25 miles) south of Wadi al-Sabu, three monuments now stand on the original west-bank site of the Temple of Amadah. The small 18th-Dynasty **Amadah Temple** ⑰ was built a couple of kilometres away by Tuthmosis III and Amenhotep II. The illustrations of planning and building the temple (in the innermost left-hand chapel) are worth finding. The nearby rock-cut **Temple of Derr** was moved 11 km (7 miles) north. Dedicated like the al-Sabu temple to Amun-Ra and Ra-Harakhte, its figures were badly damaged by Christians using it as a church. Also here is the **tomb of Penne**, a local governor (1141–1133 BC), moved from Anibaah, 40 km (25 miles) south.

Qasr Ibrim ⑱ still occupies its original position, about 15 km (9 miles) north of Abu Simbel. Now an island, before the flooding it was situated on the eastern bank of the Nile where three massive peaks of rock rose from the river. Crowning the middle peak were a ruined town and fortress, whose imposing position commanded the valley for miles around in all directions.

This *qasr* (castle) is all that emerges above the level of the lake today but it must have been a striking landmark in Roman times when the first fortress was built. A joint American/British excavation started in 1986 and aims to restore its major monuments, including a cathedral. The earliest inscriptions found so far date to the 16th century BC and there are remains of a significant Byzantine cathedral. It is known that the Romans, Saladin, the Ottoman emperor Selim and Muhammad Ali all stationed garrisons here.

Of the other temples that lined the Nile in this part of Nubia, some were

Map, page 202

Qasr Ibrim is the only site in Nubia where archaeologists are still at work.

BELOW: a calm start to a new day on Lake Nasser.

BELOW: the Temple of Ramesses II before excavation.

presented by the Egyptian government to nations that helped during the salvage operation (see, for instance, the Temple of Dandur at New York's Metropolitan Museum, the Temple of Taffah in the Leiden Rijksmuseum, the Horus Temple from Al Lasiyyah in the Turin Museum). Many others were left in place and lie beneath the cruise boats at the bottom of the lake.

The temples of Abu Simbel

The largest and most magnificent monument in Nubia, the famous **Temple of Ramesses II ⓲** (open daily; 7am–6pm in summer; 7am–5pm in winter; admission charge) at Abu Simbel, 280 km (174 miles) south of Aswan, presented a formidable challenge. Unlike other temples, Abu Simbel was not freestanding. The temple facade was, in fact, the cliff face itself hewn in imitation of a pylon, dominated by four seated statues of a youthful Ramesses II. The central hall was flanked by eight more statues of the king in a double row facing each other, against a corresponding number of square pillars. The northern wall of the hall was decorated with the Great Battle Scene, which is one of the most extraordinary and detailed reliefs to be found in the Nile Valley. There are over 1,100 figures and the entire wall, from ceiling to bedrock, is filled with activity: the march of the Egyptian army with its infantry and charioteers, its engagement in hand-to-hand combat and the flight of the vanquished prisoners, leaving overturned chariots behind them. There are also scenes of camp life.

Beyond the court, carved out of the mountain to a depth of 55 metres (180 ft), was the sanctuary, which contained seated statues of four gods, Ptah of Memphis, Amun-Ra of Thebes, the deified Ramesses II and Ra-Harakhte, the sun god of Heliopolis.

The project finally chosen entailed sawing the temple into over a thousand transportable pieces, some weighing as much as 15 tons, and placing them safely above the water level until they could be reassembled at a new site 60 metres (200 ft) higher than their original site. While the stone blocks were being treated and stored, the new site on top of the mountain was levelled. Explosives could have ruined the temples, so compressed-air drills were used instead. Studies were carried out on the bedrock to ensure that it could support the huge weight it was destined to bear, not only the mass of the reconstructed temple, but also a great reinforced concrete dome that would cover it.

The reconstruction is nearly perfect and every year on 22 February and 22 October, only one day later than originally planned, the dawn rays of the sun reach to the heart of the sanctuary to revive the cult statues. Knowing the effort that went into this massive project, the temple of Ramesses II looks almost too good to be true. The colossal statues, with finely carved faces but crudely finished bodies, and the reliefs inside the temple, never fail to impress. The tour concludes with a visit behind the scenes to the futuristic structure that was built to support the temple once it had been moved. There is something awesome about this modern achievement.

The small **Temple of Queen Nefertari** (additional admission charge) which lay to the north of the Great Temple at Abu Simbel, was also saved. Nefertari was the most beloved of the wives of Ramesses II; and the pharaoh took the unprecedented step of having the façade of this temple decorated with statues of himself, his wife, and their children. The goddess Hathor, to whom the temple is also dedicated, lovingly attends to the sun god during his day's passage, so Nefertari is depicted watching her husband kill his enemies, admiringly. ❑

Map, page 202

Hathor emblem in the small Temple of Nefertari.

BELOW: the Queen's temple at Abu Simbel.

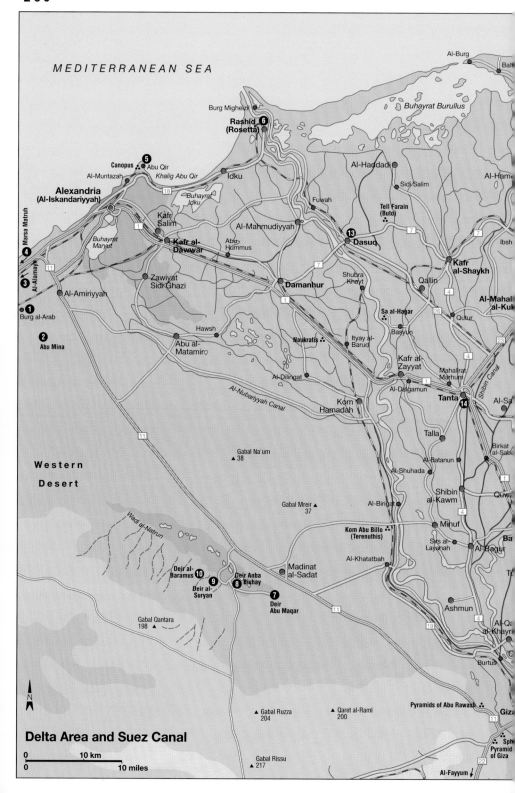

MEDITERRANEAN SEA

Al-Burg

Bal

Burg Migheizl

Buhayrat Burullus

Rashid (Rosetta) **6**

Canopus **5** Abu Qir

Al-Muntazah

Khalig Abu Qir

Idku

Al-Haddadi

Al-Ham

Alexandria (Al-Iskandariyyah)

Kafr Salim

Buhayrat Idku

Fuwah

Sidi Salim

Marsa Matruh

Buhayrat Maryut

Kafr al-Dawwar

Al-Mahmudiyyah

Tell Farain (Buto)

Abu Hummus

Dasuq **13**

Ibsh

4

3 Al-Alamayn

Zawiyat Sidi Ghazi

Damanhur

Shubra Khayt

Qallin

Kafr al-Shaykh

11

Al-Amiriyyah

Sa al-Hagar

Al-Mahal al-Kul

1 Burg al-Arab

Hawsh

Naukratis

Ityay al-Barud

Basyun

Qutur

26

2 Abu Mina

Abu al-Matamir

Al-Dilingat

Kafr al-Zayyat

Mahallat Marhum

23

4

Al-Nubariyyah Canal

Al-Dalgamun

Shibin Canal

Kom Hamadah

Tanta **14**

Al-Sa

Talla

Birkat al-Saba

Gabal Na'um ▲ 38

Al-Batanun

Al-Shuhada

Shibin al-Kawm

Quw

Western Desert

Gabal Mreir ▲ 37

Al-Biriqat

4

11

Wadi al-Natrun

Kom Abu Billo (Terenuthis)

Minuf

Sirs al-Layanah

Al-Baqur

Ba

Deir al-Baramus **10**

9

Deir Anba Bishay **8**

Madinat al-Sadat

Al-Khatatbah

Al-Qa al-Khayr

Deir al-Suryan

7

Deir Abu Maqar

Ashmun

Gabal Qantara 198 ▲

Burtus

Tr

N

Pyramids of Abu Rawash

Giza

Delta Area and Suez Canal

Gabal Ruzza ▲ 204

Qaret al-Raml ▲ 200

Pyramid of Giza

Sph

0 ____ 10 km

0 ____ 10 miles

Gabal Rissu ▲ 217

22

Al-Fayyum

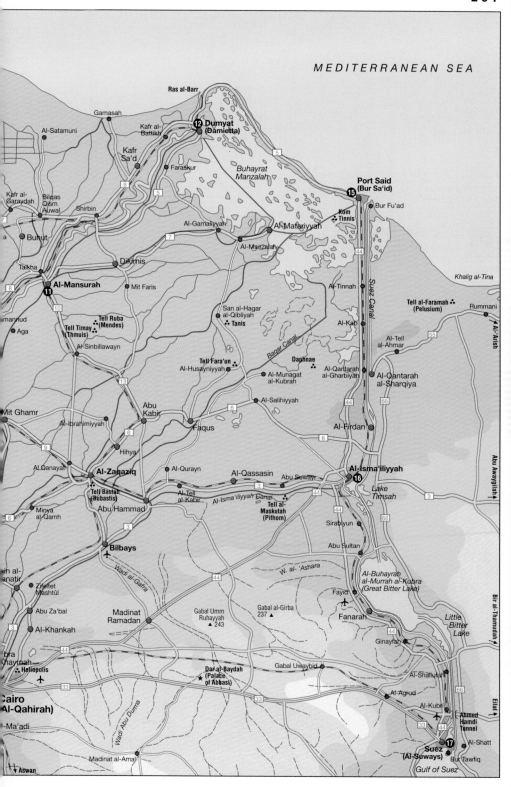

MEDITERRANEAN SEA

Ras al-Barr

Gamasah

Al-Satamuni

Kafr al-Battikh

Kafr Sa'd

12 Dumyat (Damietta)

Faraskur

Buhayrat Manzalah

15 Port Said (Bur Sa'id)

Bur Fu'ad

Kafr al-Garaydah

Bilqas Qism Auwal

Shirbin

8

5

7

Kom Tinnis

Al-Gamaliyyah

Al-Matariyyah

Buhut

Talkha

Dikimis

11 Al-Mansurah

Mit Faris

Al-Manzalah

Khalig al-Tina

8

10

amannud

Aga

Tell Ruba (Mendes)

Tell Timay (Thmuis)

Al-Sinbillawyn

San al-Hagar al-Qibliyah

❖ Tanis

Al-Tinnah

Al-Kab

Suez Canal

Tell al-Faramah ❖ (Pelusium)

Rummani

Al-'Arish

44

55

Tell al-Ahmar

Al-Tell al-Ahmar

13

Tell Fara'un

Al-Husayniyyah

Baqar Canal

Daphnae

Al-Munagat al-Kubrah

Al-Qantarah al-Gharbiyyah

Al-Qantarah al-Sharqiya

Mit Ghamr

Al-Ibrahimiyyah

Abu Kabir

Al-Salihiyyah

6

Faqus

Al-Firdan

44

66

9

Hihya

6

Al-Qanayat

Al-Zaqaziq

Al-Qurayn

Al-Qassasin

Abu Suwayr

16 Al-Isma'iliyyah

Lake Timsah

3

Tell Bastan (Bubastis)

Abu Hammad

Al-Tell al-Kabir

Al-Isma'iliyyah Canal

Tell al-Maskutah (Pithom)

44

Minya al-Qamh

6

Sirabiyun

66

Bilbays

Wadi al-Gafra

W. al-'Ashara

Abu Bultan

Abu Za'bal

Zifeitet Mashtûl

Madinat Ramadan

Gabal Umm Ruhayyah ▲ 243

Gabal al-Girba 237 ▲

Fayid

Al-Buhayrah al-Murrah al-Kubra (Great Bitter Lake)

Al-Khankah

Fanarah

Little Bitter Lake

Heliopolis

44

Dar al-Baydah (Palace of Abbasi) ★

Gabal Uwaybid

Ginayfah

Al-Shallufat

Abu Awaygilah ▶

Bir al-Thamudah ▶

33

Cairo (Al-Qahirah)

Ma'adi

33

At-Agrud

Al-Kubri

Eilat ▶

Ahmed Hamdi Tunnel

33

44

66

Madinat al-Amal

Aswan ▼

17 Suez (Al-Suways)

Al-Shatt

Bur Tawfiq

Gulf of Suez

ALEXANDRIA AND THE NORTHERN COAST

Modern Alexandria is the second largest city in Egypt. Set on the shores of the Mediterranean, it has long been a popular holiday spot, a refuge from landlocked Cairo's searing summer heat

Maps, 260–261 and 264

When emperor Alexander died in 325 BC, his mortal remains were taken to Memphis for burial, but the priests of Memphis sent the funeral cortège away. "Do not settle him here," they said, "but at the city he built at Rhakotis. For wherever his body must lie, that city will be uneasy, disturbed by wars and battles." So the conqueror of Asia was returned to the city he had established eight years earlier, where he was buried in a grave now lost somewhere below the foundations of modern Alexandria. And the priests were wrong: Memphis today is a sand heap waiting for future archaeologists, while Alexandria, although buffeted by many wars and battles, has somehow managed to stand the test of time.

Sadly, however, there is very little left of the buildings and monuments that graced it during the Hellenistic and post-Hellenistic period, making Alexandria the most renowned city of the ancient world after Athens and Rome. An odd column or two on the skyline, dank catacombs deep under modern pavements, a Roman pillar propping up the gateway to some pre-Revolutionary patrician villa and a growing inventory of masonry and statues beneath the Mediterranean are all that is left of this glorious past.

A magnificent entry

When the 25-year-old Macedonian conqueror Alexander the Great arrived in Egypt in 332 BC, he realised that he needed a capital for his newly conquered Egyptian kingdom and that, to link it with Macedonia, it would have to be located on the coast. Early in 331 he sailed northward from Memphis down the Nile, then westward along the coast. At a small fishing village called Rhakotis, on a spit of land between the sea and a freshwater lake, with limestone quarries and easy access to the Nile, he founded his city, gave orders to build it and promptly departed. He never saw his new metropolis.

After Alexander's death in 323 BC, Egypt fell to a Macedonian general named Ptolemy who had been present at the foundation of Alexandria. He made it his new capital and founded a dynasty that lasted until 30 BC.

The first Ptolemies busily set about adorning their city. They also encouraged scholarship; and under their rule Alexandria became a haven and refuge for intellectuals. The first two Ptolemies meanwhile decided that they needed a great monument in their new city, which could be seen by ships at sea and provide a guide for sailors through

PRECEDING PAGES: punts on Lake Idku. **LEFT:** boy among the typically flat irrigated fields. **BELOW:** Delta family on the move.

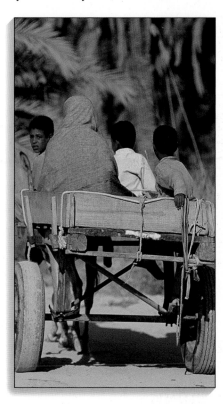

the limestone reefs that line the shore. Thus the lighthouse on the island of Pharos, one of the Seven Great Wonders of the ancient world, came into being. A fortress as well as a beacon, this huge lighthouse stood at the eastern end of Pharos, where it dominated both the Eastern Harbour, which sheltered the royal fleet, and the Western Harbour. Little remains of the lighthouse beyond a few Aswan granite blocks, although some if its statues and masonry have recently been found nearby beneath the harbour.

...few cities have made so magnificent an entry into history as Alexandria.

—E.M. FORSTER

The Mouseion

The Ptolemies' intellectual achievement was epitomised by the Great Library attached to the Mouseion in Alexandria. In many ways, the Mouseion, a shrine to the Muses, resembled a modern university, but the scholars, scientists and literary men it supported were under no obligation to teach. They could devote their entire time to their studies. The Great Library was, alas, burned down during Caesar's wars and the Mouseion's buildings have disappeared under subsequent rubble.

External threat, nationalist rebellion, intrigue at court and family strife made the Ptolemaic dynasty dependent on Rome. By 89 BC, thanks to the debts it owed to this new power, the Ptolemaic dynasty was under Roman control. In 51 BC, while rivals squabbled in the Roman Senate, a 17-year-old girl was crowned queen in Alexandria as Cleopatra VI. Three years later she was ready to play the temptress, first at Caesar's, then at Mark Antony's feet. And as long as she lived, Alexandria preserved its autonomy. At her death, it became a Roman city.

Centuries of decline

As Rome acquired increasing sway over its new colonies in the East, Christianity, a brand-new religious movement, began to find disciples. More than any other city in the Roman Empire, Alexandria was the intellectual capital of the new religion.

The conflict between the Church and State came to its height in the first years of the 4th century under the emperor Diocletian, who demolished churches, demoted all Christian officials and enslaved or killed the rest, as many as 60 a day for a period of five years, according to the traditions of the Coptic Church. This persecution prompted flight to the desert, which led to the founding of the first monasteries, and made such a strong impression on the Egyptian church that it dates its calendar from what is now called "the Era of Martyrs".

In 641, Alexandria fell to the Arab General Amr, who rode into Egypt with 3,500 Bedu horsemen. Islam, the new religion that Amr brought with him, would have been hostile to a pagan Alexandria and was uneasy with

Map, page 264

TIP

To read about the recent underwater excavations that have revealed a wealth of new information about ancient Alexandria, turn to the picture story on pages 280–281.

BELOW: late Roman council chamber excavated in downtown Alexandria.

a Christian one, but the Arab Conquest was a humane affair and no damage was done to property. The two great libraries, which the Arabs are often accused of destroying, had already been burned by pagans and Christians. It was Cairo that would develop and blossom under Egypt's Arab masters, however, while Alexandria gradually dwindled, especially after a Frankish raid in 1365, when all the public buildings were destroyed and 5,000 people were carried off to slavery.

Renaissance and revolution

Modern Alexandria really dates from the early 19th century and the reign of Muhammad Ali, who was responsible for introducing cotton and for building the Mahmudiyyah Canal. This once more linked Alexandria to the hinterland, forcing Egypt to look not only towards the Mediterranean again, but beyond it, to Europe. The later 19th century witnessed the creation of extensive wealth in the cotton trade and a steady influx of Greeks, Italians, French and English, who turned Alexandria into a pseudo-European city, complete with wide, grid-planned streets, foreign schools, clubs, restaurants, casinos, businesses and banks.

The 1952 Revolution changed all that. The new government eventually expelled most foreigners and confiscated their lands or nationalised their businesses, while Egyptian capital and enterprise fled abroad.

Using the mind's eye

Modern visitors to Alexandria will get the most out of the city if they possess lively imaginations. That is not to say that there isn't plenty to

As soon as World War II was over the writing was on the wall for Alexandria's European community, and the far-sighted were already geting out.

—DAVID HOLDEN

Letter from Alexandria

1963

BELOW: Cecil Hotel, an Alexandrian institution.

look at, for the city is still enchanting, but the visible glories of its past are few and far between and for the most part must be almost reconstructed in the mind's eye.

A good place to begin is the **Cecil Hotel** , located at the heart of the former European zone, overlooking the sea. The entrance to the hotel is on the west side of **Maydan Sad Zaghlul**, a large square between **Ramleh** (*Al Raml*) **tram station** and the **Corniche**. Here, in the lee of a few straggling palm trees, where the Romans built a temple to honour Julius Caesar, Cairo buses disgorge their passengers.

The two obelisks that once stood here, the famous Cleopatra's Needles, are now in London and New York. In the centre of the *maydan* is a **statue of Sad Zaghlul**, the nationalist hero who tried to negotiate the independence of Egypt after World War I. As you stand facing the sea, let your gaze follow the sweep of land to your left and come to rest on the Fort of Qaytbay at the western tip of the headland. The best time to see the fort is just before the sun goes down, when the warm reds and oranges of an Alexandrian sunset turn the sandstone building the colour of rich honey.

The Fortress and the Pharos

The trip out to the tip of the promontory where the **Fort of Qaytbay** **B** (open daily 9am–4pm; admission charge) stands is of no particular interest except that it stands on the site of the ancient **Pharos lighthouse**. On the Corniche side, you pass some dilapidated apartment buildings, gaily festooned with washing. On the sea side is the modern Yacht Club and a small fishing port, where brightly painted boats bob up and down on a

Map, page 264

TIP

The city is best explored on foot, but taxis, painted in distinctive black and orange, are plentiful and cheap and can be hired by the hour or by the day.

BELOW: the Eastern Harbour and the fort of Qaitbay.

dirty-looking sea and nets are hung along the jetty to dry. The fort is at the end of a breakwater and has been restored since the British bombardment of Alexandria in 1882, the preliminary to their invasion and occupation.

The lighthouse, built in around 279 BC, was a marvel of its day. It rose to over 120 metres (400 ft) and hydraulic machinery may have been used for hauling fuel to the top. Within its square base were as many as 300 rooms, to house mechanics and operators; above were an octagonal storey and a circular storey, topped by a lantern with a beacon and devices that are still a mystery. One of these was described as a mirror of polished steel, to reflect the sun by day and a fire by night, or as made of glass or transparent stone, so fashioned as to enable a man sitting under it to see ships at sea that were invisible to the naked eye. This description suggests a kind of prism, the secret of which Alexandrian mathematicians might well have discovered, only for it to be lost or destroyed when the Pharos lighthouse fell.

The lantern collapsed as early as the 8th century, followed by the circular storey. In 881 Ibn Tulun did some restoration, but in 1100 an earthquake toppled the octagonal storey and nullified his efforts. The Pharos still served as a lighthouse, however, until the square base was finally ruined in another earthquake in the 14th century. Enter Sultan Qaytbay, who in 1480 built the fort that still stands on the site, which incorporates some of the debris from the Pharos – you can make out granite and marble columns, for example, in the northwest section of the enclosure walls. The fort itself is an impressive piece of defensive architecture and inside is a revamped **Naval Museum** (additional addmission charge).

BELOW: Ras al-Tin Palace.

Ras al-Tin and Anfushi

Westward along the seafront 3 km (1½ miles) from the fort, is the19th-century **Palace of Ras al-Tin**  (Cape of Figs). Built by Muhammad Ali, but altered by later rulers of Egypt, this enormous pile is still used for official Egyptian government functions and cannot be visited. East of the Palace on Shari' Ras al-Tin, near the end of the tramline, and worth a look, are the **tombs of Anfushi** (open daily, 9am–4pm; admission charge). Ptolemaic, with decorations that marry Greek and Egyptian styles, their stucco walls are painted to imitate marble blocks and tiles.

At this point, you can turn into the old Turkish quarter of **Al-Anfushi** at the heart of what was once the island of Pharos.

Continuing southeast along Shari' Ras al-Tin you will reach **Shari' Faransa** (Rue de France). You are now in one of the most "native" parts of the city, where you may like to stop briefly to look at the 17th-century **Tirbana mosque**. It has a distinctive pale yellow exterior, with plaster overlying a red and black Delta-style facade of bricks and wooden beams. On its left side note the ancient columns at the entrance to the cellars. Two huge Corinthian columns mark the entrance to the mosque itself and support its minaret.

In ancient times Pharos was joined to the mainland by a causeway called the **Heptastadion**, which gradually became a permanent broad neck of land. Along it to the south Shari' Faransa runs into **Maydan al-Tahrir**, formerly Place Muhammad Ali. A statue of the Pasha on horseback (by Jacquemart) still graces the *maydan*. The southern end of the square marks approximately the former mainland coastline and the seafront of the village of Rhakotis.

Statue of Mohammad Ali, overlooking Maydan al-Tahrir

BELOW: tombs of Anfushi.

The southern quarter

To reach the centre of **Rhakotis**, the hub of ancient Alexandria, you must be prepared for a detour, armed with a map and on foot, through a particularly insalubrious part of town. Rhakotis is about 1.5km (1 mile) southwest from the Corniche along Shari' Salah ad-Din and Shari' Amud al-Sawari. Simplest, perhaps, is to hail a taxi and tell the driver to take you to **Pompey's Pillar** – Al-Awud as-Sawari, The Horseman's Pillar (open daily 9am–4pm; admission charge). If you survive the drive, bumping over busy tram tracks, you will reach the bottom of a rather shapeless hill surrounded by a wall – this is now all that's left of the acropolis of the Ptolemies.

Long before Alexander arrived on the scene, this hill was the citadel of Rhakotis, dedicated to the worship of Osiris. The Ptolemies in their turn constructed a temple of Serapis on its summit. Here, with a collection of around 200,000 manuscripts given to her by Mark Antony, Cleopatra endowed the second great Alexandrian library, which was to remain attached to the **Serapeum** until the temple itself was destroyed by a Christian mob. Unbelievable as it seems now, this was the most learned spot on earth for almost half a century.

Map, page 264

Today not much of the Serapeum remains: some tunnels in the rocks with crypts and niches and a few marble pillars. But the principal attraction, a solitary 22-metre (72-ft) high pillar of pink Aswan granite, seems to touch the sky defiantly and when European travellers arrived in the 15th century it caught their attention. No scholars they but, since they had heard of Pompey, they named the pillar after him and said his head was enclosed in a ball at the top. It actually has nothing to do with Pompey: according to an inscription on its base, it was dedicated to the emperor Diocletian in 297 and it may once have had an equestrian statue on top, which would explain its Arabic name.

This once-famous site has been encroached upon by a brash and often ugly modern city: hideous buildings loom around its perimeter, trams bump, screech and grind their way noisily along the street below. But a certain sense of dignity and charm lingers.

The catacombs

A short distance south of the site of Pompey's pillar are the **catacombs of Kom al-Shuqafah** ⓕ (open daily 9am–4pm; entrance fee). Come out of the enclosure of Pompey's Pillar, turn right up a small crowded street and at the top you will come to a small crossroads. Just beyond it is the entrance to the catacombs.

Immediately inside the entrance are four very fine sarcophagi of purplish granite. You are now on the Kom al-Shuqafah (Hill of Tiles) and the tombs here constitute the largest Roman-period funerary complex in Egypt. They date from about the 2nd century AD, when the old religions

BELOW: Pompey's Pillar and one of two Ptolemaic sphinxes.

began to fade and merge with one another, as demonstrated in the curious blend of classical and Egyptian designs.

The catacombs are on three different levels, the lowest being flooded and inaccessible. The first level is reached by a wide circular staircase lit by a central well, down which the bodies were lowered by ropes. From the vestibule you enter the Rotunda, with a well in its centre, upon which eight pillars support a domed roof. To the left is the Banquet Hall.

From the Rotunda, a small staircase descends to the second level and the amazing central tomb is revealed. Here the decorations are fantastic and in a hotchpotch of styles. Bearded serpents on the vestibule wall at the entrance of the inner chamber hold the pine-cone of Dionysus and the serpent-wand of Hermes, but also wear the double crown of Upper and Lower Egypt, while above them are Medusas in round shields. Inside the tomb chamber are three large sarcophagi cut out from the rock. Roman in style, decorated with fruits, flowers, Medusas and filleted ox-heads, none of them has ever been occupied and their lids are sealed on. Over each of the sarcophagi is a niche decorated with Egyptian-style reliefs.

Turn and face the entrance. On your right stands the extraordinary figure of Anubis – with a dog's head, but dressed as a Roman soldier, with sword, lance and shield. Left is the god Sobek, the crocodile god, also dressed in military costume, with cloak and spear.

In search of Alexander

Start at **Maydan Sad Zaghlul** Ⓖ and walk south along Shari' al-Nabi Danyal. The point where it meets Shari' Tariq al-Hurriyyah has been the

Map, page 264

BELOW: the catacombs of Kom al-Shuqafah.

chief crossroads of the city for over 2,300 years. Here, from east and west, the Canopic Way (Shari' Tariq al-Hurriyyah) once ran from the Gate of the Sun to the Gate of the Moon. From north to south ran a street joining the harbour and its docks with Lake Mareotis, now Shari' al-Nabi Danyal.

A short walk up Shari' al-Nabi Danyal will bring you to the Nabi Danyal Mosque, on the left side of the street with an entrance somewhat set back. Mistakenly believed to be the tomb of the prophet Daniel, it is named after Shaykh Danyal al-Maridi, who died in 1407. It is also falsely believed to be the site of Alexander's tomb, the Soma, where he and some of the Ptolemies were buried in the Macedonian manner.

Inside the mosque, an ancient caretaker will beckon you over to peer down a great square hole into the crypt where Danyal and one Luqman the Wise lie, keeping company (it is alleged) with Alexander and some of his successors. Almost straight opposite the mosque some antique columns prop up the gatepost of what is now a French Cultural Centre.

In ancient times the streets now called Shari' al-Hurriyah and Shari' Tariq al-Nabi Danyal were both lined from end to end with colonnades

Kom al-Dikkah and the Greco-Roman Museum

One block east of Nabi Danyal, on the south side of Shari' Tariq al-Hurriyyah, lie the **excavations of Kom al-Dikkah ❶** (open 9am–4pm; closed Fri; admission charge). Here Polish archaeologists have been digging up Alexandria's past since 1959. Below Muslim tombs dating from the 9th to 11th centuries, they have found baths, houses, assembly halls and the site where Christian mobs burnt objects from the Serapeum. The main attraction is the small 2nd-century threatre, with well-preserved mosaic flooring. Here also are some of the Pharos statues recently dis-

BELOW: browsing in the gold market.

covered in the waters around Qaytbay's fort. Continue east along Shari' Tariq al-Hurriyyah and you will come to the Rue du Musée and to the entrance of the **Greco-Roman Museum** ❾ (open 9am–4pm; closed Fri 11.30am–1.30pm; admission charge).

For visitors satiated with the hieratic wonders of ancient Egyptian civilisation, the Greco-Roman Museum can only come as a delightful relief. Filling the historical gap between the country's several museums of pharaonic antiquities and Cairo's museums of Coptic and Islamic art, it has recently been renovated and a charming new sculpture garden has been laid out in its grounds. Among its many treasures are some spectacular pieces of Hellenistic sculpture, but special attention must be paid to the wonderful collection of Tanagra figurines. Likewise not to be missed is a masterpiece of fresco-painting that is also the earliest depiction of an ox-powered waterwheel.

Map, page 264

Hellenistic sculpture in the Greco-Roman Museum.

Modern pleasures

This might be the time to take a break from sightseeing and to stroll back down Shari' Tariq al-Hurriyyah towards the sea, stopping off at **Pastroudis**, one of the last Greek cafés. Here you can take some refreshment while you sit at a pavement table overlooking the ruins of Kom al-Dikkah and ponder Alexandria's more recent cultural past.

During the earlier part of this century a literary revival took place. Its luminary was Constantine Cavafy (1863–1933), called "the poet of the City" by Lawrence Durrell. E.M. Forster, who lived in Alexandria and wrote its history, first met Cavafy in 1917 and was responsible for introducing him to the English-speaking world.

The Greek poet's apartment at 4 Shari' Sharm al-Shaykh became a wonderful **museum** in 1993 (open Tue, Wed, Fri, Sat 10am–3pm; Thu, Sun 10am–3pm and 6–8pm). Lawrence Durrell's *Alexandria Quartet* was to a large extent inspired by Constantine Cavafy's poetry, and all the characters in the *Quartet* meet at least once at Pastroudis for an *araq*.

Alexandria is a Mediterranean city and still has a Mediterranean café life. **Pastroudis**, the **Trianon** and the **Delices** (the last two are on Maydan Sad Zaghlul) are fine examples, if somewhat forlorn, of *fin-de-siècle* coffee houses.

Alexandria has a reputation for good food, particularly seafood. Greek *tavernas*, such as the **Diamantakis Taverna** on the south side of **Maydan Rami** (Ramleh Square), offer fried or grilled fish and Greek salads. The **Santa Lucia** on Shari' Safiyyah Zaghlul (not far from Pastroudis) is the best-known restaurant: the food is good and the atmosphere lively. A relic of the past is the **Union**, now closed, on Shari'al-Bursa just off Maydan Muhammad Ali, near where the charming Anglican **cathedral of St Mark's** is situated. As for hotels, romantics will probably favour landmarks such as the Cecil, the Metropole or the Windsor Palace, all overlooking the sea.

BELOW: patron at the Trianon café.

TIP

The train that runs
west just inland from
the Mediterranean
coast is unreliable, and
anyone interested in
exploring the region
west of Alexandria
would do best to hire a
car by the day.

Slightly out of the centre, on 27 Shari' Ahmed Yehya Pasha in Zizinia, is the imposing palace of Princess Fatma al-Zahraa, now housing the **Royal Jewellery Museum** Ⓚ. This little-visited museum (open 9am–4pm; closed Fri 11.30am–1.30pm; admission charge) has a wonderful collection of jewellery, covering a period from Muhammad Ali to the abdication of King Faruq.

A stroll in the garden

Green spaces are now a rare sight in Alexandria, but some gardens remind the visitor of its former glory. Khedive Abbas II's **Muntazah Palace** Ⓛ, now the presidential summer residence, is surrounded by 140 hectares (350 acres) of pleasure gardens (open 24 hours; admission charge). Alexandrians come for a stroll or a picnic and its private beach is cleaner than most.

Near the zoo and the Nuzha Gardens are the elegant **Antoniadis Gardens** Ⓜ in Semouha Street (open daily 8am–4pm; admission charge). These peaceful formal gardens surround the 19th-century villa of the Greek philanthropist Sir John Antoniadis.

West to Burg al-Arab

The coast road west of Alexandria is unprepossessing for the first 30 km (18 miles) until you pass the resort town of **Agami**, which began some years ago as a few bathing huts and simple beach houses in a grove of trees, but has now mushroomed into the Marbella or St Tropez of Egypt's Mediterranean coast, complete with swimming pools, discotheques, fast-food joints and a section of villas known as "Millionaire's Row".

BELOW: holiday time at Muntazah.

Before the turn-off to the village of **Burg al-Arab** on the hill on your left, is the ancient **temple of Taposiris Magna**, whose name is preserved in the modern Abu Sir. It is contemporary with the founding of Alexandria and was dedicated to the cult of Osiris. The ruined tower to the east is a Ptolemaic lighthouse, the first of a chain that stretched from Alexandria all the way down the North African coast. It looks, in miniature, very much as its big brother, the Pharos, would have appeared.

It is no longer possible to ascend to the top of the lighthouse – a great pity, as the view is magnificent: to the north, the brilliant turquoise blue of the sea is offset by its bleached white beaches, while to the south lies the dun-coloured lake-bed of **Maryut** (ancient Mareotis), vibrantly alive with wildflowers in the spring. If you leave the coast and drive south across the lake-bed, you will be able to make out the remains of the ancient causeway, to your left, which connected ancient Taposiris with the desert.

Over the crest of the hill, you will come to the curious little village of **Burg al-Arab ❶**, the brainchild of W.E. Jennings-Bramley, governor of the Western Desert under the British, who decided in the early 1920s to build a Bedu capital using stone from the ruins of Roman villas, which dotted the area. Modelling his village as a fortified medieval Italian hill town, he invited friends to build vacation houses within its turretted walls. Today the village looks like a crumbling set for a remake of *Beau Geste*, though one or two of the houses are still in private hands and the Egyptian president has a rest house there.

From here, you may want to continue inland and visit the ruins of the **monastery of Abu Mina ❷**. Drive south out of Burg al-Arab through an

Map, pages 260–1

We've driven out through Burg al Arab, and slipped down through the battlefields to a long beach where the real Mediterranean comes up in great green coasters.

– LAWRENCE DURRELL, 1944

BELOW: rural scene in the Delta.

industrial development and turn left at the first crossroads you come to. This road will take you to the turn-off to the monastery. Before long you will spot the twin towers of the new monastery, founded in 1959, on the horizon, an ugly concrete pile much favoured as a pilgrimage spot by modern Copts. Drive on by and very shortly you will see a low line of hillocks to your right. You have arrived at the site of the ancient monastery of Abu Mina (*see box below*) and the hillocks are the scrap heaps left behind by several generations of enthusiastic archaeologists.

The site has been excavated and the foundations of the primitive church and the basilica of Arcadius may be clearly discerned. The crypt where St Mina was buried lies at the foot of a marble staircase in the church, which was incorporated into the portico of the basilica, but his relics rest in the modern monastery. A baptistry with a font can be seen to the west. North of the basilica are the hospice and baths that were fed by healing springs, with cisterns for hot and cold water.

Pursuing the Desert Fox

Further along the coast road 105 km (65 miles) west of Alexandria, is **Al-Alamayn ❸** (Alamein), the site of a series of battles that began in the summer of 1942 and turned the tide of war in favour of the Allies.

Of the three main war cemeteries in Al-Alamayn, the British is the first one you come to. It is on your left as you enter the town from the east. A walk around the simple tombstones, each of which carries an inscription, cannot fail to move. In the centre of town is a **Military Museum** (open daily 8am–6pm; admission charge) housing numerous artifacts of the bat-

The distinctive little water flasks with their stamped depictions of St Mina standing between two kneeling camels have been found as far afield as France and Spain.

BELOW: the Italian memorial to the fallen.

THE CULT OF ST MINA

Abu Mina was a young Egyptian officer, martyred in 296 during his service in Asia Minor because he would not renounce Christ. When his troops returned to Egypt, they buried him at the spot where the camel carrying his remains refused to go any further. Some time after this, a shepherd noticed that a sick lamb passing over the burial spot became well; so did another lamb, then a sick princess. The saint's powers were quickly recognised by Christians far and wide. A church, built over his grave in the 4th century, was incorporated into a great basilica by emperor Arcadius in the early 5th century.

For pilgrims, the site became the Lourdes of the Western Desert. The reason for this rapid popularity was probably the local water, which must have had potent curative powers, for in the shrine's heyday pilgrims flocked here by the thousands, filling little flasks, specially stamped with the saint's image, from the sacred source that flowed by his tomb. Over time houses sprang up, a baths complex was built, the land nearby was irrigated for agriculture, and a proper settlement evolved.

Conversions to Islam eventually put an end to the cult, but as late as the year 1000 an Arab traveller saw the great double basilica dedicated to the saint still standing in the desert: lights still burned day and night at the shrine and there was a trickle of "the beautiful water of St Mina that drives away pain".

tle. Beyond stands the massive stone monument to Germany's fallen in a beautiful setting which overlooks the sea. Further on down the coast is the Italian memorial, a huge impressive white marble pile, curiously reminiscent of a railway station in a provincial Italian city.

From this point on, the coast is startlingly beautiful, although increasingly developed. On the left are the duns and ochres of the desert, enlivened by an occasional flash of colour from a gaily painted house or Bedu tent; to the right, the sea stretches towards infinity.

If you long for a day on the beach, keep going to **Sidi Abd al-Rahman**, about 25 km (15 miles) beyond Al-Alamayn: some people claim it's the best beach on the coast. There is a perfectly adequate hotel here, the Alamein Hotel, with camping facilities.

Or, alternatively, you can go all the way to **Marsa Matruh ❹**, 72 km (45 miles) farther, 280 km (175 miles) from Alexandria, which has long been a seaside resort and has some fine beaches. Its seaside is now lined with hotels, mostly aimed at Egyptian holidaymakers, but the town still has some character. There you can visit **Rommel's Cave** (open daily 9.30am–4pm summer only; admission charge), now a museum containing, among other things, the Desert Fox's own armoury, donated by his son. The beach to the east of the museum, supposedly where Rommel went for his daily swim, is popular with Egyptian families in the summer.

Eastward to Rosetta

Alexandria's **Corniche** extends some 16 km (10 miles) eastwards and there are a number of public beaches along the seafront between the

Map, pages 260–1

BELOW: Cleopatra's Baths, Marsa Matruh.

Eastern Harbour and Muntazah. But they are crowded and often dirty and incessant building has turned most of the Corniche into an ugly string of high-rise buildings, lashed into premature decrepitude by salty sea-winds.

Eight kilometres (5 miles) east of Muntazah, with the gardens of the Muntazah Palace, is **Abu Qir ❺**, famous for battles fought here in 1798 and 1799. The only real reason to come to this seaside shanty town now is its excellent seafood restaurants. One, the **Zephyrion**, bears the ancient name of the site. It is a large barn-like structure with an open-air terrace right on the sea. The fish is fresh and best eaten grilled or fried. Wash it down with the local anise drink, *zibib*, or a cold bottle of beer.

The next spot of interest is **Rosetta ❻** (Rashid), 65 km (40 miles) from Alexandria on the western branch of the Nile near the sea. It was here that the Rosetta stone, which enabled Champollion to decipher the language of the pharaohs, was discovered by a French soldier in 1799. Rosetta is famous for its 17th and 18th-century houses. The finest, the house of Ali al-Fatali (1620), has been destroyed but there are 21 others, of which three may be visited. Several 18th-century mosques may be toured, as well as a mill and a *hammam*. A **museum** (open daily 8am–2pm; admission charge) in the Arab Killy House displays coins, metalwork and ceramics.

The monasteries of Wadi al-Natrun

To the west of the Delta, beyond the ridge of desert and just off the Cairo-Alexandria desert road, the **Wadi al-Natrun**, or Valley of Natron, snuggles below sea level. It was once home to over 50 monasteries. Hundreds more monks lived in desert caves. **Deir Abu Maqar ❼**, the largest of the

A joint Franco-Egyptian project at Abu Qir is working to raise from the seabed Napoleon's fleet sunk by Nelson at the Battle of the Nile in 1798.

BELOW: inside the Deir al-Suryan.

monasteries, has in recent years been the seat of the Coptic Pope Shenouda III, who was exiled to the desert by the late President Sadat. Its oldest remains date to the 9th century. It is closed to visitors unless they can show a letter of introduction from the Coptic patriarchate in Cairo. **Anba Bishay** ❽ (open daily, summer 8am–6pm; winter 8am–5pm; free admission), founder of another monastery, was a disciple of Abu Maqar (St Macarius). A third monastery, **Deir al-Suryan** ❾ (open daily, summer 9am–5pm; winter 9am–3pm; free admission), has 10th-century paintings and ivory panels in its church of Al Adhra. **Deir al-Baramus** ❿ (open daily, summer 8am–6pm; winter 8am–5pm; free admission) is the most remote of the four.

Wadi Natrun's churches, like pharaonic temples, have three distinct areas. The outer is reserved for laymen, the middle for initiates and the inner for clergymen. Visitors should on no account venture into the curtained inner sanctuaries. Monasteries are closed to the public during periods of fast: Sexagesima Monday to Orthodox Easter (61 days), Advent (25 November–6 January), before the Feast of the Apostles (27 June–10 July) and before Assumption (7–21 August).

Map, pages 260–1

The Delta

Lush with vegetation and veined with canals, the **Nile Delta** is the flower of the Egyptian lotus. From the Barrage at **Qanatir al-Khayriyyah** in the south, where parks surround locks and sluices built under the British occupation, to the marshy waters of lakes **Idku**, **Burullus** and **Manzalah**, where smugglers live among the reeds, the Delta fans out like a palm reaching for the Mediterranean. To both the west and the east, deserts are receding in the face of vast land reclamation projects, while in the Delta *felaheen* pack their bags for Cairo or the oil-rich Gulf.

ABOVE AND BELOW: at the Monastery of St Bishay.

The prehistoric Delta was a swampy tidal estuary interspersed with islands. Centuries of effluvia built up a silty land mass that eventually split the river in two. Diligent canal building, after the union of Lower and Upper Egypt in the Old Kingdom, tamed the swamp. With the growth of Mediterranean trade and rivalry between Egypt, Phoenicia and the Greeks, the Delta grew in importance, encouraging later pharaohs to abandon the old capitals of Thebes and Memphis and establish headquarters in the Delta near the sea.

Each section of the delta has its particularity. **Al-Mansurah** ⓫, the "victorious", was founded on the site of the Mamluks' triumph over Crusaders under Louis IX. With its Nileside villas from the age when cotton was king and its fair inhabitants, the city is regarded as the Queen of the Delta. **Dumyat** ⓬ (Damietta), which rivalled Alexandria in the Middle Ages, is the home of Egypt's furniture industry; and **Disuq** ⓭ is identified with a festival (*mawalid*) in honour of its saint, Ibrahim ad-Disuqi. The Delta's largest town, **Tanta** ⓮, is known for its October *mouled*, attracting two million people for the festival of Ahmad al-Badawi. ❑

UNDERWATER ARCHAEOLOGY

Time and earthquakes brought down Alexandria's glorious waterfront, but over the past few years efforts have been made to raise it from the sea

Ancient Alexandria was one of the great cities of the world and befitting its role as a major Mediterranean seaport it had a grand waterfront, capped by the Pharos, wonder of the world. The Eastern Harbour, at whose entrance the Pharos stood, was fronted by the royal palace, which was constantly enlarged and embellished. Cleopatra built a new temple on the waterfront in honour of Mark Antony, which Augustus Caesar finished in honour of himself. In front of it stood two older obelisks brought from the south. This temple, the palace and all but a few stones of the Pharos disappeared in the aftermath of earthquakes.

RIVAL DIVERS

Alexandrians always knew they were sailing and swimming over the ruins of their city, but it wasn't until the 1960s that serious underwater exploration began. More recently, two separate teams have been at work beneath the Eastern Harbour.

The site around the Pharos outside the harbour, from where the blocks were recently lifted by a team led by Professor Jean-Yves Empereur of the Centre d'Etudes Alexandrines, was first visited in the 1960s by Kamal Abu al Sadaat. He succeeded in bringing up a colossal female statue (now in the Maritime Museum, Stanley Bay). The first underwater maps were made around that time by Honor Frost, a Briton working with UNESCO.

A second team worked inside the Eastern Harbour on what was dry land in antiquity, another site mapped in the 1960s by Abu al Sadaat. The team currently working here claim to have discovered Cleopatra's Palace, but this has yet to be substantiated.

▷ **SPHINX'S RIDDLE**
Of some 20 sphinxes discovered, only this one was intact, but even after desalination and restoration, its inscription is unreadable, its identity a riddle.

▷ **CRUEL SEA**
Excavation work was often hampered by the sea. Archaeologists had to take into account underwater currents and surface conditions.

▷ **MEN AT WORK**
A diver from the Franco-Egyptian team exploring the open-sea site in front of Qaytbay's fort, which has yielded statues believed to have decorated the Pharos.

SAVING THE SALVAGE

△ THE DEPTHS OF TIME
This obelisk was of great interest to archaeologists because under the barnacles they found an inscription bearing the titles of the New Kingdom pharaoh Seti I, who reigned *circa* 1291–1278 BC.

▽ 40-TONNE BLOCKS
Among thousands of pieces of masonry found lying on the seabed, many had come from the palace and the Pharos which collapsed in the 14th century. This 40-tonne, grooved block has no inscriptions.

The decision to raise blocks from the seabed was a controversial one, with some archaeologists arguing that conservation would be impossible.

So, having brought statues and masonry to the surface, the teams made conservation a priority. Blocks that had been soaking in salt water for a couple of thousand years needed delicate handling to stop them crumbling when they dried out. The answer was to immerse them in desalination tanks installed in Alexandria several years ago, when a French team raised the remains of Napoleon's fleet in nearby Aboukir Bay. This time the desalination was done by an Egyptian team, with technical support from members of the French Institute of Oriental Archaeology (IFAO).

The first step was to immerse pieces in water that contained the same level of salt as seawater. The salt content of the water was then gradually reduced until the blocks were left standing in fresh water and the salts absorbed by the stone had been leeched away, a process that takes about five months. Here the colossal statue of a Ptolemy is shown soaking in one of the tanks at the start of its desalination treatment.

◁ RETURN OF THE KING
This uninscribed statue of a Ptolemy was found beside fragments from other statues which Professor Empereur believes were part of a group that stood on the Pharos and overlooked the port.

▷ BACK IN TOWN
With so scant remains of their ancient culture to be seen above ground, there was a sense of excitement as the city's past and present met each other, often at unexpected moments.

THE SUEZ CANAL

The Suez Canal is arguably the single most vital traffic artery in the world. When it opened to shipping in 1869, it cut distances between Europe and India in half

Map, pages 260–1

Picture a huge ocean-going ship drifting through a sea of sand. Seen across flat desert, the hallucinatory effect of the Suez Canal underlines the revolutionary impact the waterway has had not only on the nation of Egypt, but on the structure of international commerce. By the mid-19th century, with the expansion of both trade and empires, its economic potential was becoming increasingly obvious.

An old idea

The idea of building a canal that would link the Mediterranean with the Red Sea is ancient indeed. The 26th Dynasty pharaoh Necho II first aired such a proposal at the end of the 7th century BC, with a project to join the Gulf of Suez to the Nile, down which ships could continue to the Mediterranean. According to Herodotus, an oracular pronouncement that he would merely be "labouring for the barbarians" dissuaded Necho from completing excavations. The job was therefore left to Egypt's Persian conquerors a century later; and their work was followed by Ptolemaic and Roman re-excavation.

During the centuries before the Arab conquest, however, this old canal silted up and the Muslims' brilliant general Amr ibn al-'As suggested that a new and better one should be cut across the narrow isthmus of Suez. Cautioned by the caliph Omar that it would be hard to defend and that Greek pirates might use it as a route to attack the holy city of Mecca, he had to be satisfied instead with renovating the exisiting canal. It flourished for another century before being blocked on orders of the Abbasid caliph Al-Mansur.

It was not until the 19th century, with the growth of European power and the energetic promotion of a French engineer, Ferdinand de Lesseps, that Amr's idea could be brought to fruition. A Suez Canal Company was opened by public subscription in Europe and an agreement was reached with the Viceroy Said and his successor the Khedive Ismail whereby Egypt provided both capital and labour for the job itself.

The canal opens

Construction began in 1859. It took 10 years, with 25,000 labourers working three-month shifts, to cut the 160-km (100-mile) channel. The total cost, including the building of the Sweetwater Canal for drinking water from the Nile, reached £25 million, of which Egypt put up more than two-thirds. Amid extravagant fanfare, with assorted European royalty in attendance, the canal was opened to shipping in November of 1869, transforming trade and geopolitics as dramatically as the Portuguese and Spanish discoveries of the 15th century. However, Egypt's debts forced the sale of its stake to

PRECEDING PAGES: on the waterfront, Port Said. **LEFT:** old-style architecture in Port Said. **BELOW:** Mecca-bound pilgrims beside the Suez Canal.

BELOW: visitors to
the War Museum in
Port Said.

the British government for a paltry sum of £4 million sterling. As London's *Economist* drily commented in the year of its opening, the canal was "cut by French energy and Egyptian money for British advantage". The strategic importance of the canal to the British Empire was one of the excuses for occupying Egypt in 1882.

The fortunes of five wars

Britain imposed draconian measures on Egypt while defending the canal in both world wars. For Egyptians, foreign possession of the canal came to represent the major reason for anti-imperialist struggle. Not until 1954 did Nasser arrange for the withdrawal of British troops occupying the Canal Zone.

In 1956, hard up and seeking to finance the High Dam, Nasser turned as a last resort – having been refused financing by the United States – to nationalising the canal, from which Egypt received only a tiny portion of the revenue. Unreconciled to the rapid decline of its empire, Britain responded by invading, with the collusion of Israel and France. Only the intervention of the two superpowers resolved the crisis, which marked a turning point in world affairs. Ten years later, all that remained of Britain's empire were Gibraltar, Hong Kong and a few remote islands, while Egypt had become dependent upon the Soviet Union.

In 1967, the Israelis again attacked Egypt, and held the Sinai Peninsula up to the edge of the canal. Heavy bombardment during the "War of Attrition" that followed the Israeli conquest shattered the canal cities and made refugees of their 500,000 inhabitants. For six years, until the successful Egyptian counter-attack of 1973, the waterway was closed to traffic. Reopened in 1975, it has since been widened and deepened.

The canal cities

Port Said ⓑ sits on an artificial landfill jutting into the Mediterranean. From here convoys of ships pass the green domes of the Suez Canal Authority building to begin the journey to the Red Sea. Once the major point of entry for tourists stepping off the great Peninsular and Orient (P & O) passenger lines, Port Said is now the Hong Kong of Egypt, where Cairo consumers flock for duty-free goods. Despite the damage of three wars and the current emporium atmosphere, this resilient town retains a good deal of character.

Situated on **Lake Timsah** halfway between Port Said and Suez, **Al-Isma'iliyyah** ⓰ is the queen of the canal cities. With its tree-shaded avenues and colonial-style houses, it retains a certain gentility from the 1950s when British officers escaped the hardships of their desert postings to relax here at the French and Greek clubs. It is the cleanest city in Egypt. There are a number of fairly good hotels and restaurants; and from uncrowded lakeside beaches ships transiting the canal can be watched.

South of Al-Isma'iliyyah the canal enters the **Great Bitter Lake**, a small inland sea bordered by holiday villas and military installations. Halfway between the lake and Suez, the 5-km (3-mile) long **Ahmed Hamdi tunnel** provides the only permanent bridge across the canal.

Suez (Al-Saways) ⓱, the canal's southern terminus, was Egypt's major Red Sea port for hundreds of years. Its harbour is now at **Bur Tawfiq**, an artificial peninsula where the canal meets the **Gulf of Suez**. Israeli bombardments flattened the town in the 1967 war; and hasty rebuilding has not enhanced its beauty. Suez is best observed from the Sinai side of the canal, where scores of ships can be seen lining up in the Gulf ready to make the northward passage. ❑

Map, pages 260–1

In Ismailia... you would be tempted... to imagine that you were in some country quarters of "La belle France"...
– WILLIAM HOWARD RUSSELL
A Diary in the East, 1869

BELOW: gone fishing.

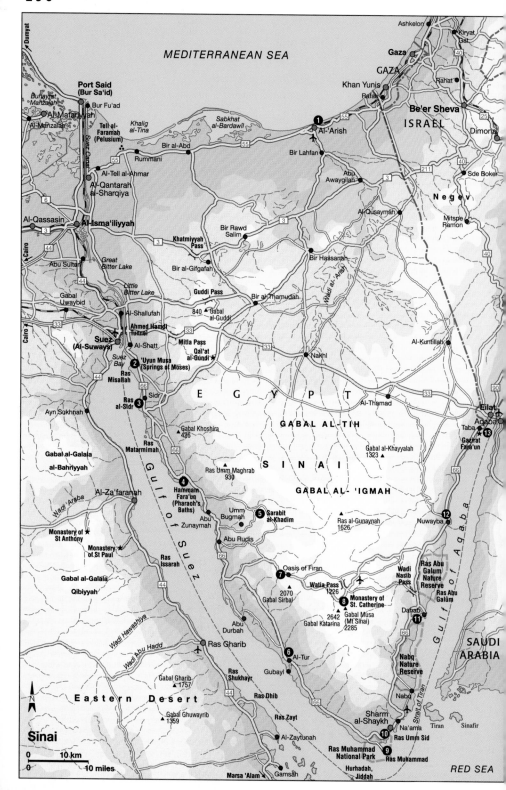

MEDITERRANEAN SEA

Ashkelon
Kiryat Gat
Gaza
GAZA
Rahat
Port Said
(Bur Sa'id)
Khan Yunis
Rafah
Be'er Sheva
Dimona
ISRAEL
Bur Fu'ad
Buhayrat
Manzalah
Al-Matariyyah
Al-Manzalah
Tell al-
Faramah
(Pelusium)
Khalig
al-Tina
Sabkhat
al-Bardawil
Al-'Arish
Bir al-Abd
Bir Lahfan
Sde Boker
Rummani
Al-Tell al-Ahmar
Abu
Awaygilah
Al-Qantarah
al-Sharqiya
Negev
Al-Qassasin
Al-Isma'iliyyah
Al-Qusaymah
Mitspe
Ramon
Abu Sultan
Great
Bitter Lake
Khatmiyyah
Pass
Bir Rawd
Salim
Bir al-Gifgafah
Bir Hassanah
Gabal
Uwaybid
Little
Bitter Lake
Guddi Pass
Bir al-Thamudah
Al-Shallufah
840 Gabal
al-Guddi
Ahmed Hamdi
Tunnel
Suez
(Al-Suways)
Al-Shatt
Mitla Pass
Qal'at
al-Gundi
Al-Kuntillah
Suez
Bay
'Uyun Musa
(Springs of Moses)
Nakhl
Ras
Misallah
Sidr
Al-Thamad
Ayn Sukhnah
Ras
al-Sidr
Eilat
Aqaba
Taba
Gazirat
Fara'un
Gabal Khoshira
426
GABAL AL-TIH
Ras
Matarmimah
Gabal al-Galala
al-Bahriyyah
Ras Umm Maghrab
930
Gabal al-Khayyalah
1323
SINAI
Hammam
Fara'un
(Pharaoh's
Baths)
GABAL AL-'IGMAH
Wadi 'Arba
Al-Za'faranah
Umm
Bugman
Sarabit
al-Khadim
Ras al-Gunaynah
1626
Nuwayba
Abu
Zunaymah
Monastery of
St Anthony
Monastery
of St Paul
Abu Rudis
Ras
Issarah
Wadi
Nasib
Pass
Ras Abu
Galum
Nature
Reserve
Ras Abu
Galum
Gabal al-Galala
Qibiyyah
Oasis of Firan
Watia Pass
1226
Monastery of
St. Catherine
Dahab
2070
Gabal Sirbal
Gabal Musa
(Mt Sinai)
2285
2642
Gabal Katarina
Abu
Durbah
Ras Gharib
Al-Tur
Gubayl
Nabq
Nature
Reserve
Ras
Shukhayr
Gabal Gharib
1757
Ras Dhib
Nabq
Eastern Desert
Gabal Ghuwayrib
1359
Ras Zayt
Sharm
al-Shaykh
Na'ama
Tiran
Sinafir
Al-Zaytunah
Ras Umm Sid
Ras Muhammad
National Park
Ras Muhammad
Sinai
0   10 km
0   10 miles
Marsa 'Alam
Gamsah
Hurhadah,
Jiddah
RED SEA

Dumyat
Suez Canal
Cairo
Cairo
Gulf of Suez
Wadi Abu Hadd
Wadi Hawashiya
Gulf of Aqaba
Strait of Tiran
SAUDI
ARABIA
EGYPT
Wadi al-'Arish

SINAI

*Whether treated as holy ground or as a battleground
fought over by classical empires and modern nation states,
the Sinai Peninsula has always been special*

Map,
page 290

Volumes have been dedicated to this small jewel of a desert poised delicately but obstinately between two continents. As a passage between Asia and Africa, it has weathered as many military crossings as it has peaceful occupations, thanks in part to a climate that precludes all but the sparsest settlement. Even its few prehistoric, ancient and medieval remains, however, have only been scratched at by archaeologists, while Biblical geographers' controversies over problematical routes and sites have created an academic kaleidoscope of fact and fantasy.

It is only in the years since the latest of more than 50 recorded invasions that Sinai has ceased to be regarded by non-inhabitants as an empty buffer zone, as a dangerous crossroads where native Bedu or foreign powers controlled all access, or as a barrier separating the two halves of the Arab world.

Sinai's 25,000 sq km (10,000 sq miles) of desert, ranging from the spiky granite mountains of the south to the central plateau of Al-Tih, then to the rolling dunes of the northern coastal plain, are now fair game to back-packers, camel trekkers and camera-happy busloads of tourists. The shock of the recent occupation and the Israelis' opportunistic development of the peninsula's tourist potential prodded Egypt towards a fierce determination to bind Sinai once again to the Nile valley, this time inextricably. Although the hotel infrastructure was originally geared to low-budget kibbutznim, the Sinai now has some of Egypt's finest hotels and the country's best-maintained roads and most-efficient bus services. Daily flights connect the capital to Al-'Arish, St Catherine's and Sharm al-Shaykh, while a ferry and two flights a week link Sharm al-Shaykh with Hurghadah. Although public transport is reliable, there is no substitute for having one's own car – preferably with four-wheel drive.

PRECEDING PAGES:
fine views from
Mount Sinai.
BELOW: exploring
the canyons
of Sinai.

North Sinai

Aside from seasonal Bedu encampments, North Sinai's population is concentrated around the provincial capital of **Al-'Arish** ❶. From Cairo the main Isma'ilia highway leads to the Suez Canal. At **Qantarah**, north of Al-Isma'iliyyah, crossing to Sinai is made by ferry.

The road continues across the desert to the northeast, skirting the marshy lagoon of **Lake Bardawil** to reach Al-'Arish after 130 km (85 miles). This town of 40,000 is the biggest in the peninsula and much recent effort has been made to turn it into a palm-fringed resort with plenty of reasonably priced hotels and restaurants, though the once-beautiful beaches are hemmed in with concrete. The local Friday *suq* has some good Bedu finds. Bedu crafts and jewellery are also on display at the local museum.

Just east of the town, the bare dunes begin. A few

olive trees appear, marking the decline of the desert and the beginning of the fertile Palestine coastal plain. At 50 km (30 miles) the town of **Rafah** marks the current border. Beyond lies **Gaza**. Rafah's population is a mixture of local Bedu and Palestinian refugees. Their camp – built with Canadian government aid and consequently called Canada – was brutally bisected by the border fence erected after the area's return to Egypt in 1983.

Between Al-'Arish and Rafah a number of *wadis*, seasonal watercourses, lead back from the sea into the desert interior. The laid-back Bedu graze their goats and camels extensively in this region. Friendly and hospitable, they are wont to invite travellers into their ramshackle settlements – shacks slapped together with cans, boxes and the debris of four wars – for a glass of tea. The desert-dwelling women of North Sinai wear gorgeous embroidered dresses and heavy silver jewellery, so the opportunity to mingle should not be missed.

Put off thy shoes from off thy feet, for the place whereon thou standest is holy ground.

—EXODUS 3:5

South Sinai

With its two coasts, oases, mountains and historic sites, South Sinai is a more popular destination. North of Suez, the **Ahmed Hamdi tunnel** carries traffic under the Canal. Turning south, the main road follows the Canal, veering eastwards opposite Suez. From here it descends 320 km (200 miles) along the breezy Gulf of Suez to Sharm al-Shaykh.

Along this route are **'Uyun Musa** ❷, the Springs of Moses, a palm grove fed by brackish water where the prophet is said to have rested with his flock, reached after 40 km (25 miles). Thirty-three kilometres (20 miles) farther on, the road nears the coast at the wide sandy beach of **Ras al-Sidr** ❸, a favourite stopping place, and for some people worth the day trip from Cairo. Unlike the Gulf of

BELOW: Bedu in northern Sinai.

Aqaba on Sinai's east coast, the Gulf of Suez is shallow and sandy-bottomed; the marine life is abundant, but there are no major coral reefs this far north. Moon Beach in Ras al-Sidr is one of Egypt's premier windsurfing destinations.

Beyond Ras al-Sidr the road bends away from the coast up into the mountains. A track to the right at this turn leads after a few hundred yards to **Hammam Fara'un ❹**, the hot springs known as Pharaoh's Baths. The seven springs produce boiling-hot mineral-rich waters that bubble from the base of the mountains right into the sea, and are said by local Bedu to cure rheumatism.

About 16 km (10 miles) into the mountains above Hammam Fara'un, a track leads left among palm trees. Negotiable only by four-wheel drive vehicles, it continues for 32 km (20 miles) to the site of **Sarabit al-Khadim ❺** (no facilities, ask for a Bedu guide at Abu Zunaymah), a 12th-Dynasty temple that serviced workers in the region's mines and was dedicated originally to the goddess Hathor. A second shrine, for the patron god of the Eastern Desert, Sopdu, was later added. The site, which covers approximately 0.4 hectares (1 acre), has yielded over 400 inscriptions, some of which praise Hathor, Hatshepsut or Tuthmosis III, and others give instructions regarding the turquoise mines.

More important are the graffiti of the workers, some written in unknown scripts called protosinaitic. They form the link between hieroglyphics and the Phoenician alphabet from which our own script is developed. Also discovered here was the bust of Queen Tiy of the Old Kingdom, now in the Egyptian Antiquities Museum, Cairo.

Inscriptions at the **mines of Wadi Maraghah**, south of Sarabit al-Khadim, date back to the 4th Dynasty and the reigns of Snefru and Khufu (Cheops), builder of the Great Pyramid. Turquoise, malachite and copper were mined in the

Map, page 290

BELOW: war wreckage abandoned in the Sinai Desert.

region. The British caused much damage to the inscriptions here when they tried to reopen the mines in 1901.

From Wadi Maraghah a track running down the **Wadi Sidri** for 24 km (15 miles) rejoins the main road at **Abu Zunaymah**, where it descends again from the mountains to the coast. Beyond this ramshackle frontier settlement, where manganese from local mines of recent date is processed, the road continues to **Abu Rudis**. The Gulf of Suez is at this point dotted with beetle-like rigs shooting flames into the haze: this is the centre of Sinai's oil fields, most of them offshore. Pipes, fences, tanks and prefabricated housing clutter the shore town to **Balayim** 50 km (30 miles) farther on.

The road again leaves the coast, heading towards the mountains of the Sinai range. A checkpoint marks the turn-off to St Catherine's monastery, while the main road continues south to **Al-Tur** ❻ and Sharm al-Shaykh. Tur, the capital and largest town in South Sinai, is reached after 75 km (45 miles) of hot driving through a wide valley. Settled in ancient times because of its good water supply and excellent harbour, it was the chief quarantine station for pilgrims returning to Egypt from Mecca. Modern Al-Tur, despite scattered palm groves and a beautiful beach, retains this way-station atmosphere. A peculiarity of the town is the racial mix of its inhabitants, many of them descended from Berber and African immigrants. From Al-Tur it is 100 km (60 miles) to Sharm al-Shaykh.

Going to St Catherine's

Turning instead up toward St Catherine's, you enter the **Wadi Firan**. Narrowing as it mounts, after 33 km (20 miles) the dry ravine suddenly blossoms into a river of date palms. This is the **Oasis of Firan** ❼, the largest and most fertile

patch of cultivation on the peninsula. Parched for most of the year, winter rains and melting snow send down short-lived torrents to water the valley. Scattered throughout the palm groves are clusters of Bedu huts. The *wadi* may have been the site of the biblical battle between the Amalakites and the Israelites. Within the mountain are the scattered remains of monasteries, chapels and hermit cells of early Christian monks who believed this to be the Elim of the Bible. Tranquil and serene, it is difficult to imagine that Firan was a bustling cathedral city in the Middle Ages.

South of the oasis, approached most easily up the **Wadi 'Aleayat**, rises the peak of the **Gabal Sirbal**. At 2,070 metres (7,000 ft) it is not high for the Sinai range, but its isolation makes the view from its summit extensive. One school of Biblical speculators claims it as the true **Mount Sinai**.

From Firan the road climbs into an open plain and after 32 km (20 miles) reaches the settlement of **Santa Katarina**. Here there are numerous hotels, a campsite and the bus stop. The famous **monastery** ❽ sits in a *wadi* between **Gabal Musa** – most popular candidate for the site of the delivery of the Ten Commandments – and the **Gabal al-Dayr** just up the hill to the south.

The Roman emperor Justinian ordered the building of a fortress monastery on the site in 537 AD in order to protect the Sinai passes against invasion. Originally dedicated to the Transfiguration of Christ, the church built within the fortress was renamed after St Catherine (a 4th-century Alexandrian martyred for her derision of Roman idol-worship), after her body miraculously appeared atop the Sinai's highest peak, apparently looking none the worse for wear. This miracle, coupled with the Crusaders' occupation of nearby Palestine, ensured the support of Christian rulers. The monastery's fame spread, so much so that by

Map, page 290

Some scholars believe that the local tamarisk trees may be the source of the manna that supported Moses and his followers in the desert.

BELOW: St Catherine's, founded by the Emperor Justinian.

the 14th century up to 400 monks lived there, as the grisly collection of skulls attests. In recent centuries Russia was the chief benefactor. The monastery, with its 20 resident monks, remains the property of the Greek Orthodox Church.

The monastery and its treasures

The path to St Catherine's leads past a walled orchard and an outer complex of buildings before reaching the monastery itself. An old basket-and-pulley system of entry has been abandoned and visitors now enter by simply walking through a portal. (Note that the monastery is closed on Friday and religious holidays and that modesty of attire is required. The best time for a visit is between 9.30 am and noon.) A small building on the left inside the wall is one of the original structures, diplomatically converted into a mosque in the 12th century. The **Church of St Catherine** is down the steps to the left just behind the mosque.

The church, built by order of Justinian in 527 AD, is basilical in form, with great granite columns supporting the nave. The marble inlay floors will be familiar to anyone who has visited the mosques of Cairo. The wooden bracing beams of the reconstructed ceiling are original and beautifully carved, one of them with a foundation inscription dating to Justinian. The doors leading to the sanctuary are flanked by two silver chests inlaid with precious stones. Both were donated by members of the Russian royal family, one in the 17th century, the other in the 19th. The sanctuary is adorned with 6th-century mosaics that are the monastery's greatest treasure. Within the arch and semi-dome of the apse is a portrayal of the Transfiguration of Christ. To his left stand Moses and St James, and on his right are Elijah and St John the Apostle.

Side aisles, lined with chapels dedicated to varied saints and decorated with

BELOW:
the Chapel of the
Burning Bush.

ancient and modern icons, lead off from either side of the church. At the sanctuary end of the building a small alcove opens into the **Chapel of the Burning Bush**. Here, on a site marked by a small silver plate, God spoke to Moses disguised as a flaming shrub. The monastery's other treasures are off-limits to run-of-the-mill tourists. They include a library of rare manuscripts and a museum stocked with a superb collection of icons.

Just behind the monastery a well-worn path begins, leading ultimately to the summit of **Gabal Musa**. Steps mounting the cliff to the right should be avoided for the ascent. Instead, continue on the gently sloping main track, which curves behind the southern slope. All but the most feeble should be able to manage the way up – coming down is trickier, and care needs to be taken. The view from the top is magnificient, particularly at dawn or sunset. **Gabal Katarina**, the highest point in Egypt at over 2,640 metres (8,500 ft), has an even better view. It is approached up the *wadi* on Gabal Musa's western side.

Sinai's mountains are very ancient, and their variety, in terms of texture, colour, shape and vegetation, is eternally fascinating – especially in the very early morning or early evening when their contours and colours are seen most clearly. The descent from St Catherine's to the east traverses enthralling landscapes all the way to the sea. The Gulf of Aqaba, one of the earth's most dramatic interfaces, is only 16 km (10 miles) wide, but in places as much as 1,800 metres (6,000 ft) deep. Indeed, it marks a long geological fault, running from the Dead Sea in the north to Africa's Great Rift Valley in the south.

Coral reefs line the shores of the Gulf from Ras Muhammad at the peninsula's extremity to Taba on the Israeli border. Teeming with life and colour, they provide a striking contrast to the desolation of the land.

Map, page 290

Map, page 290

TIP

Enthusiasts who are really keen to see the rare manuscripts and icons at St Catherine's Monastery should arm themselves with a letter of introduction from the Greek Patriarchate in Cairo.

BELOW: the ossuary at St Catherine's houses the skulls of former monks.

The Gulf of Aqaba

Ras Muhammad ❾ is a coral peninsula thrusting its head into the Red Sea. It is a nature reserve and one of the most oustanding snorkelling and diving areas in the world. At the **Shark's Observatory** a coral ridge falls over 80 metres (262 ft) into the open sea and the wary diver can float along its edge (under 1 metre/3 ft deep at high tide) and look out into an underwater paradise. Although a haven for large fish, especially sharks, there has been no reported shark attack in the Red Sea for 25 years.

North of Ras Muhammad, on a beautiful natural harbour much damaged by the ill-planned building of successive occupants, is the town of **Sharm al-Shaykh ❿**. Five miles farther on, **Na'ama Bay** is the local tourist centre, with hotels, restaurants, camping grounds and diving shops. Overdeveloped, it makes a good base for visiting local beaches. Some of the best for diving and snorkelling are **The Tower**, **Ras Umm Sid**, **Ras Nasrani** and **Nabq**. Equipment can be rented at one of several diving centres, where boat trips to **Gazirat Tiran**, an island in the middle of the straits with superb corals, can also be arranged. Shipwrecks dot the shoreline, testifying to the difficulty of navigation between the reefs.

Hotel complexes spread further and further toward the airport, but the next major coastal settlement lies 56 miles (90 km) north at **Dahab ⓫**. Sediments washed down from the mountains have created a broad sandy plain here. A model Israeli-built town on a sandy cove, it has a few hotels, a cafeteria and camping and diving facilities.

Across the plain a mile (2 km) to the west, the Bedu village of Assalah sits next to a palm-lined horseshoe bay. Here low-budget travellers stay in reed huts on the

BELOW: Nuwayba.

beach and live on grilled fish. The locals are laid-back – frequently horizontal in fact – so outsiders are often surprised to find that many of them speak perfect English. Camel treks into the interior can be arranged here. Many of Dahab's fertile *wadis* are stunningly beautiful.

Nuwayba ⑫ is 75 km (45 miles) farther north, a slightly upmarket resort, although the reefs are not as good as farther south. There are wide sandy beaches, a few hotels and a campsite. The hotels offer tours by Land Rover to the **Oasis of 'Ayn al-Furtaga**. If the preferred vehicle is the camel, arrangements, including food and a guide, can be made with the Bedu at their settlement a few miles south of the hotel strip, where palms mingle with shacks along the beach. The Bedu offer a choice of trips, depending on how many days you want to spend.

Taba ⑬ is 60 km (38 miles) north of Nuwayba and offers a five-star hotel and domestic airport. Two hundred metres/yards beyond the hotel is the Israeli border. **Gazirat Fara'un**, an island just offshore, is a recently restored fortress built by Saladin to protect the overland route of the Haj, the annual pilgrimage to Mecca. Smack in the middle of the peninsula, and difficult to access, lie the ruins of a second medieval fortress, **Qala'at al-Gundi**. Built by Saladin to protect trade and pilgrimage routes, these fortifications attest to the importance Muslim rulers attached to Egypt's Asian gateway.

Although no-one needs to be warned of the danger of sharks, swimmers should be aware that coral reefs can hide unpleasant as well as pleasant surprises. The spine of a sea urchin, for example, is most unfriendly on the feet and the sting of the well-camouflaged stone fish can be fatal. It is advisable to wear shoes or flippers and to swim in pairs. Above all, be aware that corals take thousands of years to form and should never be removed. ❏

Map, page 290

TIP

Ferries from Nuwayba's port leave daily for Aqaba in Jordan, a journey taking three hours. At Aqaba excursions to the famous rock city of Petra, an hour or so north of Aqaba, can be arranged.

BELOW: diving in the Gulf of Aqaba.

THE RED SEA AND EASTERN DESERT

Map, page 304

The beauty of the landscape and an excellent climate are obvious reasons for this region's ever-increasing popularity, especially as a winter sun destination

T he **Red Sea coast** of Egypt runs for 1,600 km (1,000 miles) in a southeasterly direction from Suez. Despite the many offshore oil wells and numerous oil depots, petrol stations are few and far between and trips by car must be planned with foresight. Once assured of freedom from mechanical worries, however, the happy motorist is rewarded with a glorious sense of infinite space. For most of its length, beautiful but desolate limestone and granite mountains border the coast. Range rises upon range as a thousand peaks harmonise their purples with the blue of the sky. Sandy coves and beaches edge a brilliant sea. Within its coral reefs the water is a light blue-green, while beyond them a deep dark blue stretches to the distant coasts of Sinai and Arabia.

But how long can this coast remain idyllic? Apparently the entire 1,600-km (1,000-mile) stretch has been sold to developers and many large-scale tourist projects, from the basic to the luxurious, have already been built or are underway. The landscape, climate and increasingly sophisticated facilities are obvious attractions, but many tourists also prefer coming to the Red Sea because it is considered safer from the point of view of terrorism than resorts along the Nile.

In the vicinity of Suez, the sea is liberally strewn with tankers and other ships converging on the canal, and the road along the coast has received a good deal of wear and tear from heavy trucks. Both sea and land traffic soon thins out, however, and the beaches improve near Ayn Sukhnah.

A spectacular drive

South of Ayn Sukhnah the rocky skirts of the North Galala Plateau come right down to the edge of the sea and the drive along here is spectacular. Several new hotel complexes and holiday villages are being built and a good coastal highway has been constructed. At **Al-Za'faranah** (80 km/50 miles) south of 'Ayn Sukhnha, is a junction with another good road across the desert from the Nile Valley 290 km (180 miles) to the west.

The new resort of **Al-Gouna ❶**, 21 km (13 miles) north of Hurghadah, is Egypt's most luxurious holiday village to date. A Cairene millionaire, Samih Sawiris, bought the plot of land on which Al-Gouna is rising with the intention of building a few holiday homes for family and friends, but before long his business instincts got the better of him, and he seized the opportunity to create something unique in Egypt. Unlike the miles of often unattractive concrete structures further south in Hurghadah, Al-Gouna has been planned as a community, served by its own little airstrip. Gardens and an 18-hole golf course have been skilfully landscaped out of

PRECEDING PAGES: the not-so-Red Sea; the Monastery of St Anthony. **BELOW:** Hurghadah beach party.

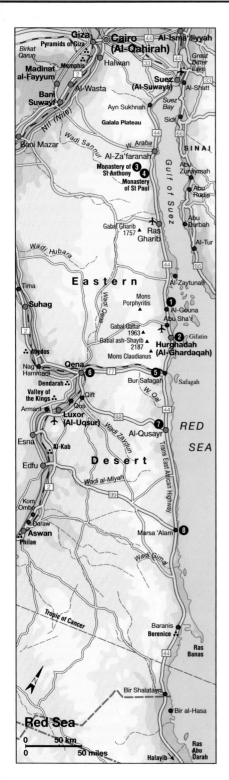

the barren desert sands, and several man-made lagoons add to the peacefulness of the place.

Wealthy Cairenes have hurried to buy the expensive beach-front villas, while visitors can stay in one of several attractive hotels ranging from three to five stars. The inspiration for most of the design has come from traditional Nubian architecture, revived by the late Egyptian architect Hassan Fathy, and from the Mediterranean – there's plenty of whitewash and some corners could be mistaken for old towns on the Cycladic Islands in Greece.

The spectacular five-star Miramar Hotel, managed by the Sheraton chain and designed by the celebrity American architect Michael Graves, is a unique sight in Egypt. The hotel was built as a giant toy town where blue, red and yellow buildings contrast with the bright turquoise of the lagoons and the deep purple of the mountains in the background. The village at the centre of the development is **Kafr al-Gouna**, which has several restaurants and a small museum (open daily 10am–2pm and 4–9pm; admission charge) displaying good replicas of many precious examples of ancient Egyptian art.

Hurghadah

In recent years the small fishing village of **Hurghadah ②** (Al-Ghardaqah), 420 km (250 miles) south of Suez, has been developed into one of Egypt's most popular destinations. It has its own airport served by several European charter operators and by domestic flights from Cairo (one hour) and Sharm al-Shaykh (35 minutes). The town itself has a large range of accommodation, from some basic and cheap hotels catering for back-packers, to upmarket resort hotels. A long strip of holiday villages continues to spread further south and has now reached way past the airport. Many of these villages, which rival each other for splendour, the size of their pools and the number of rooms, are operated by international four and five-star hotel chains.

Hurghadah's pleasures are the ideal antidote to an overdose of antiquities. Instead of monuments it offers golden sands and a sea full of exquisite tropical fish, which swim in and around the plentiful coral beds. The water is warm all the year round except for a few weeks in December and January; the sun is always shining and even in the hottest months there is a breeze, which can sometimes turn into a strong wind.

Holiday villages are staffed by cheerful youngsters of many different nationalities who work as instructors in scuba diving, snorkelling, sailing, surfing, archery and other sports. For the fisherman, all-day or overnight fishing trips to the offshore islands can be arranged either through the hotels or privately with individual boat owners at the harbour.

The modern town of Hurghadah is not a pretty sight and the public beach here is often littered with garbage. The large *suq* area offers the usual souvenir shops filled with cheap leather, brasswork, papyrus, furry camels, statuettes and so on.

Map, page 304

For those who missed out on snorkelling or diving, a small **aquarium** at 6 Corniche Street (open daily 9am–10pm; admission charge), offers an insight into the area's rich marine life. Five km (3 miles) north of town, the **Museum of Marine Biology** (open daily 8am–5pm; admission charge) has a fine collection of corals and an aquarium. But more revealing are the glass-bottomed boats and the Sindbad Submarine which make several trips daily. Both can be booked at any of the hotel receptions.

Monasteries in the Eastern Desert

As a popular daytrip from Hurghadah, the Monasteries of St Paul and St Anthony have lost much of their original remoteness. Two hundred kilometres (130 miles) east of Bani Suwayf in the rugged hills at the foot of the South Galala Plateau, looking out over the desolate Wadi Araba stands the **Monastery of St Anthony ❸**, the 4th-century Christian hermit, whose temptations are so enthusiastically illustrated by European painters of the Renaissance. An hour's drive further on by car is the monastery of his contemporary, **St Paul ❹**, tucked into a fold of the Red Sea Mountains. Both monasteries are open daily from 9am to 5pm, but close during Christian festivals and periods of fast.

Hurghadah is perfect for water sports of all kinds.

The Monastery of St Anthony was founded by the followers of St Anthony after his death in AD 356, and is often regarded as the oldest monastery in the world. The oldest building in the compound is the Church of St Anthony with

BELOW: Sindbad's Submarine.

A visit to St Paul's.

murals from the 13th century onwards. A path from the west side of the monastery climbs steeply up to St Anthony's cave where the saint lived as a hermit until the age of 105. His life was the inspiration for monasticism, which soon found many followers throughout the Christian world.

Smaller, more dilapidated and more remote, the Monastery of St Paul the Hermit sees fewer visitors. St Paul (AD 348–228) was the earliest-known hermit but, when he was visited in his cave at the age of 113 by St Anthony, St Paul recognised him as being spiritually his superior. St Paul's cave is in the Church of St Paul, where his remains are buried.

The monks here today lead a quiet life of work and prayer, very much as they did 15 centuries ago, when the original Desert Fathers retired from the injustice of the world to seek a better way of life.

Ancient Egyptian ports

Further on down the coast the famous ancient ports, which were thriving even after the discovery of the Cape route in the 15th century, have largely fallen into disuse since the inauguration of the Suez Canal. Some are still visible as little ghost harbours with the skeletal hulls of old wooden boats whitening in the sun; and others have completely disappeared under the sand.

BELOW: keep at the Monastery of St Anthony.

Bur Safagah ❺, however, which is 70 km (45 miles) south of Hurghadah, is still very much alive. Its deepwater facilities have been expanded and it has retained the role it played in the past as the nearest port to **Qena** ❻ (177 km/110 miles) to the west. The old caravan trail leading through the mountains has now been replaced by an excellent paved road to the Nile valley which carries truckloads of wheat and raw aluminium off-loaded at Bur Safagah. It is also con-

venient for those who want to make the round trip from Cairo down the Nile to Luxor, across the mountains to the sea, returning north up the coast. Bur Safagah is being developed for tourism and already has several hotels.

and it won't be long before upmarket resort hotels appear here too. Foreigners who want to venture further south do still need to apply for a military pass in Cairo.

Except for the remote mountainous area known as Gabal Elba on the Sudanese border in the far south, which receives monsoon rains and has a unique eco-system supporting forest and pasturage, the coastal plain and the Red Sea mountains are almost entirely devoid of vegetation. What rain there is falls only a few times a year and then often in the form of violent storms, which carry all before them as water pours off the mountains into the sea.

Some water gathers in potholes among the granitic rocks and, together with the ancient wells, amounts to enough to support the scattering of Bedu and the animals that live there. Until recently fresh water had to be shipped in for the villages along the coast, and the natives lived on a simple diet of bread and fish.

Realms of gold

In pharaonic times the **Eastern Desert**, particularly the mountains, was thoroughly searched for gold and other precious metals, for ornamental stone and for building materials. These resources contributed greatly to the wealth and prestige of the pharaohs and were later coveted by Assyrians, Persians, Greeks and Romans.

Thousands of prisoners in chains were used for the extraction of these riches. More often than not they died in the mines and quarries. The gold was arduously mined and smelted, and both granite and limestone were quarried and transported to Thebes for the construction of temples and other monuments.

The indefatigable Romans established permanent quarrying camps in the mountains, visible from the stretch of road between Hurghadah and Safagah.

BELOW: desert explorations.

They were particularly partial to the purple stone known as porphyry, which comes from **Gabal Abu Dukhan** (Father of Smoke). It was in great demand for the adornment of palaces and temples and was brought out of the Egyptian mountains until as late as the 5th century AD. Great blocks were quarried and then dragged the 180 km (112 miles) through the mountains and over the desert to Qena, whence they were transported down the Nile and then across the Mediterranean to Rome. Another famous mountain nearby, known as **Mons Claudianus**, yielded superlative white granite.

Map, page 304

Desert flora and fauna

Apart from east of Cairo, where semi-suburban industrial zones sprawl out to the east, eventually joining up with the pock-marked battlegrounds of recent wars in the canal area, the transition from the green valley is abrupt. Suddenly the lush cultivated land gives way to stony wilderness, where the rocks rise up in extraordinary formations, reminiscent of the Pyramids and Sphinx, the sand blows and spills, and there is hardly a sign of human life for hundreds of miles.

The geological formations are endlessly various and strange, yielding stones and sands of amazing shapes and colours. The flora and fauna, though sparse and timid, are all the more wonderful for their tenacious hold on life. There are numerous species of birds, some resident and some migratory, and occasionally in spring and autumn a skein of migrating cranes can be seen high overhead. Once in a while a gazelle or a wild goat streaks across the open plain and disappears among the rocks; and often a sandy picnic place is crisscrossed with the embroidery of bird and animal tracks. Jerboas, jackals and foxes leave dainty padmarks, while rabbits, gazelles and hyenas leave heavier prints. ❑

A variety of plants, some of them aromatic, grow on the flanks and bottoms of the wadis. Once in a while a lone tamarisk or wild fig casts a bit of shade.

BELOW: posing for the camera.

SCUBA DIVING AND WATER SPORTS

*Gorgeous corals, shooting damsel fish, brightly coloured
parrot, butterfly and angel fish – Egypt's
Eastern coasts teem with brilliant life*

The climatic and geographic position of Egypt's eastern coasts is ideal for the formation of coral, which cannot grow at temperatures of less than 18.5°C (65°F) or at depths of more than 22 metres (70 ft). Though the Gulf of Aqaba and the Red Sea attain a depth of 1,850 metres (6,000 ft) in the middle, where the tectonic plates of Africa and Asia have drawn apart to form a great rift, relatively shallow seas cover the continental shelf that runs along the shores, which are interrupted only by occasional wadis, formed by infrequent but torrential rains. The sunshine that penetrates the very salty water for many hours each day enables the coral to build up its formations.

Colonies of coral

There are basically four types of reefs. Fringing reefs and barrier reefs run parallel to the coast, usually with shallow sandy-bottomed lagoons between the land and the coral, which then drops by as much as 22 metres (70 ft) in a cliff-like formation. There are no atolls (the third type) in the Egyptian part of the Red Sea, but the fourth type, roughly distinguished as a patch formation, is common.

BELOW: preparing to dive in.

Mounds of coral build up on the sandy floor of the sea like islands, the tips of which are barely skimmed by the waves. Patch formations occur at Nuwayba on the Sinai coast, off Hurghadah and at spots further south.

Each coral accretion consists of numerous minute anemone-like individual polyps, growing together in a colony. When one colony dies, a new one grows on top, attached to the skeletons of its defunct ancestors. Two thousand species have been identified and christened with complex names. Even the amateur can find as many as 100 types. Some corals are soft and undulating, like the sea anemones; some are hard and solid, squat and rounded like brains or mushrooms; some branch like elkhorns, or stack up like fortifications, spires and pinnacles; others are fan-shaped and perforated like Elizabethan lace collars.

The corals feed, mostly at night, on organisms trapped on their multiple surfaces. These organisms in turn are nourished by sunlight, which is the base of an ecosystem that supports a rich variety of marine life and furnishes a living laboratory for both professional and amateur biologists. Some creatures live off algae and plankton trapped by the coral, others actually eat and digest the coral itself. These characters are in turn hunted and eaten by a progressive chain of predators, the biggest of which are the prowlers of the open sea.

Slugs, snails, shellfish, shrimps and crabs live in the nooks and crannies of the coral or in the sandy patches within the lagoons. But it is, above all, the fish that liven the coral beds, with their tremendous beauty and variety, their curious relationships and habits.

The most common inhabitants are the thousands of little damsel fish, including green chromis and blue fusiliers, which graze peacefully or shoot up suddenly in a great sparkling cloud. Flame-coloured coral fish, only about 2.5 cm (an inch) long, hover close to the shadows in ones and twos.

Butterfly and angel fish form a large and easily distinguishable family because of their oval shape, snub noses and gorgeous lemony colouring, enhanced by blue and black stripes and patches: they swim in pairs and stick to the same territory. Other easily recognisable types are the disc-shaped sergeant major, which sports appropriate stripes, and his cousins the dascylus and bi-coloured chromis, which parade in regiments, turning together like lazy pieces of a Calder mobile.

More gorgeous greens and blues occur in the families of wrasses and parrot fish, which can reach a fair size if they survive the many hazards of predatory society; the giant humphead wrasse can be as big as 1.5 metres (5 ft) long. These families eat coral with their beaks and the crunching of their jaws can be heard as they chew up the madrepore. Grinding plates in their throats break down the coral. After they have extracted the nourishing material, they excrete great quantities of coral sand.

Next up the ecological ladder come the groupers, jacks, skates and other predators, who feed on the little fish. Their bodies are mottled or blotched brown, red, or blue and they have big mouths, which can stretch wide to swallow their dinner. They hunt singly, swimming with their pectoral fins and hovering steadily, ready to pounce on their prey.

Whales and sea-cows (dugongs) inhabit the deep sea and are not carnivorous, but ingest gallons of plankton. The only danger from these species is that they may accidentally give a small boat a mighty wallop.

The more scary monsters of the deep are not normally encountered by the ordinary snorkeller and rarely by scuba divers. Only very experienced pros engage in debates with moray eels, lionfish, barracuda, sting rays or sharks.

Diving facilities

Most hotels on the Sinai and Red Sea coasts have affiliated diving centres with resident instructors, boats and equipment for hire. Nuwayba, Dahab and Sharm al-Shaykh, for example, have diving centres with hotels and camping grounds in the vicinity. The Hurghadah InterContinental, Jasmine Village, Sonesta, Marriott, Giftun Village, and other hotels are all well-equipped. Trained supervisors can initiate novices into what to look for, where to see it and how to manage their gear.

Reasonably efficient snorkelling equipment – mask, snorkel and flippers – can be rented or bought. Serious participants should buy gear before coming.

An acronym for "self-contained underwater breathing apparatus", scuba enables the diver to submerge completely for up to 30 minutes at a time, to depths of 22 metres (70 ft) or more. Besides the mask and flippers, a dive tank, consisting of two cylinders of compressed oxygen, attached to a harness, worn on the back and connected to the mouth by tubes, a regulator and a weight belt comprise the essential equipment. A wet suit, or part of one, is advisable, particularly during the winter months. It has the added advantage of protecting the wearer from the coral. ❑

BELOW: snorkelling opens up a bright new world.

New Insight Maps

Maps in Insight Guides are tailored to complement the text. But when you're on the road you sometimes need the big picture that only a large-scale map can provide. This new range of durable Insight Fleximaps has been designed to meet just that need.

Detailed, clear cartography
makes the comprehensive route and city maps easy to follow, highlights all the major tourist sites and provides valuable motoring information plus a full index.

Informative and easy to use
with additional text and photographs covering a destination's top 10 essential sites, plus useful addresses, facts about the destination and handy tips on getting around.

Laminated finish
allows you to mark your route on the map using a non-permanent marker pen, and wipe it off. It makes the maps more durable and easier to fold than traditional maps.

The first titles
cover many popular destinations. They include Algarve, Amsterdam, Bangkok, California, Cyprus, Dominican Republic, Florence, Hong Kong, Ireland, London, Mallorca, Paris, Prague, Rome, San Francisco, Sydney, Thailand, Tuscany, USA Southwest, Venice, and Vienna.

𝄪 INSIGHT GUIDES
The world's largest collection of visual travel guides

CONTENTS

Getting Acquainted

Area: 1,002,000 sq. km (626,000 sq. miles).
Capital: Cairo.
Longest River: The Nile.
Population: 61.5 million, (estimated 1996).
Language: Arabic (official), English and French are widely understood by educated people.
Religion: Muslim (mostly Sunni): 90 percent, Coptic Christian and other: 10 percent.
Time Zone: GMT plus 2 hours.
Currency: Egyptian pound of 100 piastres.
Weights and measures: metric.
Electricity: Power supply in Egypt is 220 volts.
International Dialling Code: 20.

Egypt links the northeastern corner of Africa and the southwestern edge of Asia. Its longest distance north-south is 1,025 km (640 miles) and widest distance east-west is about 1,240 km (775 miles).

The **deserts** of Egypt comprise over 90 percent of the land surface. They are part of an arid region that stretches from the Atlantic coast in the west to Central Asia in the east. Though extremely sparsely populated (they are inhabited by less than 1 percent of the population), they

Temperatures

Average Year-round Temperatures (max/min, in celsius)

	winter	summer
Alexandria	21/11	30/21
Cairo	21/11	36/20
Luxor	26/6	42/22
Aswan	26/9	42/25

contain six inhabited depressions known as oases.

The **Eastern** or **Arabian Desert** is east of the Nile Valley and extends to the Red Sea. It is far higher than the **Western Desert**, rising to a series of ranges, parallel to the sea, called the Red Sea Mountains. It covers approximately 223,000 sq. km (86,101 sq. miles), or 21 percent of the land mass of Egypt.

The Arabian Desert has two distinct areas, the northern Al Ma'aza Plateau, which is composed primarily of limestone, and the southern Al 'Ababda Plateau. Water is very scarce in these areas.

The Western or Libyan Desert is much larger than the Arabian Desert, covering 681,000 sq. km (332,434 sq. miles) and comprises two-thirds of Egypt. It is separated from the North African or Great Sahara by highlands and is composed primarily of Nubian sandstone and limestone.

South of the Qattarah depression there is a band of north-south sand dunes that continue as far south as the Kharga Depression, where they flatten out. The Western Desert is the most arid region of Egypt.

The **Red Sea** is 2,359 metres (7,785 ft) deep, 1,932 km (1,207 miles) long from north to south and 306 km (191 miles) from east to west. Cutting through the Gulf of Aqaba from the Dead Sea and continuing south through the Red Sea and on into East Africa is the **Great Rift Valley**, the juncture of the African and Arabian Tectonic plates. The Red Sea is highly saline with small tides and exquisite coral shelves and reefs.

Climate

Summers are hot and dry in Upper Egypt, humid in the Delta and along the Mediterranean Coast. In recent years the humidity has spread to Cairo and the city swelters in August. Winters are mild with some rain, but usually there are bright, sunny days and cold nights.

Spring and autumn are short, and during the 50 days (*khamseen*)

between the end of March and mid-May, dust storms can occur sporadically. The creation of Lake Nasser has had an effect on the climate of the whole Nile Valley.

Women in Society

Before the famous Egyptian feminist Hoda Shaarawi deliberately removed her veil in 1922, veils – which had no religious significance – were worn in public by all respectable middle-class and upper-class women, Muslim, Jewish or Christian. By 1935, however, veils were a comparative rarity in Egypt, though they continued to be worn in neighbouring countries like Syria and Jordan for 30 more years and have remained obligatory in the Arabian Peninsula to this day.

Nowadays in Egypt, veils are worn only by Bedu women, who are the inheritors of the urban fashions of a century ago, or by younger middle-class urban women demonstrating Muslim piety. Feminine modesty alone – not necessarily identified with any religion – is shown by wearing a covering over the head. One reason for the latter is that it tends to discourage male advances.

From the 1930s onwards, Egyptian women began to enter into businesses and professions. Thus by 1965, thanks in part to social changes effected in the course of the July Revolution, Egypt could boast a far higher proportion of women working as doctors, dentists, lawyers, professors, diplomats or high officials than might have been found in the US or in any European country outside of Scandinavia. Egyptian women still do not have equality with Egyptian men, however, either in law or by custom; and no matter how much they may rule the roost in the home, Egyptian public places are still fundamentally male preserves.

The Economy

Since 1979 there has been a massive influx of foreign aid into Egypt. As a result infrastructure has improved: there are new roads linking all areas of the country. Villages up and down the Nile and in the deserts have now got electricity, new schools and hospitals, and other services have sprung up by the dozen. Telephone systems continue to undergo renovation and expansion, and investment has been encouraged in the private sector. The change in Egypt has been dramatic.

For the tourist there are dozens of new hotels and restaurants, monuments have been restored and their environments spruced up, tour guides are licensed, and retail shops are bursting with good quality products.

The Egyptian pound has been floated, with an exchange value fixed daily, and has shown itself to be remarkably stable. For Egyptians, however, life is expensive. Rents are high, food though abundant is costly, and salaries lag behind the cost of living.

Until the Gulf War, remittances from Egyptians working abroad were amongst Egypt's largest foreign currency earners, but now tourism and revenues from the Suez Canal generate more.

The Government

Egypt is officially known as the Arab Republic of Egypt (ARE). Its capital city is Cairo and other major cities include Alexandria, Giza, Port Said, Asyut, Suez, Minya and Aswan. It is a republic with an elected president, who is commander in chief of the Army, and leader of the National Defense Council. The prime minister and cabinet are appointed by the president.

There is one legislative body: the National Assembly, composed of elected representatives from all districts of the country, 50 percent of whom must be from the working class or farmers. Copts and women are elected according to a quota. The Shura Council is an advisory body with 140 elected members and another 70 appointed members.

Culture & Customs

Whether Muslim or Copt, the Egyptians as a whole tend to be religious, and piety is important in their daily lives. So is commitment to the extended family. Each family member is responsible for the integrity of the family and for the behaviour of other members. Certainly, one result of these concerns is that the city of Cairo is safer than any western metropolis.

Yet when westerners visit Egypt they are often apprehensive. Their views of Egyptians and Arabs, fomented by unkind and exaggerated media stories, often bear no relation to reality at all. Travellers normally receive friendly, hospitable treatment and take home with them good feelings about the warmth and goodwill of the Egyptian people.

Planning the Trip

What to Bring

Almost everything is available in Cairo, but may be cheaper at home. Special medication should be brought with you. A small supply of plasters, antibiotic ointments and anti-diarrhoea tablets may well come in handy. If you have a favourite sun lotion, make-up, toothpaste or shampoo that you cannot possibly live without, bring some with you.

What to Wear

Be modest, be sensible and travel light. Egypt is a conservative country. It is an affront to your hosts to appear in a mosque or even on the street in clothing that is considered immodest. Women should keep shoulders and upper arms covered. Neither men or women should wear shorts except at resorts or on the tennis court. No topless or nude bathing is permitted.

On the practical side, leave your synthetics at home as they will prove too hot in the summer and not warm enough in the winter. Cotton is suitable for all seasons; wool for winter and many summer nights.

Loose and flowing garments are not only modest, but also extremely practical in a hot climate. Hats are vital and necessary, to protect against heat stroke and so are sunglasses, to defend the eyes against the glare.

Bring stout, comfortable shoes. You will be doing a lot of walking and neither Cairo's streets nor Luxor's temple floors are friendly to feet.

Disabled Facilities

Few hotels or cruise boats and no public buildings, restaurants, theatres or historical sites provide any facilities for the infirm or disabled. Major airlines, however, provide services both entering and leaving the country that match worldwide standards. Dr. Sami Bishara of ETAMS tours , 13 Sharia Qasr en-Nil, Cairo (02-575 2462) specialises in making travel arrangements for individual disabled travellers or groups.

Entry Regulations

VISAS & PASSPORTS

All travellers entering Egypt must have the appropriate travel documents: a passport with at least 6 months to run and a valid visa. Lost or stolen passports must be reported to the police immediately. New passports can be issued in a matter of hours at the consular office of your embassy in Egypt but procedures will require a copy of the police report verifying the loss. Tourist visas are also routinely issued at Cairo International Airport and the Port of Alexandria, but may also be acquired in advance at any Egyptian Consulate.

See **Useful Address** (*page 318*) for Egyptian consulate addresses.

Extension of Stay

Visas can be renewed at the Mugama'a (Cairo's central administrative building on Maydan at-Tahrir), usually after a long wait. Visas are usually considered valid for 15 days after the expiry date, but if not renewed then a letter of

Porter Service

For a rental of 2LE, baggage trolleys are available at Cairo International Airport. There are also porters with larger trolleys to service individuals and groups.

apology from your embassy must be presented to the Mugama'a or you will have to pay a small fine.

Customs

A visitor is permitted to enter the country with 250 grammes of tobacco, or 50 cigars, one litre of alcohol and personal effects. Animals must have a veterinary certificate certifying good health and a valid rabies certificate.

Duty-free purchases of liquor (3 bottles per person) may be made within a month of arrival twice a year at ports of entry or at the tax-free shops in Cairo, Luxor or Hurghadah.

Persons travelling with expensive electronic equipment may be required to list these items in their passports so that authorities can ensure that they will be exported upon departure.

On Departure

Although the traveller is free to buy and export reasonable quantities of Egyptian goods for personal use, the export of large quantities of items requires an export license. Egyptian-made items over 20 years old are not permitted to leave the country. Nor are foreign-made items deemed to have "historic value". Export of carpets, Egyptian-made or not, is restricted. Travellers may be requested to show bank receipts as proof of payment for other valuable items. Excess pounds may be changed back at the airport on showing valid bank receipts.

Animal Quarantine

It is not wise to bring a pet to Egypt on holiday. Rabies is a problem in the country and very few hotels have facilities for animals.

Health

Evidence of yellow fever and cholera immunisation may be required from persons who have been in an infected area up to six days prior to arrival.

Money

Airport Exchange

Banks are available at the airport for currency exchange. Egyptian money, with both Arabic and English numerals, consists of these denominations:
Pound notes: 100, 20, 10, 5, 1.
Piaster notes: 50, 25.
Coins: 20, 10, 5.

Credit cards are used in most major hotels, but not always in shops. Bring some traveller's cheques.

Public Holidays

There are six official government holidays a year when banks, government offices, many businesses and schools are closed. In addition there are Islamic and Coptic holidays spread throughout the year.

New Year's Day. Public holiday.

Coptic Christmas, January 7. Copts observe the birth of Christ on the same date as all other Orthodox churches except the Armenian. Prior to the feast they abstain from animal flesh and animal products for 43 days.

Feast of Breaking the Fast, 'Id al-Fitr, celebrates the end of Ramadan, the month of fasting. During daylight hours, Muslims will have abstained from food, drink, sex and violence for some 30 days. Business hours are shortened during Ramadan and social life, centring on the meal eaten after sunset, called iftar, becomes nocturnal and intense. 'Id al-Fitr is a happy celebration with new clothes, gifts, and plenty of good food. Festivities usually last for three days.

Feast of the Sacrifice, 'Id al-Adha, begins approximately 70 days after the end of Ramadan and commemorates Abraham's sacrifice of a sheep in place of his son, Isaac. It is traditional to kill a sheep and share the meat with the extended family, neighbours and the poor. Festivities last for four days.

Coptic Easter ends the Coptic Lenten season. Usually celebrated one week after Western Easter,

Coptic businesses are closed.

Sham an-Nissim, "sniffing the breeze", is a holiday celebrated the Monday after Coptic Easter. Dating from Pharaonic times, it is celebrated by all Egyptians regardless of their religious affiliation. The entire population goes to the countryside or to some urban green space for a day-long outing, with picnic baskets filled with hard boiled eggs and pickled fish. Businesses are closed.

Liberation of Sinai Day, April 25. Public holiday.

Labour Day, May 1. Public holiday.

Islamic New Year, Ras al-Sana al-Higriya. Public holiday.

Anniversary of the 1952 Revolution, July 23. Businesses are closed.

Prophet's Birthday, Mawlid al-Nabi, is celebrated in honour of the Prophet Muhammad. A parade complete with drums and banners is held in the historic zone of Cairo. Public holiday.

Armed Forces Day, October 6. Public holiday.

Calendars

The business and secular community in Egypt operates under the Western (Gregorian) calendar. But other calendars have official status in Egypt. The Islamic calendar is used to fix religious observances, and is based on a lunar cycle of 12 months of 29 or 30 days. The Muslim year is thus 11 days shorter than the year in the Gregorian calendar and months move forward accordingly.

In the Gregorian calendar, for example, April is in the spring, but in the Muslim calendar all months move through all seasons in a 33-year cycle.

The Coptic calendar is the Julian calendar, which was replaced in the West by the Gregorian calendar between 1582 and 1752, but the months carry their current Egyptian names. The Coptic year consists of 12 months of 30 days and one month of 5 days. Every four years a sixth day is added to the shorter month. An adaptation of the Coptic

calendar is often used for planting and harvesting crops. It is used by the authorities of the Coptic Orthodox Church.

Muslim Calendar	Coptic Calendar
Muharram	Toot (begins Sept 11 or 12)
Safar	Baaba
Rabi' il-awal	Hatour
Rabi' it-tani	Kiyaak
Gamada-l-uula	Tuuba (mid-Jan)
Gamada-l-ukhra	Amshir
Ragab	Baramhat
Sha'aban	Barmuda
Ramadan	Bashans
Shawal	Bauna
Dhu'l	Abiib
Dhu'l	Misra
	Nasi (5–6 days)

Getting There

BY AIR

Egypt is served by international airports at Alexandria, Cairo, Luxor and Hurghada on the mainland, and at Sharm al Shaykh on the Sinai peninsula.

Return tickets must be confirmed before departure. Check with a travel agent in your hotel or contact the airline office in Cairo. Most major airlines have offices located at the Cairo International Airport

and in and around Maydan at-Tahrir in downtown Cairo.

Cairo International Airport is now a first class facility. Despite the fact that it is located to the north of the city, most airlines from Europe approach the air field from the south. In daylight passengers are offered a magnificent view of Cairo, the Nile, and the Giza Pyramids.

Alexandria airport is served by Olympic Airlines and Egyptair. **Luxor** Airport now has direct flights from several European cities via Air France, Lufthansa and several charter companies. **Hurghada** Airport is also serviced by Lufthansa while **Sharm el Shaykh** Airport receives charter flights from all over Europe.

Other airports in Egypt are Asyut, Aswan, Abu Simbel, Al Arish, St Catherine's, Al-Khargah Oasis and Siwa Oasis.

Domestic Airlines

Egypt has two national carriers for internal flights, Egyptair and Air Sinai. Egyptair flies daily from Cairo to Alexandria, Luxor, Aswan, Abu Simbel, Sharm al-Sheikh and Hurghadah, and twice a week to Al-Khargah Oasis. Air Sinai flies from Cairo to Hurghadah, Sharm al-Sheikh, St Catherine's Monastery, Al Tor and to Tel Aviv, Israel.

Type of Visa

Single entry visas are good for one entry into Egypt for a period of up to one month. If you require a longer stay than this, request it at the time of application.

Multiple entry visas should be requested if you plan to exit and re-enter Egypt during your visit.

Student visas for people studying in Egypt are valid for one year and are not issued until verification of registration at an Egyptian university.

Business visas are issued to persons with business affiliations in Egypt.

Tourist Residence visas are extended to persons wishing to

visit Egypt for an extended period of time. Holders are not permitted to work in Egypt and must be prepared to present evidence of having exchanged $180 a month for up to six months at a time. This type of visa is only issued in Egypt at the Passport Department of the Mugama'a. Persons holding a Tourist Residence visa must apply for a re-entry visa whenever they plan to leave the country. All visas may be renewed up to 15 days beyond their expiration date. If not renewed during that time a fine is imposed and a letter of apology from your embassy must be taken to the Mugama'a.

Cairo Terminals

Terminal 1: Egyptair domestic and international flights.
Terminal 2: International Airlines.
Terminal 3: Saudia Arabia Airline.
Terminal 4: International cargo. English language information, Tel: 291-4255.

Egyptair Offices
www.egyptair.com.eg
Alexandria: 19 Midan Zaghlul
Tel: 483-3357, 390-0999
9 Taloot Hoib Street
Tel: 393-2836
Cairo: 6 Adli Street
Tel: 920-000
12 Qasr al Nil Street
Tel: 750-600
Nile Hilton Hotel
Tel: 574-7322
Cairo Sheraton
Tel: 348-8630
Heliopolis: 22 Ibrahim al Lakani
Tel: 290-8453
Luxor: Winter Palace Arcade
Aswan: Corniche
Tel: 575-4984
Hurghadah: Tourism Center near the National Hotel
Tel: 447-501
Sharm al-Sheikh: Mövenpick Hotel, Naama Bay
Tel: 600-314

Private Airlines
In November 1997 the Egyptian Government gave permission for private airlines to begin operations and announced that they would build more domestic airports. One of the first of the new, independent operators was **Orascom Air**, which operates regular flights from Al Gouna to Luxor and Cairo. Orascom Cairo office, tel: 02-301 5632.

BY SEA

Alexandria and Port Said on the Mediterranean Sea, and Suez and Nuweiba on the Red Sea are ports of entry. Services vary according to the time of year. More information is available from the ports and the larger travel companies.

BY LAND

From Israel
Private vehicles are not permitted to enter Egypt from Israel; however travellers may use public transport and enter Egypt via Rafah on the northern coast of Sinai or from Eilat on the Red Sea. Buses run regularly from Tel Aviv and Jerusalem to the border at Rafah. Passengers disembark from the Israeli vehicle, go through customs and take an Egyptian bus or taxi. There are no facilities for issuing visas at the border. In Eilat, Israeli buses are permitted to enter Egypt and travel as far as Sharm al-Sheikh at the southern tip of Sinai.

From Sudan
The only overland route in operation between Egypt and Sudan at present is by ferry from Suez, via Jeddah in Saudi Arabia, to Port Sudan. The trip should take four days. Information and tickets are available from Yara Tours and Shipping, 38 Sharia Mohammed Sabri Abu Alam, or Misr Travel in Port Tawfiq, Suez Canal. All arrangements to enter Sudan, including visas, must be made in Cairo. You must have a valid passport and either a transit or tourist visa to Sudan. If you plan to pass through the Sudan you must have a valid visa for your next destination.

From Libya
The border with Libya is open and buses and taxis make regular runs between Alexandria and Sollum. However, there are some travel restrictions for Westerners. Consult your, or the nearest Libyan, embassy for details.

Motoring to Eygpt
All private vehicles entering Egypt must have a triptyque or *carnet de passage en douane* from an automobile club in the country of registration or pay customs duty which can be as high as 250 percent. Emergency triptyques are available at the port of entry via the Automobile and Touring Club of

Egypt. This permits a car to enter Egypt for three months with one extension. The extension is available from the Automobile and Touring Club of Egypt, Qasr al Nil, Cairo. All persons travelling in the vehicle must have a valid passport and the driver must also have an International Driver's Licence. (*See Getting Around, Private Transport, page 324* for additional details on driving in Egypt.)

Useful Addresses

Tourism websites
www.touregypt.net
www.tourism.egnet.net

Egyptian Tourism & Information Centres
Athens: 10 Amerikis St
Tel: 360-6906
New York: 630 Fifth Ave
Tel: 332-2570
San Francisco: Suite 215, 83 Wilshire Boulevard, Wilshire San Vincente Plaza, Beverly Hills
Tel: 280 4666
London: 3rd floor Egyptian House
170 Picadilly, W1
Tel: 020 7493-5282
Rome: 19, Via Bissolati
Tel: 482-7985
Paris: 90, Avenue de Champs-Elysées
Tel: 45-62-94-42
Frankfurt: Kaiserstrasse 64, Bürohaus A
Tel: 23-98-76

Egyptian Consulates Abroad
Canada: 454 Laurier Ave. East, Ottawa; 1, place Sainte Marie, Montreal
France: 58, avenue Foch, Paris
Germany: Waldstrasse 15, Berlin; Eysseneckstrasse 34, Frankfurt
UK, 2 Lowndes Street, London SW1
Tel: 0891-887777
www.egypt-embassy.org.uk
United States:
3521 International Court NW, Washington DC 20008;
1990 Post Oak Blvd., suite 2180, Houston TX 77056;
500 N Michigan Ave., suite 1900, Chicago IL60611

Practical Tips

Islam is the official religion of Egypt, but there is a large Coptic community and other Christian sects represented in the country. There is also a small Jewish community. Islam is part of the Judaeo-Christian family of religions and was revealed to the Prophet Muhammad in what is now Saudi Arabia.

Islam has five major principles, known as "pillars", which form the foundation of the religion. The first principle is the belief that there is only one God and that the Prophet Muhammad is the messenger of God. The second is prayer, which should be performed five times every day. Almsgiving is the third principle and Muslims often donate

Business Hours

Banks: 8.30am–1.30pm daily, closed Friday, Saturday and most holidays.
Businesses: Business hours throughout the week are flexible. Few businesses function before 8am; many are open until 5pm, but some close during the after-noon and then re-open at 5pm. Clinics are customarily open from 5–8pm.
Government offices: 8am–2pm daily, closed Friday, Saturday, most holidays.
Shops: Shops keep hours according to demand. In central Cairo, many shops, including those owned by Muslims and Jews, are closed on Sunday.
Khan al-Khalili bazaar: open 10am–7 or 8pm daily and most shops close Sunday.

a percentage of their earnings to others.

The fourth pillar is fasting during the holy month of Ramadan. The fifth pillar is the pilgrimage to Mecca, *haj*, which all Muslims hope to perform at least once. The pilgrimage is performed during the month of Dhu'l-Higga, which begins 70 days after the end of the Ramadan fast.

COPTIC ORTHODOX

The Copts, a large minority in Egypt, are a Christian sect which separated from the Byzantine and Latin churches in AD 451 over a disagreement in religious doctrine. Copts founded the world's first monasteries, and the monastic tradition is an important part of the Coptic faith.

Religious Observances

Visitors may attend any Coptic serv-ice. Non-Muslims should not enter mosques while prayers are in progress, and may be asked, in mosques listed as antiquities, to pay entry fees. Muslims may enter any mosque free of charge. Listed below is a selection of Christian services. Hours should be checked against the weekend newspapers.

CATHOLIC CHURCHES

Church of the Annunciation
36 Muhammad Sabri Abu Alam, near Maydan Talaat Harb
Tel: 393-8429
Armenian Rite. Holy Liturgy Sunday 8.15am (in Coptic with Arabic read-ings); 9.30am, 10.30am and 6.30pm.
Our Lady of Peace
(Melkite, Greek Catholic), 4 Maydan al Sheikh Yusef, 96 Qasr el Aini
Byzantine Rite in Arabic. Holy Liturgy Sunday at 8.30am, 10.30am, and 6pm.
Holy Family Catholic Church
55 Road 15, Maadi
Latin Rite. Daily Mass in French or English Mon-Thur–6.15am, Fri 9am. Family Mass 5.30pm Saturday in

English, 6.30pm in French. Sunday Mass 9.30am in French, 6pm in English.
St Joseph's Church
(Italian and Egyptian Franciscan Friars), 2 Bank Misr at corner of Muhammad Farid
Tel: 393-6677
Latin Rite. Holy Mass Sunday 7.30am. 8.30am in French; 10am in Arabic; 12pm in Italian; 12.30pm in French; 4.30pm in English; 6.30pm in French. Weekdays 7.30am and 6.30pm in French.
St Joseph's Roman Catholic Church
4 Ahmed Sabri, Zamalik
Tel: 340-8902
Latin Rite. Holy Mass Sunday 8.30am in Arabic; 11am in French; 6pm in English. Weekdays 6pm in French. Saturday 6pm in Italian (sometimes Spanish).

ORTHODOX CHURCHES

Armenian Orthodox
Cathedral of St Gregory the Illuminator, 179 Ramesses near Coptic Hospital
Armenian Rite in Armenian. Holy Liturgy Sunday 9–11am.
Abu Serga Church
Old Cairo
Coptic Rite in Coptic and Arabic. Holy Liturgy Sunday 8am–noon.
St Mark's Cathedral
222 Ramesses, Abbassiyah
Coptic Rite in Coptic and Arabic. Holy Liturgy Sunday 6–8am.
Church of the Virgin Mary
6 Muhammad Marashli
Zamalik
Tel: 340-5153
Coptic Rite in Coptic and Arabic. Holy Liturgy Sunday 7.30–9.30am and 9.30–11am.

PROTESTANT CHURCHES

All Saints' Cathedral
5 Michel Lutfallah
Zamalik, behind the Marriott Hotel
Tel: 341-8391
Episcopal/Anglican.
Services in English: Sunday 8.30am, 10.30am and 7.30pm.
Mon–Thur 9am, Fri 9.30am, 6pm.

Christian Science Society
3 Midan Mustafa Kamil
Service and Sunday School, Sunday
7.30pm. Testimony Meeting
Wednesday 7.30pm. Reading Room
with Bible references and Christian
Science literature open Wednesday
and Sunday 6–7.20pm and Friday
11am–2pm.
Church of God
15 Emad al Din, Apt. 45
Sunday service 10.30am.
**Church of God Cairo Christian
Fellowship**
St Andrew's Church, corner of
Galaa and 26 July
Sunday service 6pm in English.
**Church of Jesus Christ of Latter-
Day Saints** (Mormon)
21 Road 17, Maadi
Weekly sacrament service Friday at
9.30am.
Maadi Community Church
(The Church of St John the Baptist)
Corner of Port Said and Road 17,
Maadi
Services in English Friday 8.30am
and 11am, with nursery; Sunday
7pm.
Saint Andrew's United Church
38, 26 July and Ramesses Street
Service in English Friday and
Sunday 9.30am.
Seventh Day Adventist Church
16 Kubba, Roxi Heliopolis.
Tel: 258-0292, 258-0785

Media

RADIO

European Radio Cairo 557 AM and
95 FM, 7am–midnight, is a station
playing European classical music,
pop, and jazz. News in English at
7.30am, 2.30pm, and 8pm; in
French at 8am, 2pm and 9pm; in
Greek at 3pm; in Armenian at 4pm;
in German at 6pm.
BBC World Service broadcasts to
Egypt on 639 kHz and 1323 kHz.
The higher metre band provides
better reception between sunrise
and sunset. There are also
shortwave alternatives. News is on
the hour.
The **VOA** (Voice of America)
broadcasts on a variety of
wavelengths from 3–10am daily, on
1290khz.

TELEVISION

The arrival of satellite TV, and more
recently cable TV have
revolutionised viewing in Egypt.
Most hotels, even the more down-
market ones, offer satellite TV and
satellite dishes now top many of
Cairo's apartment blocks. Local TV
is rarely exciting.
Channel 1: on the air from

3.30pm–midnight (local time), and
found on 1 and 5 on the dial, is
mainly in Arabic.
Channel 2: broadcasting from
3pm–midnight daily, and also from
10am–noon on Fridays and
Sundays, has many foreign
language programmes.
Channel 3: is a Cairo-only station
broadcasting, in Arabic, from
5–9pm.
CNN: arrived in Egypt in 1991. It
broadcasts to subscribers 24 hours
a day with an uncensored
programme.
See the *Egyptian Gazette* for daily
television schedules. Schedules
vary during Ramadan and in the
summer.

NEWSPAPERS

In Cairo all major English, French,
German and Italian daily
newspapers are available at larger
hotels and at newsstands in
Zamalik and Maadi usually a day
late. The two most important local
dailies are *Al-Ahram* and *Al-Akhbar*.
Al-Ahram, "The Pyramids", was established in 1875, making it the
oldest newspaper in Egypt.
Published daily, it also has a UK
edition, a weekly English-language
edition, *Al-Ahram Weekly* and a

Postal and Courier Servcies

The Central Post Office at Maydan
al Ataba in Cairo is open 24 hours
a day except Friday and occasional
holidays. All other post offices are
open from 8.30am–3pm daily,
except Fridays. Mailboxes, found
on street corners, and in front of
post offices are red for regular
Egyptian mail, blue for overseas
airmail letters and green for Cairo
and express mail within Cairo.
Allow seven days for air mail post
to Europe, 14 days to America.
Mail sent from hotels seems to go
quicker.

Express Mail Agencies
The major post offices, marked
with the EMS sign, offer an

Express Mail Service (EMS), which
is more expensive but much faster.
In addition to this there are various
international courier services:

DHL
20 Gamal al Din Abdul Mahasen,
Garden City
Tel: 355-7118
34 Abdel Khalek Sarwat
Tel: 393-8988
35 Ismail Ramzi, Heliopolis
Tel: 246-0324
Federal Express
1079 Corniche al Nil, Garden City
Tel: 355-0427
24 Syria Mohandeseen
Tel: 349-0986
31 Golf, Maadi

Tel: 350-7172
TNT International Express
33 Dokki, Dokki
Tel: 348-8204/348-7228
World Courier Egypt
17 Qasr al Nil
Tel: 777-678/741-313

Mail can be received at American
Express offices, you don't need to
be a cardholder to use the mail
pick-up service. Letters can also
be sent poste restante to most
Egyptian cities or to 15, Sharia
Qasr al-Nil, Cairo, A.R.Egypt. Bring
your passport to pick up your mail.
Some embassies may offer a mail
holding service for their nationals,
but check in advance.

weekly French-language edition, *Al-Ahram Hébdo*. Other English-language weeklies include the *Middle East Times* (online at: metimes.com), the *Cairo Times* (online at: www.cairotimes.com) and the *Arab Times*. *Al Akhbar al Yawm*, "The News", established in 1952 offers a weekly edition in Arabic.

The *Egyptian Gazette*, established in 1880, is the oldest foreign language daily newspaper still in operation in Egypt.

In French there are *Le Progrès Egyptien* and *Le Journal d'Egypte*; in Greek, *Phos*; and in Armenian, *Arev*.

Informal newsletters serve to keep the foreign residents in Egypt in touch: the *British Community Association News* for the British community; *Helioscope*, serving the residents of Heliopolis; the *Maadi Messenger* for foreigners in Maadi, and *Papyrus* for the German community.

English-language magazines include *Arab Press Review*, a biweekly political magazine, *Business Monthly*, featuring business news, *Cairo's*, a monthly what's on, *Egypt Today*, a monthly general interest magazine, *Places in Egypt*, designed for tourists, and *Prism*, a literary quarterly.

Telecoms

Most 5-star hotels offer a direct dial service. The Central Telephone and Telegraph offices (8 Shari Adli, on Maydan Tahrir, 26 Ramesses) are open 24 hours a day, as are many branch exchanges. Others are open from 7am–10pm daily. Telex and fax services are also available from the above, and fax facilities in particular are available at business centres dotted around the city.

Orange card phones are increasingly common; cards are available from the telephone offices.

Calls booked at telephone offices must be paid for in advance, with a three minute minimum. Between 8pm and 8am the cost of phone calls is greatly reduced.

If your have an AT&T calling card it is possible to charge a call from Egypt to the United States to a US account. You may place a call with a New York operator by dailing 356-0200 or 510-0200. You must supply both the American number and the number of your AT&T account.

Internet facilities are available through both commercial offices and educational institutions.

Emergencies

SECURITY AND CRIME

Like many other countries, such as Italy and the USA, Egypt has been troubled in recent years by right-wing extremists and radical Islamic terrorists. Like the US in the late 1960s, Germany in the 1970s, the UK and France throughout the 1970s, 80s and early 90s, it has also suffered from terrorist violence. In 1997 two attacks specifically targeting tourists – one outside the Egyptian Museum in Cairo and another at Hatshepsut's Temple, Luxor – significantly raised the overall death toll. These attacks appear to have been the work of a breakaway group from the main terrorist organisation. A heavy military response from the government designed to protect tourists and deter further terrorist activities cannot guarantee security and this further clamp-down may exacerbate the situation. However, even during the violence of 1991–2 tourists were statistically safer in Egypt than in many American cities and Egyptian drivers presented a greater threat than terrorists.

Visitors from abroad should nevertheless be warned that there may be restrictions on travel into or through Middle Egypt, the zone along the Nile in Upper Egypt between Al-Minya and Luxor. This region is beautiful, but poverty-stricken, and historically given to violence, much of it directed against officialdom or formal authority. It also contains many of Egypt's most interesting and least spoiled ancient sites, some of them only recently opened to visitors.

Elsewhere, common caution is advised. Social restrictions on women in Egypt can make foreign women seem particularly enticing to young Egyptian men, who may have heard lurid stories about sexual encounters (a situation not helped by the insensitive dress of some tourists). Care should be taken. Also, as Egypt's economic reforms have created great hardship, the number of petty thefts have increased although you are still more likely to have a lost wallet returned intact than in many countries.

If you do experience serious difficulties, you should report immediately to the nearest tourist police post or police station.

HOSPITALS

There are good hospitals in Cairo and Alexandria. However, they operate on a cash basis and patients cannot use foreign medical insurance plans. Some hospitals are:

Anglo-American Hospital Zohoreya next to the Cairo Tower, Zamalik
Tel: 340-6162
As Salam International Hospital Corniche al-Nil, Maadi
Tel: 363-8050/363-4196/363-8424
Shaalan Suificenter 10, Abal El-Hmid Lofi Street, Mohanandesseen
Tel: 360-5180
Al Salam Hospital 3 Syria, Mohandeseen
Tel: 346-7062/3

Telephone codes

Alexandria	03
Aswan	097
Asyut	088
Cairo	02
Fayyum	084
Hurghada	065
Ismailia	064
Luxor	095
Port Said	066
Suez	062

For general enquiries tel: 140.

PHARMACIES

Pharmacies are usually open from 10am to 10pm and are staffed by competent professionals. Both locally made and imported medication is subsidised by the government and is inexpensive. Some medication requiring prescriptions abroad is sold over the counter in Egypt.

24-hour pharmacies in Cairo include:

Attaba
Attaba Pharmacy
17 Midan Attaba

Central Cairo
Isaaf Pharmacy
3, 26th July
Seif Pharmacy
Qasr al Aini
Tel: 354-2678

Maadi
As Salam International Hospital
Maadi Corniche
Tel: 363-8050

Esam Pharmacy
101 Road 9
Tel: 350-4126
Mishriki Pharmacy
81 Road 153
Tel: 350-3333

Zamalik
Zamalik Pharmacy
3 Shagaret el Dorr
Zamalik
Tel: 340-2406

LEFT LUGGAGE

At the airport luggage is claimed via airline offices. In hotels consult the manager.

Photography

Egypt is a photographer's paradise. The best film speeds for daylight outdoors are low (100 and under), but fast film (400, 1000) is necessary for interiors, high-powered lenses and night shots like the moon over the Nile. Photography is forbidden in security zones, often curiously defined, and a variety of rules pertain to Pharaonic monuments. Signs are usually posted in restricted areas. In other areas photography is permitted for a fee. Fees for still cameras run as high as LE50, for video cameras up to LE200. There are no restrictions on photography anywhere in Cairo.

Scholars and professional photographers working on projects may apply for a special permit to take pictures from the Supreme Council for Antiquities. The procedure may well take some time, and passes are not given out freely.

Photographing individual people requires a bit of consideration. The Egyptian people are constantly having cameras pushed in their faces, so be courteous and ask first. If a person does not want you to take his or her photo, do not take it. If he or she wants to be paid, pay. If you don't want to pay, don't take the picture. You will find plenty of good shots elsewhere.

Getting Around

From the Airport

All airports in Egypt have a taxi service to city centres, operated on a flat fee basis (ask your airline). In Cairo transport includes limousine, taxi and bus. A curbside limousine service is offered by Misr Limousine (tel: 285 6721).

Official Cairo taxis are predominantly black and white and Alexandria taxis are black and orange. There are also larger Peugeot taxis in a variety of colours, but they all have an emblem and number painted on the driver's door. Fees are the same as the limousine service.

The Airport Bus Service operates from Terminal 1. The bus leaves when full and stops at Maydan Tahrir in downtown Cairo, in Mohandeseen, and along Pyramids Road in Giza.

Public Transport

BY RAIL

The Egyptian State Railway is a government-owned system founded in 1851 which services the entire Nile Valley down to Aswan, the Red Sea cities of Suez and Port Said, the Delta and Northern Coast cities of Alexandria (two stops) and Marsa Mutrah. There are at least half a dozen through trains a day on major routes. Fares are inexpensive, but unless one is travelling with a tour, tickets must be purchased at the main railway stations (in Cairo at Ramesses Station at Maydan Ramesses).

The privately-owned Wagon-Lits train company runs three fast turbo-trains a day from Cairo to

Alexandria (2 hours). Booking should be done in advance at Ramesses Station, Cairo or at Alexandria station. Wagon-Lits also operate trains and sleepers between Cairo and Luxor (10 hours) and Aswan (15 hours). For reservations and information, tel: 02 574-9474.

BY BUS

Air-conditioned buses link most parts of Egypt to Cairo and Alexandria. Seats may be reserved up to two days in advance. There is also a fleet of cheaper non-air-conditioned buses. Although bus times may change without any notice, departures are so frequent that schedule changes are not a problem at all.

Tickets for air-conditioned buses should always be booked in advance.

The fastest buses to Alexandria (3 hours) are operated by the Superjet and Golden Rocket companies. Buses for Alexandria and Mersa Matruh leave from the Abdel Mouneem Riyad Terminal near the Ramses Hilton.

The principle carrier to Aswan and Luxor is the Upper Egyptian Bus Company, 4 Sharia Yussef Abbas, tel: 260-9304/260-9297/8. Departures are from 45 Sharia al Azhar and the terminal at Maydan Ahmed Helmi. Two buses a day complete the run to Aswan, departing early morning and arriving in the evening.

Air-conditioned Superjets to Luxor and Aswan are not advisable as the services involve overnight travel with loud and rarely interesting end-to-end videos.

The East Delta Co covers the Canal zone and most of the Delta; buses leave from the Koulali Terminal. Buses for the Western Desert Oases leave from the scruffy Al Azhar terminal, near Maydan al-Ataba.

By Bus Around Cairo

The large red-and-white and blue-and-white buses are usually so over-

Orientation

The Nile flows through the country from south to north. Upper Egypt is therefore the south, Lower Egypt the Delta. Upstream is south, downstream north. Many good maps are available.

crowded they assault one's sense of private space. They also provide ample opportunity for petty theft and unwelcome sexual encounters. But here are a few interesting routes for the adventurous tourist:
- Number 400 from the airport to downtown.
- Number 66 from the Nile Hilton in Maydan Tahrir to the Khan al-Khalili.
- Number 72 from the Nile Hilton in Maydan Tahrir to the Citadel.
- Numbers 800 and 900 from the Mugama'a in Maydan Tahrir to the pyramids.

More comfortable are the smaller orange-and-white buses which do not permit standing. Here are a few major routes (from Maydan Tahrir):
- Number 24 to Ramesses statue, Abbassiyah and Roxi.
- Number 27 to Ramesses statue, Abbassiyah and the Airport.
- Number 82 to the Pyramids.

METRO & TRAM

Both Alexandria and Cairo have tram or metro systems that run through at least part of the city. Trains run every few minutes from early morning (5.30am) to midnight and fares are inexpensive, usually under a pound to the furthest destination.

By Tram Around Alexandria

Tram lines in Alexandria run only between Ramleh Station (called "Terminus") near the Cecil Hotel and destinations to the east of the city.
- Tram 1 (Bacos line), Ramleh Station to Sidi Bishr.
- Tram 2 (El Nasr line), Ramleh Station to Sidi Bishr.
- Tram 3, Ramleh Station to Sidi Gaber.

- Tram 4, Circular route: Sidi Gaber, Ramleh Station, Sidi Gaber.
- Tram 5, Ramleh Station to San Stefano via Bacos.
- Tram 6, Ramleh Station to Sidi Bishr via Glym.

By Metro Around Cairo

In Cairo the metro system is identified by circular signs with a big red M. The metro is clean and efficient, and an easy way to get around. Note that every train has a special carriage for women. The system runs north–south from Heliopolis to Helwan through the heart of the city. Another line was opened from the northern suburb of Shubra el-Kheima to Bulag al-Dakrour and other lines are currently under construction. Additional routes, east and west, are currently under construction. Useful stations:

Mubarak Station Ramesses Square with access to the main

Travel Agents

Abercrombie and Kent
5A Sharia Bustan Flat 14,
3rd floor
Tel: 393 6255
E-mail: akegypt@attmail.com
American Express
Nile Hilton, Maydan Tahrir
Tel: 578-0444
Also at 15, Sharia Qasr al-Nil
E-mail: aets@ritsec2.com.eg
Bestours
37 Qasr el Nil
Tel: 392-4741
Eastmar
13 Qasr el Nil
Tel: 574-5024
E-mail: eastmar@es.egnet.net
Egypt Panorama Tours
11 Tourist Center,
Zamslek Club, Mohandeseen
Tel: 344-9590
E-mail: ept@intouch.com
Misr Travel
1 Talaat Harb
Tel: 393-0010
E-mail: misrtrav@link.com.eg
Thomas Coo
4 Champollion
Tel: 574-3776
E-mail: tcintlsales@attmail.com

train station and bus stations to Upper Egypt and the Oases.

Urabi Station Sh Gala'a. *Al Ahram* newspaper.

Nasser Station Maydan Tawfiqiyyah.

Sadat Station Maydan Tahrir with 10 entrances and access to Egyptian Antiquities Museum, the American University in Cairo, Nile Hilton, all major airline offices and the Mugama'a (central administrative building).

Mar Girgis at Old Cairo with access to the Coptic Museum, Coptic churches and Roman fortress.

Zaghlul Station The National Assembly. Zaghlul monument.

By Tram Around Heliopolis

Cairo also has tram systems and Heliopolis is served by six tram lines. The major three lines are:

Abd el Aziz Fahmi line (green) from Midan Abd el Monim Riad (behind the Egyptian Museum) via Ramesses to Roxi, Merryland, Mahkama, Heliopolis Hospital to the Shams Club;

Nuzha line (red) runs Midan Abd el Monim Riad, Ramesses, Roxi, Heliopolis Sporting Club, Salah al

By Taxi

For one of the experiences of your life, take an Egyptian taxi. Taxi drivers seem to need to fill every empty space on the road (and sometimes the pavement). All taxis have orange licence plates and are identified by a number on the driver's door. Drivers are required to have their licence and identity numbers displayed on the dashboard. Sharing a taxi is not unusual. In Cairo and Alexandria taxis ply the streets at all hours of the day or night and can be flagged down. There are also taxi ranks at all the major hotels and public squares.

Official or metered prices are unrealistic and meters are seldom used. The fare should be agreed beforehand. The majority of taxi drivers are honest, but some try to cheat unwary foreigners, espe-

Din and Maydan al Higaz to Nuzha; **Mirghani** line (yellow) Midan Abd el Monim Riad, Ramses, Roxi, Sharia el Merghani, Saba Emarat, Midan Triomphe, Military College.

BY SERVICE TAXI

Collective service taxis are a faster alternative to the bus, and will get you just about everywhere in Egypt. The fare is about the same as for the bus, and on the main routes there are several departures daily. These taxis, often estate Peugeots – hence their pet name of 'Beejoo' – seat six or seven and leave as soon as they are full. Drivers are renowned for their speed, since the sooner they arrive the sooner they can load up again. The service station is usually beside the bus or train station.

Private Transport

CAR RENTAL

Driving in Egypt is very demanding (*see Driving Conditions below*). The best alternative is to hire a driver

cially between five-star hotels and such destinations as the pyramids or Khan al-Khalili. Do not hesitate to ask for assistance from the tourist police. At your destination, pay the fare in exact change and walk away. No tip is expected.

Taxi drivers are friendly, many speak English, some are college graduates moonlighting to supplement their incomes, and most are very eager to be hired by the day. The fee is negotiable, something in the region of £15 (LE82) per day. Such an arrangement is ideal for shopping or for seeing several scattered monuments.

Taxis in Luxor and Aswan are easier to find (they line up outside all the hotels), but for the distance travelled they work out more expensive than those in Cairo.

and car together, thus freeing yourself to enjoy the scenery.

Car rental agencies exist at most major hotels. Foreigners must have an International Driver's Licence and be at least 25 years of age to rent a car in Egypt. Some agencies offer four-wheel drive vehicles, with or without driver, for desert travel. You will need your passport, driver's licence and a prepayment. Credit cards are accepted.

Rental Agencies

Avis
16 Maamal el Sukkar
Garden City
Tel: 354-8698
Budget
5 Sh el Maqrizi
Zamalik
Tel: 340-0070/340-9474
Max Rent-a-Car
27 Sh Lubnan
Mohandeseen
Tel: 347-4712/3
Fax: 341-7123
Europacar
5, el-Fallah street
Mohandeseen
Tel: 303-5125
Also for four-wheel drive vehicles with or without experienced desert drivers. Branch office in Sharm al Sheikh.

Limousines

Limousines are available for those who want to travel in style:
Bita Limousine Service
Gazirah Sheraton
Tel: 341-1333/341-1555
Marriott Hotel
Tel: 340-8888
Budget Limousine Service
Semiramis Intercontinental Hotel
Tel: 355-7171 x 8991
Limousine Misr
7 Aziz Bil-Lah, Zeitoun
Tel: 259-9813/4

Driving Conditions

The roads that go from Cairo to Upper Egypt are the longest, most congested, and most dangerous in Egypt. Most traffic moving south from Cairo must travel a route along the western shore of the Nile.

It is not advisable to drive at night; vehicles stop dead on the road and turn out their lights; unlit donkey carts move at a snail's pace and are usually not seen until it is too late; and long distance taxis and overloaded trucks travel too fast, often without lights, and are driven by drivers who use "stimulants".

There are petrol stations throughout the country, with those operated by Mobil, Esso, and Shell offering full service with mini-markets on the premises. Fuel, inexpensive and sold by the litre, is available in 90 octane (*tisa'iin*) which is super, or 80 (*tamaniin*), regular. Super is better for most purposes.

Road signs are similar to those used throughout Europe. Driving is on the right-hand side of the road. Speed limits are posted on major highways and are enforced by radar.

Desert Travel

Use commonsense. Bring a compass. Check your car. Be sure to have a good spare tyre. Drive on loose sand as you would on snow. If your wheels get stuck in soft sand, put a rug under the back tires and move out slowly. If you spin your tyres, you will sink deeper into the sand. If your car breaks down along the road, don't abandon your vehicle; even in remote areas another vehicle will pass by. If you break down on a desert track (you should never leave the main road for long distances with only one vehicle), hike to the nearest road and wait. On all desert travels, have ample food, water, salt tablets, a hat and sunglasses. Cover the head and the back of the neck.

Top up your tank at every petrol station, as the next one may be hundreds of miles away. If your tank is small, carry a jerry can on long hauls like Dakhla to Farafrah (390 km/243 miles). Dehydration can sneak up on you in desert travel. In an emergency one teaspoon of salt and two tablespoons of sugar in a cup of water will revive you.

Desert driving is very monotonous. Remember you are still on a highway. When you wish to pass, sound your horn very deliberately, in order to make it clear that you are going to do something extraordinary. Egyptian drivers need an extra signal, since nearly all of them over-use the horn even when no-one is around. Another bad habit is misusing lights at night, either leaving them off or flickering the high beams dangerously. When a car is approaching he may blind you. Blink back and he may stop. He may be checking to see if you are awake.

Nile Cruises

A cruise on the Nile still is one of the best ways both to visit the temples and ancient sites and sample the peaceful life along the river. Hundreds of ships now cruise along the Nile following more or less the same itinerary but offering a wide choice of accommodation, suitable for every budget. Most people book cruises before they leave for Egypt, which is advisable as it is usually cheaper to buy them as part of a package. Most boats travel between Luxor and Aswan in 3-4 days, sometimes for 6 days to include Abydos and Denderah, and only occasionally sail the whole way from Cairo to Aswan (8 days).

Differences in price usually reflect the standard of service, the numbers and the size of the cabin and the quality of the food. More expensive boats tend to have fewer

Felucca Trips

A felucca trip is still the best way to get a feel of the Nile. Felucca boats can be hired for 2–4 days and temples are visited along the way. The boatman may cook and will point out places where it is safe to swim. If the wind is unreliable, you are advised to sail from Aswan to Luxor, so at least the current will carry you downstream (it's a long way to row). To find a felucca, ask along the Corniche in Luxor or Aswan.

Distances from Cairo

Distances between Cairo and other cities

North to Alexandria
225 km/140 miles (Delta road)
221 km/138 miles (desert road)
to Damietta
191km/119 miles
to the Barrages
25km/15 miles

South to Al-Minya
236km/151 miles
to Asyut 359km/224 miles
to Luxor 664km/415 miles
to Esna 719km/449 miles
to Edfu 775km/484 miles
to Kom Ombo 835km/521 miles
to Aswan 880km/550 miles

East to Port Said 220km/137 miles
to Ismailia 140km/87 miles

west to Fayyum 103km/64 miles
to Baharia Oasis 316km/197 miles
to Farafrah Oasis 420km/262 miles
to Dakhla Oasis 690km/413 miles
to Kharga Oasis 586km/366 miles

and larger cabins and will make the effort to prepare good food. All boats provide guides to accompany passengers to the sites and some have small libraries on Egyptian history and culture.

But there is no doubt that cruising is no longer as romantic as it used to be. There are often delays at Esna due to the large number of boats passing through the lock, forcing some companies to transfer their passengers to a sister boat on the other side of the lock. For the same reason not all boats dock in the centre of Aswan or Luxor; cheaper boats are often moored further along the river bank, or will be wedged between other boats and therefore without any Nile views from the inside. Your

travel agent should know if you will
have a Nile view.

To get a real feel of what cruising
used to be like before the traffic
jams on the Nile, a cruise on Lake
Nasser is much recommended. Two
companies now offer the 3–4 day
cruise, visiting the Nubian
monuments on the shores of Lake
Nasser. Watch Abu Simbel at dawn
before breakfast (and the crowds)
or take an apéritif at one of the
rarely visited Nubian temples. The
beautifully decorated MS *Eugenie* is
run by Belle Epoque Travel in Cairo,
tel:02-352 4775, and 352 8754
and the larger MS *Prince Abbas* is
operated by the Nile Exploration
Corporation, tel:02-340 7308 and
341 7865. Some more upmarket
tour operators in Europe and the
United States offer the cruise in
their brochures.

There are scores of Nile cruise-
companies, here are some of the
boats and operators:

★★★★★
Alexander the Great
Jolley Travel and Tour Company
23 Qasr el Nil
Tel: 393-9390
E-mail: atg@jolleys.com
This cruise ship was featured in the
American series The Love Boat.
Anni, Aton, Hotp, and Tut
Sheraton Management Corporation
48B Sharia Giza, Dokki
Tel: 348-8215
Golden Boat
International Nile Cruise
87 Sharia Ramses
Tel: 760-198
Isis and Osiris
Hilton International Company
Nile Hilton Hotel
Tel: 740-880
The first modern day cruise boats
on the Nile, these sister ships offer
5-day cruises.
Neptune
Trans Egypt Travel Company
37 Qasr el Nil
Tel: 392-4313
Seven-, 10-, and 11-day cruises.
**Nile Admiral, Nile Emperor, Nile
Legend, Nile President, Nile
Princess, Nile Ritz, Nile Symphony**
Presidential Nile Cruises

13 Marashli
Zamalek
Tel: 340-0517
4-, 7-, and 10-day cruises.
Nile Majesty I, Nile Majesty II
Mo Hotels Travel and Nile Cruises
41 Sherif
Tel: 392-5674
Nile Queen, Nile Sphinx
Sphinx Tours
2 Behler Passage
Qasr el Nil
Tel: 392-0704
**Oberoi Shehrayar, Oberoi
Shehrazad**
Oberoi Corporation Ltd
Mena House Hotel
Tel: 387-1225
Ra
Eastmar Travel
13 Qasr el Nil
Tel: 753-216
E-mail: eastmar@eis.egnet.net
Seti II, Seti III
Magdy G. Henein
16 Ismail Muhammad
Zamalek
Tel: 341-9820

★★★★
Atlas, Nile Star
Eastmar Travel
13 Qasr el Nil
Tel: 753-216
E-mail: eastmar@eis.egnet.net
Fleur
International Nile Cruises Company
3 Monshat el Katab
Tel: 392-4656
Horus
International Company for Hotels
and Nile Cruises
23B Ismail Muhammad
Zamalek
Tel: 340-0675/6
Seti I, Seti IV
Magdy G. Henein
16 Ismail Muhammad
Tel: 341-9820/2
Part of a fleet of six ships ranging
from 5-star to unclassified.

★★★
Abu Simbel, Aswan, Nile Delta
Hapi Travel and Tourism Company
17 Qasr el Nil
Tel: 393-3611/93, 393-3562
E-mail: bbg@ritsec3.com
7- and 14-day cruises

**Karnak, Pyramids, Queen Nefertiti,
Akhenaten**
Pyramids Nile Cruise Company
56 Gamet el Dowal el Arabia
Mohandeseen
Tel: 360-0146/7
Nefertari
Eastmar Travel
13 Qasr el Nil
Tel: 753-305
E-mail: eastmar@eis.egnet.net
13-day cruises.

Unclassified
Unclassified cruise ships may be
3–5 star and above. This is a
selected list.
Aida I, Aida II
Nile Valley Tours
80 Gamel el Dowal el Arabia,
Mohandeseen
Tel: 349-5482, 349-3768
Ambassador I, Ambassador II
Ambassador Nile Cruises Company
33 Hosny Saleh
Mohandeseen
Tel: 347-1015
Excelsior, Seti the Great
Magdy G. Henein
16 Ismail Muhammad
Zamalek
Tel: 341-9820/2
**Nile Pullman Fleurette, Nile
Pullman L'Egyptien**
Pullman International Hotels
9 Menes St, Heliopolis
Tel: 290-8802/3

Where to Stay

In 3-, 4- and 5-star hotels payment for non-Egyptians and non-resident foreigners must be made in foreign currency, by credit card or in Egyptian currency with a bank exchange receipt. Motels do not exist in Egypt. Booking a hotel as part of a package reduces the rates considerably.

Abu Simbel

★★★★
Nefertari Abu Simbel
Abu Simbel
Tel: 400-508
For those who want to spend longer on the site than the one or two hours usually allowed for an excursion, an overnight stay is the answer. About 400m from the temple, set in a garden, The Nefertari offers smallish air-conditioned rooms and a swimming pool. In winter it is advisable to book in advance.

★★★
Nobaleh Ramses
Abu Simbel
Tel: 400-294
Although located further away, about 1.5km, from the site, this hotel has larger, more comfortable rooms which are equipped with air-conditioning and a fridge.

Alexandria

★★★★★
Helnan Palestine Hotel
Montazah palace grounds
Tel: 547-3500
E-mail: reshp@helnan.com
An Alexandrian institution, very popular with ex-pat residents and local families, who come on weeekends the enjoy the peaceful

bay and to swim in a slightly cleaner sea. Rooms are worn, but the view makes it worthwhile.
Sheraton Muntazah
Corniche Muntazah
Tel: 548-0550
The most upmarket of Alex's hotels, with a pool and private beach across the road. A long drive from the centre, near Muntazah.

★★★★
Paradise Inn Metropole
52 Sharia Saad Zaghlul
Tel: 482-1465
Recently renovated period hotel with lots of atmosphere, mouldings and antiques in the reception, now also comfortable beds and all mod cons. Much cheaper than the Cecil. Highly recommended.
El-Salamlik Palace Hotel
El-Montazah Palace
Tel: 547-3585
E-mail: salamek@sangiovanni.com
The recently renovated Salamlik (guest house) of the Montazah palace provides peaceful rooms in great surroundings.
Sofitel Alexandria Cecil Hotel
16 Midan Saad Zaghlul
Tel: 483-7173
The Cecil is haunted by the ghosts of Noel Coward, Somerset Maugham and others, including Lawrence Durrell who immotalised it in *The Alexandria Quartet*. The glamour has long gone, but the charm of the place, and views over the bay still pull the romantics. The coffee shop is a popular rendezvous for a cup of tea.

★★★
Agami Palace
El-Bittash Beach
Agami
Tel: 433-0230
Spacious but basic rooms with balconies overlooking the beach and swimming pool.

★★
Ailema
21 Sharia Amin Fikry, Downtown
Tel: 482-7011
Old-style, adequate rooms in a quiet, downtown backwater, overlooking Ramlah Square.

Price Guides

Price ranges for double rooms with bath are:

★	$10–20
★★	$20–30
★★★	$30–100
★★★★	$50–180
★★★★★	$100–400

Seastar
24 Sharia Amin Fikry
Tel: 483-1787
Modernised spacious rooms, great value.

Unclassified
Acropole,
27 rue Chambre de Commerce
Tel: 480-5980
No stars, but the rooms in this atmospheric, clean, Greek-owned pension enjoy the same views as the much more expensive Cecil Hotel.

Aswan

★★★★★
Aswan Oberoi
Elephantine Island
Tel: 314-667
Luxurious spa-hotel with a good swimming pool, set in a garden on the tip of Elephantine island.
Sofitel Old Cataract
Sharia Abtal et Tahrir
Tel: 316-002
For old-style, Agatha Christie nostalgia and the smell of polished wood there is nowhere quite like the Old Cataract in Aswan. Rooms are cosy and tastefully furnished. North-Wing, Nile-side rooms overlook the temple on Elephantine Island, part of the town and has a magnificent river view. Breakfast is served in the splendid Moorish room, once the ball room, and the Belvedere terrace is still the place to watch the sunset.

★★★★
Amoun Hotel
Amoun Island
Tel: 313-800
A favourite hotel, now run by Club Med, with peaceful rooms

overlooking the river and the desert with the Aga Khan mausoleum. A great place to relax for a few days, with good food.

Basma Swiss Inn
Sharia el-Fanadek
Tel: 310-901/2/3
E-mail: sst@ritsec1.com.eg
One of the more recent arrivals in town, a full-blown resort hotel with all you would expect, including a huge swimming pool. Most rooms overlook the river.

★★★
Cleopatra
Sharia Sad Zaghloul
Tel: 324-001
Very clean rooms with phone and private bathroom, near the *suq*, with a small pool on the roof.

★★
Ramses
Sharia Abtal et-Tahrir
Tel: 324-000
Modern hotel with well-kept rooms all with phone and private basthroom, offering very good value.

★
New Abu Simbel
northern end of the Corniche in the Atlas area
Tel: 312-143
Modern carpeted rooms with private bathrooms, some with balconies overlooking the Nile, and a pleasant garden terrace that serves cool beers.

Asyut

★★★★
Badr Touristic Hotel
Sharia et-Thallaga
Tel: 329-811
So-called best hotel in town, though both the modern architecture and tasteless decor can be immensely depressing.

★★★
Assiutel
146 Sharia en-Nil
Tel: 312-121
This hotel has comfortable rooms and all the usual amenities.

Cairo

★★★★★
Cairo Marriott,
Sh. Saray al Gazirah
Zamalik.
Tel: 340-8888
E-mail: marriott@ritsec3.com.eg
The Marriott Hotel has built this facility around the former palace of the Khedive Ismail, built to commemorate the opening of the Suez Canal in 1869. Antique furniture graces the halls and public rooms. The Eugénie's Lounge, an elegant cocktail bar in the former rooms of the Empress Eugénie, and the Garden Promenade, the open air café in the Khedive Ismail's garden make this a good place to recover from Cairo's hustle and bustle. There are several other restaurants and the popular Harry's Pub.

El-Gazirah Sheraton
Gazirah
Tel: 341-1333/341-1555
South of the Cairo Opera House, on the southern tip of the island, the Gazirah Sheraton has excellent Nile views. In summer there are several outdoor riverside restaurants. The later Oriental show at the nightclub usually has one of Cairo's best belly dancers, while the Kebabgy al-Gazirah restaurant offers excellent Middle Eastern food. Has an excellent view of the Nile.

Mena House Oberoi
end of Sharia al-Haram
(Pyramid's Road)
Giza
Tel: 383-3222
E-mail: obmhobc@oberoi.com.eg
A historic landmark refurbished by the Oberoi chain, the Mena House is the only hotel in Egypt to have a golf course. The rooms in the 19th-century khedival hunting lodge are tastefully decorated with antiques, but most rooms are in the less-characterful modern garden wing. Lunch by the pool is recommended after visiting the Giza Pyramids. The elegant Moghul Room is the best Indian restaurant in town, with live music. Outlets include: the Greenery Coffeeshop, a buffet in the garden; Khan al Khalili, a

Price Guides

Price ranges for double rooms with bath are:

★	$10–20
★★	$20–30
★★★	$30–100
★★★★	$50–180
★★★★★	$100–400

coffeeshop featuring international and Middle-Eastern entrées; the Mogul Room offering Indian food and one of the best restaurants in Egypt; the Rubayyat, the main dining room with continental and Middle-Eastern meals and live entertainment. Bars include the Mameluke Bar and El Sultan Lounge. Nightclubs are Oasis Summer Nightclub and Abu Nawas Nightclub. The disco is The Saddle.

Le Meridien Heliopolis
51 Sharia Oruba
Heliopolis.
Tel: 290-5055/290-1819
One of Cairo's best hotels, a short ride from the airport, offers luxurious accommodation and a selection of excellent restaurants, including the Pool restaurant and Marco Polo, where Italian dishes have a delicate touch of Middle Eastern cusine.

Nile Hilton
Corniche
Maydan Tahrir
Tel: 578-0444/578-0666
E-mail: rhilton@brainy1.ie-eg.com
This was one of the first international hotels in Cairo, the Hilton, located on the Nile in the city centre, has an authentic ancient Egyptian statue in the lobby. Abu Ali's Café serves *sheesha*, green tea, and light snacks on the terrace and is a popular meeting place in downtown Cairo. Jackie's is one of the best discos in town, and when it closes the casino continues. The Safari Bar on the first floor offers cosy armchairs, a nostalgic atmosphere and good cocktails, while the Taverne du Champs de Mars, a genuine Art Nouveau Pub shipped in pieces from Brussels, is a more casual place for drinks and snacks.

★★★★
Atlas Zamalek
20, Sharia ad-Duwal al-Arabiya
Mohandeseen
Tel: 346-4175
Modern hotel in this upcoming part of town with a swimming pool on the roof and one of the most popular discotheques in town. All business facilities.

Golden Tulip Flamenco Hotel
2 Sharia Al-Gezirah al-Wusta
Tel: 340-0815
E-mail: cairo@flamenco.com.eg
Modern hotel in a quiet, tree-lined street in the residential part of Zamalik, with some rooms overlooking the Nile and even the Pyramids on a clear day. The Florencia restaurant serves excellent paellas.

★★★
Cosmopolitan
1, Sharia Ibn Tahlab
Downtown
Tel: 392-3845
A grand Art Nouveau building offering spacious, comfortable rooms with all modcons. Surprisingly quiet.

Horus House
21, Sharia Ismail Muhamad
Zamalik
Tel: 340-3977
A home away from home, the Horus is often booked up by returning guests. The restaurant offers a good-value lunch, popular with older Zamalik residents.

President
22, Sharia Dr. Taha Hussein
Zamalik
Tel: 340-0652
More like a four-star hotel, this efficient, friendly hotel with a good business centre is a well kept secret in a quiet Zamalek street. The Cellar Bar, always crowded, serves good *mezze*.

Windsor
19, Sharia Alfi Bey, Downtown
Tel: 591-5277
For nostalgic souls, this is a place to sniff a Cairo that is no more. Faded but clean rooms and friendly service. The bar, with its old waiters, sunken sofas and heavy air, is an institution.

★★
El Hussein,
Maydan al-Hussein
Al Azhar
Tel: 591-8664, 591-8089
A noisy affair during religious festivals, this hotel is the place to stay if you want to get lost in Cairo's old city. Clean but basic rooms.

Lotus
7th floor
12 Sharia Talaat Harb
Tel: 575-0966
Good value and as central as it gets. Airy, clean rooms with balconies and air-conditioning.

★
Garden City House
23, Sharia Kamal ad-Din Saleh
Garden City
Tel: 354-4969
Pleasant, dusty pension, popular with scholars and archaeologists, with large clean rooms. Half board is compulsory but meal times provide a good opportunity to meet some interesting people.

Mayfair
9, Sharia Aziz Osman
Zamalik
Tel: 340-7315
Tranquil hotel with tidy rooms overlooking a tree-lined street. Pleasant terrace for an afternoon drink.

Pension Roma
169 Sharia Muhamad Farid
Downtown
Tel: 391-1088
This is a popular hotel with travellers. All rooms have shiny wooden floors and old-style furniture. Book ahead.

Unclassified
Pension Oxford
32, Sharia Talaat Harb
Downtown
Tel: 391-1088
One of the cheapest and oldest of the backpacker haunts with more or less clean dormitory beds, and belly-dancers and Italian hairdressers amongst the residents.

Ismailia House
8th floor

1 Maydan Tahrir
Tel: 356-3122
Recent arrival and already very popular with backpackers on account of its clean white rooms, many communal bathrooms and most of all its view

Hurghadah & Red Sea

AL-GOUNA

All hotels in Al-Gouna have a central reservation system.
Tel: 065 545-060, fax: 545-061, or through the Cairo Office, tel: 02 336-5202, fax: 02 336-9049.

★★★★★
Al-Gouna Mövenpick
Tel: 544-501
Huge resort hotel where you could easily get lost. Despite its large number of rooms, there is plenty of space for everyone around one of the pools, the lagoons, or on the large stretch of beach. Good selection of bars and restaurants within the compound.

Al-Gouna Paradisio (Sonesta)
Tel: 547-934
Built in traditional style, rooms in this resort hotel are set in landscaped gardens around lagoons, and two swimming pools. Good windsurfing centre.

Miramar (Sheraton)
Tel: 545-606, 545-680
Unlike any other hotel in Egypt, the latest arrival in Gouna offers world-class architecture by celebrity American architect Michael Graves, who was inspired by the work of the late Egyptian architect Hassan Fathy. Painted in muted primary colours and built in a low simple style, the hotel feels like a toy town surrounded by turquoise lagoons.

★★★★
Dawar al Omda
Kafr el-Gouna
Tel: 545-060
Built in the traditional style of a 'House of the Mayor', rooms in domed bungalows around pool and lagoon, elegantly decorated with new and period furniture, antique objects, tiles and local crafts.

Price Guides

Price ranges for double rooms
with bath are:

★	$10–20
★★	$20–30
★★★	$30–100
★★★★	$50–180
★★★★★	$100–400

★★★
El-Khan
Kafr el-Gouna
Tel: 545-060
Smaller hotel, beautifully decorated,
with rooms around a pleasant
courtyard, or overlooking the
lagoon. Heated swimming pool in
winter.

HURGHADAH

★★★★★
Intercontinental Hurghadah
Tel: 443-911
Large resort hotel with rooms
overlooking a garden, the swimming
pool and the bay. Large private
beach, one of Hurghada's best
watersports facilities and a marina
as well as a swimming pool. There
are also several good restaurants
and although there is a free shuttle
bus into Hurghadah town, many
people never leave the hotel.

★★★★
Sonesta Beach Resort
Tariq el-Matar
Hurghadah
Tel: 443-664
Deluxe resort hotel with well-
equipped rooms and offering all
sports facilities, a private beach
and swimming pool.

★★★
Giftun Village
Tel: 442-665
Large resort hotel with an excellent
diving and windsurfing centre and
bright whitewashed rooms with tiled
floors.
La Bambola
Sheraton Road
Tel: 442-085
Clean and cosy. Not on the shore,

but a regular bus shuttles guests to
a private beach.
Shedwan Golden Beach
Sharia el-Corniche
Tel: 447-044
Typical package tour hotel catering
mainly to divers, with a good beach
and swimming pool.

Unclassified
California
Tel: 549-101
Very good value rooms, recently
refurbished with good beds, funky
murals, and some with a private
bath room.
El-Arousa
Hurghada town
Tel: 548-434
One of the best mid-range hotels
with impeccable rooms with
bathroom, phone and balcony with
sea view. It has an Indoor pool and
guests have free access to the
beach of the Geisum Village across
the road.

AL-QUSAYR

★★★★★
Movenpick Resort Jolie Ville Tel:
432-10010
Beautifully designed hotel with
domed rooms built and decorated in
traditional style, excellent service
and very good facilities.
Recommended for a few days of
peace and quiet.

Luxor

★★★★★
Movenpick Jolie Ville Luxor
Crocodile Island, 6km (4 miles) out
of town
Tel: 374-855
E-mail: mpluxor@intouch.com
The best hotel in town, Swiss-
managed, with excellent service,
good food, relaxed atmosphere and
simple, comfortable rooms set in a
splendid garden, most overlooking a
beautiful stretch of the Nile.
Sofitel Winter Palace
Sharia Corniche en-Nil
Tel: 380-422
Old-style hotel, recently refurbished
to some of its former splendour.

The rooms in the old building have
more character than the new
garden wing, but service
everywhere can be slow at times.

★★★★
Akhtetaton Village (Club Med)
Sharia Khaled Ibn Walid
Tel: 380-850
Comfortable rooms set in a garden
on the Nile, typical Club Med
facilities and good food.
Mercure Luxor Hotel
10, Sharia Maabad Luxor
Tel: 580-944
The old-Etap hotel offers adequate
and clean rooms though liitle
atmosphere. Half the rooms
overlook the river and West Bank
mountains. The terrace is popular
for a sunset drink.

★★★
Emilio Hotel
Sharia Yousef Hassan
Tel: 373-570
This is a very good mid-range hotel
with comfortable rooms that are
equipped with all modcons. There is
a rooftop pool and sundeck. Book in
advance in winter, popular with tour
groups.
Philippe
Sharia Labib Habashy
Tel: 372-284
Excellent three-star hotel offering
spotless aircon rooms, TV, fridge
and some balconies. The pleasant
roof terrace has a small pool and
bar. Recommended, but book
ahead, especially in winter.

★★
Horus
Sharia el-Maabad
opposite Luxor Temple
Tel: 372-165
Rooms overlook either the temple
or the lively suq. Central, well-kept,
with recently renovated bathrooms.
Mina Palace
Sharia Corniche en-Nil
Tel: 372-074
Good value and friendly, on the
Corniche, recently refurbished air-
con rooms and private bathrooms.
Some corner rooms have balconies
overlooking the Nile and Luxor
Temple.

Unclassified
Habu Hotel
opposite Medinat Habu
Nag Lolah
West Bank
Tel: 372-477
Very basic rooms but popular for
the price, the village atmosphere
and a spectacular view over
Medinet Habu temple from the
large upper terrace.
Mersam Hotel
also known as Sheikh Ali's Hotel,
opposite the Tombs of the Nobles,
West Bank
Tel: 372-403
In 1881 the Abdul Rasoul family
discovered the Deir el Bahri cache
of royal mummies, which are now
on show in the Cairo Museum. The
late Sheikh Ali's son now runs this
simple hotel. The tranquil garden
has views over green fields.
Pharaoh's
near the ticket office on the West
Bank
Tel: 374-924
This is the only mid-range hotel on
this side of the Nile with clean
rooms some with private
bathrooms and a pleasant garden
bar/restaurant.

Al-Minya

★★★★
Mercure Nefertiti/Aton
Sharia Corniche en-Nil
Tel: 341-515
This is the most upmarket hotel in
the area with comfortable rooms –
some of these face the Nile. There
is also the luxury of a swimming
pool in the garden. Functioning
restaurant and bar.

★★
El-Shatee (Beach Hotel)
31 Sharia al-Gumhuriya
Tel: 322-307
Pleasant and clean rooms with fan
or air-conditioning.
Lotus
1, Sharia Port Said
Tel: 324-500
Clean rooms with fans and a good
bar-restaurant frequented by beer-
drinking locals.

Sinai

SHARM AL SHAYKH

★★★★★
**Intercontinental Resort
and Casino,**
Sharm al-Maya Bay
Tel: 601-291
One of the most recent arrivals on
the luxurious side of the market,
this resort-style hotel offers
spacious accommodation and a
good choice of restaurants as well
as a lively casino. A free shuttle bus
goes frequently to Naama Bay but
the hotel has an excellent pool and
a private beach.
Mövenpick Jolie Ville
Naama Bay
Tel: 600-100/5
Good resort hotel with bungalows
set in a beautiful garden and with
several restaurants, in the heart of
Naama Bay.

★★★★
Fayrouz Hilton
Naama Bay
Tel: 600-136
One of the first upmarket hotels in
the bay, the Hilton continues to
offer an efficient service. The
bungalows are set in a lovely
garden. The stables organise
horseriding in the desert.

★★★
Clifftop
Naama Bay
Tel: 770-44
Air-conditioned bungalows and
rooms with bathroom and a
pleasant garden, overlooking the
beach and the bay.
Sanafir
Naama Bay
Tel: 600-197/8/9
One of the most charming and
relaxed hotels in the bay, run by
Adly al-Mestekawi. Not on the
beach, but with an internal
courtyard and swimming pool.
Guests get a free pass to use the
beach at the nearby Aquanaute
Diving Club. Comfortable rooms in
an attractive Moorish style. The
staff has plenty of experience in
diving and desert trips.

Unclassified
The Pigeon House
northern edge of Naama Bay
Tel: 600-996
Best of the few budget hotels in
town with basic but clean bamboo
huts with fans, some smaller rooms
and communal bath rooms. It is
advisable to book in advance as it
fills up quickly.

REST OF SINAI

★★★★★
Helnan Dahab
Dahab
Tel: 640-425
A real resort hotel, but like most
places in Dahab it caters for
package tours and is seriously
lacking in atmosphere.
Taba Hilton
Taba
Tel: 530-140
This luxury hotel is about all there
is in Taba, on the border with Israel.
The hotel has several restaurants
and a diving centre.

★★★★
Hilton Coral Nuwayba
Nuweiba
Tel: 520-320
Just north of the port this resort-
style hotel offers characterless but
comfortable accommodation, a fine
beach and a range of food outlets.

★★★
Helnan Nuwayba
Nuweiba
Tel: 500-401
Formerly the Holiday Village, also
hotel that caters mostly to package
tourists, with air-conditioned
bungalows set in a garden along the
beach.

★
Elsebaey
Tarabin, Nuweiba
Tel: 500-373
Brand-new hotel in Tarabin, with
basic but clean rooms, shared as
well as private bathrooms and a
pleasant rooftop bar.
Starcosa
south of Assalah, Dahab

Tel: 640-366
A modern and pleasant place to stay. Comfortable rooms with bathroom and fan.

Unclassified

Basata

23km (14 miles) north of Nuwayba
Tel: 500-481, or 02 350-1829 in Cairo
Clean and very relaxed camp with simple bamboo huts, a bakery and communal kitchen.

Bedouin Village (Dahab)

Most travellers head for the so-called Bedu Village where Bedu run camps of concrete (hotter!) and reed (less secure) huts with mattresses and some with electricity and fans. One of the better camps is **Mirage Village** (tel: 640-341), which has both huts and, more expensive, proper rooms.

Gulf Hotel

near el-Masbat, Dahab
Tel: 640-147
Basic clean rooms but nothing special.

St Catherine's Monastery Hostel

Tel: 770-945
Monastic rooms, some with private bathroom, overlooking a tree-lined courtyard in an annex just outside the monastery proper. The place to stay for an early ascent of the mountain, three solid meals are included in the price. Book well ahead.

Price Guide

Price ranges for double rooms with bath are:

★	$10–20
★★	$20–30
★★★	$30–100
★★★★	$50–180
★★★★★	$100–400

Where to Eat

Cairo and Alexandria have a good selection of restaurants, but smaller towns have a rather limited choice. Set menus and buffets in hotels offer an international cuisine with the occasional Egyptian dish, but Egyptian food is definitely worth trying out. Apart from the regular fare, 5-star hotels often fly in European chefs for week-long ethnic extravaganzas. Hotel restaurants will only be mentioned here if they are really notable. In recent years prices have risen steeply in Egyptian restaurants, and a good meal can cost almost as much as in London or New York although the more basic restaurants are still a bargain. Cheaper restaurants often don't serve alcohol, while more upmarket places may only serve the much more expensive imported wines. Local Stella beer is good, and is often preferred to Stella Export and the new Stella Premium.

Drinking Notes

The traditional **hot and cold drinks** served in coffeehouses are delicious and thought to be health-giving. The usual idea of American coffee is instant Nescafé. If you want decaffeinated coffee then you will have to bring your own.

Fresh juices such as orange, mango, strawberry, pomegranate, lime or whatever, depending on the season, are available in juice bars everywhere *except* in major hotels.

Internationally formulated drinks made and bottled locally under li-cense include a range of Schweppes and Canada Dry mixers, Coca-Cola, Seven-Up, Sport and Pepsi-Cola.

The local **beer** is Stella, a lager that comes in two varieties: Stella Export and ordinary Stella, which is less sweet and therefore usually preferred to Export. The adventurous may encounter a mild home-brew called buza, which is recorded to have been made in the Third Dynasty.

Egyptians were making **wine** even earlier. Reds include Omar Khayyam, Pharaohs and Château Gianaclis; there is one rosé, called Rubi d'Egypte. Among the whites – Gianaclis Village, Cru des Ptolemées, Castel Nestor, Nefertiti and Reine Cléopatre – Gianaclis Village (ask for Qaryah) is the driest and is preferred with fish or seafood. Reine Cléopatre (ask for Kliobatra), sweeter and fruitier, is a suitable accompaniment to turkey or veal. Caution is advised when dining out, however, since Egyptian wine has only recently recovered from several years of faulty manufacture and quality is still apt to vary from bottle to bottle. If there is a risk of spoiling an evening, the worst should be sent back immediately. Mediocre French or Italian wine is available in the major hotels, at prices roughly 10 times their maximum value on the western market.

Imported spirits are also available, although they are relatively expensive. Local spirits are quite popular among Egyptians. They include several kinds of brandy and various versions of **zibeeb** or **araq**, the Arab World's heady and dangerous version of ouzo.

Alexandria

EGYPTIAN/LEVANTINE

Tikka Grill

Al-Kashafa el-Baharia Club no.26 on the Corniche
Tel: 480-5114
Excellent fish kebabs and meat dishes, a salad bar and good views over the bay.

Hassan Bleik

opposite 18 Sharia Saad Zaghloul
Tel: 484-0880
Old fashioned and cheap Lebanese restaurant with a large menu of delicacies including stuffed pigeon

Street Food

Streetfood in Egypt is often delicious but take care if your stomach is unacclimatised. *Koshari*, a mixture of rice, macaroni, fried onions, lentils and chickpeas, topped with a spicy tomato sauce, is popular, as are *ful* and *tamia*. A wide variety of sandwiches are available, filled with *pasturma* (a local dried meat), white cheese, chopped liver, kidneys and *tameya*. Roast corn, chicken soup and baked sweet potatoes are popular snacks in winter.

and chicken with almonds. Lunch time only.

Mohamed Ahmed
17 Sharia Shakour
Tel: 483-3576
By far the best *ful* and *tamia* in town, known as the Great Pyramid of Alexandria. No alcohol.

SEAFOOD

Adoura
33 Sharia Bayram al-Tonsi
Tel: 480-0405
Popular cheap outdoor restaurant in a quiet back street with an excellent selection of fresh fish, but no alcohol. They even have a sister branch in Brooklyn New York.

Fish Market
Al-Kashafa al-Baharia Club
no.26 on the Corniche
Tel: 480-5114
A more upmarket fish restaurant with a huge display of fresh fish, which is then cooked the way you want it. Good service, excellent salad bar and a perfect view of the harbour.

Sea Gull
al-Maks, on the road to Agami
Tel: 445-5575
Famous fish restaurant in a mock medieval castle with a playground for children. Lobster and shrimps are a speciality.

Shaaban Fish
behind Rex cinema in al-Manshia
Tel: 484-1629

Extremely popular but very basic fish restaurant in the centre, which advertises itself, quite rightly, as "the fish restaurant everyone talks about".

Zephyrion
41 Sharia Khalid ibn Walid, Abu Qir
Tel: 560-1319
The only reason to venture to Abu Qir is to go to this excellent fish restaurant, perched over the Mediterranean and run since 1929 by Greeks. It becomes very busy at weekends with Alexandrian families.

COFFEEHOUSES/BARS

Athineios
21 Maydan Sad Zaghlul
Tel: 482-0421
This is an old-fashioned patisserie, nightclub and pleasant restaurant with Levantine and Mediterranean fare.

Cap d'Or
4 Sharia Adib
off Sharia Saad Zaghlul
Tel: 483-5177
Wonderful art nouveau bar serving the best squid stew in town and good fried fish. Difficult to find, but attracts a loyal crowd of lcoals and ex-pats who come for a beer and vintage French pop.

Pastroudis
39, Sharia al-Hurriya
Tel: 492-9609
Another famous patisserie with a large terrace overlooking the excavations at Kom al-Dikka. The dark red plush restaurant is perfect for that illicit rendez-vous or for some typical Alexandrian fare. A must.

Spitfire Bar
7 Sharia al-Bursa al-Qadima
Tel: 480-6503
Smoky and fun rock and roll bar with walls full of memorabilia and a mixed crowd of local die-hards, ex-pats and a few American sailors if the fleet is in town.

Trianon
Maydan Sad Zaghlul
Tel: 482-0986
Wood-panelled elegant restaurant with Mediterranean-Levantine food and occasionally live music. The next-door a patisserie serves good

Middle eastern Food

Egyptians, like other Arabs, enjoy eating *mezze* whilst chatting around a table with family and friends. *Mezze* are hors d'oeuvres, salads and dips, served as a starter with drinks or as a meal. Dishes keep on arriving, hot or cold, an endless variety, and are eaten with the fingers or scooped up in pieces of flat bread. For newcomers, there follows a list of the most common dishes:
tahinah (a sesame paste mixed with water, oil and lemon juice) served as a dip or a sauce,
baba ghanough is tahinah mixed with garlic and roasted eggplant,
hummus is a paste of chick peas, garlic, *tahinah* and lemon topped with parsley, and sometimes served topped with tiny bits of fried lamb,
ful mesdames is a stew of fava beans, Egypt's national dish, served with egg, meat, yoghurt or white cheese,
tamiya are deep-fried fava-bean balls,
kibda is fried chopped calf's or lamb's liver,
torshi are pickled vegetables,
salata baladi is chopped lettuce, tomato and cucumber with lots of parsley and lemon,
waraa eynab are stuffed vine leaves,
kofta is minced meat,
kibbeh is a fried ball of cracked wheat stuffed with ground beef.

pastries and a large, good value breakfast.

GREEK/EUROPEAN

Elite
43 Sharia Safia Zaghlul
Tel: 482-3592
Endless menu of Greek and Egyptian dishes and windows with a view on the world. Cheap.

Mamma Mia
Sheraton Hotel, Muntazah
Tel: 548-0550

Good Italian restaurant with fresh pastas and pizzas, served in a kitsch Italian decor.

Santa Lucia
40, Sharia Safia Zaghlul
Tel: 482-0332
Not as glamorous as it used to be, but the staff tries hard to keep up standards and the food is still far better than in most places.

Aswan

Aswan Moon
Corniche an-Nil
Floating restaurant on the Nile which attracts many *fellucciyas*. Beer, fresh fruit juices and standard Egyptian fare in a relaxing atmosphere.

Al-Misri Tour Restaurant
Sharia al-Matar, off Sharia al-Suq.
Not easy to find but everyone knows the restaurant as it serves the best *kofta* and kebab in town. The decor is Islamic kitsch and there is a family room for couples at the back.

La Trattori
Isis hotel, Corniche an-Nil
Tel: 315-500
Standard Italian restaurant, but still a good option when you get tired of too much kebab.

Old Cataract Terrace
Old Cataract Hotel
Tel: 316-001
English tea is served on the terrace from 4pm onwards, following an old tradition of watching the sun set on the West Bank.

Cairo

EGYPTIAN/LEVANTINE

Abou Shakra
69 Sharia Qasr al-Aini
Tel: 364-8811
Known as 'the King of the Kebab' this is one of the best places to eat kebab, and prices are very reasonable.

Alfi Bey
3 Sharia al-Alfy, Downtown
Cheap 1940s restaurant with wonderful decor, antiquated waiters and traditional Levantine fare. No alcohol.

Andrea's Chicken and Fish Restaurant
on the left bank of the Maryutiya Canal heading towards Kerdassa, Giza
Tel: 851-133
Some of the best *mezze* in town and certainly the best grilled chicken. Mostly outdoors under the trellices, with simple wooden and bamboo furniture. Recommended.

Arabesque
6 Sharia Qasr an-Nil, Downtown
Tel: 574-7898
E-mail: arabesq@ritsec1.com.eg
Even though this restaurant with adjacent art gallery serves some of the best French food in town, it is worth trying the Egyptian dishes like *meloukhia* or grilled pigeon with rice. Whatever your main course, leave space for their Umm Ali dessert.

Casino des Pigeons
On the Nile south of Abbas Bridge Giza.
Specialities are pigeon, cooked in many ways, and *mezze*.

Egyptian Pancake House
Between Sharia al-Azhar and Maydan al-Husayn.
Delicious and cheap *fateers*, a cross between a pizza and a pancake that can be sweet or savoury. No alcohol.

Fatayri at-Tahrir
Sharia et-Tahrir, near Maydan Tahrir.
Excellent sweet and savoury *fatir*.

Felfella
15, Sharia Hoda Shaarawi
Tel: 392-2751
The original Felfella restaurant, which now has several branches in Cairo and other Egyptian cities. Started as a cheap vegetarian restaurant, it still serves plenty of cheap vegetable dishes and *mezze* beside the traditional *kofta, kebab* and stuffed pigeon. The Cafeteria around the corner serves good *ful* and *tamia* sandwiches.

Al-Omdah
6 Sharia al-Gazair (next door to the Atlas Hotel).
One of the best places to eat a superior version of *kushari,* the national dish of rice, macaroni, lentils, fried onions and a spicy tomato sauce.

Papillon
Tirsana Shopping Centre
26 July Street
Mohandiseen
Tel: 347-1672
Another good place to sample a wide selection of *mezze*, especially popular with vegetarians. Excellent for lunch.

Il-Yotti
44 Sharia Mohi al-Din Abu el-Ezz
Dokki
Tel: 349-4944
This is not so easy to find but worth the effort of braving the heavy wooden door, behind which a wide selection of excellent *mezze*, grills and drinks are served in a clubby atmosphere.

SEAFOOD

Flying Fish
166 Sharia an-Nil, Agouza
Tel: 349-3234
Aquariums filled with fish, stained glass windows with mermaids and candlelight make for a relaxed ambience, in which an extensive menu of fish dishes is served, from Egyptian fish kebab to British-style fish fingers. Excellent.

Seahorse
Corniche an-Nil (opposite the Badrawi Hospital), Maadi
Tel: 363-8830
Waiters dressed up as fishermen serve fresh grilled fish and giant shrimps with Oriental rice. In summer, food is served on a large terrace overlooking the Nile.

FRENCH

Champollion
Meridien Le Caire Hotel
Corniche al-Nil, Garden City
Tel: 362-1717
Cairo's finest French cuisine served in plush surroundings, overlooking the Nile, with a few specialities for the weight conscious.

Justine
Four Corners
4 Sharia Hassan Sabri, Zamalik
Tel: 341-2961
Creative French cuisine and a cosy

luxurious atmosphere in the most upmarket of the Four Corners restaurants.

ITALIAN

La Piazza
Four Corners, 4 Sharia Hassan Sabri, Zamalik
Tel: 340-4385
Good and easy-going Italian restaurant with fresh pasta and superb desserts like profiteroles and chocolate tiramisu.

INTERNATIONAL

El-Greco
1 Maydan Amman, Mohandisseen
Tel: 336-1883
A chic Greek restaurant decorated in a style that hints at the Greek Islands. Excellent food and perfect service.
Estoril
12 Sharia Talaat Harb, Downtown
Tel: 574-3102
Tucked away in a passage, the Estoril has been going for many years and has a loyal clientele of Cairene actors and intellectuals as well as expats.
Le Steak
Le Pacha 1901 boat
Sharia Saray el-Gezirah, Zamalik
Tel: 340-6730
Excellent *mezze* served with an apéritif. Those with a larger appetite can tuck into a tender steak with several sauces or grilled seabass.
Le Tabasco
8 Amman Square, Mohandeseen
Tel: 336-5583
One of the trendiest bar-restaurants in town. Good modern Mediterranean dishes accompanied by swinging music. After 10pm the music and air-con are turned on full, and in come Cairo's young, rich and beautiful.

ASIAN

Buo Khao
9 Road 151, Maadi
Tel: 350-0126
Genuine and well-prepared Thai

food served in the typical blue and white china.
Peking
14 Sharia Saraya el-Ezbekiya Downtown
Tel: 591-2381
Well-prepared and fresh Chinese food served in a pleasant decor. The strange house speciality is Irish coffee served with much drama and accompanied by taped bird-song.
Taj Mahal
5 Sharia Lebanon
Mohandeseen
Tel: 302-5669
Some of the best Indian food in town is served in a stark black and white room. Vegetarians will be particularly happy with the wide selection of vegetable curries.

CAFÉS/BARS

Absolut
10 Amman Square
Mohandeseen
Tel: 336-5583
Trendy bar taking the overflow of the next door restaurant Le Tabasco, run by the same owner.
Deals
2 Sharia al-Maahad al-Swissri Zamalik
Tel: 341-0502
Tiny bar decorated with vintage film posters is popular with 20- and 30-something expats attracted by the casual atmosphere and good prices. Good mezze.
The German Corner
Balmoral Hotel, 26 July Street (near the Abu al-Ela bridge) Zamalik
Latest hang out for hardened ex-pats, pool-playing *Zamalikawis* and Sudanese girls.
Groppi
MaydanTalaat Harb
Downtown
Tel: 574-3244
Only vaguely reminiscent of its former grandeur, the tearoom now serves increasingly stale pastries, but the old waiters are still smiling.
Harry's Pub
Cairo Marriott Hotel
Zamalik
Tel: 340-8888
Popular English pub.

Piano Piano
World Trade Center
1191 Corniche an-Nil, Bulaq
Tel: 762-810
Glitzy bar with windows overlooking the Nile and a menu with French and Chinese dishes.
Simmonds Coffee Shop
112, 26 July Street, Zamalik
Meeting place for locals, Ethiopian students and foreign correspondents. Good cappuccinos and fresh juices.

Luxor

Brasserie 1886
Winter Palace Hotel
Corniche en-Nil
Tel: 380-422
This smart new restaurant is elegant, though the food is not always up to standard and service can be slow.
Kushari Sayyida Nefisa
Sharia Mustapha Kamel, near the suq. Famous for the best *kushari* in town.
La Mamma
Sheraton hotel
Sharia Khaled Ibn Walid
Tel: 374-544
Italian restaurant in a quiet garden with pelicans and ducks, and live accordion music in the evening.
Møvenpick restaurants
Crocodile Island
Tel: 374-855
The pleasant terrace restaurant serves fresh pasta, salads and grills as well as excellent Møvenpick ice-creams. Two indoor restaurants serve a good buffet or expensive French à la carte.
Tutankhamun
At the public ferry landing on the West Bank. Simple but clean serving good food as the chef trained at one of the five-star restaurants. Worth crossing the Nile for.

Red Sea

AL GOUNA

Zeytuna
on the small island south of the Miramar Hotel (reached by water

taxi from the dock in front of the Al Gouna Museum). Funky and relaxed bar with its own beach for day and night entertainment.

Café des Artistes
Kafr al-Gouna. Simple Italian pastas with vegetables served under the stars.

Al-Hanim
Al-Khan Hotel
Tel: 545-060
Good Turkish food.

Sayadeen Fish Restaurant
Huge fish restaurant on the beach with grilled fish and seafood.

Morgan's
Paradisio Hotel. Small and cool barbecue fish restaurant on the beach which has a touch of the Greek Islands about it.

HURGHADA

Belgian Restaurant
Empire Hotel Shopping Centre Al-Dahar
Good French and Belgian restaurant, run by the same Belgian family who owns the Three Corners Hotel.

El-Sakia
On the beach in Sekala
Tel: 442-497
Spacious surroundings, popular with better-off Egyptians and foreigners. One of the best places to eat fish and seafood in Hurghadah. Private beach.

Felfella
Tariq al-Sheraton
Tel: 442-411
Part of the Cairene chain serving reasonably priced Egyptian food.

Italian restaurant
Intercontinental Hotel
Tel: 443-911
Excellent and inventive Italian food served on the romantic garden terrace.

Portofino
General Hospital Street
Al-Dahar
Tel: 546-250
Good Italian food and seafood specialities; nice atmosphere.

Young Kang
5 Sharia al-shaykh as-Sebak
Tel: 446-623
Chinese and Korean food with

seafood and Peking Duck as specialities.

SHARM AL SHAYKH

Beach BBQ
Fayruz Hilton, Na'ama Bay
Beach restaurant serving a buffet of salads, pasta prepared to order and grilled fish and meats. Good for lunch and dinner.

Beach BBQ
Møvenpick Hotel, Na'ama Bay.
Good beach restaurant for lunch with a salad bar and fine grills.

Pizzeria
Intercontinental Hotel
Sharm al-Maya Bay
Tel: 601-291
Well-prepared pasta and pizza served outdoors, friendly service.

Sanafir Bar
Sanafir Hotel, Na'ama Bay
Tel: 600-197
Pleasant and popular bar with reasonably priced drinks and good music.

Sites

Museums

ALEXANDRIA

Greco-Roman Museum
5, Sharia Al-Musthaf
Tel: 482-5820
The only museum in Egypt to honour the Hellenistic and Roman-period heritage of the country is justly placed in Alexandria, the intellectual centre of Hellenistic civilisation. The collection includes mosaic pavements, glass, coins, sculpture, sarcophagi and the wonderful Tanagra figures. 8am–4pm daily, closed Fri from 11.30am–1.30pm.

Marine Life Institute and Aquarium
Near the Qaitbay Fort
There are two buildings here, the Museum of Hydro-Biology, with a collection of boats, and the Aquarium with fish and other marine species found in Egyptian waters. Daily 9am–2pm.

Royal Jewellery Museum
21 Sharia Ahmed Yehya Pasha
Zizinia
Tel: 586-8348
Jewellery and other luxury items of the Muhammad Ali family. 9am–4pm daily, closed Friday from 11am–1.30pm.

Cavafy Museum

Sharia Sharm ash-Shaykh
Alexandria
Housed in this flat for 25 years, this small museum pays tribute to Constantine Cavafy (1863–1933), one of Alexandria's major poets. Daily 9am–2pm, and on Tue and Thurs 6–8pm. Closed Mon.

CAIRO

The most famous of the city's museums is the Egyptian Museum full of antiquities, but many others are well worth visiting. The usual hours are from 9am to 4pm daily except Friday, when all museums are closed between approximately 11.30am and 1pm.

Agricultural Museum
Ministry of Agriculture, Dokki
Tel: 702-933
The oldest in the world (founded 1938), with 27 acres (11 hectares) of garden, contains a **Museum of Ancient Egyptian Agriculture, a Natural History Museum, a Museum of the Social Life of the Arab Nations** and a **Cotton Museum.** Open Tue-Sun 9am–1.30pm.

Bayt Gamal ad-Din
east of the Qasabah between the Fakahani Mosque and the Ghuriyyah. Residence of a 17th-century gold merchant.
Bayt al-Kiridliyyah (See Gayer-Anderson House.)

Bayt Ibrahim Katkhuda as-Sinnari
17 Harat Monge, off Shari an-Nasiriyya, Sayyidah Zaynab
An 18th-century townhouse, one of three requisitioned for Bonaparte's savants in 1798, now used as a centre for research in applied arts from the pharaonic period to the present. Open Sat–Thurs 9am–2pm.

Bayt as-Sihaymi
Darb al-Asfar
Gamaliyyah
An Ottoman-period townhouse, largely intact, with Chinese porcelain made for the Arab market.

Cairo Tower
Gazirah island Built in 1961. Has a revolving restaurant on top and excellent views when the smog allows.

Citadel
Tel: 926-187
Muhammad Ali's Citadel *salamlik* (reception palace), restored since 1971 and fitted with furniture formerly owned by the Muhammad Ali family. The name of the palace means bijou or jewel, but there has never been a "jewel collection" in it.

Gayer-Anderson House
Adjoining Ibn Tulun Mosque
Tel: 364-7822
Two houses, 16th- and 17th-century, joined together and furnished with his collections by Major Robert Gayer-Anderson Pasha, who lived here 1935–42.

Gazirah Museum
Planetarium building, Gazirah Exhibition Grounds, next to the National Cultural Centre
Paintings, bibelots and objets d'art. Some confiscated from the Muhammad Ali family.

Islamic Art Museum
Corner of Sharia Port Said, Sharia Qala'a (Sharia Muhammad Ali), and Sharia Sami al-Barudi, Abdin
Tel: 390-9930
Important collections of arms and armour, ceramics, coins, carpets and textiles, manuscripts and printed papers, metalwork, stonework and woodwork from the period of the city's greatest glory.

Manastir Palace and the Nilometer
Southern end of Rawdah Island. Restored in 1990, this early 19th-century *salamlik* is the public portion of a palace complex that belonged to a distinguished Cairene Turkish family. The Nilometer is the oldest intact Islamic monument in Cairo.

Manyal Palace Museum
Rawdah Island
A complex of gardens and buildings constructed between 1901 and 1929 and bequeathed to the nation in 1955 by Prince Muhammad Ali, younger brother of Khedive Abbas II Hilmi and first cousin of King Faruq. Apart from the prince's residence with all its furnishings, there are buildings housing splendid collections of family memorabilia, costumes, calligraphy, glass, porcelain, silver and trophies of the hunt.

Military Museum
Citadel
Housed in the Harim Palace Chief residence of rulers belonging to Muhammad Ali's family from 1827–74. Collections include uniforms, weapons and models.

Muhammad Ali Museum
Qasr ash-Shubra, Shubra
Closed to the public at time of press.

Mar Girgis
Old Cairo
(Misr al-Qadimah)
Arts of Egypt's Christian era: textiles, metalwork, woodwork, ceramics, glass.

Muhammad Mahmud and Emilienne Luce Khalil Collection
Giza Corniche (Sharia Gamal Abd an-Nasir), Giza
Tel: 336-2358
Open Tue–Sun
Paintings. Chiefly 19th- and 20th-century French, including works by Ingres (2), Delacroix (8), Corot (12), Daumier (4), Courbet (4), Millet (6), Renoir (6), Degas (2), Fantin-Latour (2), Manet, Monet (5), Pissarro (6), Sisley (5), Toulouse-Lautrec, Gauguin (3), van Gogh and others, sculpture (Houdon, Barye, Carpeaux, and Rodin), chinoiserie, japonaiserie, and turquoiserie. Bequeathed with their house to the nation by Muhammad Mahmud Khalil (died 1955), landowner, industrialist, and politician, and his French wife, Emilienne Luce Khalil (died 1962).

Mukhtar Museum
Tahrir street, Gazirah (near Galaa Bridge)
Tel: 340-2519
Open: 10am–1pm, 5–9pm on Fri 9am–noon, closed on Mon.
Designed by Ramses Wissa Wasif, founder of the Harraniyyah weaving project, and dedicated to Mahmud Mukhtar, sculptor of Awakening Egypt, the monument at the Giza end of the Kubri Gaamah (University Bridge), as well as the monumental

Egyptian Antiquities Museum
Maydan Tahrir
Cairo
Tel: 575-4319
The world's greatest collection of Pharaonic antiquities, including the Menkauré triads, the finds from the tomb of Hetepheres and the treasures of Tutankhamun.

Solar Boat Museum

Solar Boat Museum
Beside the Great Pyramid, Giza
Tel: 385-7928
Houses the Old Kingdom boat
found on the site and
painstakingly reassembled.

statues of Saad Zaghlul in Cairo
and Alexandria.
Musafir-khana
Darb at-Tablawi, Gamaliyyah, behind
the mosque of Sayyidna Husayn.
Townhouse built in 1779, birthplace
of Khedive Ismail. Open daily
9am–4pm
Museum of Hygiene and Medicine
Maydan Sakakini, Abbasiyyah
Housed in the extraordinary
Sakakini Palace, built in 1898 by
the Syrian financier Henri Sakakini
Pasha, head of the firm of Sakakini
Frères, Cairo agent for the Dervieux
(Paris) and Oppenheim (London)
banks.
Museum of Modern Art
Tel: 341-6665
Gazirah Exhibition Grounds. Moved in
1991 to new quarters opposite the
Opera House – an old Exhibition
Ground display pavilion lavishly re-
built for the purpose – the museum
houses a collection of representative
works by 20th-century Egyptian
artists. Outstanding are the paintings
of Mahmud Said (1897–1964), who
was for three decades one of Egypt's
best known painters.
Mustafa Kamil Museum
Maydan Salah ad-Din (below the
Citadel)
Tel: 510-9943
Houses the tomb and memorabilia
of the founder of the Nationalist
Party.
Muhammed Nagi Museum
9, Sharia Mahmoud al-Guindi (off
Cairo-Alexandria road near the
Pyramids)
Dedicated to the life and work of
Muhammad Nagi (1888–1956),
Alexandrian neo-Impressionist
painter.
National Police Museum
The Citadel
Uniforms, weapons and various
criminological exhibits, including the

full selection of drugs available in
Cairo.
October War Panorama
Junction of Oruba and Ismail
al-Fangari Streets, Heliopolis
Visual demonstration of the October
1973 War depicting several scenes
of the battle. Very popular with
Egyptian school groups.
Ornithological Museum
Giza Zoo, Sharia Giza (Sharia Murad)
Outstanding collection of insects
and migrant and native birds.
Dr. Ragab's Papyrus Institute
Corniche an-Nil on a boat docked
near the Cairo Sheraton
Tel: 348 8676
Open: daily 9am–9pm
Dr Ragab, who rediscovered the
ancient art of papyrus rolling,
opened this museum with displays
explaining the process of making
papyrus sheets. Also art gallery
where a better quality papyrus is on
sale.
Dr Ragab's Pharaonic Village
Jacob's island, Sakiet Miky
Tel: 571 8675
A guided tour by floating
amphitheatre through the 'Canal of
Mythology', past scenes reenacted
from Ancient Egypt and
reconstructions of houses, temples
and tombs. Kitsch in conception
and execution but fun for kids.
Sad Zaghlul Museum
Bayt al-Umma
2 Sharia Sad Zaghlul, Munira
Tel: 534-5399
Residence of the nationalist leader
who inspired the 1919 Revolution,
founder of the Wafd (opposition
party), Prime Minister 1924–25.
Shawqi Museum
6 Sharia Ahmad Shawqi, between
Sharia Giza (Sharia Murad) and the
Giza Corniche (Sharia Gamal Abd
an-Nasir).
Elegant residence of Ahmad Shawqi
(1868–1932), court poet to
Khedive Abbas II Hilmi, exiled by the
British between 1915 and 1919.
State Railway Museum
Sharia Bab al-Hadid
(Ramesses Railway Station)
Tel: 763-3793
A splendid collection of viceregal
rolling stock and British-made mod-
els. A must for any railway

enthusiasts. Open Sun–Thur
8am–5pm.
**Suzanne Mubarak's
Children's Museum**
34 Sharia Abu Bakr al-Seddiq
Heliopolis
Tel: 249 9915
Wekalat el-Ghouri
Next to the Al-Azhar Mosque
Tel: 511 0472
Well-preserved caravanserai now
used as workshops for painters and
artisans, with traditional handicrafts
on sale. Open: daily 8am–midnight

LUXOR

Luxor Museum
On the Corniche
A small but excellently laid out
museum with an excellent collection
of Amarnah art and royal statues of
the 18th Dynasty. Open: 4–9pm in
winter and 5–10pm in summer.

Historical Sites

ALEXANDRIA

Ancient Monuments
Pompey's Pillar
Sharia Ahmed el Sawari, in the
southwestern part of the city
This Aswan rose granite pillar, built
in AD 297 in memory of the Roman
Emperor Diocletian, stands on the
site of the Serapeum, one of the
greatest temple complexes of the
ancient world. Open 9am–4pm
daily. Small entrance fee.
Catacombs of Kom esh-Shawqafa
South of Pompey's Pillar in the
southwestern section of the city
Discovered in 1900, the catacombs
are dug one hundred feet into the
rock bed and date back to the
second century AD. The reliefs are
a blend of Greek and Egyptian
symbolism. Open 9am–6pm daily.
Small entrance fee.

Medieval Monuments
Fort of Qaitbey, located at the
northern tip of the eastern harbour,
the 15th-century fort stands on the
site of the Pharos, the ancient
lighthouse. Open 9am–3pm daily. A
small entrance fee.

Palaces

Antoniadis Villa and Gardens, in the southern central section of the city along the Mahmoudieh Canal. Mansion and gardens open daily 8am–4pm.

Muntazah Palace Complex, set in a seaside park, was a summer residence of Abbas II Hilmi (1874–1944, Khedive 1892–1914). At the outbreak of World War I, the British deposed Abbas and seized his estate which they used as a military hospital until 1919. It later belonged to King Fa'ad. The park is open to the public.

Day-trips

Abu Qir, located to the east of the city of Alexandria along the shore of the Mediterranean. This was the site where Nelson destroyed Napoleon's fleet in 1798.

Al Alamein, situated 62 miles west of Alexandria along the Mediterranean coast, was the site of the decisive battle for North Africa in World War II. Commonwealth, Italian and German cemeteries open during daylight hours, if closed look for the guard. No entrance fees.

CAIRO

Pharaonic Monuments

Cairo did not exist as a city during pharaonic times, but the area surrounding was dominated by Memphis, one of the most important administrative centres of ancient Egypt.

Sakkara, 15 miles (26 km) southwest of Cairo along the western bank of the Nile, is part of a long cemetery which runs from Giza to Maidum. It is the greatest burial site of ancient Egypt. Included in standard tours are the Funerary Complex of Zoser with the Step Pyramid, The Pyramid of Unas, the Tombs of Ptah-Hotep, Ti and Mereruka, and the Serapeum. Open daily from dawn to sunset. Allow at least 4 hours to tour Sakkara. Photography restrictions within the tombs. Fees for videos. Entrance fee.

A few miles south and east of Sakkara, **Memphis** was the capital of the Old Kingdom. Most of this once magnificent city is buried under the village of Mit Rahina, but sites to visit include the Colossus of Ramses II, Temple of Ptah and the Temple of Hathor. Open daily from dawn to sunsetset. Allow 1 hour to tour Memphis. Small entrance fee.

South of Sakkara along the same road, the four pyramids of **Dahshur** represent royal burial sites of the Old and Middle Kingdoms. The most interesting complex contains the Bent Pyramid.

The highlight of any tour of Egypt, must be the **Giza Plateau**. This is located at the end of Pyramids Road. Sites include the three pyramids, Boat Museum (special fee), the Sphinx and various tombs. Allow at least 4 hours to tour the area. Photography permitted in outdoor areas. Fees for videos. Entrance fee.

Old Cairo

Most of the monuments of early Christianity in Egypt are found in Old Cairo, to the south of the modern city. Accessible by Metro (Mari Girgis Station), sites to see include the **Fortress of Babylon**, the **Convent of St George, Hanging Church**, church of **Abu Serga**, the **church of Saint Barbara**, and the **Coptic Museum**. Area open 24 hours. Churches open from dawn to sunset, but discretion is advised during religious ceremonies. Allow 2–3 hours. Small entrance fees at various sites.

North of Fustat is a crowded area filled with modern and medieval buildings called the **Southern Cemetery**. The most important monuments in the area are the **Mausoleum of Imam al Shafi'i**, a shrine, a pilgrimage site and a functioning mosque originally built by Salah el Din in 1211, and **Hauosh al Basha**, a multi-domed tomb housing the graves of the Mohammed Ali dynasty. Both buildings are open from sunrise to sunset. There is an entrance fee for Hauosh el Basha.

Medieval Cairo

Cairo was founded by the Arab invaders in the 7th century and its fortunes grew with their successes. They ruled the city for nearly 1,000 years and left behind a dynamic legacy in stone. Left to languish when the city expanded and came under Western influence in the 19th century, many of the architectural features have recently been restored and rise gloriously from the medieval streets. Tourists touring the medieval city should dress modestly (no shorts, no sleeveless dresses, no short skirts) and use common sense when taking photographs. Although most mosques are open to visitors, non-Muslims should not enter when religious services are taking place.

The **Mosque of Amr ibn al-As** (Old

Sound & Light Shows

The Pyramids

Every evening three performances of a one-hour sound and light show are held on the Giza Plateau in front of the Sphinx. English language shows are held every night apart from Sundays (consult the Tourist Office or your hotel for the timetable). Photography is permitted but no video cameras are allowed.

Luxor

The Karnak sound and light show is one of the best in Egypt. It is held three or four times a night, with a daily English language performance. It lasts around 90 minutes and some walking is involved. To get to Karnak in the evening, hire a taxi, the driver will wait for you.

The Temple of Isis

This rescued temple, rebuilt on Aqilqiyyah Island near Aswan, also has a light and sound show outlining its history. English language shows are held every evening except Sunday and Thursday. For further details contact the Tourist Office in Aswan.

Cairo) was the first to be built in Egypt. It was named after the Arab soldier who conquered Egypt and founded Cairo. It is a functioning mosque and open from sunrise to sunset. Allow 1 hour. Entrance fee.

The graceful and serene **Mosque of Ibn Tulun** is one of the most impressive buildings in the world. It is an architectural masterpiece of Islamic art. Beside it is the **Gayer-Anderson Museum**. Allow 1–2 hours. Entrance fee.

The **Citadel**, begun by Salah el Din in the 12th century, was the headquarters of government until the 19th century. Located on a spur of the Muqattam Hills overlooking Cairo, it houses a host of museums and mosques. In the square below, once used as a race course, stand the **Madrasah of Sultan Hasan** and the **Rafa'i Mosque**, where Khedive Ismail and the Shah of Iran are buried. Allow 3–4 hours. Open daily 9am–4pm. Entrance fees.

The **Bab Zuwayla** is one of the main gates to the medieval city. The area around the gate is rich in medieval architecture including the **Qasaba of Ridwan Bey**, the last existing example of a covered bazaar, and the **Mosque of Maridani**, one of the most exquisite 14th-century mosques in the city. The area is open 24 hours a day. Allow at least 3 hours. Photograph at will, but be aware of people's sensitivities. Entrance fees to some monuments.

The **Northern Cemetery** is the best place to see an oriental skyline. Minarets and domes from mortuary buildings of the 14th and 15th centuries stretch for several miles. Two monuments must not be missed: the **Mausoleum of Barquq** and the **Mausoleum of Qaitbey**. In the Mausoleum of Barquq everything is in duplicate: two minarets, two domes, two sabils and two delicate wooden screens. The Mausoleum of Qaitbey was built near the end of the Mamluk era and epitomises the power and exquisite taste of Egypt's slave dynasty. Area open 24 hours. Monuments open 9am–4pm. Do not enter during religious services. Photographs,

particularly of people, should only be taken with discretion. Entrance fees to monuments.

MINYA

Travel and tourism in the zone between Minya and Luxor is currently restricted though it includes some of the most interesting and least spoiled sites in Egypt.

Beni Hassan is located on the east bank of the river. Signs along the main highway mark the way to the river crossing. A local felucca watertaxi crosses the river. On the east bank one may walk the mile or so to the tombs or ride a donkey, tractor, or car. The 39 tombs of the 11th and 12th Dynasty are cut into the side of the mountain. Area open 24 hours. Monuments: 9am–4pm. Allow half a day. Photography permitted. Videos for a fee. Entrance fee.

Tel el Amarna is the most important site in Middle Egypt. The area contains the site of the town of **Akhet-Aten**, the capital of ancient Egypt during the short reign of Amenhotep IV, the Pharaoh Akhenaten. Now a ruin, foundations of palaces, temples and houses can be seen. In the tombs located in the mountains to the east are wall illustrations executed in the naturalistic style of the Armana period. The most interesting are the **Tomb of Aye** and the **Tomb of Merire**. To get to Tell el Amarna cross the river by ferry. Area open 24 hours. Monuments: 9am–4pm. Allow half a day. Photography permitted. Entrance fee to tombs.

ABYDOS

The most impressive monument is the **Temple of Seti I**, with a hypostyle hall, seven shrines and the Corridor of Kings. Abydos is often included on tour itineraries combined with a visit to Dendera. Area open 24 hours. Monuments: 9a.m–4pm. Allow half a day. Photography permitted. Fee for video. Entrance fee.

DENDERA

Parts of the Graeco-Roman **temple of Hathor** at Dendera (4th century BC) still stand. The zodiac on the roof and the crypts below the temple are particularly interesting. There is also the ruin of a Christian basilica. Dendera lies on the west bank of the Nile 60 km (37 miles) north of Luxor and can be visited by bus or taxi. Allow at least a day for Dendera and nearby Abydos, which are often visited together. Area open 24 hours. Monuments: 9am–4pm. Photography permitted. Fee for video. Entrance fee.

LUXOR

Great Temple of Amun at Karnak, not to be missed are the first pylon, the temple of Ramses III, the hypostyle hall, the obelisks of Hatshepsut, the sacred lake and the festival hall of Thutmosis III. Karnak is north of Luxor and can be reached by car, horse carriage or bus along the Corniche. Allow 3–4 hours. Open 9am–4pm. Photography permitted. Fee for video. Entrance fee.

Luxor Temple, situated in the heart of modern Luxor. Allow 1 hour. Open 9am–11pm. Photography permitted. Fee for video. Entrance fee.

The West Bank, cross the river via tourist or local ferry. Tickets are available to all sites at the kiosk near the tourist ferry. Tickets cannot be purchased at the various sites. Taxis, donkeys and bicycles

Valley of the Kings

There are 62 known tombs in this desert valley. Several have electricity and are open to the public on a continuous basis. Among the most famous tombs are: Tutankhamun, where the famous treasures were found; Ramses VI, with its vaulted ceiling; and Seti I, the largest and finest tomb in the valley.

can be rented to visit the West Bank at the ferry landings. A superficial tour visiting 1 mortuary temple, 3–4 tombs in the Valley of the Kings, a quick trip to Deir el Medina and 2–3 tombs in the Valley of the Nobles is all that can be accomplished in a day.

Valley of the Queens, although there are over 70 tombs of queens and royal children of the 18th and 19th Dynasties here, few are open to the public.

Tombs of the Nobles at Qurnah, many of these 400 noblemen's tombs are closed to the public but not to be missed are the tomb of Nakht with scenes of planting, harvesting, banqueting, hunting and fishing; the tomb of Menna with fishing and fowling scenes; and the tomb of Ramose with the famous mourning scene.

Mortuary Temples, four mortuary temples remain standing: Seti I with very good reliefs; Ramses II, called the Ramesseum, Ramses III, the most intact; and Deir el Bahri, the temple of Hatshepsut. Of the Mortuary Temple of Amenhotep III, only a stela and the two statues of the king remain. The latter are known as the Colossi of Memnon.

FROM ESNA TO KOM OMBO

Most tour boats ply the river between Luxor and Aswan stopping at the Ptolemaic temples along the way. Visits are usually an hour long, entrance fees are included. Open 9am–4pm. Photography permitted. Fee for videos.

From north to south: the Temple of Esna, the least impressive of the group; the Temple of Edfu, the best preserved Ptolemaic temple in Egypt; and the Temple of Kom Ombo.

ASWAN

Elephantine Island is accessible by felucca. It was the original site of ancient Aswan. Modern excavations have unearthed interesting sites

including the Temples of Khnum and Satis, the complex of Hekayib and the Necropolis of the Sacred Rams. There is also the ancient Nilometer and the Aswan Museum. Allow 2–3 hours. Site open dawn to dusk, museum from 9am–2pm. Photography permitted. No entrance fee to the island, small entrance fee to the museum.

Tombs of the Nobles, on the west bank of the river along the mountain Qubbet el Hawa, Dome of the Wind, are tombs of Aswan noblemen. The best are the Tombs of Kehayib, Harkhuf, Mekhu and Sabni, Sarenput II, and Khunes. Allow half a day. Accessible by felucca and a steep climb. Open 9am–4pm. Photography permitted. Small entrance fee.

Philae rises from the lake on its new home between the High Dam and the Aswan Dam. Sites to see include the Temple of Isis, the Gateway of Hadrian, the Temple of Hathor and the Kiosk of Trajan. Allow half a day. Open dawn to dusk. Accessible by motor launch. Photography permitted. Entrance fee. Sound and light show at sunset.

ABU SIMBEL

Abu Simbel is south of Aswan on the western shore of the Lake Nasser. Two magnificent temples await the visitor, the Temple of Ramses II and the Temple of Nefertari. This site was the object of the greatest salvage operation in history. Abu Simbel is serviced by flights from Cairo, Luxor, and Aswan. It is also accessible by car. Allow at least 2 hours. The temple is open 9am–4pm, but the grounds are accessible from dawn to dusk. Photography permitted. Entrance fee.

Culture

Art Galleries

Alef
14 Sharia Mohamed Anis
Zamalik
Tel: 340-3690
Daily 10.30am–2pm and 5–8pm, closed on Sunday
Furniture, lighting and textiles by young artisans, often inspired by pharaonic and Islamic motives.

Arabesque
6, Sharia Qasr an-Nil
Downtown
Tel: 574-7898
Open daily. Smart art gallery with works by Egyptian painters

Atelier du Caire
2, Sharia Karim ad-Dawla
Downtown
Tel: 574-6730
Open daily 10am–1pm and 5–11pm, closed Friday. Egyptian and foreign artists.

Cairo-Berlin Art Gallery
17, Sharia Youssef al-Guindi
Bab al-Louq
Tel: 393-1764
Contemporary art from Germany and Egypt.

Centre of Arts, Akhnaton Halls
1 Sharia Maahad as-Swissri
Zamalik
Tel: 340-8211
Often stages very interesting exhibitions.

Hanager Arts Centre
Opera House Grounds, Gazirah
Tel: 340-6861
Open daily 10am–10pm.

Mashrabia
8, Sharia Champollion
Downtown
Tel: 578-4494
Contemporary Egyptian artists.

Sony Gallery
Adham Center for Television Journalism, American University

Tahrir Square
Tel: 354-2964
Open Sun–Thurs 9am–noon and
9–9pm. Photo exhibitions

Music

Arabic Music Troupe
(Shirket al Musiqa al Arabia)
Al Galaa Building, Sharia Galaa
This all male choir performs group
songs and solos.
Cairo Conservatoire, City of Art
Pyramids Road
Tel: 385-1475
Egypt's leading music school has
instruction in composition,
musicology, percussion, piano,
singing, strings and wind, and
offers concerts at the Sayed
Darwish Concert Hall.
Cairo Symphony Orchestra
Performs at the Cairo Opera House
every Friday at 8.30pm from
September to mid-June.
**Umm Kalthum Classical Arabic
Music Troupe**
Performs classical Arabic music
September–May, Thursdays 8.30pm
at the Sayed Darwish.

Cultural Centres

Cultural centres tend to be very
active in Cairo, putting on
concerts, lectures, film, theatre
and exhibitions. For non-Arabic
speakers they may be good
places to soak up some Western
culture. For programmes check
with the daily English-language
Egyptian Gazette, or the *Al-Ahram
Weekly*.

American Cultural Center
U.S. Embassy
5, Latin America Street
Garden City
Tel: 354-9601
**American Research Center
in Egypt**
2, Midan Simon Bolivar
2nd floor,
Garden City
Tel: 354-8239
Excellent library for researchers,
lectures, films.

Ballet & Dance

BALLET

Egyptian ballet dancers are trained
at the National Ballet Institute in
the City of Art complex on the
Pyramids Road. The Institute was
founded with Russian help in 1960
and staffed with Russian experts.
In 1966 the Institute's first
graduating class premiered with *The
Fountain of Bakhchiserai* in the old
Cairo Opera House. The Cairo Ballet
currently includes Russian and
Italian dancers and performs in the
new Opera House.

TRADITIONAL DANCE
TROUPES

Folk dance is very popular in Egypt
and there are over 150 troupes in
the country. The most prominent
are the National Troupe and Reda
Troupe which perform in Cairo and
Alexandria.
**Al-Tannoura Egyptian Heritage
Dance Troupe** performs every

British Council
192, Sharia en-Nil,
Agouza
Tel: 347-6118
Centre Français de Culture
1, Sharia Madrasset al-Huquq al-
Faransiya, Mounira
Tel: 355-3725
**Egyptian Center for International
Cooperation**
11, Sharia Shagaret ad-Dorr
Zamalik
Tel: 341-5419
Goethe Institut
5, Sharia Abd al-Salam Arif
Downtown
Tel: 575-9877
Good films and concerts.
Netherlands Institute
1 Sharia Mahmoud Azmi,
Zamalik
Tel: 340-0076
Very interesting lectures every
Thursday evening on Egyptian
history or archaeology.

Opera

Cairo Opera Company
From 1869 to 1971 Cairo was
regularly visited by foreign opera
troupes, which performed in the
old Opera House. A local
company has performed in
Arabic since 1961, and features
fine individual singers.
Performances are at the Cairo
Opera House.

Wedneday and Saturday evening
from 9pm (9.30pm in winter) at the
Madrasa of Al-Ghouri, near the
pedestrian bridge on Sharia al-
Azhar. Islamic Cairo. They perform
raks sharqi (eastern dance) and/or
Sufi dancing, a form of ecstatic
mystical dance, though here it is a
cultural performance

Venues

Balloon Theatre
(Om Kalthum Theatre)
26 July and Sharia Nil
Agouza
Tel: 347-1718
Various performances, mostly in
Arabic, fill this vast theatre from
October to May. A favourite venue
for folklore troupes.
Cairo Opera House
(The Egyptian Education and Culture
Centre) Gazirah
Tel: 342 -0598
In 1971 the Cairo Opera House, an
elegant wooden structure with
perfect acoustics built to celebrate
the opening of the Suez Canal in
1869, burned to the ground along
with the scenery, costumes and
props of 100 years. Included in the
loss were the original costumes for
the first performance of *Aida*. In
1988 a new facility opened at the
Gazirah Exhibition Grounds on
Gazirah Island and the performing
arts of Egypt are enjoying season
after season of first class entertainment. Built with the cooperation of
the Japanese, the new facility includes three theatres (the largest
containing about 1,000 seats), an
art gallery, conference rooms and a
library.

Gumhuria Theatre
12 Gumhuria
Cairo
Tel: 391-9956
Used as temporary quarters for the performing arts in Egypt until the Cairo Opera House was built, the Gumhuria Theatre is still a venue for performing arts.

Sayed Darwish Concert Hall
Gamal al Din al Afghani, Giza
Tel: 385-2473
There are two Sayed Darwish Concert Halls, one in Cairo and another in Alexandria in the old Alexandria Opera House. This one is used by the ballet, opera company, student performers of the conservatory and the Academy of Arts. It is a showcase for performers of traditional Arabic music and composers working to develop new music with classical themes. There are Classical Arabic Music concerts every Thursday at 9.30pm.

Cairo International Conference Centre (CICC)
Tel: 263-4632/4631/4637
Fax: 263-4640
On Sharia an-Nasr, next to the Monument of the Unknown Soldier and the Sadat Memorial in the northeastern suburb of Madinat Nasr. Magnificently set in an unusually large tract of land, it was presented to Egypt in 1991 as a gift from the Chinese people, who also gave the surrounding park, with a landscape and buildings in the style of the Emperor K'ang-Hsi.

Al Warsha (The Workshop)
10a Abdel Hamid Sayed
Tel: 779-261
The repertory of this exploratory troupe includes translated and new Egyptian plays.

The American University in Cairo Theatre Company
Tel: 354-2964
Performs in the Wallace Theatre and Howard Theatre on the AUC campus.

Avant Garde Theatre
Talia Theatre
Maydan Attaba
Tel: 937-948, 763-466
This large company performs modern Arabic plays and western

plays in translation in two halls, the Zaki Tolaimat and the Salah Abdel Sabour (Pocket Theatre).

Cairo Puppet Theatre
Azbakkiyah Gardens
Tel: 591-0954
Dialogue is in Arabic, but the gestures and meanings are not too difficult to follow. Thursday to Saturday at 6.30pm, Friday and Sunday at 11am.

Comedy Theatre
Star-studded casts perform at the Muhammad Farid, tel: 377-0603, and at the **Floating Theatre**, next to University Bridge, Manyal, tel: 364-9516.

Modern Theatre
Al Salam Theatre
101 Qasr al Alini
Tel: 355-2484, 354-3016
The hardworking cast performs contemporary Arabic plays in three nightly shows beginning at 5.30pm.

Hilton Ramses Theatre
Hilton Ramses Annex
Tel: 574 7435
Regular performances of good Egyptian plays.

The Floating Theatre
Next to University Bridge, Manyal
Tel: 849-516
Star-studded casts perform at the Muhammad Farid Theatre.
Modern Theatre

Al Salam Theatre
101 Qasr al Aini
Tel: 355-2484/354-3016
The cast performs contemporary Arabic plays in three nightly shows beginning at 5.30pm.

National Theatre
(Qawmi), Maydan Attaba
Tel: 917-783, 911-267
Arabic and western plays in translation at the George Abiad Theatre.

Samir Ghanem Troupe
Bab al Luq Theatre, Maydan Falaki
Tel: 355-3195
Named after the famous comedian who is often the star of the show.

Cinemas

Most cinemas are old with poor acoustics. A few new venues have opened in recent years, most featuring western films.

Theatre

Theatre season in Cairo is September–May. There is a summer season in Alexandria. Curtain is at 9.30pm, 10.30pm during Ramadan. Theatres are dark on Tuesday or Wednesday. Except at the American University or the Brtitish Council, all performances are in Arabic.

Commercial cinemas change their programmes every Monday. Films are listed in the daily *Egyptian Gazette* or in *Al Ahram* weekly.

Cairo Sheraton Cinema
Sharia el-Galaa
Giza
Tel: 360 6081

Hyatt al-Salam Hotel
65 Sharia Abdel-Hamid Badawi
Heliopolis
Tel: 293 1072
Mainly foreign films

Karim I & II
15, Sharia Emad ed-Din
Downtown
Tel: 591 6095

Ramses Hilton Cinema
Sharia Corniche en-Nil
Downtown
Tel: 574 7435

Tahrir
112 Sharia Tahrir
Dokki
Tel: 335 4726

Casinos

Gambling is only available for foreigners, only in 5-star hotels. Most casinos are in Cairo, but there is one at the Hilton International, Luxor. They offer roulette, black jack, chemin de fer and slot machines until the early hours. (Note: in Cairo casino otherwise means "teahouse").

Shopping

Amber

Pale yellow, honey, brown, red, white and almost-black amber can be found in shops in the Khan al Khalili in the form of beads, necklaces, pipe parts and cane handles. The most famous shop is Mohammed R. El Kady.

Antiquities & Antiques

Pharaonic and Islamic antiquities can only be exported though a few shops. Each sale should be accompanied by a letter of authenticity and permission to export the item. Street vendors selling antiquities are selling fakes, worth purchasing for their own merit, but not as authentic articles. In fact, the best buys in Cairo are European antiques. There are many

Jewellery

From modern pharaonic cartouches to antique Turkish, Art Deco and Art Nouveau, jewellery is one of the best buys in Egypt. Gold is sold up to 21 carat for traditional jewellery, and 18 carat for modern jewellery of chains and charms. One of the best places to shop is the Suq al Sagha in the Khan al Khalili. Here you will find traditional designs coveted by the farmers' wives in the form of necklaces, earrings and bracelets. Special shops sell 21 carat handtooled or stamped Nubian designs. Shops that sell gold plate are identified by a large gilded camel in the window. Modern designs are found in jewellery stores throughout the city. Many

are found on Abdel Khalek Sarwat west of Opera Square in Cairo.

In Luxor the jewellery bazaar is just behind Luxor Temple to the north of the Luxor Hotel. In Aswan look for jewellery shops in the *suq*.

Although gold is the preferred metal today, silver traditionally dominated the market. Designs tend to be large and heavy, and are therefore too costly to be made in gold.

If you are interested in Bedu ware, ask, for these wonderful items are often hidden away in giant sacks under the counter. Silver items are sold in all shopping areas and *suqs* in Egypt but predominate in the Khan al Khalili in Cairo.

little antique shops in Cairo around Sh. Huda Shaarawi in Zamalik, and in Maadi. In Alexandria the Attarin district around the street of the same name is popular with antique-hunters.

Appliqué

The Tentmakers' Bazaar (Suq al Khiyamiyyah), the only covered bazaar left in Cairo, is the place to buy appliqué tenting. This wonderful craft, probably traceable to ancient Egypt, when appliqué banners billowed from the tops of temple gates, comes in Pharaonic and Islamic designs in the form of pillow cases, tablecloths and wall hangings.

Senouhi on the 5th floor, 54 Sharia Abd el-Khaled Sarwat, Downtown Good selection of appliqué work and hand-woven carpets from the Wissa Wasef school in Haraniyya.

Baskets

Every region has its own distinct type of basket. it is best to buy them in the village *suqs*. In Aswan, the flat Nubian baskets are still available. The oases crafts shops have an abundance of baskets.

Exporting

If your items cannot be easily carried it is best to let the merchant handle the export. Items over LE200 may require export licences.

Brass & Copper

The Suq au-Nahhasiin in the Qasabah near Khan al Khalili is the best place in Egypt to buy brass and copper, both antique and modern.

Clothing

The world's finest cotton is Egypt's major export product, but it can be hard to find good quality cotton inside the country. Imported designer wear and casual wear are now available in the cities. On Safari (branches in the major tourist resorts) sell good, locally-produced cotton holiday wear. The **World Trade Center** on 1191 Corniche en-Nil in Bulaq, Cairo is the largest shopping mall in Egypt, where most chains are represented.

For lounging around there is nothing like an Egyptian *gallabiyya*. A good place to buy them as well as cotton fabrics is **Ouf** in the alley beside the Madrasah of Barsbay off Sharia al-Muizz, Islamic Cairo. Most popular are red and white striped *gallabiyyas* from the northern coast; the most difficult to find are green and orange diamond patterns from Sinai.

Designs or can be made to order in a day. Bedu dresses are handmade. Those from Northern Sinai are cross-stitched in reds, oranges and yellows, or blues and pinks. They can be bargained for in villages on the way to Al Arish, or in Khan al Khalili, or at Kirdassah, or bought in the more upmarket shops like Nomad in the Cairo Mariott.

Furniture & Woodwork

Mashrabiyyati, traditional screens of turned wood, covered the windows of old-fashioned Cairene houses and shielded the sanctuaries of mosques.

Alif, 14 Sharia Mohamed Anis, Zamalik (tel:340 3690), is a good place to look for old or new furniture. Even better is the shop of interior designer **Zaki Sherif** on 18B Sharia Marashli, Zamalik (tel: 341 5250). Zaki, who has styled some of the country's hippest bars and hotels, sells old furniture as well as his own designs, inspired by his pharaonic and Ottoman predecessors.

Leather

Everything from large and small pieces of luggage to clothing is found in many designs. Leathers include buffalo, gazelle, crocodile, serpent, lizard, cow, moose and goat.

Musical Instruments

Middle Eastern musical instruments of all qualities are made in Cairo along Shari Muhammad Ali near the Citadel.

Muski Glass

Recycled glass products come in six main colours: navy blue; brown; turquoise; green; aqua; and purple. The glass is hand-blown into pitchers, beakers, cups, tumblers, vases, dishes, Christmas ornaments, and amulets. The imperfections and bubbles make this inexpensive glass extremely fragile.

Papyrus

The cultivation of papyrus has been revived by the Dr Raghab Papyrus Institute. Shops all over Egypt now sell hand-painted papyrus sheets. Designs are quite stunning and many duplicate famous ancient wall paintings.

Perfume

Perfume shops with their beautifully decorated bottles are easy to spot. Egypt grows and exports jasmine, geranium, rose, violet, camomile and orange for the major perfumiers

in France, from whom essence is then re-imported.

Weaving

Kirdassah, on the western fringes of greater Cairo, has a large market where weaving is sold. Harranniyyah, on the Saqqarah road, is world-famous for its tapestries, woven by villagers using naturally dyed wools. Bedu rugs, made on small looms in the desert, vary in design between tribes.

Bookshops

Cairo is the publishing capital of the Middle East and there are hundreds of bookshops. English language books can be found in all major hotels. For rare books try The Orientalist, 15 Qasr en-Nil Street, tel: 575-3418. Some bookstores that offer foreign language publications are:
Ahram
Outlets at: 165 Muhammad Farid; Cairo Sheraton; Cairo International Airport; Meridien Hotel; Semiramis Inter Continental Hotel; Nile Hilton Hotel; Ramses Hilton Hotel Annex; Maadi Club.
American University in Cairo Bookshop
113 Qasr al Aini
Tel: 357-5377
Excellent collection of English language books on Egypt.
Livres de France
36 Sharia Qasr en-Nil, Downtown
Tel: 393 5512
French and English books.
Lehnert and Landrock Bookshop
44 Sherif
Tel: 393-5329
German and English books, maps, and old postcards.
Madbouli
6 Midan Talaat Harb
Tel: 756-421
Arabic, English, French and German.
Reader's Corner
33 Sharia Abdul Khalek Sarwat
Tel: 392-8801
General English.
Zamalik Bookshop
19 Shagaret el Dorr, Zamalek
Tel: 341-9197

Sport

Participant

FISHING

The Nile, Lake Nasser and the lakes along the northern coast support commercial fishing. Fishing is forbidden off Sinai, but is a thriving sport elsewhere in the Red Sea and in the Mediterranean. Boats and guides can be hired at Hurghada. For information about international tournaments contact: **The Shooting Club** Shari an Nadi as Sayd Dokki. Tel: 337-3337, 337-4678.

GLIDING

For a spectacular view of the pyramids and portions of the city of Cairo, gliding excursions are available on a hit and miss basis on Thursday and Friday at the Imbaba Airfield to the west of Cairo. The Egyptian Gliding Institute and the Egyptian Aviation Society offer motorgliders and lessons.

GOLF

There are two nine-hole courses in Cairo, at the Gazirah Club in Zamalik and at the Mena House Oberoi in Giza (with the pyramids as a backdrop). Equipment can be rented, but the courses are extremely busy.

PHARAOH'S RALLY

The Pharaoh's Rally has earned a niche in the rally world and is second in endurance and difficulty only to the Paris–Dakkar Rally. It is

Football

Professional football has been known to cause traffic jams, slow down service in restaurants and empty the streets. It is the national pastime of Egypt. Three leagues compete at 3pm each Friday and Sunday afternoon from September to May at various stadiums throughout Egypt. Among the top teams in Egypt are Ahly, Zamalik and the Arab Contractors.

a 12 day, 4,500 km (2,790 mile) endurance race through the deserts of Egypt for dirt bikes, cars and trucks.

RIDING

There is little to compare with a dawn or dusk gallop through the desert. The Bedu at the Giza Pyramids have been catering for eager riders for generations and there are several good stables in the area. Horses and camels are on offer. Lessons are available. Overnight trips to Saqqarah can be arranged. Stables include MG, KM, SA, AA (tel: 850531), M6 (tel: 385-1241) and FF stables.

ROWING

There are 10 rowing clubs in Cairo, and almost all are located on the west bank of the Nile from Giza to Imbaba. Competitions start in November and run through April. They are held every Friday on the Nile. Schedules can be obtained from any rowing club and lessons are available at some clubs.

For information see the **Egyptian Rowing Club,** 11 Sharia al Nil, Giza, near the Cairo Sheraton, tel: 373-1639.

ON AND UNDER WATER

Diving and snorkelling in the Red Sea are among the best sports offered in Egypt. On good days, the sea is calm, the visibility near perfect and the currents mild. However, swells do develop and it is easy to lose sight of the boat after swimming below the surface. All diving should be done in the company of experts after suitable instruction, which is available at many hotels (see "Scuba Diving and Water Sports", p.310–11). Dive shops exist at Hurghadah and Safaga on the mainland and at Sharm al Shaykh, Nuwayba and Dahab in Sinai. Most of the resorts on the Red Sea provide lessons for windsurfing. Equipment can be rented.

YACHTING

Docking facilities exist at major ports in Egypt and along the Nile at major cities. Yachts may enter the country through the various ports if they have the proper documents. The Egyptian Tourist Information Centres throughout the world have a booklet for yacht enthusiasts entitled *Egypt for Yachtsmen* giving entry information and maps. See Useful Addresses. p.318, for listing.

Spectator

HORSES

There are several spectator equine sports. Horse racing takes place on Saturday and Sunday, mid-November to May, at the Heliopolis Hippodrome Course in Heliopolis, Cairo, and at the Smouha Race course in Alexandria. Races begin at 1.30pm.

Arab horses are known through-out the world for their beauty, stamina and intelligence. Originally bred on the Arabian Peninsula, stud farms for Arab horses now exist worldwide. Characteristics include a compact body with a straight back, a small head, wide eyes, wide nostrils, a wide forehead, small ears and a wide jawbone.

There are many stud farms in Egypt, but only four major ones. The biggest, with 300 horses, is the government-owned Egyptian Agricultural Organisation (EAO), El Zahraa Station, Sharia Ahmad Esmat, tel: 243-1733. This farm has only pure-bred bloodlines and is the home of the most famous Arabi-an stallion of this century, Nazeer. Every important stud farm in the world has some of his offspring.

Language

Sounds

Many sounds in spoken Arabic have not been represented by the transliteration used in this book. A particularly characteristic Arabic sound, however, is *cayn*, represented in the following list as ᶜ. All Arabic-speakers, native and otherwise, delight in producing the appropriate noise, described as a guttural hum or a voiced emphatic "h", which occurs in such common names as ᶜAbbas, ᶜAbdallah, Ismaᶜil and ᶜAli. Non-Arabic-speakers generally find pronouncing ᶜ impossible without instruction and practice; and if it seems too difficult, it may be ignored. One will merely be marked as a non-Arabic-speaking foreigner.

Most Cairenes speak English to some degree, though real ability to use languages other than Arabic is confined to the educated. A few words of colloquial Egyptian Arabic are therefore useful.

The words and phrases listed below are not transliterated strictly, but spelt more or less phonetically. Take care over long and short vowel sounds, which may alter the meaning of a word substantially.

Pronunciation

Vowels
c = *cayn*, as explained above
' = glottal stop
a = a as in cat
aa = a as in standard English castle or bath
e = e as in very

i = i as in if, stiff
ii = ee as in between
o = o as in boss
u = u as in put
uu = o as in fool

Consonants
(all emphatic consonants have been omitted):
All consonants are pronounced individually and as they normally are in English with these exceptions:
kh = ch as in Scottish loch,
sh = sh as in shut,
gh = Arabic *ghayn*, usually described as resembling a (guttural) Parisian r,
q = Arabic qaf, frequently pronounced in Cairo as a k or a glottal stop.

Vocabulary

airport *matár*
boat *mérkeb*
bridge *kubri*
car ᶜ*arabiyya, sayára*
embassy *sefára*
hospital *mustáshfa*
hotel *fúnduq*
post office *bosta*
restaurant *matáam*
square *maydan/midáan*
street *shaaria*
right *yemiin*
left *shemáal*
and/or *wa/walla*
yes/no *aywa/laa'*
please/thank you *minfadlak/shukran*
big/little *kibiir/sughayyar*
good/bad *kwáyyis/mish kwáyyis*
possible *mumkin*
impossible *mish mumkin*
here/there *hena/henáak*
hot/cold *sukn/baarid*
many/few *kitiir/olayyel*
up/down *fo' (foq)/taht*
more/enough *kamáan/kefáya*
breakfast *íftar*
dinner *asha*
today *innahárda*
tomorrow *okra*
yesterday *embáareh*
morning *is-sobh*
noon *id-dohr*
afternoon *bᶜad id-dohr*
at night *belayl*
next week *il esbuul-iggáy*

next time *il mara-iggáya*
last time *il-mara illi fáatit*
after a while *bᶜad shwayya*
I/you *ana/enta*
he/she *huwwa/hiyya*
they/we *humma/ehna*

Common Expressions

Hello, welcome *ahlan wa sahlan*
Good morning *sabáh-il-kheyr*
Good evening *masáal-kheyr*
Goodbye *mᶜas-saláama*
What is your name?
(to a male) *íssmak ey?*
What is your name?
(to a female) *íssmik ey?*
How are you?
(to a male) *izzáyak*
How are you?
(to a female) *izzáyik*
I am fine
kwayiss (M), *kwayíssa* (F)
Thank God *il-hamdo li-lah* (standard reply)

Often heard is "*insha'Allah*", which means "God willing" and is a reminder that all things are ultimately in the hands of Providence. The standard reply to a casual "see you tomorrow", for instance, is "*insha'Allah*".

Numerals

1 *wáhid*
2 *itnéyn*
3 *taláatah*
4 *arbᶜá*
5 *khamsa*
6 *sitta*
7 *sébᶜa*
8 *tamánya*
9 *tíssah*
10 *áshara*
11 *hedásher*
12 *itnásher*
13 *talatásher*
14 *arbatasher*
15 *khamastásher*
16 *sitásher*
17 *sabatásher*
18 *tamantásher*
19 *tissᶜatásher*
20 *ashríin*
30 *talatíin*
40 *arbaᶜíin*
50 *khamsíin*
60 *sittíin*

70 *sabaˁíin*
80 *tamaníin*
90 *tissaˁíin*
100 *miiya, miit*

Money

money *filúus*
50 piastres
khamsíin ˁersh (qersh)
75 piastres *khamsa wa sabaˁíin*
ˁersh (qersh)
change/no change
fakka/mafiish fakka
the bill *al hesáb*
this/that *di/da*
how much? *bekáam?*
how much do you want?
(to a male) *ˁayiz kaam?*
how much do you want?
(to a female) *ˁayza kaam?*
all/half *kull/nus*

Days/Months

Sunday *yowm al had*
Monday *yowm al-itnéyn*
Tuesday *yowm it-taláat*
Wednesday *yowm al-árba*
Thursday *yowm al-khamíis*
Friday *yowm ig-gómˁa*
Saturday *yowm is-sabt*
January *yanáyer*
February *febráyer*
March *máris*
April *abreel*
May *mayuu*
June *yuunyuu*
July *yiilyuu*
August *aghustus*
September *sibtímbir*
October *októbir*
November *nofímbir*
December *disímbir*

Further Reading

General

Ammoun, Denise *Crafts of Egypt.* Cairo, 1991.
Biegman, Nicolas *Egypt: Moulids, Saints, Sufis.* The Hague/London, 1990.
Bloom, Jonathan and Sheila Blair *Islamic Arts.* London, 1997.
Buonaventura, Wendy *Serpent of the Nile: Women and Dance in the Arab World.* London, 1989.
Danielson, Virginia, *The Voice of Egypt: Umm Kulthum, Arabic Song and Egyptian Society in the Twentieth Century.* Chicago, 1997.
Herodotus *The Histories.* London, 1996.
Hoath, Richard *Natural Selections: a Year of Egypt's Wildlife.* Cairo, 1992.
Mitchell, Timothy *Colonising Egypt,* Cairo, 1988.
Moorehead, Alan *The White Nile* London, 1973.
The Blue Nile. London, 1984.
Roden, Claudia *A New Book of Middle Eastern Food.* London, 1986.*The Book of Jewish Food.* London, 1997.
Rodenbeck, Max *Egypt from the Air.* London, 1991.
Sattin, Anthony *Lifting the Veil.* London, 1988.

Cairo

Behrens-Abouseif, Doris *Islamic Architecture in Cairo.* Cairo, 1996.
Cooper, Artemis *Cairo in the War, 1939-45.* London, 1989.
Lane, Edward William *Manners and Customs of the Modern Egyptians.* London, 1833–5.
Raafat, Samir *Maadi 1904–1962: Society and History in a Cairo Suburb.* Cairo, 1994.
Rodenbeck, Max *Cairo.* New York/London, 1998
Stewart, Desmond *Great Cairo, Mother of the World.* Cairo,1996
Williams, Caroline *Islamic*

Monuments in Cairo: a Practical Guide. Cairo, 1993

Alexandria

Bowman, Alan K. *Egypt After the Pharaohs: 332BC–AD642 from Alexander to the Arab Conquest.* London, 1986.
Ellis, Walter *Ptolemy of Egypt.* London, 1993.
Forster, E.M. *Alexandria, a History and Guide.* London, 1986.
Grant, Michael *Cleopatra: a Biography.* London 1992.
Haag, Michael *Alexandria, City of Durrell, Forster and Cavafy.* London, 1998.
Pinchin, Jane Lagudis *Alexandria Still: Forster, Durrell and Cavafy.* Cairo, 1989.
Whitehorne, John *Cleopatras.* London, 1994

The Oases

Bagnold, R.A. *Libyan Sands.* London, 1987.
Belgrave, C. Dalrymple *Siwa: the Oasis of Ammon.* London, 1923.
Fakhry, Ahmed *Siwa Oasis.* Cairo, 1973.

Sinai

Buckles, Guy *Dive Sites of the Red Sea.* Cairo, 1995.
Carletti, Alessandro and Andrea Ghisotti *Red Sea: Diving Guide.* Cairo, 1994.
Jahn, Wolfgang and Rosel *Sinai and the Red Sea.* Cairo, 1997.
Siliotti, Alberto *Guide to the Exploration of the Sinai.* Cairo,1994.

Ancient Egypt

Andreu, G *Egypt in the Age of the Pyramids.* London, 1997.
Baines, John and Jaromir Malek *Atlas of Ancient Egypt.* Oxford, 1980.
Bauval, Robert and Adrian Gilbert *The Orion Mystery.* London, 1994.
Clayton, Peter *The Rediscovery of Ancient Egypt.* London, 1990.
Clayton, Peter *Chronicle of the*

Pharaohs. London, 1994.
Edwards, IES The Pyramids of
Egypt. London, 1991
Lichtheim, Miriam Ancient Egyptian
Literature. California, 1975–80.
**Reeves, Nicholas and Richard
Wilkinson** The Complete Valley of
the Kings. London/Cairo 1996.

Travellers

Duff Gordon, Lucy Letters from
Egypt, 1862–69. London, 1986.
Edwards, Amelia A Thousand Miles
Up the Nile. London, 1982.
Flaubert, Gustave Flaubert in
Egypt. London, 1983.
Frank, Katherine Lucie Duff
Gordon, a Passage to Egypt.
London, 1994.
Ghosh, Amitav In an Antique Land.
London, 1992.
Manley, Deborah A Traveller's
Amthology. London, 1991.
Nightingale, Florence Letters from
Egypt. London, 1987.
Pick, Christopher Egypt, an
Anthology. London, 1991.
Pye-Smith, Charlie The Other Nile.
London, 1986.

Fiction

Abdullah, Yahya Taher The
Mountain of Green Tea and Other
Stories. Cairo, 1991.
Christie, Agatha Death on the Nile.
London, 1995.
Durrell, Lawrence The Alexandria
Quartet. London, 1968.
Ghali, Waguih Beer in the Snooker
Club. London, 1987.
al-Ghitani, Gamal Zayni Barakat.
London, 1988.
Lively, Penelope Moon Tiger
London, 1989.
Mahfouz, Naguib The Cairo Trilogy,
Miramar and many others.
Cairo/London.
el Saadawi, Nawal Woman at Point
Zero. London, 1983.
Soueeif, Ahdaf In the Eye of the
Sun. London, 1999.

Other Insight Guides

Other books in the 190-title **Insight
Guides** series which highlight
destinations in this region include
The Nile, Cairo, Jordan, Israel,
Jerusalem and Oman & the UAE.

Each contains the same standard of
insightful text and lavish
photography as the present book.
 A companion series, **Insight
Compact Guides**, includes a book
on Egypt. This is essentially a mini-
encyclopedia packed with facts and
comprehensively cross-referenced
to make it ideal for on-the-spot use.

ART & PHOTO CREDITS

INSIGHT GUIDE EGYPT

Maps **Colourmap Scanning**
Cartographic Editor **Zoë Goodwin**
Production **Mohammed Dar**
Design Consultant **Klaus Geisler**
Picture Research **Hilary Genin**

Picture Spreads

ndex

Note: *Numbers in italics refer to illustrations*